WARS IN THE MIDST OF PEACE

Pitt Series in Policy and Institutional Studies

Bert A. Rockman, Editor

Wars in the Midst of Peace

THE INTERNATIONAL POLITICS OF ETHNIC CONFLICT

EDITED BY

David Carment and Patrick James

University of Pittsburgh Press

Published by the University of Pittsburgh Press, Pittsburgh, Pa., 15261

Copyright © 1997, University of Pittsburgh Press

Manufactured in the United States of America

Printed on acid-free paper

10 9 8 7 6 5 4 3 2 1

Library of Congress Cataloging-in-Publication Data

Wars in the midst of peace: the international politics of ethnic conflict / edited by David Carment and Patrick James.

     p.   cm. — (Pitt series in policy and institutional studies)

  Includes bibliographical references and index.

  ISBN 0-8229-3975-4 (cloth : acid-free paper). — ISBN 0-8229-5626-8 (pbk. : acid-free paper)

  1. Ethnic relations. 2. Ethnicity. 3. International relations. 4. Secession 5. Culture conflict. 6. Conflict management.

I. Carment, David, 1959– . II. James, Patrick, 1957– .

III. Series.

GN496.W37   1997

305.8—dc21   96-51262

A CIP catalog record for this book is available from the British Library.

CONTENTS

ACKNOWLEDGMENTS

The editors are grateful to several organizations and people who helped to bring the volume to completion. We are grateful to the Canadian Department of Foreign Affairs and International Trade for a very generous grant that permitted us to hold two conferences. At these gatherings, six months apart from each other, drafts of the respective chapters developed and all those in attendance benefited from a lively exchange of ideas. We are grateful to Florida State University and McGill University, respectively, for hosting these events. The authors also wish to thank the Cooperative Security Programme, under the direction of Roger Hill, at the Canadian Department of National Defense; the Social Sciences and Humanities Research Council of Canada; the Fonds pour la Formation de Chercheurs et l'Aide à la Recherche; and NATO for financial support. David Carment appreciates the support provided by the Hoover Institution during his year as a visiting fellow.

The authors also would like to thank the very fine scholars who read and supplied valuable commentaries on various chapters in this volume: Mark Brawley, Arlene Broadhurst, Andre Donneur, David Goetze, Ted Robert Gurr, Fen Hampson, Frank Harvey, David Lake, Douglas Lemke, David Long, Zeev Maoz, Pierre Martin, T. V. Paul, James Lee Ray, and Dale Smith. We are also grateful to Scott Jenkins for excellent service as a research assistant. David Davis, Keith Jaggers, and Will Moore are grateful to Ashley Leeds and Chris McHorney for their help with data preparation. In addition, Davis (at Emory) and Moore (at Riverside) received research support from the University Research Committee, Emory University, and the Institute on Global Conflict and Cooperation and the Academic Senate of the University of California, Riverside. The data used in their study are available via the Worldwide Web at: http://wizard.ucr.edu/~wm/wm.html.

An earlier version of Robert A. Young's chapter appeared in the *Canadian Journal of Political Science* 27 (1994): 773–92.

WARS IN THE MIDST OF PEACE

Ethnic Conflict at the International Level

THEORY AND EVIDENCE

David Carment and Patrick James

This is the beginning of the final days. This is the apocalypse.
—A resident of Goma, Zaire, in *Time*

The conflicts which are of global concern involve deep issues of ethnic
and cultural identity, of recognition and of participation that are
usually denied to ethnic minorities in addition to issues of security and
other values that are not negotiable.
—John Burton, "The International Conflict Resolution Priorities"

From magazines such as *Time* (which recently featured a horrific scene from
Rwanda on its cover) to the most arcane academic publications, the subject
of ethnic conflict has appeared with renewed vengeance. The creation of jour-
nals such as *Nationalism and Ethnic Politics* and *Nations and Nationalism* reflects
both popular and academic interest in this subject matter. The causes of violent conflict are being redefined as the cold war recedes and a New World Order
fails to emerge. No longer can potential or ongoing strife be subsumed under
the ideological competition between East and West, which shaped perceptions
for almost half a century. Previously repressed by authoritarianism, dormant
conflicts have come to the fore. Without an ideological framework, new and
emerging issues take on an increasingly ethnic character because political leaders find it relatively easy to mobilize populations by stimulating a sense of
collective identity. Appeals to ethnicity, in fact, have been crucial in the ousting
of some entrenched elites. In other cases the rallying cry of "democratization"
has resulted in something other than effective pluralism; by-products include
upsurges in rampant ethno-populism, replacement of elites, or the shattering
of fragile democratic institutions (Rupesinghe 1990; International Alert 1993a).

Ethnic politics may become even more pervasive, given the current geopolitical map: among over one hundred and eighty states in the international system, only a small number are ethnically homogeneous. The critical features of an ethnic group are ascription and exclusivity: its continuity depends on the maintenance of a boundary based on values and identity. Nelson Kasfir's exegesis of ethnic political participation provides an excellent starting point for analysis because it recognizes the need for both objective and subjective criteria: "(1) Particular objective indicators associated with common ancestry (2) become the focus of subjective perceptions among both members within the unit and by non-members (3) through social solidarity created by a resurgence, or the fictive creation, of traditional unity (4) so that in certain situations political participation will occur" (Kasfir 1979, 373).

According to some estimates there are over *five thousand* minorities and approximately eighty ethnically oriented protracted conflicts around the globe. Approximately thirty-five internal wars were under way in 1994; if the usual threshold used to define such wars, one thousand battle-related casualties, is set aside, the number increases to somewhere between one hundred and fifty and two hundred and forty (Gurr 1993a).

Data from various sources also show that these events, which can easily spill over into the international arena, are no longer restricted to the southern hemisphere. Violent conflicts are raging in the former Soviet Union, the southern Balkans, Africa, Asia, and the Pacific. At least forty-eight existing or potentially violent conflicts are in progress; the list includes those in Romania, Mauritania, Rwanda-Burundi, Senegal, Togo, Nigeria, Kenya, Papua New Guinea, Fiji, Algeria, Egypt, China, Bhutan, Brazil, Mexico, India, Kosovo, Albania, Greece, Bulgaria, the Republic of Macedonia, and Tajikistan (*New York Times*, 7 February 1993). States, by contrast, rarely go to war with each other anymore. Since 1980, the only interstate wars have been Britain and Argentina over the Falklands/Malvinas, Iraq with Iran, China's border skirmish with Vietnam, and the Gulf War.

Lagging behind this emerging reality are theory and evidence. Agreement exists that some combination of economic, political, and psychological factors can explain ethnic conflict. Consensus, however, ends at that point. The primary antecedents will vary, depending on the case(s) at issue. Conflicts can arise when ethnic groups are geographically concentrated, in backward or advanced regions. One argument is that ethnic conflict becomes likely only when certain structural elements (such as a core-periphery differential) coincide with regional disparities and intense nationalism among communal groups. Alternative interpretations focus on the class-based reinforcement of cleavages, relative equality in the size and number of groups within states, unequal resource mobilization, labor market division along ethnic lines, differential activity of elites, and responses to uneven state policies (see Carment and James 1994b).

Conflict in the former Yugoslavia serves as an excellent example of how much theoretical and practical work is needed. The difficulties encountered in anticipating and understanding the scope and intensity of this conflict and its impact on the international system are directly linked to the changing nature of sovereignty. The central issues are the proper conduct for states external to a conflict and the implications of internal changes (most notably democratization) for outside intervention.

In this volume, we focus on the theory and evidence of an international politics of ethnic conflict. Theory, comparative case studies, and aggregate data analysis are combined; an eclectic approach is appropriate at a time when change is rapid and existing frames of reference are increasingly questionable. In general, the early chapters present a range of theoretical perspectives, while the later ones focus on reproducible evidence. It might be more accurate to say that the mixture of theory and evidence, generally speaking, becomes more heavily weighted toward evidence as the volume unfolds. The concluding chapter serves as a foundation for more applied investigations of peacekeeping and policy.

John F. Stack Jr. argues in chapter 2 that ethnicity challenges traditional assumptions about international relations. Ethnicity should not be regarded as an atavistic force destined to be superseded by supposedly more enduring factors, such as socioeconomic class. Liberalism and Marxism share the view that ethnic attachment is by definition transitional, an example of false consciousness. Experiences such as the establishment of civil societies and secular polities within the expanding Westphalian international system provide evidence that ethnicity is ephemeral. In sum, theories of international relations fail to examine ethnicity as a meaningful force at either the domestic or international levels.

Despite the importance of a global balance of power, nuclear weapons, and transnational economic relations, ethnicity remains a critical factor. A *primordial* outlook provides insight into the nature of ethnicity and the intensity of related conflicts. Although cultural approaches to international relations were long held in disrepute, a review of recent scholarship and events supports a different point of view. Whether at the level of the clash between civilizations, among states, or within national societies, ethnicity constantly reemerges as an important social force.

In chapter 3, Gerald Alfred and Franke Wilmer focus on the conflict between indigenous peoples and the state and world system. Although scholars now widely agree that politics is about the allocation of values or, taking it a step further, the distribution of resources according to values, virtually all social scientific thinking about ethnicity emphasizes identity, often to the exclusion of the normative dimension. However, in terms of ethnicity, it is the profound distance between the core values of indigenous ways of life and those of "modernizing" societies that lies at the heart of the conflict of indigenous peoples with the state, and with the world system in which the state's legitimacy is embedded. The most significant conflict between indigenous and modernizing ways of life derives from fundamentally different ways of understanding the relationship between human beings and the resource base on which they depend for their continued existence. Modernization entails an instrumental and objectified view of natural resources, a hierarchy of values in which the creation of surplus wealth is paramount, and the development of complex hierarchical social structures to manage people and resources within a globally connected system of exchange.

Indigenous peoples and states are in basic conflict over values used to allocate resources. The fundamental issue raised by indigenous political activism is whether national and international political institutions, which allocate resources according to the primacy of industrial economic expansion, ought to be constrained. In other words, how can (and should) states deal with indigenous peoples' right to a material basis sufficient for the perpetuation of their ways of life?

Robert A. Young's central purpose in chapter 4 is to arrive at empirical generalizations about the politics of secession. He explores how secessions have unfolded in the past and searches for general patterns in the political dynamics. Evidence from comparative experience that suggests how the process might occur peacefully is of interest to both aggregate analysts and area specialists. Three cases provide the basis for a focused comparison of peaceful secession: Hungary from Austria in 1865, Norway from Sweden in 1905, and Singapore from Malaysia in 1965. Although these cases hardly exhaust the potential choices, the time periods and locations are fairly diverse. Thus development of a more general model from these instances should have reasonable prospects for success.

Young identifies seven stages in the process of secession. First, secession follows protracted constitutional and political disputes. Second, the secessionist region declares its intention to withdraw. Third, within the context of values, secession becomes a momentous, galvanizing event. Fourth, in peaceful instances only, the predecessor state accepts the principle of secession and negotiations ensue. Fifth, the government is broadened and strengthened on each side; there is a premium on solidarity. Sixth, the negotiations involve few participants. Seventh, the settlement is made quickly and involves a relatively short list of items. Among the features shared by the various cases are a constitutional mechanism and important roles for foreign powers in the secession.

Peaceful secession can in principle occur within a context of ethnic diversity. It may be possible to transfer the lessons of the three cases studied to contemporary settings, where the process of secession usually involves significant violence.

In chapter 5, Manus I. Midlarsky considers two instances of communal strife preceding World War I—Bosnia-Herzegovina and Macedonia—and compares them to the unfolding events in the former Yugoslavia. The analysis identifies the current strife as a species of *systemic war* confined to a particular region. Midlarsky then invokes a theoretical framework to explain systemic war (Midlarsky 1988a).

When ethnic conflicts are critical to actual or anticipated changes in the balance of power among contending international actors, the likelihood of internationalization is greatly increased. Bosnia's presence on the Austro-Hungarian border made it a likely subject for disputes about its political future among Austria-Hungary, Serbia, and Russia, once Bosnia was removed from direct Ottoman administration (in 1878 at the Congress of Berlin). Geographic and social proximity to Slavic peoples made Bosnia a more likely source of overlap in disputes between major powers involving a small power, and between major powers alone, as in the variable sequence conventionally associated with systemic war. Its status attracted both the South Slavs in Austria-Hungary (who confronted an enlarged Serbia) and Germany (which faced a potentially disintegrating great power ally).

Currently, Bosnia is in no sense critical to the European "balance of power," if such a concept is even relevant at the present time. However, the intensity of this communal strife can be explained as a systemic war within small confines. Under conditions of economic decline and support for one side from the emerging dominant European power, the three communities in a state of conflict facilitated both the Serbo-Croatian War and the overlap of this conflict with the Serbian-Muslim and Croat-Muslim hostilities. Within this system, the balance of power among the three communities and especially between the Serbs and Croats is of critical importance. It is possible, then, to relate the concept of systemic war to this more localized conflict and use it to explain the intensity of the strife. A direct implication of this framework, however, is that the structural systemic war is likely to be followed by a mobilization conflict initiated by one of the current protagonists. Unfortunately, neither the timing of this future conflict nor the precise mobilizing entity is apparent from prior research. Questions of this type provide a fruitful avenue for future study of the origins of systemic war in the context of underlying ethnic conflict.

In chapter 6, Monty G. Marshall presents a theoretical explanation of group dynamics and supporting empirical evidence, which is directly relevant to international ethnic conflict. While the use and magnitude of violence experienced in conflicts that involve identity-based social groups have increased suddenly and dramatically, much of the perceived change simply represents a shift away from ideology-based conflicts. The general level of violence in the world does continue to increase, but it is the perception of ongoing conflict processes and the actors involved that is fundamentally different.

Much of the confusion and resulting disagreement over the dynamics of group conflict stem from differences in underlying assumptions about "human nature." Questions about whether human beings are essentially cooperative or conflictual, social or individualistic, active or passive, aggressive or acquiescent, are most often answered by universal postulates of either a unitary or a dual nature, as in realism, liberalism, Marxism, and feminism. The theory presented in this chapter posits that human nature is a variable that is both relationally and relatively determined. While each individual nature is malleable and adaptable and, therefore, always in a state of flux (and, as a result, difficult to detail or predict), the influence of human nature on political behavior is given stability and continuity through social aggregation and the structure of group dynamics.

Crisis modes (insecurity) and noncrisis modes (security) of group political behavior are fundamentally different. Crisis modes emphasize exclusivity, enmity, and coercive (or violent) strategies of conflict management, while noncrisis modes stress inclusiveness, amity, and cooperative strategies. Since conflict is an inevitable condition of political relations, the main theoretical problem is to understand why political relations become violent, as in certain ethnic conflicts. The existence of violence—especially systematic violence (i.e., protracted social conflict)—creates or reinforces a social psychology of insecurity that tends to be diffused through the network of social ties. The perceptions and priorities of political actors most closely affected by the threat of violence (i.e., all actors in affective proximity, the protracted conflict region) are altered. A growing sense of insecurity leads to increasing exclusivity, enmity, and violence in political relations among all groups in proximity to the source of political violence.

While there has been increasing interest in diffusion processes in political research, studies have looked primarily at temporal and spatial diffusion patterns of categorical events such as war. Extending that work to systemic diffusion of insecurity requires analysis of the uses of violence in every political interaction (interstate, civil, and communal) and between all groups at any level of aggregation. Marshall uses political relations in the Middle East from 1945 to 1990 to assess the theory. The findings strongly support the diffusion hypotheses. The implications for issues related to ethnic strife range from the role of the UN to the nature of an early warning network.

In chapter 7, Zeev Maoz examines the impact of internal strife, such as ethnic conflict, on a state's international relations. Maoz focuses on the effects of changes taking place in the politically relevant international environment (PRIE) of states on their strategic behavior. Three types of response are examined: military allocations, alliance formation, and international conflict involvement. The PRIE of a given state includes all states that are directly or indirectly contiguous, great powers with global reach capacity, and regional powers with regional reach capacity.

Maoz's empirical analysis of all states in the international system from 1816 to 1986 supports expectations about national perspectives. Increases in the level of democratization within a state's PRIE generally reduce its perception of threat and are associated with a decline in military allocations, alliance formation, and conflict involvement. By contrast, increasing domestic instability in states' PRIE typically results in heightened strategic responses. The findings suggest that democratization in the global system should have positive implications, most notably for the reduction of military allocations.

Maoz effectively demonstrates that, if current patterns of ethnic conflict continue, political leaders in the West may have to find more decisive ways of dealing with this problem. The findings of this chapter suggest that increasing internal conflict will stimulate militarization and international instability. Ethnic strife is likely to escalate into international tension. Most notably, it increases the risk of systemic conflict.

In chapter 8, David R. Davis, Keith Jaggers, and Will H. Moore examine the impact of ethnic conflict within states on the occurrence and escalation of interstate strife. While the resurgence of ethno-nationalism throughout eastern Europe and the former Soviet Union has refocused scholarly attention on the ethnic dimensions of international conflict, the linkage remains underdeveloped. Few studies consider the basic question: What are the implications of research findings for general theories of international politics? While the statistical analysis of this chapter focuses explicitly on the effects of ethnic hostilities within states on interstate conflict, the general concern is with how domestic and international authority patterns overlap and interact. This approach implicitly challenges realist assumptions that have traditionally guided the study of international cooperation and conflict. In particular, the belief that sovereign states represent the fundamental building blocks of international relations needs further consideration. Competing authority patterns may cut across territorial boundaries and influence the interaction of states in the global arena. Ethnicity provides an alternative authority pattern to the territorial state, a pattern that, at least in principle, can affect the dynamics of interstate relations.

Realist theory suggests that the international system is driven by its state of anarchy. There is no government or established authority that rules the international state system. Any given state's first priority is self-preservation and hence national security. Thus, realists contend, international politics is "high politics," and domestic considerations (e.g., interest groups, coalitions, etc.) have only marginal impact on foreign policy behavior because the stakes are too high. States instead follow their self-defined national interest, at the heart of which is self-preservation.

If the realist view is correct, ethnicity should not influence international behavior, especially in terms of conflict. While leaders might empathize with the plight of ethnic brethren in another state, they will not pursue a risky venture simply because of public pressure. Four interrelated hypotheses emerge from this line of reasoning. H_1: Conflict levels (including war) between any two states will be higher if there is a minority at risk in at least one of them. H_2: Conflict levels (including war) between any two states will be higher if there is a minority at risk in one state and members of the same minority group are in power in the other. H_3: When the same minority is at risk in two states, the intrastate conflict levels will be high and those states will exhibit more cooperative interaction patterns. H_4: The higher the level of discrimination or magnitude of grievances experienced by the minority group, the higher the level of international conflict, including war, between any two states. The data analysis supports H_2 and H_4. Realist theories cannot account for these results and need to be revised. States do seem to take domestic concerns—such as ethnic ties to a disadvantaged group in another state—into consideration when constructing and implementing foreign policy.

Michael Brecher and Jonathan Wilkenfeld explore the causal link between ethnicity and international crisis in chapter 9. They present a model of ethnicity and crisis, which produces both a general proposition and a series of specific hypotheses. They test the propositions against the international crisis behavior (ICB) system-level data set over a period that covers most of the twentieth century.

The guiding research questions are as follows: Are there differences between international crises with and without an ethnic dimension? Specifically, does the attribute of ethnicity affect any or all of the crucial dimensions of crisis, from onset to termination? Furthermore, are the effects of ethnicity upon crisis accentuated or moderated by a setting of protracted conflict? Underlying these questions is a general perspective on ethnicity and crisis, which generates a set of hypotheses. Brecher and Wilkenfeld propose that ethnic international crises differ from nonethnic crises in a number of ways, including type of trigger, values at stake, the role of violence in crisis management, the extent of external involvement by the major powers and by the global organization, and type of crisis outcome, both its content and its form. They expect that a setting of protracted conflict will *sharpen* the difference between ethnic and nonethnic crises.

Ethnically driven behavior, based on the results of the aggregate analysis, seems to coincide with system transformation. The findings imply that the scope and intensity of both secessionist and irredentist conflicts will increase in the next decade and beyond.

In chapter 10, David Carment and Patrick James approach the interstate dimension of ethnic conflict from two directions, addressing both its secessionist and its irredentist forms. They review conventional perspectives on interstate relations, including neoliberalism and realpolitik, as they relate to third-party involvement in ethnic strife. They then introduce an alternative model, based on the concept of a two-level game. They focus on affinity and cleavage, which play important roles in mediating the potential for intervention in ethnic conflict and present directions for further research.

The investigation of ethnicity and foreign policy begins with the assumption that developed and integrated political institutions can restrain states from belligerence and adventurism. Carment and James assess the effects of an additional constraining mechanism, namely, a state's ethnic diversity, on three measures of interstate ethnic conflict: crisis management technique, severity, and protractedness. They argue that, in conjunction with institutions, diversity can restrain states from pursuing involvement in ethnic strife under certain conditions. A related concern is to identify factors that increase the potential for interstate ethnic strife and violent (and even unmanageable) conflict. Carment and James identify two variables—cleavage and affinity—as important mediators that influence a leader's preference for involvement in ethnic strife. Taken together, the independent and mediating variables move toward a more precise delineation of the causal relationship between ethnic and interstate conflict.

Aggregate testing suggests that ethnic conflict, whether it results in a crisis that leads to war or in future cooperation, is not a culture-specific phenomenon. (Of course, there may be a fundamental difference between ethnic conflict in postcolonial societies and in societies without that experience.) Future international incidents will likely involve ethnically divided states attempting to make the transition to systems that are both more economically open and more democratic. These states will succumb to the politics of intransigence, confrontation, and conflict if the political system is arranged along ethnic lines *and* one ethnic group is allowed to become dominant. Over the short term, leaders of ethnically based political parties will lack the capacity to widen the policy agenda to encompass nonethnic issues. When other bases of mobilization are weak, ethnic elites will depend on direct support from their constituencies and, in turn, will seek to control and influence these groups. The Soviet successor regimes represent prime examples of how that process may unfold. These states are potential objects for renewed and vigorous collective efforts at conflict management.

Louis Kriesberg explores a variety of ideas about preventing and resolving destructive communal conflicts in chapter 11. He focuses on successes, not just failures, in conflict management. Kriesberg outlines a range of communal relations in terms of their degree of interdependence and unilateral imposition. The result is a taxonomy consisting of fifteen intercommunal relationships, with forced assimilation and agreed-upon self-determination being at the extremes. Kriesberg then turns to policies to prevent destructive conflicts, in the process identifying four phases: conflict emergence, threat or isolated destructive acts, extensive destructive acts, and protracted and extensive acts. Within each phase he isolates five preferred goals: to correct underlying conditions, prevent destructive acts, prevent escalation, end fighting, and move toward resolution.

Cases of varying success in preventing destructive conflict escalation are used by Kriesberg to illustrate the range of policies that have been pursued around the world. Quebec separatism in Canada, racial tensions in South Africa, and events in the former Yugoslavia reveal a wide range of options for conflict prevention, as well as the fact that the outcome of any given case of communal strife is far from preordained.

In chapter 12, Carment and James discuss the concept formation and theorizing produced by this wide-ranging collection of innovative ideas. Primordialism, indigenous versus modernizing political economies, systemic war, diffusion processes, and minorities at risk are among the most significant contributions. These ideas are tested against the evidence from multiple geographic regions, time frames, and degrees of aggregation. The resulting overall contribution to theory and evidence creates a solid foundation for subsequent inquiry into peacekeeping and policy.

The Ethnic Challenge to International Relations Theory

John F. Stack Jr.

It is always possible to bind together a considerable number of people
in love, so long as there are other people left over to receive the manifestations of their aggressiveness.
—Sigmund Freud, *Civilization and Its Discontents*

The virus of tribalism . . . risks becoming the AIDS of international
politics—lying dormant for years, then flaring up to destroy countries.
—*The Economist*

The study of ethnicity is more akin to Freud's notion of love as a mechanism
of group mobilization than students of international relations would ever
want to admit. "Ethnicity" is a term with so much baggage that most social
scientists, and especially, students of international politics, have failed even to
consider it a significant dimension. Ethnicity is as alien to the study of international relations as are Freud's musings in *Civilization and Its Discontents*.

With the disintegration of the Soviet Union and the tragic conflict in the
Balkans, ethnicity has become relevant to any discussion of world politics. But
ethnicity is held in such disrepute that for many it resembles a deadly political
virus. For them, the problem is to isolate the pernicious virus of tribalism
before it proliferates further. There is an explicit assumption that ethnicity has
no place in international relations theory. As Donald Horowitz notes:

> The increasing prominence of ethnic loyalties is a development for which
> neither statesmen nor social scientists were adequately prepared. . . . The
> study of ethnic conflict has often been a grudging concession to something

distasteful, largely because, especially in the West, ethnic affiliations have been in disrepute. (Horowitz 1985, 13; quoted in Moynihan 1993, 157)

Yet ethnicity is increasingly a major force within world politics—among states, in the foreign policy–making process, among nonstate actors, and within and between societies around the globe—despite the difficulty, and in many cases the unwillingness, that students of international relations have had in getting a conceptual handle on it for decades on end. From this perspective, ethnicity may be akin to Justice Stewart's often paraphrased definition of pornography: you know it when you see it. Scholars of international relations have not known what to do with ethnicity any more than the United States Supreme Court has known what to do with pornography in the context of the First Amendment.

Ethnicity and World Politics

For nearly twenty years, a number of scholars have attempted to demonstrate why ethnicity is important in world politics. The work of Cynthia H. Enloe (1973, 3), Walker Connor (1972, 319–55; 1984a, 324–57; 1984b), Horowitz (1985, 13–21), Joseph Rothschild (1981, 173–89), and Crawford Young (1976, 505–29), to name only a few, demonstrates why ethnicity was relevant to the actions of states in the northern and southern hemispheres throughout the cold war.

Notwithstanding the impressive scholarship produced, the dominant approaches to the study of international relations—realism and neorealism—have hardly considered ethnicity. For Hans Morgenthau (1977), E. H. Carr (1939), Henry Kissinger (1974), Hedley Bull (1977), Robert Gilpin (1981), Robert Keohane (1986a), Stephen Krasner (1985), Kenneth Waltz (1979, 1986), and John Gerald Ruggie (1986), ethnicity has no real place among studies of the great powers or of the global balance of power (Chatterjee 1975 is a rare exception). When one considers the fundamental importance of ethnicity in the nature of the changes that have swept the Soviet Union and eastern Europe, it is extraordinary that ethnicity has not been seen as a major dimension of change. Such a perspective led Senator Daniel P. Moynihan (1993, 145–46) to declare that realism "proved altogether out of touch with reality!" The fact that scholars and policy makers limited their assessments of the USSR to "'hard' quantifiable . . . measures that made no provision for the passions—the appeal of ethnic loyalty and nationalism, the demands for freedom of religious practice and cultural expression, and the feeling that the regime had simply lost its moral legitimacy" suggests that realism asks the wrong questions (Moynihan 1993, 146).

The influence of realism has extended far beyond studies of the superpowers. Students of comparative politics approach modernization and devel-

opment throughout the world as an extension of the process of nation building and state building in the United States and western Europe. The successful
creation of a civic culture in the United States and the reconstruction of integrated national societies in Europe following World War II suggested that ethnic differences could likewise be overcome throughout the world. Perhaps it
was a sense of inevitability—that if the United States could merge millions of
diverse immigrants into one nation in its short history, then other countries
could do the same—or perhaps it was a sense of mission, which cold war in-
ternationalism mandated. In any case, scholars such as Gabriel Almond and
Sidney Verba (1963) and Almond and Powell (1966) tended to ignore "the
question of ethnic diversity or to treat the matter of ethnic identity superficially
as merely one of a number of minor impediments to effective state-integra-
tion" (Connor 1994, 318). The failure to study ethnicity as a central dimension
of the post–World War II international system, whether in superpower relations or in the southern hemisphere, is striking and now appears to be an
almost inexplicable oversight. In what is arguably the most important reinter-
pretation of realism since the publication of Morgenthau's *Politics Among Nations*, Keohane (1986a) and his contributors say hardly a word about ethnicity,
while the index lists only two references to nationalism. In summarizing his
unease with Waltz's neorealism (1979), for reasons ranging from economic
and ecological interdependence to the role of international institutions and
regimes, Keohane (1986b, 25) does not mention ethnicity.

The publication of Samuel Huntington's "Clash of Civilizations?" (1993,
22–49), with its hypothesis that ideology and economics would no longer be
the central sources of conflict in international politics, constitutes an alternative (if long overdue) recognition of the nature of conflict in international
relations: "It is far more meaningful now to group countries not in terms of
their political and economic systems or in terms of their level of economic
development but rather in terms of their culture and civilization" (ibid., 23).
Much of the firestorm of criticism that greeted Huntington's essay had to do
with his emphasis on culture—the least respectable way to analyze differences
among groups within political systems. A good deal of the disfavor that the
study of ethnicity encounters is based on the philosophical underpinnings of
liberalism. Moynihan (1993, 27), citing Milton Gordon, calls this outlook the
liberal expectancy that ethnicity is "recessive, readily explained by immigrant
experience, but essentially transitional." The very ascriptive nature of ethnicity
points out the vast gulf separating it from the rational positivism of the en-
lightenment. As an atavistic force, ethnicity is seen as a premodern holdover
that risks plunging individuals and societies into the nonrational, anti-intel-
lectual circumstances that eighteenth-, nineteenth-, and twentieth-century
politics have sought to move beyond. This is one reason that Western scholars,

those of the United States in particular, seem so dismayed by the increase of intractable ethnic conflicts since World War II.

As Anthony Smith persuasively argues, liberalism assumes that the movement from primitive tribal organizations to industrial and postindustrial structures will render ethnic attachments obsolete (Smith 1981, 2). The inexorable process of economic growth that liberalism champions will result in the proliferation of the rational and universal values of capitalism, which are antithetical to the premodern basis of ethnicity. Liberalism also holds that worldwide communication and transportation patterns and the creation of a global economy will reduce the attractiveness of ethnic attachments to parochial communities around the globe. Finally, liberalism entails the belief that the authority of nation-states will become increasingly irrelevant in meeting the basic needs of all peoples. The global economic system will ultimately supplant the role of states in meeting individual needs, thereby resulting in a shift in allegiance to the institutions of global capitalism (Smith 1981, 2–4).

The timing of the transition from ethnic politics to nation-state politics remains unclear. Scholars of world politics look to the formal institutional birth of the state system—the Peace of Westphalia in 1648—as the dawn of a new era. For others, the French Revolution and the triumph of Napoleon's army of citizens marked the birth of the national state. Marxism links the development of the modern state to nineteenth-century industrial capitalism. The ideological character of the birth of nationalism and the attenuation of ethnic politics make attempts to pinpoint the time when nationalism putatively superseded ethnic politics very difficult. That date, as Connor (1990, 99) indicates, is very murky at best and historically suspect at worst.

Ethnic Group and Nation

For the United States, which has a political culture that emphasizes assimilation, there would appear to be a vast difference between the formation of ethnicity and the crystallization of nationalism. In fact, I follow Moynihan's view that ethnicity and nationality occur along a continuum—they are a "question of degree" (Moynihan 1993, 4). The nation constitutes the most politicized form of ethnicity, "denoting a subjective state of mind as regards ancestry, but also, almost always, an objective claim to forms of territorial autonomy ranging from a regional assembly to full-blown independence" (ibid., 4–5). Rupert Emerson's definition of the nation captures the intensity of primordial sentiments common to both the ethnic group and the nation. For Emerson (1967, 95–96), the nation is "the largest community, which when the chips are down, effectively commands men's loyalty, overriding the claims of both lesser communities within it and those which cut across it or potentially enfold it within a still greater society." Contemporary ethnic conflicts live up to Emerson's definition—they are the kind of conflicts that divide groups fundamentally. One of the most perplexing issues is why ethnicity is so potent now, at the end of the twentieth century, as opposed to ten, fifteen, or fifty years ago? If ethnicity is as important as it appears, why does it cast such a long shadow now, when it did not in the past?

The answer is that there is a time lag between the crystallization of national consciousness among elite sectors of the society and its spread outward to the masses; this process can sometimes takes centuries to occur (Connor 1990, 99). The key to understanding this phenomenon is to recognize that the formation of a national identity is not an isolated event but an ongoing process. For Connor, the series of events that established the nations of Europe is of very recent date, "In the matter of nation-formation, there has been far less difference in the timetables of Western and Eastern Europe than is customarily acknowledged, and the lag time between Europe and the Third World has also been greatly exaggerated. Indeed, in the case of a number of putative nations within Europe, it is problematic whether nationhood has ever yet been achieved" (ibid.). This is a controversial proposition because it sees nationalism as a far less stable and predictable development than was previously thought.

There remains considerable resistance to such a perspective, notwithstanding the fundamental transformation of the landscape of world politics in the past seven years. For example, Liah Greenfeld has recently dismissed ethnicity as a meaningful identity, when considered alongside nationalism, because the possession of ethnic attributes such as language, customs, territory, and phenotype are so ubiquitous among individuals as to be "quite irrelevant to their motives and actions, and seen, if at all noticed, as purely accidental" (Greenfeld 1992, 12–13). Ethnicity does not qualify as an identity in this sense because "an essential characteristic of any identity is that it is necessarily the view the concerned actor has of himself or herself" (Greenfeld 1992, 12–13). Thus, Greenfeld seems to be implying that identity formation requires some affirmative act to establish that identity for an individual and that ethnicity does not qualify as a meaningful identity because it constitutes an ephemeral residual category shared by everyone.

It is difficult to accept Greenfeld's conceptualization, first, because of the universality of ethnic conflicts, and second, because the nationalism of which she writes is now so tattered. We do well to recall Bell's characterization of the primordial bases of ethnic conflict:

> The strength of a primordial attachment is that emotional cohesion derives not only from some "consciousness of kind," but from some external definition of an adversary as well. Where there are *Gemeinde,* there are also *Fremde.* And such divisions, when translated into politics, become, like a

civil war, *politique à l'outrance.* It was once hoped that the politics of ideology might be replaced by the politics of civility, in which men would learn to live in negotiated peace. To replace the politics of ideology with the politics of ethnicity might only be the continuation of war by other means. And those are the drawbacks of ethnicity as well. (Bell 1975, 174)

The Primordial Basis of Ethnicity

The primordial approach to the study of ethnicity could not be further removed from the concerns of traditional theorists of international relations. This approach is largely indebted to the work of Harold Isaacs (1975) and Clifford Geertz (1973). For Isaacs (1975, 42–43), a sense of belonging and the level of an individual's self-esteem form the essence of a basic group identity. "An individual *belongs* to his basic group in the deepest and most literal sense that he is not *alone*, which is what all but a very few human beings fear to be." Geertz (1973, 259) underscores the importance of the "assumed 'givens'—of social existence." He notes the importance of region, shared religion, language, and kin connections that bind people together: "These congruities of blood, speech, custom, and so on are seen to have an ineffable, and at times overpowering coerciveness in and of themselves." A community of fellow believers is therefore created "as the result not merely of personal affection, practical necessity, common interest, or incurred obligation, but at least in great part by virtue of some unaccountable absolute import attributed to the very tie itself" (ibid.).

The primordial approach is not favored by social scientists, because the very term suggests a romanticization and mystification of individual and collective behavior not appropriate for social science. Further, there is a reluctance to view ethnicity in terms of primordial dynamics because of the danger of embracing a form of cultural determinism. There is also a concern that primordial arguments constitute a deus ex machina that frees one from having to engage in a rigorous assessment of ethnicity.

Yet Geertz seems able to capture the intangible, even nonrational, essence of primordial attachments:

> The general strength of such primordial bonds, and the types of them that are important, differ from person to person, from society to society, and from time to time. But for virtually every person, in every society, at almost all times, some attachments flow more from a sense of natural—some would say spiritual—affinity than from social interaction. (Ibid., 259–60)

Geertz's emphasis on such intangible factors as "spiritual affinity" is a start at conceptualizing the resilience of ethnicity throughout the world. Ethnicity has proven to be incredibly resistant to assimilation in the form of urbanization, education, and exposure to the mass media, and to the power of egalitarian values such as class and occupational identities. In weighing the differences between class conflict and ethnic conflict, Nathan Glazer argues:

> Ethnic conflict, however, seems to have become more effective in reaching and drawing upon the more emotional layers of human and social personality than class conflict. Class conflict is rational—it is based on the defense and expansion of interest. Ethnic conflict is rational in this sense, too—but it fuses with the rationality of class conflict a less rational, an irrational appeal, that seems to connect better with powerful emotions. (1981, 79)

Connor also recognizes the incredible power of the social-psychological dimensions of ethnic conflict:

> In summary, ethnic strife is too often superficially discerned as principally predicated upon language, religion, customs, economic inequity, or some other tangible element. But what is fundamentally involved in such a conflict is the divergence of basic identity which manifests itself in the "us-them" syndrome. And the ultimate answer to the question of whether a person is one of us, or one of them, seldom hinges on adherence to overt aspects of culture. . . . But an individual (or an entire national group) can shed all overt cultural manifestations customarily attributed to his ethnic group and yet maintain his fundamental identity as a member of that nation. Cultural assimilation need not mean psychological assimilation. (1972, 341–42)

The social-psychological dynamics of primordial attachments form a very powerful basis for the articulation of a sense of group consciousness. Ethnicity comes to resemble a double-edged sword in that it reassures the individual that he or she is not alone, "which is what all but a very few humans beings most fear to be," yet it may be just as easily used as a vehicle for mobilizing "us" against "them" (Isaacs 1975, 43). Once primordial attachments are mobilized, they will not easily abate, but will provide ethnic conflicts with their seemingly intractable character. The intensity of ethnic conflicts led Geertz to observe (1973, 260): "In modern societies the lifting of such ties to the level of political supremacy . . . has more and more come to be deplored as pathological."

A primordial approach need not conceptualize ethnicity in terms of immutable characteristics. The upsurge of ethnic conflicts since World War II suggests that ethnic groups respond to a broad spectrum of structural changes. The anthropologist Charles Keyes (1981) compares ethnic identity to a gyroscope that changes form and boundaries over time. The structure of a society—indeed, the structure of the international system—is critically important in determining how ethnicity manifests itself over time and from society to society. The issue is not ethnicity or class alone, but the mutually reinforcing *dynamics* of both ethnicity and class. Social structures matter within states as they do in the global balance of power. Ethnicity, like class, is affected by such external forces, though the primordial perspective disputes the notion that ethnicity is subservient to class attachments.

Ethnicity and Realism

Realists compare global politics to a billiard game: the table represents the global political environment in which nation-states, the most important actors, lie; the balls represent the sovereignty and differential powers of states as expressed in the Westphalia system. The game of international politics is made up of the interactions among states, that is to say, the balance of power is based on shifting coalitions that are fueled by a state's pursuit of its national interest. The balls colliding with one another represent this interaction of states—the irreducible essences of the realist perspective—from which new configurations and alliances emerge. The game of world politics is dominated by those states capable of marshaling superior resources to attain their objectives. Speculation as to what goes on inside states is less relevant than how states interact with allies and adversaries at any given point in time. Thus, realists necessarily focus their attention on what happens on the billiard table, because of the fast-paced nature of the game and because the risks of failing to pay attention are so costly to the survival of states.

The classical realists such as Carr (1939), Morgenthau (1977), and Bull (1977) see the foreign policy–making process through which states shape their formal relations with one another as the central way to influence world politics. States use their foreign policy to structure decisions in the international arena through the exercise of power. Politics in the global arena becomes state politics writ large. Explanations and predictions about world politics must of necessity focus on the goals of states, with the most powerful units defining the rules of the game. Central concerns encompass the size and effectiveness of a state's war-making capacity, the nature of alliance structure, and the effectiveness of its leverage vis-à-vis other states in military and nonmilitary contexts—for example, international organizations, regional organizations, and bilateral relations with individual states.

With their near exclusive focus on the forging of a national society, realists view the unadorned state as the basic building block of international politics, which resembles a Hobbesian state of nature. Supranational and transnational influences are considered unimportant in the age of superpower confrontation. For example, Morgenthau writes (1977, 338):

> The supranational forces, such as universal religions, humanitarianism, cosmopolitanism, and all other personal ties, institutions, and organizations

that bind individuals together across national boundaries, are infinitely weaker today than the forces that unite peoples within a particular national boundary and separate them from the rest of humanity.

Realism's emphasis on sovereignty, military power, and the control of foreign policy channels discounts the importance of ethnicity as a factor in international politics. Its preoccupation with state actors, best expressed in the notion of the balance of power, critically underestimates the power of ethnicity over human minds and its capacity to affect not only domestic politics but regional and global politics as well.

Such a policy predilection has entirely missed the significance of ethnicity as a growing force within eastern and western Europe and around the world. Morgenthau provides an illustration:

> This weakening of the supranational forces, which must be strong in order to impose effective restraints upon the foreign policies of nations, is but the negative by-product of the great positive force that shapes the political face of our age—nationalism. Nationalism, identified as it is with the foreign policies of individual nations, cannot restrain these policies; it is itself in need of restraint. Not only has it fatally weakened, if not destroyed, the restraints that have come down to us from previous ages, it has also supplied the power aspirations of individual nations with a good conscience and a Messianic fervor. It has inspired them with a thirst and a strength for universal dominion of which the nationalism of the nineteenth century knew nothing. (Ibid.)

The foreign policy–making process is a crucial dimension of political realism because it emphasizes the importance of national elites in achieving consensus on fundamental foreign policy goals. Ethnicity is rendered irrelevant both as a dimension of international politics and as a part of the foreign policy process, as a result of the shared experiences of modern nationalism. As Morgenthau explains:

> In preceding periods of history, the collectivity with whose power and aspirations for power the individual identified himself was determined by ties of blood, of religion, or common loyalty to a feudal lord or prince. In our time the identification with the power and policies of the nation has largely superseded or, in any case, overshadows those older identifications. . . . Power disguised by ideologies and pursued in the name and for the sake of the nation becomes a good for which all citizens must strive. The national symbols, especially in so far as they have reference to the armed forces and relations with other nations, are instruments of that identification of the individual with the power of the nation. (Ibid., 108–09)

In the United States, ethnic involvement in foreign policy has been only as effective as the national security elite allowed it to be, with the exception of Jewish-American support for Israel. In rare cases, cold war politics dovetailed with the demands of an ethnic group; such was the case for the United States's support of the captive nations of Latvia, Estonia, and Lithuania, and its anti-communist stand against Cuba. Another exception is the case of Greek-Americans, whose efforts in the United States Congress to shape American policy in favor of Greek interests in Cyprus were successful but limited (Paul 1982, 74–75).

For American foreign policy makers, an ethnic agenda was anathema to the explicit values of cold war nationalism. Ethnic group involvement in foreign policy was de facto proof that assimilation had failed, as Louis Gerson's attack on ethnic involvement in American foreign policy, *The Hyphenate in Recent American Politics,* amply demonstrates. This is especially the case since Anglophilia and nativism have dominated the foreign policy agenda of the national elite since the 1880s (Higham 1974, 141–42). The elites' sympathy for the British cause was easily mobilized as anti-German sentiments increased in intensity. War propaganda was skillfully used on behalf of Britain and the stereotype of the respectable, hardworking German was transformed into that of the barbarian Hun. For the American elite, the ties to British political and legal institutions and culture were not expressions of ethnicity but lines of demarcation between American civilization and the barbarian hordes of immigrants, whose massive numbers threatened to overwhelm the Anglo-American political and cultural inheritance. Both Woodrow Wilson's and Franklin D. Roosevelt's support for Britain during wartime underscored a profound cultural affinity. The cultural dominance of Anglo-American values was so pronounced and so accepted that it could scarcely be described in ethnic terms. It was, as Andrew Greeley aptly describes it, Anglo conformity, the benchmark against which all the myriad "newcomers" would judge themselves (1977, 9–21). For American foreign policy elites, their own ethnicity was never the issue.

Realism's emphasis on the primacy of national constituencies as the basis of interstate relations fused with the development models of Western theories of modernization, which negate the importance of ethnicity within states. The rise of fundamental ethnic conflicts in Northern Ireland, Belgium, Spain, France, and Germany was something that realists found troubling and certainly did not anticipate. This liberal viewpoint envisioned the progressive incorporation of smaller groups into larger groups until fully developed national consciousness emerged. But the salience of ethnicity increased as the remote technocratic state created conditions conducive to politicized ethnicity in the societies of western Europe, as Smith's work illustrates (1981, 165).

The frustrated attempts of educators and intellectuals to attain status and a measure of political power to combat the entrenched power of national and supranational bureaucracies served as the catalyst for the articulation of a powerful "ethnic historicism" (ibid., 105). A multiclass appeal provided an antidote to the alienation individuals feel when encountering impersonal and seemingly uncaring government authorities. Ethnic affiliation provided groups with an interest and an affective tie, as Bell notes, thereby furnishing ethnic groups with the ability to place collective demands within the policy-making processes of postindustrial societies and providing a means of nurturing isolated individuals (1975, 151–52). Realism's emphasis on state power and pursuit of the national interest fails to account for the resurgence of ethnicity in western Europe.

The limitations of the state-centered paradigm have been challenged by the transnational relations perspective proposed by Nye and Keohane (1973, ix–xxix). In proposing a broad and inclusive definition of transnational relations as the "movement of tangible and intangible items across state lines when at least one actor is not an agent of government or intergovernmental organization" (ibid., xii), Nye and Keohane offer a framework that encourages the study of a plurality of actors affecting world politics. Realists, however, have viewed the explanatory power of transnational relations as limited, because of the continued primacy of states (Bull 1977, 278). Notwithstanding the reservations of some realists, transnational relations, especially in the areas of bureaucratic and nongovernment relations, seem to have initiated a new era of global interactions.

As Chadwick Alger suggests, there is nothing new about the way individuals and ethnic groups interact in world politics (1984, 326):

> With the incorporation of transnational relations into the state paradigm, the impression has been created that so-called nonstate actors are entirely new, a product of modern transportation and communications. Certainly, jet engines and satellite communications have greatly changed the nature of global interactions among peoples. But sustained contact between local peoples over long distances is not new.

The diffusion of peoples, ideas, and goods through evolving patterns of global interdependence proceeded long before the Westphalia system solidified. The problem for international relations theories is that "this more encompassing perspective has not been incorporated into mainstream international/global research, thus serving to wall off people from understanding the historical links of their local communities in what William McNeil has called the 'ecumene'" (ibid.). James Rosenau's powerful assessment of change and continuity in global politics, *Turbulence in World Politics* (1990), is the most recent and basic attack on all forms of realism. No study of world politics is more open to the possibilities of global transformation based on the centrifugal force of a disintegrating globalized system.

In underscoring limitations of the state-centered model, transnational relations theory encourages us to consider ethnicity the result of complex patterns of global interdependence (Stack 1981, 17–19). As emerging transnational actors, ethnic groups seem destined to play a more significant role in world politics: "The ethnic nation cannot yet compete with the state in nuclear warheads and warships, but it continues to exercise formidable influence over the primary authority patterns of men. It is from this exercise of power that revolutions are born" (Said and Simmons 1976, 14). Global patterns of interdependence provide ethnic groups and other nonstate actors with additional techniques in attempting to influence states or international organizations (Rosenau 1990, 5–10, 388–415). For most mainstream theorists of the late 1970s and 1980s, however, ethnicity appeared to be a trivial concern, when considered alongside the issues of nuclear war and economic survival. The hope placed in the explanatory power of transnational relations was short-lived. Realism in a slightly altered form triumphed.

With the deterioration of United States–Soviet relations in the late 1970s and early 1980s, scholars reassessed the usefulness of realism. The limitations of the state-centered model of world politics and the awareness of increasing levels of global interdependence led to this reappraisal. The neorealists approached world politics with a profound respect for state power and for the centrality of states within a decentralized global system (Waltz 1979, 88–89). Realists, however, tended to underestimate the importance of economic forces and the power of informal regimes, which played a role in agenda setting, especially for medium-sized powers and nontraditional actors (Gilpin 1981, 35–36, 95–96). Neorealism extended its analytical reach by providing assessments of power from political and economic perspectives, but remained within the philosophical orbit of realism, very much a part of the distinctive political and economic climate of the late 1970s and early 1980s. As Robert Cox points out (1986, 248):

> Neorealism, both in its Waltzian structuralist form and in its game-theoretic interactionist form, appears ideologically to be a science at the service of big-power management of the international system. There is an unmistakably Panglossian quality to a theory published in the late 1970s which concludes that a bipolar system is the best of all possible worlds. The historical moment has left its indelible mark upon this purportedly universalist science.

From a neorealist perspective, ethnicity did not count in assessments of super-power and great power national security elites. The importance of ethnicity, one of the most significant forces in the formation of the post–cold war international system and now a central dimension in the articulation of major power foreign policies, was simply marginalized.

The contributions of Marxists, like their neorealist counterparts, left little room for the consideration of ethnicity. For Marxists, the vertical appeal of ethnicity was by definition subservient to the power of horizontal socioeconomic interests (Connor 1984a, 353). The philosophical underpinnings of Marxism, as of liberalism from which it is derived, postulate a unilinear model which views ethnicity as a "transitional phenomenon" (Smith 1981, 4). For example, if ethnic conflict results from modernization, then once the process of modernization runs its course, Marxism assumes, ethnic conflict will abate— probably to be replaced by class or some more legitimate, objective basis of group mobilization (ibid.) For Connor, the central failure of class-based theories is their reliance on causality and their attempt to place ethnic mobilizations within a historical process that will inevitably eliminate ethnic conflict: "It is likely that the tendency to perceive economic causation behind ethnonational developments is in large part due to a fortuitous accident of chronology. . . . Causal connection between economic force and ethnonationalism should not be inferred simply from the fact of coexistence" (1984a, 355). The history of Marxist attempts to subordinate ethnicity is instructive. Lenin's appeal to ethnic nationalism in 1924 played a vital role in the assumption of power by the Communist Party in the Soviet Union, the People's Republic of China, Vietnam, and Yugoslavia (ibid., 354). The rising tide of ethnic nationalism within Slavic Russia, the ethnic conflicts that now divide the Caucasus, and the ongoing slaughter in the Balkans are stark testaments to the failure of material interests to overcome primordial attachments. In a synthesis of the contributions made by dependency theorists to international relations theory, Harry Targ argues that the global dominance system of the future will engender a homogeneous global culture defined in the following terms (1976, 473):

> The new global culture would manifest patterns of consumption much like middle class patterns with the Center today. It would endorse and sustain the commitment to scientism and rationalism, and most importantly, it would accept the legitimacy of technocrats as men of power and authority. All of these would destroy the salience of heterogeneous elements of world culture.

Ethnicity challenges traditional assumptions of international relations theory, which views ethnicity as an atavistic force destined to disappear once it has run its course, at which time more enduring factors (such as socioeconomic class and state structure) will take hold. Such a perspective sees ethnicity as irrelevant. Ethnic attachments are by definition transitional, and ethnicity constitutes a false consciousness that will become readily apparent as individuals, states, and the global system move to other stages. Liberalism and Marxism share this perspective, drawing on the shared experience of the establishment of civil societies and secular political systems under the umbrella of the expanding Westphalian international system.

The problem with conventional interpretations is that ethnic conflicts have increased worldwide in the north and the south, within the states of western and eastern Europe, and throughout the world. More than twenty years ago, Connor described the pervasiveness of multiethnic societies and predicted the declining congruence between the nation and the state (1972, 319–55). Connor (1990, 99; 1984, 342–59) and Smith (1981; 1986b; 1991) have consistently, if not inexorably, demonstrated the conceptual problems that ethnicity continues to present to liberal theories of nationalism and modernization. Yet the importance of the ethnic group and the likelihood that ethnicity in its most politicized form will become a species of *ethnic nationalism,* with all the intensity that term conveys, appear to have been lost among the most prominent students of nationalism, the state, and the international system.

One way to extract oneself from such a conceptually impoverished perspective is to envision the creation of national societies in the West as very much an ongoing process, just as it is in eastern Europe, the former Soviet Union, and most of the rest of the world. Such a perspective virtually guarantees that ethnicity will become more relevant to the development of theories of international relations and will address the greatest single challenge confronting world politics—the issue of conflict resolution in ethnic and racially divided societies. Thus, the study of nineteenth-century nationalism is likely to yield insights that explain why contemporary ethnic nationalism challenges the legitimacy of the nation-state (Smith 1986b, 129–73).

The importance of states and the need for domestic and international order are beyond doubt. The failure of international relations theory to examine ethnicity as a meaningful force domestically and internationally goes hand in hand with a preference for studying material conditions, such as class, as determinants of individual and group behavior within states and for examining the critical role of states and economic forces in an anarchical global system. Despite the near universal refrain from proponents of realism that the issues surrounding global balances of power, the prospects of nuclear warfare, or the collapse of the global economic system were *the only important reality* of the cold war, the pervasiveness of deeply rooted ethnic conflicts throughout the world underscores why the study of ethnicity must be incorporated into the study of world politics as a key conceptual building block.

In sum, a primordial perspective to the study of ethnicity provides insight into the nature and intensity of ethnic conflict. Although cultural approaches to international relations have long been held in disrepute, Huntington's recent work reminds us that we can no longer afford to ignore culture as a dimension of world politics, whether in the clash between civilizations, among states, or within putatively well-integrated national societies.

Stanley Hoffmann has argued that the study of international relations is an American social science (1977, 41). The global importance of ethnicity challenges American scholars of international relations to confront the reality of ethnicity as a powerful global force, notwithstanding the liberal expectation that ethnicity should simply wither away.

Indigenous Peoples, States, and Conflict

Gerald R. Alfred and Franke Wilmer

In this chapter, we examine some of the core differences between indigenous and Western systems of thought regarding the intersection of political identity and issues of state sovereignty. A particular form of European ethnic identity lies at the core of the state, and state institutions support the values of the powerful ethnic group while delegitimizing the bases of alternative indigenous ethnic affiliations, which challenge the hegemony of the dominant group's values. Particular values flowing from a European culture have become entrenched, to the exclusion of those derived from indigenous cultures.

The first task is to explain the key differences between indigenous and European perspectives regarding the various aspects and elements of sovereignty. While we focus primarily on the case of indigenous peoples in the Americas, the common perspectives and concerns of indigenous peoples worldwide have been acknowledged at numerous international meetings among indigenous representatives (Wilmer 1993). The world system that has evolved based on European conceptions of sovereignty and territoriality embraces values that contrast with those presenting themselves in indigenous systems. It is the activism of indigenous groups that raises the issue of the dominance of European "ethnic states" and undermines the legitimacy of a system that marginalizes these groups culturally and politically. A number of policy implications arise out of the effort to accommodate and legitimize indigenous peoples' values within the state.

Among ethnic groups in the First World, indigenous peoples are the only ones whose political demands are firmly grounded in an international legal tradition. That tradition includes both a historical claim to sovereignty and a title to territory. Although aboriginal title is a controversial basis for indigenous land claims and many courts view it as inferior to the "proprietary" title claimed by European settler states, it has been recognized by those states. In addition, indigenous peoples who are parties to treaties with European governments are on equal legal footing with the European and settler states, which are also parties to such agreements. While these treaties did not *create* native sovereignty, they do constitute recognition of native sovereignty by Euro-American governments. And all indigenous peoples, whether parties to treaties or not, enjoy inherent and unextinguished sovereignty and the international right of self-determination.

From discussions among Spanish theologians in the sixteenth century to recent work of the United Nations Commission on Human Rights in the past two decades, indigenous peoples have been treated as subject to international law (Barsh 1986). Indigenous peoples are often also viewed as among the most successful ethnic groups making demands for self-determination, gauged by the extent to which demands are met with policy responses in the form of legislative or constitutional change (Werther 1992; Rudolph and Thompson 1985).

Worldwide, there are some 300 million persons who consider themselves indigenous. This status is defined in relation to a power-dominant, national political culture controlled either by descendants of European settler populations in the First World, or by politically decolonized "modernizing" elites in the Third World (Wilmer 1993). The first question raised in most discussions among nonindigenous people about indigenous peoples' politics is: Who are indigenous peoples? The best answer to this question, we believe, is that given by Robert T. Coulter, a lawyer and international advocate of indigenous peoples' rights: "Indigenous peoples are American Indians and people like them." The United Nations Working Group on Indigenous Peoples struggled for years with the issue of definition to develop international standards for the protection of indigenous peoples' rights. The definition that has emerged from this process, which included the participation of literally hundreds of indigenous peoples from around the world, stipulates three conditions: first, they are descended from the original inhabitants of the geographic area they continue to occupy, hence, they are aboriginal; second, they wish to live in conformity with their continuously evolving cultural traditions; and third, they do not now control their political destiny, and consequently are frequently subjected to policies arising from the cultural hegemony originally imposed by an "outside" force.

There is perhaps no issue of ethnic conflict that so cuts to the heart of politics than that of indigenous peoples' rights. According to Carment (1994a, 15, emphasis added), "The critical features of an ethnic group are that it is ascriptive and exclusive: its continuity depends on the maintenance of a *boundary based on values* and identity." Political scientists now widely agree that politics is about the allocation of values (Easton 1959, 1971; Easton 1966; Deutsch

1970; Gunnell 1988; Warren 1992), or, taking it a step further, about the allocation of resources according to values. And yet, virtually all social scientific thinking about ethnicity emphasizes the issue of identity, ignoring the importance of values and value conflicts.

With regard to indigenous ethnicity, however, it is the profound distance between the core values of traditional indigenous ways of life and those of the "modernizing" societies that lies at the heart of indigenous peoples' conflict with the state, and with the world system in which the state's legitimacy is embedded. "Modernization" refers to a program involving the economic mobilization of people and resources for the purpose of creating a capitalistic and industrialized infrastructure within the state, which in turn can be incorporated into a global capitalist system. In that system, both European societies and others emulating the European social model constitute a core elite group (Wilmer 1993). This global system has its roots in the development and expansion of European commercial economies and in four centuries of colonization. Modernizing societies have rationalized the appropriation of indigenous peoples' land and resources on the grounds that indigenous values are inferior to the capitalistic value of creating surplus, which vests in entrepreneurs a superior claim to land and property title that derives from a Lockean tradition.

Indigenous ways of life *prior* to contact with Europeans linked the acquisition of surplus wealth to certain beliefs about the necessity of balancing resource use with a sustainable environmental ethic. Indeed, many indigenous cultures contained specific practices to reinforce an ethic of generosity and exercised restraint on the acquisition of surplus by individuals as an end in itself. Ritual expressions of generosity, such as potlatches in the Pacific Northwest and giveaways among the Plains peoples, promoted mutual obligation and the strengthening of clan and family structures.

This is not to say that indigenous peoples' claims to sovereignty rest on the necessity of maintaining distinct or even traditional values. Instead, there has been a continuous claim to sovereignty from the earliest points of contact with Europeans and there is now claim to *internationally defined* self-determination. In exercising self-determination, indigenous peoples may choose to maintain or adapt systems of self-governance derived from traditional values or may devise entirely new institutions. However, it is the perception that *indigenous values, as distinct from European values, are inherently inferior* that rationalizes the preemption of indigenous self-determination and sovereignty by the presumed superior authority of the state. This presumption is the basis for the plenary power claimed by the United States government and for the priority of proprietary over aboriginal title asserted by the Canadian government. In both countries, the state has integrated within its legal and structural framework the set of beliefs that informed the initial interactions between indigenous and European peoples, and an inherently racist presupposition of the superiority of European values has become entrenched.

Conflicts between indigenous peoples and the state raise serious normative questions about national versus local or transnational configurations of identity. Although for analytical purposes we discuss the ways in which values and identity are distinct, in reality no such neat distinction occurs. Perhaps the most significant conflict between indigenous ways of life and the Western colonizers' program of national and global industrial development is the result of fundamentally different ways of understanding the relationship between human beings and the resource base on which they depend for their continued existence. Modernization requires an instrumental and objectified view of natural resources, a hierarchy of values in which the continuous and virtually limitless creation of surplus wealth (the constant growth assumption) and the development of complex hierarchical social structures to manage people and resources within a globally connected system of exchange are paramount. The traditional values of indigenous cultures, notwithstanding the tremendous variations of cultural practice and social organization among them (Deloria 1994, 1993a, 1993b; Akwesasne Notes 1978; Gawitrha' 1991; Suzuki and Knudtson 1992), contrast sharply with the values of modernization.[1]

Indigenous peoples may *choose* to adopt or adapt to values more consistent with modernization than what are here termed "traditional" values. Important and contentious discourses within many indigenous communities address the issue of adaptation and tradition, as communities seek a new or renewed consensus and normative basis. Their claim to self-determination and rights flowing from inherent sovereignty are unimpaired by the possibility of deviating, for whatever reason, from a purely "traditional" value orientation. We are not primarily concerned with the legal rights of indigenous peoples, but rather with the general nature of their conflict with states, which may include battles fought in legal and linguistic arenas.

According to the views of indigenous cultures, human beings exist within a web of life—there is no distinction between the human and natural worlds. Hence, "natural resources" or the "natural world" are experienced subjectively as well as objectively. Other elements and actors within the natural world have the right to control their destiny apart from human influence. The natural world—all its plants, animals, and minerals—has a mind of its own, so to speak.

Although surplus wealth may be created, at the collective cultural level its creation does not have primacy over other values. In fact, a different hierarchy exists altogether, which posits the predominance of human responsibility for taking care of the natural world. Most indigenous cultures are based materially on sustainable rather than surplus economies, or they balance sustainable and surplus values.

Of course, just as there are Western societies characterized by a greater or lesser degree of egalitarianism, some indigenous cultures do establish a certain hierarchy, proving once again that throughout history people the world over have experimented with all forms of social order and authority. Evidence for hierarchy, organizational complexity, and self-destructiveness through internal war or resource depletion abounds in the indigenous civilizations of the Mayans, the Anasazi, and the "mound builders." However, the tendency toward increasing complexity, incorporation, and centralization of control that enabled the state to emerge in Europe and the Far East has not generally been present in indigenous social structures in the past millennium or so.[2]

It is because these differences are of crucial political—and more to the point, economic—significance that conflicts arising out of indigenous ethnic activism go beyond the question of identity. Although certain kinds of cultures can exist without a material basis, indigenous cultures cannot, in that their boundaries are delineated by values regarding the use of resources. Indigenous ethnic activism calls into question nothing less than the underlying global process of economic incorporation of resources, which is carried out in local contexts by the policies of "modernizing" states.

The economic conflict over values and the centrality of these issues to the concept of indigenous ethnicity is an inevitable topic in discussions with indigenous peoples about politics. In interviews, Mohawk traditionalist Kevin Deer, who lived at the time in Kahnawake, six kilometers from Montreal, echoed many indigenous activists around the world: "I know what the white man wants, he wants my land. And he won't be satisfied until he has it all." Another traditionalist, Charles Patton, put it this way:

> Those people around us, their objective is to take away our land. The governments of Canada and the United States, their basic function is to eliminate us from the surface of the land. To eliminate us, our title of ownership of this land, control of the earth, so they can own it, finally. They will allow us to be ethnic peoples, they will allow us to have our little ethnic party on the riverfront on July 1st [Canada Day], but to concede that we still have ties and we are still the original people of this land, they won't ever do that. (Interview, 12 June 1992)

The conflict between indigenous peoples and the state and world system takes the form of a clash over the values invoked to allocate resources. The fundamental questions raised by indigenous political activism are: Should national and international political institutions allocating resources according to the primacy of industrial economic expansion be constrained by certain fundamental limitations? And should the right of indigenous peoples to a material basis sufficient for the perpetuation of their ways of life be among these limitations? Finally, what are the policy implications of indigenous ethnic activism and what national and international strategies can resolve the conflict and lead to a new partnership with indigenous peoples, based on their inclusion in international community building and on respect for their right to pursue a distinct path of cultural evolution?

Indigenous Identity: The Right to a Distinct Cultural Existence

The identity dimension of indigenous ethnicity is quite distinct from other kinds of ethnic identity, for two reasons. First, it is impossible to separate the fulfillment of indigenous identity needs from an attachment to certain geographic spaces (Deloria 1994). This includes not only "sacred places" but economic resources. Indigenous identity is perpetuated through the expression of unique values related to these resources, including values originating from a chosen path distinct from that of Western societies and modified through a process controlled by the indigenous people themselves.

Second, indigenous peoples are uniquely perceived *in the minds of policy makers controlling state institutions* to be in opposition to modernization (progress) or to be inferior to those pursuing such a program. Accordingly, they have been called "backward," "savage," or other similarly pejorative terms. Because of this perception, indigenous peoples in every part of the world have been consistently subjected to policies that are inherently degrading and destructive to their identity, and frequently to their physical survival as well. Thus, it is not only the Swedish or Thai immigrant in the United States or Canada who is forced to speak English at school, work, and in the public sphere in general. Among indigenous peoples, children were removed from their homes to grow up in a distant, culturally remote boarding school where authority figures believed at best that it was their duty, in the best interests of the children, to eliminate all vestiges of native cultural practices and beliefs. While these policies have been abandoned in the United States and Canada (though adoption policies have had the same effect on a smaller and less public scale until very recently), boarding schools and similar institutions are now on the rise in South America (Lizot 1976; Krueger 1986).

Clearly, Patton's statement that "they will allow us to be ethnic peoples, they will allow us to have our little ethnic party on the riverfront" points to the inadequacy of policies addressing only the identity dimension of indigenous peoples' concerns. Such policies are incapable of resolving fundamental conflicts over values. "Cultural pluralism" or policies concerned with protecting "ethnic diversity" are promoted only to the extent that they do not conflict with values invoked by the state to allocate economic resources. The conflict with indigenous peoples, as Patton, Deer, and many other indigenous activists have noted, is "about land" (Akwesasne Notes 1978; Deloria 1994; and Wilmer 1993).

In this sense, the political significance of ethnic identity as a problem of state policy is frequently viewed from the perspective of how individual members of ethnic groups are adversely affected by formal and informal political and economic discrimination. From this perspective, once the political and economic inequalities and discriminatory practices against *individuals* are addressed, the issue of ethnic identity will lose its political significance. We would like to cast the problem differently by posing the question: What is the political significance of ethnic identity in relation to the state as a set of governing institutions?

Part of the problem in attempting to come to terms with the pervasiveness of ethnic conflict today is that the rhetoric of modernity denies the ethnic basis of the state by putting forth images of a society organized more in terms of economic and social cleavages than in terms of ethnic ones. The state as we know it today is not and never has been an ethnically neutral actor. Instead, the state consists of a set of institutions, backed by coercive power, authoritatively allocating resources according to values. These institutions are in turn controlled predominantly by members of a particular ethnic group, who get to decide what official language(s) will be used, what cultural/symbolic practices will represent national political culture, what values will be invoked to allocate resources, and what terms and conditions, if any, for protecting diversity and promoting religious and ethnic tolerance and nondiscrimination will be set. This is true from Rwanda to Russia, from the United States to the People's Republic of China, with the only possible exception being those states where political cohesiveness is based on religious (not necessarily theocratic) rather than ethnic homogeneity among the "ruling class." The lack of ethnic neutrality simply becomes more obvious when we attempt to understand the policies of moral exclusion and coerced assimilation that have been implemented by states toward indigenous peoples.

The attempt to develop a policy of multiculturalism in Canada is a case in point. The official policy of the Multiculturalism Act of 1981 is to incorporate ethnic minorities and their cultures intact into Canadian society. The ideal is to promote the persistence of distinct cultural groups within Canada. Yet despite the existence of an act to promote multiculturalism, the reality is that Canada remains a dualistic country, officially bilingual, in which ethnic minorities are appeased by a policy that amounts to nothing more than folklore tokenism embracing superficial symbols of alternate ethnicities. In spite of the official policy, the "two founding nations" myth has remained unchanged, ethnicity has been stripped of its political component and power, and the preservation of institutions and value structures built on Euro-American (British and French) cultures has been achieved.

Ethnicity, the Multinational State, and the World System

Prior to the emergence of the nation-state in Europe and parts of Asia, the construction of collective, ethno-cultural identity was an exclusively "bottom-up" and localized process, created, transmitted, and transformed through the extended family, the clan, and the systems of interlocking clan and community alliances, which Western anthropologists often called "tribes."[3] Ethno-cultural identity throughout the world—in premodern Europe, Scandinavia, the Middle and Far East, as well as throughout the present-day Americas, Australasia, Africa, and the Pacific archipelagos—is clearly grounded in such primordial association (Condren 1989; Gimbutas 1982). Well into the first half of the twentieth century, European and Euro-American ethnographers made the assumption that, since such affiliations provided the basis for the development of cultural practices (including beliefs about and institutions of governance), and because sometime within the past millennium in Europe these bottom-up processes came under the control of hierarchical and incorporative political and religious institutions, similar developments were inevitable—and desirable—everywhere and for all peoples. In other words, since family, clan, and tribe preceded nation-state as the locus of political control in Europe, and since Europeans regarded their own path of cultural evolution as superior to all others, all peoples were believed to be following essentially the same path, though they were moving at a somewhat slower pace (explained by the "inferiority" of the non-European "other") (Sanders and Price 1968). Europe's "civilizing mission" would take the form of helping others to accelerate their own cultural evolutionary processes (Wilmer 1993). Once we abandon these ethnocentric axioms, however, different interpretations of the process of nation-state formation are possible.

The mobilization of a world system organized around a relatively small number of politically autonomous nation-states affects the political dimension of ethno-cultural identity in four ways: first, it reduces the number of political units in which ethno-cultural identity is the basis for self-government, by replacing ethnicity with statehood as the basis for sovereignty;[4] second, it destroys local self-governing communities since state building requires a hierarchical social order and an incorporative process for expanding influence to a degree not found within small, ethnically based local societies; third, it legitimizes claims by the nation-state to the loyalty of citizens so that the state can control critical economic and military resources to a greater extent than in ethnically based local communities; and fourth, it legitimizes national policies of cultural assimilation.

While there are between three thousand and four thousand distinct ethnic groups that have experienced the greatest portion of their histories as self-determining, self-governing peoples prior to European colonization, there are now only about one hundred and ninety nation-states acknowledged as politically sovereign equals within the world system (Connor 1972; Nietschmann 1987). This represents a noteworthy reduction in the number of self-governing political communities. The nation-state, which has become the basic unit of international political order, is predicated on the notion that the nation is an expanded form of ethnic association, and that within the context of that form, the set of governing institutions we refer to as "the state" emerge in response to environmental factors of increasing complexity in both economic and social terms. Thus there is a presumed continuity, first between ethnicity and nationhood, and then between nationhood and statehood. Of course, in reality, the process of incorporation was more revolutionary than evolutionary, and took place primarily in Europe, China, and Japan.

The emergence of the nation-state in Europe occurred only after nearly a millennium of subjection to outside influences—the conquest first by the Roman Empire, then by the Holy Roman Empire. When the Holy Roman Empire collapsed, it left behind a Christian Europe, and Christianity thus became the basis for membership in the European moral community (Wilmer 1993). From this basis, then, there ultimately emerged a system of European nation-states, or, as European leaders came to refer to them, of "civilized nations." The political restructuring that took place in Europe ultimately shaped the world system we know today, and in the process mounted a direct assault on the physical and cultural viability of indigenous peoples. In addition, that religious restructuring meant that, when assessing the moral competence of non-European peoples, Europeans ultimately evaluated both their own moral responsibilities and the rights of others in terms of Christian discourse. That discourse rationalized much of the harm done by European colonialists to indigenous peoples, including their baptism and subsequent execution by the European invaders in the Americas (Heizer and Almquist 1971).

In addition to a political restructuring and an emerging Christian basis for a European moral community, Europe as it emerged from the Dark Ages experienced an economic restructuring, first through commercialization and mercantilism, then through industrialization, both at home and in the first British colonies to be settled. Populations burgeoned among people whose immunities were strengthened in the aftermath of widespread epidemics, and the economic surplus was able to support a much larger population. Europe overflowed with people, whose materialistic worldview was increasingly devoid of moral restraint; yet ironically, these people also possessed the belief that the religious basis of their own moral community could include "others," if only those others were willing to assimilate through conversion. This was the Europe that literally set out to conquer the world in the sixteenth century. If anyone should doubt that this conquest formed the basis to rationalize doing harm to indigenous peoples, consider the response of the United States

State Department to complaints on behalf of indigenous peoples, presented to the United Nations Human Rights Commission in 1987: The continuing subjection of indigenous peoples to the ultimate authority of the United States government was said to be based legitimately on the law of conquest (United Nations 1987).

How does this affect the identity of indigenous peoples? Although China occupies Tibet, and Britain occupies Northern Ireland, only the United States has asserted in international forums that its legal claim to jurisdiction over indigenous peoples rests today on an international law of conquest (Wilmer 1993, 58). Furthermore, conquest has been the pretext for intrusion into every area of public and private life in indigenous communities: the boarding or adoption of children outside the community; policies of forced assimilation; forced removal from territories occupied "since time immemorial"; the outlawing of indigenous political institutions and religious practices. The legacy of conquest survives in the form of "plenary power" and the ward-guardian relationship derived from the international colonial law of trusteeship. American Indians, for instance, are the only "citizens" of the United States for whom the protections of the Constitution itself can be superseded by an act of Congress, undertaken under the (self-proclaimed) authority of plenary power. American Indians cannot sell, build on, or improve in any way land owned individually without approval from the Bureau of Indian Affairs; they cannot even harvest the land's natural resources such as timber. On the other hand, the bureau can approve plans to build on or improve land leased by an Indian "landowner" to a non-Indian, or to harvest its resources.

The Earth Is a Living Being

Issues related to state control over indigenous identity, however, cannot be fully appreciated without a consideration of the link between identity and values and the fundamentally different ways that the state and indigenous peoples relate to the physical or natural world. As a consequence of the spread of European economic interests throughout the world via colonization, "modernization," and "development" (as contexts of meaning) refer to the physical, natural world as one of "resources" that are to be used to maximize surplus value. The only hint of restraint in what has come to be known as the "industrialized world" has emerged quite recently in the form of environmental considerations.

The restraint with which indigenous peoples have traditionally exploited the earth's resources to meet their needs—what some might regard as an environmental ethic—should not be trivialized. It is precisely this restraint that stands as the most striking and contentious point of conflict between indigenous nations and nation-states. In the first place, immigrating newcomers should exercise restraint by showing respect for aboriginal inhabitants of an area and for their right to perpetuate a distinct cultural existence and control the resources necessary to do so. This kind of restraint was promised repeatedly in the treaties negotiated between the settlers and the indigenous peoples in North America, but many times these promises were broken.

In other parts of the world, including Australia and much of the Third World, there have been no such formalized promises. The Australian government has discussed negotiating a treaty with aboriginals, but as yet has not done so. An Aboriginal Reconciliation Commission has also been established in the prime minister's Office of Natives. It is geared toward resolving some of the disputes that arise in the process of implementing greater self-determination for aboriginal communities. Australia has also decentralized its aboriginal administration and incorporated aboriginal participation in decision making and implementation at all levels. Nonetheless, it has yet to deal with the basic issue of land title in contested areas.

The problem of broken treaties and the lack of respect for indigenous sovereignty is directly linked to the general issue of restraint, in that these legal encroachments into the political, self-governing status of indigenous communities, including physical invasions of indigenous territories were—and ultimately continue to be—motivated by economic forces. The continued expansion of control over resources for the creation of surplus value functions as a kind of "prime directive." Thus indigenous peoples' "backwardness" (frequently represented in images of indigenous identity) is juxtaposed with the "progressiveness" of Western-style resource exploitation, and that juxtaposition rationalizes the destruction of indigenous peoples' ways of life as a necessary step toward their "modernization."

Contrasting views embedded within indigenous cultures on one hand, and within modernizing cultures on the other, come sharply into focus in relation to the physical, natural world. Modernizing cultures seem to have a very narrow view of the natural world. When viewed in solely economic terms, the earth or physical world becomes simply a set of "resources." Even the definition of a state as "institutions exerting ultimate control over people and resources within a given territory" reveals this tendency toward a materialistic conception of the physical world.

Indigenous worldviews are also territorial and regard the various realms or kingdoms of the physical world—mineral, plant, and animal—as resources. Prior to contact with Europeans, indigenous peoples also used resources to create trade surpluses. Indigenous peoples today consider their worldviews to be continuous with pre-European indigenous worldviews. This does not mean they are the same; indeed, like all worldviews, they are continually adapting to changing circumstances. Worldviews cannot be considered bounded and fixed; like "culture," they are fluid, intermingling, and intersecting, even overlapping and layered. Some might even argue that many indigenous peoples today hold a worldview that is not distinguishable from a Western one. Nonetheless, we wish to focus on those aspects of indigenous worldviews that, according to persons from those communities, are distinct. That is, we focus our analysis on points of *conflict* rather than *convergence*. It is necessary to generalize about both the "Western" and "indigenous" views from the perspective of these conflicts, while acknowledging that within both categories there are diverse representations and variations of the larger commonalities.

Two things distinguish resource use among indigenous peoples from that among Europeans. First, indigenous peoples exercise restraint in the exploitation of resources; second, they believe that the earth is not only a set of resources but an organically integrated and interdependent whole and, on a local level, the site of sacred places, often viewed as essential to the spiritual survival of the people, and in some cases, to the whole of humanity (Waters 1963).

The interdependence of the natural world, including human beings, is not only represented by indigenous writers and activists. A young environmental engineer—a traditionalist—employed by the Mohawk Band Council at Akwesasne, explains the differences between Mohawk society and the dominant culture. According to him, the two cultures differ in language, the use of money (the Mohawks prefer bartering), and the relationship to the environment or resources (interview with Jim Ransom, 5 June 1993). The most important difference between traditional Mohawk society and the dominant society derives from the "psychological and social impacts of two different ways of life." Ransom explains:

> The difference can be thought of in terms of the difference between a Circle of Life versus a straight line of hierarchy with people at the head of the system and resources commanded or controlled by people. In a circle system people understand that everything that happens to resources comes back to the people. Understood as a Circle of Life, people and resources are continuously interrelated.

In a book originally written on the topic of sacred places, and recently expanded to include a more extensive discussion of the implications of differences in American Indian and Western metaphysical systems, Deloria (1994) discusses the linear versus circular orientations, arguing that one worldview is organized in temporal terms, the other in spatial terms. "Western European peoples," he says, "have never learned to consider the nature of the world discerned from a spatial point of view."

> American Indians hold their lands—places—as having the highest possible meaning, and all their statements are made with this reference point in mind.... The structure of their religious traditions is taken directly from

the world around them, from their relationships with other forms of life. Context is therefore all important for both practice and the understanding of reality.... The vast majority of Indian tribal religions, therefore, have a sacred center at a particular place, be it a river, a mountain, a plateau, valley, or other natural feature. This center enables the people to look out along the four dimensions and locate their lands, to relate all historical events within the confines of this particular land, and to accept responsibility for it. Regardless of what subsequently happens to the people, sacred lands remain as permanent fixtures in their cultural or religious understanding. (Deloria 1994, 65)

He contrasts this indigenous orientation with what he sees as the essential nature of the European identity, with its assumption of a linear progression in time and history, and with European societies as the culmination of the process.

Prior to the emergence of environmental activism, the Western (and industrialized) societies' view of the physical world as a set of resources was entirely one-dimensional. Indigenous worldviews pertaining to the physical world are much more complex. The issue is not which view is "better," or whether all resources should be used in a manner advocated by one view or the other. The issue is simply one of *restraint*. Should global and national political and economic institutions be held to some basic considerations of restraint in their ever expanding "development" schemes, which for centuries have rationalized destruction of indigenous self-determination? And should the rights of indigenous peoples to perpetuate a distinct cultural existence according to their own self-determined values (and adaptations of values) be among those restraints?

The Nature of Indigenous Peoples' Political Activism

Indigenous resistance to colonization, conquest, and forced assimilation has been a persistent feature of indigenous-European relations from the earliest days of contact (Wilmer 1993). Although international appeals were made to the British Commonwealth during the nineteenth century, and later an attempt was made to bring the issue of abrogated treaties before the League of Nations and the United Nations, the most intense international and coordinated transnational activism has occurred within the past two decades. Because in most cases the colonizing/settler populations quickly obtained a numerical advantage and brought with them sophisticated weapons against which indigenous peoples had no long-term chance of defending themselves and their territories,[5] most indigenous resistance has taken the form of political activism, with only occasional or relatively brief armed confrontations.

Indigenous activism varies according to the purposes and tactics used: assertions of sovereignty, litigation, alliances, protest activism, proactive "consciousness raising," and metapower (Wilmer 1993; Kane 1993; Darling et al. 1993).

Assertions of sovereignty often occur through legal battles, but may also take the form of sustained protest. One example is the recent reoccupation by the Guarani Indians of Takuaryty Ivykuarusu in the central region of the Mato Grosso do Sul in Brazil. When legal channels are nonexistent, unavailable, or persistently unresponsive to indigenous concerns, assertions of sovereignty may turn from resistance to violence. The armed indigenous resistance to the Chico dam project in the Cordillera region of the Philippines illustrates this kind of activism.

One of the most flagrant examples of how "development," as conceived by a dominant European-oriented or Western society, continues to rationalize intrusions into indigenous self-determination occurred in 1989 and 1990. Plans were announced to expand a private golf course just outside Oka, Quebec, into an area that Kanesatake Mohawks claimed as a Mohawk burial ground (Hornung 1991). This led to an armed standoff in the summer of 1990. The issue might be understood as being over who has "legal title" to the land—but whose legal system would be used to make such a determination? Viewed from the standpoint of the above arguments, however, the question is this: Should the dominant society of Quebec observe some restraint against the "development" of (or encroachment on) the several thousand acres of territory claimed by the Kanesatake Mohawks as their aboriginal lands and burial sites? Such assertions of sovereignty often grow out of or develop in conjunction with protests over specific developments.

Litigation is a strategy not only for asserting sovereignty, but also for enforcing domestic and international laws that do not directly raise questions of sovereignty. Although the bulk of this kind of litigation deals with land title, the case against Manoel Lucindo da Silva in Brazil raised charges of genocide—an international crime—against the Oro-Win Indians. A jury convicted him. The Brazilian Nucleus for Indigenous Rights and the Washington-based Environmental Defense Fund succeeded in obtaining an injunction against roads illegally opened by logging companies on indigenous land. Ecuadorian Indian groups, along with United States environmentalists, have filed a suit in United States federal district court against Texaco for damage to the Ecuadorian Amazon.

Another strategy is alliance making. For example, a Tribal Lands conference was held at Smith College in 1989, entitled "From Arctic to Amazonia: A Conference on the Industrialized Nations' Exploitation of Tribal Lands." The conference was attended by indigenous activists from Scandinavia, the United

States, South and Central America, and by environmentalists and academic researchers. The "Proyecto Ikam Ayamjut" (Project We Defend the Jungle) is a Peruvian native initiative linking the conservation concerns of Western environmentalists to issues of autonomy and ecologically sustainable development, for which the Amazonian peoples seek protection. Indigenous peoples form alliances among themselves and with nonindigenous groups, including environmentalist and human rights organizations. Alliances also form around specific protest movements.

Protest activism usually occurs in response to a specific action that encroaches on indigenous self-determination, or that is perceived as a threat to traditional indigenous values, as is often the case in various development schemes in the Third World. Some recent examples include protests against further oil drilling in the rain forests among Ecuadorian Indians, a massive Indian-orchestrated march on Quito in 1992, a sit-in by Tzeltal Indians in San Cristobol de las Casas in the summer of 1992, and the march in Guatemala City by more than three thousand Indians in February 1993. The James Bay Great Whale hydroelectric power project has been continually hampered over the past two decades by political and direct action protest, legal maneuvering, and alliance building between native and environmental activists in Canada and the United States. During the summer of 1995 Canadians witnessed a thirty-day armed standoff at Gustafsen Lake in British Columbia, and the occupation of Ipperwash Provincial Park. In the winter of 1995–1996, the Nuxalk Hereditary chiefs in British Columbia became involved in a political and legal conflict over the status of what the chiefs claim is unceded land, on which their people live. Examples of alliance-based protest include a June public meeting entitled "Exxon's Wisconsin-Colombia Connection"—a presentation by a Colombian Indian organizer cosponsored by the Madison Treaty Rights Support Group and the University of Wisconsin Greens and held at the Mole Lake Sokaogon Chippewa Community in Wisconsin.

In 1993, representatives (elders) from Huichol, Maya, Iroquois, Miqmac, Algonquin, Hopi, and other indigenous nations met at the United Nations for a historic "Cry of the Earth" conference to discuss their prophecies and concerns regarding the state of the global environment. Other prominent examples of consciousness raising include the First Continental Encounter of Indigenous Peoples in Quito, Ecuador, in July 1990 and the Encounter II of Indigenous Peoples, Nations, and Organizations in 1993; and the Peoples' International Tribunal, Ka Ho' Okolokolonui, held in Hawaii, which charged the United States with violating the human rights of the Kanaka Maoli Nation and People in Hawaii in 1993. The Fourth Russell Tribunal held in Rotterdam in 1980 heard more than fourteen cases involving the rights of the Indians of the Americas. Much of indigenous peoples' participation at the United Nations over the past seventeen years, and their involvement in the nongovern-

ment meetings coinciding with the Rio Earth Summit, is also of a conscious-
ness-raising nature.

Metapower activism has been described by Krasner (1981) as efforts directed toward altering existing institutional relationships. As a result of activism,
indigenous rights are protected in the Brazilian and the Colombian constitutions. Indigenous activists also engage in lobbying efforts within parliaments
and legislative bodies, send representatives to international organizations, and
make appeals to the World Bank and other development institutions. Eleven
indigenous organizations have "observer status" at the United Nations. Indigenous activism led the International Labour Organization in 1989 to revise its
1957 Convention on Indigenous and Tribal Populations in order to remove
the paternalistic tone and take into account such populations' existence as
peoples. In 1993 the United Nations Working Group on Indigenous Peoples
approved a set of draft principles for the protection of indigenous peoples'
rights. These principles are headed for the General Assembly where, it is hoped,
they will be passed as a declaration. The group immediately began work on
drafting a treaty based on these principles, which also eventually will be offered to the international community for ratification. This is the international
"legislative" path for the set of treaties and conventions that currently constitutes the body of international human rights law. These strategies represent a
growing sophistication among indigenous activists regarding the need to fundamentally alter the distribution of political power in national and international settings.

Policy Implications

Recent developments in the Mexican state of Chiapas notwithstanding, political conflicts with the state and state system rarely involve direct violence initiated by indigenous peoples. The policies of states and of international institutions such as the World Bank, however, have been marked by a long history of
devastating structural violence toward indigenous peoples, to such a degree
that such actions are sometimes characterized as genocidal (Jaimes 1992). The
80–90 percent decline in the indigenous population of North America, including the deaths of several million persons during the nineteenth century, is
not simply a tragic chapter in American history (Thornton 1987; Jaimes 1992).
It is representative of a pattern of destruction that follows from the expansion
of industrial economic activities—particularly those involved in the development of infrastructure and raw materials—such as mining and deforestation
or "timber harvest." These activities not only bring the spread of alien diseases
into vulnerable indigenous population areas; on the "development frontier,"
they also bring high levels of private violence by settler populations against
the indigenous peoples for whom these "resource frontiers" are an ancestral

homeland. These acts of violence are frequently ignored or condoned by state government authorities. In other words, the millions of indigenous people killed during the first century of American state building is being replicated in many areas of the Third World today, including Central and South America, India, and Southeast Asia.

Although policy analyses are often implicitly driven by a rational calculus, and in spite of the overwhelming imbalance of power and often unilateral direction of violence, there are at least four reasons why individuals involved in state and international policy making should take indigenous peoples' assertions seriously.

First, indigenous activism expands the principle of self-determination and asks us to consider how it can be applied beyond the limited case of decolonized territories, where boundaries were determined in a colonial office thousands of miles away. The United Nations and its judicial organ, the International Court of Justice, has thus far restricted the application of the principle of self-determination to the former trust territories under the United Nations mandate system. Yet the draft principles for the protection of indigenous peoples, after much contentious deliberation in the working group and after reassurances that the right of self-determination does not itself constitute or imply a right of secession, do acknowledge indigenous peoples' right to define self-determination in international terms. Self-determination at best means that individuals who identify themselves collectively as a "people" may control their political destiny. If the right of self-determination is granted to an expanding number of ethnic groups, we need to ask: How can this principle be realized by indigenous and other ethnic groups in a manner compatible with the basic state structure of the world system?

Here the experience of First World nations may be instructive. In the United States, for example, courts have recognized state and native sovereignty in addition to federal sovereignty. State and native sovereignty is inherent and reserved, while federal sovereignty consists of certain independent powers and of some powers shared or concurrent with state and tribal sovereignties. It becomes increasingly clear that sovereignty is no longer assumed to be either absolute or nonexistent (if it ever was, outside the writings of political scientists and philosophers). We might instead speak of more or less complete forms of sovereignty, with all sovereignties—including the international sovereignty of the nation-state—compromised by the force of some law that represents a political reality in which sovereignty is restrained. Federal (nation-state) sovereignty may be more *complete*—just as the sovereignty of more powerful nation-states may be more complete—than state or native sovereignty, but that does not mean that these forms of sovereignty are nonexistent. Federal sovereignty is itself limited by the reserved and inherent sovereignty of states and native nations. Rather than absolute sovereignty, we have a set of negotiated relationships in which power is shared, reserved, concurrent, and restrained by principles, norms, rules, treaties, constitutions, and compacts.

Second, indigenous ethnic assertiveness attests to the bankruptcy of cultural diffusion models, which assume that the assimilation of minorities into a national culture is inevitable, given an overall environment of equal economic and political opportunity for individuals. The melting pot has turned out to be a myth. The reason that persisting indigenous ethnicity is such a powerful test of the melting post hypothesis is precisely that it remains a viable source of both identity and values within the powerful states of the First World, in spite of centuries of persistent and well-funded efforts by these state governments to eliminate all signs of indigenous ethnicity—language, religious and cultural practice, family (by encouraging the adoption of native children), and distinct resource base. It thus seems more likely that the state must be adjusted to the reality of ethnic pluralism than assimilation into a national culture can be accomplished, even with the state's formidable coercive power.

Third, it is possible that the state can adjust peacefully to the reality of ethnic pluralism and can reach beyond ethnic tolerance and equal opportunities for individuals in order to achieve that adjustment. State-sanctioned harm against indigenous peoples has been perpetrated in virtually every form of discriminatory practice—from genocide and ethnocide to inequalities of economic and political opportunity. Transformation of the dominant society's perceptions of the moral competence and therefore moral equality (and entitlement to equality) of indigenous peoples is often painfully and dangerously slow. If the inclusion of indigenous peoples in domestic and global societies is to be based on an acknowledgment of their moral equality, then state and international political institutions must undertake policies aimed at racial reconciliation between indigenous nations and state societies. Racial reconciliation is needed in the large number of cases for which state building has involved, either officially or de facto, racial and ethnic oppression. Since some four thousand nationalities live in one hundred and seventy-five or so states, there is an enormous need to understand the necessity and dynamics of successful reconciliation. Indigenous activism offers special insights into peaceful change precisely because indigenous peoples must rely on such means to achieve their goals when confronted with the overwhelmingly superior weapons of Western, industrial societies. And because indigenous peoples' distinctiveness derives both from their identity and values, indigenous ethnicity can only be secured through the further legal development of group rights.

In light of the proliferation of ethnic conflicts during the second half of the twentieth century, and in view of the role ethnicity and nationalism played in both world wars, it is time to acknowledge that the state is not an ethnically neutral actor. Rather, it is a set of institutions controlled by individuals who conceive of themselves as constituting a kind of moral community whose boundaries are often delineated by ethnicity, which may include racial and cultural attributes. State institutions are used to organizing people and resources according to the values and identity of a dominant culture. In the case of indigenous peoples it makes sense to consider the possibility of denationalizing and deterritorializing political power. This could take the form of developing parallel indigenous parliaments that would have the power to review and ultimately veto any legislative initiatives involving or affecting indigenous interests. This also would provide an incentive for governments to involve indigenous peoples *in* the parliamentary processes where such policies are formulated in the first place, and thus avoid the potential for problematic reviews. This process would acknowledge the aboriginal interests of indigenous peoples and address the need to reconcile the structural and systemic effects of centuries of marginalization. Another possibility is represented by the New Zealand provision for four permanently "Maori" seats in the Parliament. Although it is not without controversy in New Zealand and in Canada (where some proposals for aboriginal electoral reform have referred to the New Zealand model), it does provide an example of how ethnic participation can be protected even as representation is denationalized (Fleras 1991). Experimentation with models of indigenous representation can also provide some insight into possibilities for negotiating new relationships between the state and ethnic groups in a variety of settings.

Finally, while their protests may have little substantive significance, indigenous peoples have policy relevance in relation to the world system as a whole because within that system, as Cohen (1960) has said, they are like Ghandi's "miner's canary"—they are the most vulnerable to its destructive influences. The negative consequences of a world system mobilized for the purpose of creating an ever increasing surplus wealth *without restraint*—the effects of excessive industrialization—affect everyone on the planet, or, from the viewpoint of traditional indigenous peoples, all the animals, plants, and minerals that make up life on the planet. Indigenous people may simply be more vulnerable to these effects in the short run.

How Do Peaceful
Secessions Happen?

Robert A. Young

The phenomenon of secession has recently attracted the attention of scholars working within a variety of theoretical perspectives. Spurred by events in the former USSR, specialists in comparative politics have returned to classic questions about nationalism and state viability (Schroeder 1992; Etzioni 1992; Bookman 1993). Studies of the legal and moral issues around secession have begun to proliferate (Buchanan 1991; Heraclides 1992). Political economists have attacked a process that lends itself well to calculation and strategic games (Wittman 1991; Simard 1991; Young 1994a; Carment and James 1994b). And theories both deductive and inductive are emerging on the causes and processes of secession (Buchanan and Faith 1987; Hechter 1992; Dion 1993). Of course, in particular countries such as Canada, where secession is a burning public issue, scholarly attention to all its causes, features, and likely effects is intense.

Within that context, my central purpose in this chapter is modest and straightforward. It is to arrive at empirical generalizations about the politics of the secession process. The objective is not to investigate the causes or consequences of secession; it is not to formulate theories about the relations between economic and social factors and political events; nor, finally, is it to predict when and how particular secessionist movements may achieve their ends. The purpose is simply to explore how secessions have occurred in the past and to search for general patterns in the political dynamics.

This is worth doing for several reasons. First, it is important to study the transition from a single sovereign unit to two or more states, because the outcome may be highly path-dependent. That is, the nature of the "new" polities and the economic and political relations between them may depend critically on the process through which secession took place. Second, a primary focus on politics is justified to the extent that political actors possess a high degree of autonomy in making decisions about secession and how to respond to it. The societal constraints on decision makers negotiating a new trade agreement, for example, may be far more binding than the constraints sensed by politicians, who must decide how far to push secessionist demands, how to respond to them, or how to negotiate the transition to separate sovereign entities. Finally, for analysts interested in particular cases, empirical generalizations about secession may assist in predicting how the process might unfold in other countries. Every country and every secessionist movement is unique, but this is precisely what renders predictions about each case unreliable (and contestable). Any evidence from comparative experience that suggests how the process might occur should be welcome to those who analyze particular systems. It is in fact possible to identify general patterns in the transition processes by which peaceful secessions have taken place. Whether these generalizations illuminate other contemporary cases remains to be seen.

Two basic limitations in this discussion should be noted. The most serious is that few cases are considered here. Most attention is devoted to only three—the secession of Singapore from Malaysia in 1965, of Hungary from Austria in 1867, and of Norway from Sweden in 1905. There are a handful of other cases to which some reference can be made, but these are primarily breakups of short-lived colonial federations, those countries outfitted by the receding British Empire with generic (or "neoclassical") federal systems that did not long endure (Franck 1968). Other cases include the breakup of the West Indian Federation, the nonformation of the East African Federation, and the disintegration of Rhodesia and Nyasaland (the Central African Federation). The secession of Iceland from Denmark in 1944 is of some interest as well.

This small sample also excludes contemporary secessions from the former USSR, not because withdrawal from a Communist empire is less relevant than some of the cases explored here—there undoubtedly is much to be learned from the CIS—but because time and linguistic constraints have not allowed me to gather reliable information. The breakup of the Czech and Slovak Federal Republic is of even greater interest, but I have treated it elsewhere in much more depth, using the same framework laid out here (Young 1994b).

Our confidence in the robustness and validity of the empirical generalizations is heightened by the fact that they accommodate the Czech-Slovak case very well, and therefore fit a modern, industrial, eastern European, and fully democratic country. Since the only commonalities among the cases, which differ widely in level of economic development, geographic location, cultural traditions, and political institutions, are that two sovereign states were formed where one had existed previously, our approach is oriented toward "most different systems" (Przeworski and Teune 1970, 31–39). Thus any commonalities in the political process through which secession occurred are all the more remarkable.

Another limitation is that this survey covers only cases of peaceful secession and excludes contested secessions. This is not because those cases are irrelevant; on the contrary, useful lessons and analogies have been drawn from them (Watts 1971; Nafziger and Richter 1976). Moreover, contested secessions are far more numerous than peaceful ones. But they fall into a different category from that of interest here. For many purposes, it may be more fruitful to examine cases of "success," and to look for patterns in the transitions, than to focus on instances of civil war in the hope of discovering salutary lessons. I also do not deal with a third class—the few instances, like Western Australia in 1933–1935 and Nova Scotia in 1868, where secessionist movements attained majority support among populations or elected representatives, but were simply ignored or "waited out."

So how has peaceful secession occurred in the past? What features have characterized the process?

Secession Follows Protracted Constitutional and Political Disputes

While the event of secession is always abrupt, cases of peaceful secession have capped long periods of disagreement between the constituent units of a federation or empire. In a sense, secession results from an impasse on an important matter of principle, even though this may be only one of many irritants, or one that becomes important as the symbolic focus of autonomist yearnings.

In 1867, Hungary and Austria were separated through the Ausgleich (Compromise), which was finally sealed by its acceptance by the Austrian Reichstat on 21 December (Tihany 1969). This agreement provided a durable arrangement for the coexistence of territories that had been united but riven by fundamental conflict for almost two decades. As part of the 1848 revolutions that swept Europe, Hungary first achieved a separate ministry responsible to the national Diet, and then declared formal independence in April 1849. This revolt was crushed by the Russians, who returned the errant state to the Austrian emperor. After a period of authoritarian rule in the 1850s, a brief flirtation with a decentralized structure was followed in 1861 by a centralized, bicameral system. This the Hungarians boycotted for some years in a struggle for greater autonomy. Their local diets generally refused to raise taxes or military recruits for the imperial authorities. In April 1865, Francis Deák and other Hungarian moderates published a program for reform that envisaged a largely autonomous country, and the emperor encouraged discussions to be held with Hungarian leaders because the central authorities were weakened by the boycott and by rapidly rising debt (May 1951, 495, n. 22; Huertas 1977, 37–38, table 8). In early 1866 a new Hungarian Diet was called, and it worked out a program for negotiations. But bargaining became serious only toward the end of the year, after Austria was defeated by the Prussians at Sadowa and the Treaty of Prague dissolved the Germanic Confederation, essentially removing Austria from the Germanic system and making an internal reordering highly advisable (May 1951, 34–36).

Norway, a Danish possession, was united with Sweden under King Karl XIII in 1814. While each country maintained separate citizenships, ministries, civil services, and courts, and while there was (formally) no joint legislature, there were important joint and common functions. The king appointed each of the ministries, could veto legislation, and, most critically, conducted war and foreign policy.

Despite the fact that Sweden's main economic links were to Germany while Norway's were to England, there was also substantial economic integration. A common coinage was introduced in 1875, and a joint tariff law prevailed after 1825. The tariffs covered a few items only, but were a cause of continuing dispute as Sweden sought to increase protection toward the end of the century; in the absence of an agreement, the joint laws lapsed in 1897 (Wendt 1981, 21). But there were no serious economic disputes between the countries.

Deeper political integration was resisted, primarily by Norway. An 1850s plan for a confederal legislature failed, and Norway also blocked moves toward closer cooperation in 1871, causing much bitterness (Lindgren 1959, 49–51). As under the Austro-Hungarian Ausgleich, it was the common royal prerogative that ensured some internal policy harmonization, through the veto power and the authority to select ministries. More important in an era of very limited government, the Crown's control over war and foreign policy enabled the countries to operate as a unit on the international stage, and although such an arrangement was not envisaged in the Riksakt (the Act of Union), the king was working through a joint council for diplomacy and foreign affairs by the late nineteenth century (Lindgren 1959, 62–65). In the case of Sweden and Norway, however, growing nationalism and liberal demands for a fully responsible government led to the secession.

The immediate issue of contention was the Norwegian demand for a separate consular service. This nearly led the countries to war in 1895. Further negotiations over the issue opened in 1902. The stakes escalated in a bitter election campaign, won by the Norwegian Conservatives, who then had one last chance to find a negotiated solution (ibid., 95–111). In February 1905, however, the Norwegians refused the Swedish proposals; in March a coalition government was formed in Norway; then a consular bill was passed with the knowledge that the king would veto it and precipitate a crisis.

The secession of Singapore from Malaysia on 9 August 1965 was remarkable for the speed with which it was accomplished. But the final, very brief negotiations put the seal on a disengagement motivated by acrimony on several fronts. Discord had been growing almost since Malaysia was formed in September 1963. Although this federation was very young, and in part a product of British imperial withdrawal, the sovereign Federation of Malaya had been formed in August 1957, building upon the four-state Federated Malay States (1895) and the Federation of Malaya Agreement (1948). More important, under colonial rule, Singapore and the Malay states had been governed as an economic unit since the nineteenth century. The common Malayan dollar, for instance, had been issued by a currency board since 1906 (Drake 1966, 28). Interrupted by World War II, (British-led) defense cooperation between the colonies had been close since 1951.

In this case, protracted and tense disputes about central-bank arrangements remained unresolved at the time of secession (Chan 1971, 36–37). In addition, Singapore, which had supported the federation in part to gain fuller access to the Malayan market, was disappointed by the slow progress toward the goal of a full common market, which was enshrined in Annex J of the 1963 constitution (Fletcher 1969, 12–16). Other causes of friction included the distribution of tax revenues in the federation, economic favoritism toward the Borneo territories (Sabah and Sarawak), and Singaporean underrepresentation in Parliament and the Cabinet (a consequence of the asymmetrical powers that Singapore possessed under the constitution) (Watts 1966, 177, 257). All these were aggravated by an undeclared war with Indonesia—the Confrontation—which put pressure on expenditures and led to the imposition of emergency power rule (Fletcher 1969, 16–23; Vreeland et al. 1970, 74; Ongkili 1985, 181; Lee 1986, 134–56).

The major incompatibility between the units, however, concerned race and the deeper ideology that would underpin the federal political system. The accession of Singapore (80 percent Chinese) to the Federation of Malaya posed a threat not only to the special privileges of the Malays (who became a minority overall), but also to the communitarian system through which the country had traditionally been governed. This was a system of elite accommodation between racial groups, largely achieved within the Alliance between the United Malay National Organization and the Malayan Chinese Association (UMNO-MCA). The Indian community, about 10 percent of the population, was also incorporated into this system. But communitarianism was challenged by Lee Kuan Yew of Singapore, through his People's Action Party (PAP), which advanced an ideology of progressivism, individualism, and pluralism, under the slogan "Malaysian Malaysia" (Ongkili 1985, 184–85). While the long-standing conflict was expressed through partisan competition, it went to the cultural and systemic foundations of the federation. PAP swept the 1963 elections in Singapore, then contested the 1964 elections on the mainland, though with little success. Undeterred, Lee Kuan Yew continued in 1965 to press for noncommunal equality and spearheaded the Malaysian Solidarity Convention to fight the Alliance, targeting the sensitive states of Sabah and Sarawak (Fletcher 1969, 50–51, 56–66). In the summer of 1965 there were serious race riots in Singapore, but even before this manifest unrest, it seems, Tunku Abdul Rahman, prime minister of Malaysia, had concluded that Singapore's secession would be desirable for Malaysian stability (Lyon 1976, 74–76); Lyon considers the possibility that the secession was a "contrived withdrawal" by Lee Kuan Yew. On balance, however, he agrees with most analysts that the event was an eviction.

The Secessor State Declares Its Intent to Withdraw

In the West Indies, the Jamaican referendum of September 1961 was immediately followed by a declaration that it would quit the Federation of the West Indies. In the case of Singapore, the situation was reversed: the Malaysian leader consulted his inner cabinet about Singapore's exit in July 1965, and declared his decision to the government of Singapore upon his return to Kuala Lumpur on 5 August. The announcement that Singapore would leave the federation was made in Parliament on 9 August.

In the Austria-Hungary case, the Hungarian Diet drew up and approved a program for independence in early 1866. But war with Prussia was declared the following day. In July 1866, after the empire's stunning defeats, Deák, the leader of the Hungarian moderates, met the emperor and in a famous interview was asked what Hungary wanted now that the realm was so weakened. He replied, "No more after Sadowa than before" (May 1951, 34).

In the Norwegian case, the declaration took two forms. The first was a Storting vote in favor of the principle of dissolving the union, passed under the new coalition government in March 1905. Then the consular bill was passed in May, and it was duly vetoed. The Norwegian ministry resigned. The final act came on 7 June, when the Storting passed a resolution authorizing the ministry to continue as the government and to exercise the authority granted to the king under the constitution. It also dissolved the union (Lindgren 1959, 130–31). This resolution passed unanimously.

Secession Is a Momentous, Galvanizing Event

Despite contemporary slogans such as the "velvet divorce" or the *rupture tranquille*, even peaceful secessions are times of much disruption and uncertainty. They mark profound changes in the relations between peoples and between states, and this is fully recognized at the time. Secession opens new possibilities and closes off options, and it does so in a compressed time period, when the actors and arguments and choices are known to have serious long-term consequences. Even peaceful separations are marked by considerable ferment.

There are always changes at the elite level. In the Hungarian case, for example, new leadership emerged in the moderate party during the early transition (in the person of Count Andrássy), and in Austria the minister-president resigned in some confusion after the major elements of the Ausgleich had been agreed upon. Coalitions formed and re-formed in both Norway and Sweden. Reflecting the turmoil of the transition, the internal politics and policies of the defederating units changed a great deal.

There is also considerable mass unrest and excitement. In Singapore, racial tension and conflict continued after secession. In Austria, the Czechs and other minorities saw new opportunities for autonomy during the uncertainty of 1866–1867, a prospect that led to external appeals to Russia and internal agitation by Prussia (May 1951, 50–51; Tapie 1971, 304–05). And in Norway-Sweden, secession was marked by huge public demonstrations in both countries, much chauvinism and tension, and the mobilization of defensive forces while the negotiations on disengagement were taking place (Lindgren 1959, 189–90).

The Predecessor State Accepts the Principle of Secession: Negotiations Follow

The most profound decision on the part of the leadership of the predecessor state is to accept the fact that secession will occur. In the cases examined here, this was a bitter and very difficult decision. But it marks the fundamental difference between peaceful secessions and those that are violent. This immense concession then sets in motion all that follows, and the first item is negotiation.

In the case of the breakups of colonial federations, it was the imperial power that generally had to accept the fact that secession would occur. In late 1962, for instance, Britain recognized the right of Nyasaland (later Malawi) to secede from the Central African Federation: this led directly to a similar demand by Northern Rhodesia, and to the Victoria Falls Conference in June 1963. Similarly, the British government accepted both the Jamaican referendum result and the decision of Trinidad to seek its own independence (Watts 1966, 311–12). In Malaysia-Singapore, the normal situation was reversed. It was Lee Kuan Yew who had to swallow the bitter pill presented by Malaysia and to negotiate as well as possible around the terms of secession presented to him and his colleagues (Ongkili 1985, 186). The acceptance in Austria-Hungary was through the emperor, who had come to the conclusion that the weakened realm could only be salvaged by placating the Magyars through recognition of the principle of Hungarian independence. Negotiations were opened after his meeting with Deák.

Acceptance was most difficult in Sweden, where the populace, the government, and the king were all shocked by the Storting's vote to sever the union. On the same day, however, despite some ministers' advocacy of war, the cabinet decided to proceed peacefully. This decision was confirmed by an extraordinary meeting of all party leaders the following day. Norwegian opinion was solid for sovereignty, war would be ruinous, and the great powers would isolate Sweden if it tried forcibly to maintain the union. Negotiation represented the only viable course of action. Even Conservative newspapers accepted, after the Storting vote, the fact that the union was "devoid of value for Sweden and, therefore, the use of force was unthinkable" (Lindgren 1959, 133–34).

The Government Is Broadened and Strengthened on Each Side

In order to undertake fundamental constitutional change, the governments of both the predecessor and successor state must be strengthened. Attention focuses on the immediate need to reach a settlement rather than on other constitutional matters. Hence, it is the leaders in place who assume responsibility for negotiating secession. And in nonbipartite cases, it is the central government that negotiates. In the extreme case, Malaysia-Singapore, the state governments—including Sabah and Sarawak, which had entered the expanded federation with Singapore—were not even informed about the secession arrangements (Ongkili 1985, 187–90).

But the national governments seek to augment their authority by broadening their bases of support. This occurs both in the period leading to the declaration of intent to secede and in the transitional period of negotiations. In Hungary, for example, the platform of demands issued by the Diet in 1866 was forged by a special committee of sixty-seven members, representing all factions, and by a strong executive committee of fifteen members. In Singapore and Malaysia, PAP and the Alliance, respectively, had overwhelming majorities; therefore, broadening was not necessary. But in Norway and Sweden, where the transition was particularly tense, this process was very evident.

In Norway in the spring of 1905, there was a tremendous premium on solidarity as the crisis developed. This is not to say that partisan considerations were entirely forgotten, for the radical Venstre Party pressed a hard line on the consular issue. Once that matter was decided, however, Norwegian politicians submerged their differences. A Special Committee of the Storting was established and took a great deal of initiative. Then a new coalition government was formed with broad representation; until the 7 June vote and during the subsequent negotiations, this ministry relied heavily on the committee

(Lindgren 1959, 128). The committee refused to abide by the views of the ministry just before the decisive vote, but there was no ministerial crisis: "The times demanded that there be no constitutional or parliamentary conflicts."

In Sweden after the vote, an Extraordinary Committee of the Riksdag was formed. It helped frame the national response to the Norwegian declaration, which consisted of a set of conditions to govern the secession. Then, in July, a coalition cabinet was assembled. This incorporated the opposition Liberals, and thus had a much broader composition than any preceding government (ibid., 149–51).

The crisis of secession, then, solidifies each side politically. And the sides polarize. These effects are undoubtedly less thoroughgoing than what occurs in contested secessions, when war entirely divides the states and forces internal unity. Nevertheless, those responsible for negotiations seek truly national support by submerging partisan and ideological differences for the duration of the crisis. And this effect is not confined to political elites. The secession plebiscite forced upon the Norwegians by the Swedes as a precondition of negotiations carried by 367,149 to 184 votes. Such a margin could never have been achieved six months earlier. The process of secession, or the crisis of the transition, itself generates internal unity.

The Negotiations Involve Few Participants

The cases examined here involve quasi democracies characterized by a limited franchise and deference to regal or charismatic leaders. Nevertheless, it is striking that the negotiating teams have been very small in number, and this is the more remarkable when combined with the broadening of support discussed above. The paradox vanishes when one realizes that the teams incorporate the strongest leaders of all factions. Furthermore, the same solidarity that arises from the national dimension of the crisis permits the delegation of substantial power to a very few representatives.

In Singapore-Malaysia, only the prime ministers were involved, aided by a few key members of their cabinets (Fletcher 1969, 3; Vreeland et al. 1970, 75). In East Africa, just as the Nairobi Declaration was the product of the anticolonial leaders from each state, so were the failed negotiations about federation conducted by them. In Austria-Hungary, the predecessor state was effectively represented by the minister of foreign affairs, Baron Ferdinand Beust, who was appointed in November 1866 and who alone conducted the serious negotiations that began in January 1867. In the case of Norway and Sweden, one immediate and critical issue to settle was whether Norway should invite a member of the Swedish Royal House (the Bernadottes) to take the throne: secret negotiations undertaken by one man produced a solution—Prince Carl of Denmark—within a month (though confirmation was delayed until after the main negotiations were finished, because the election of a king had implications for international recognition) (Lindgren 1959, 155–66). The main negotiations about secession and its terms, conducted at the Karlstad Conference, involved Norwegian and Swedish delegations of only four members each.

The Settlement Is Made Quickly

Negotiations about secession are not protracted. When a unit breaks up peacefully, the two sides disengage quickly, and the negotiations concern a relatively short list of items that are settled in principle. Singapore-Malaysia is the extreme case. Tunku Abdul Rahman returned from London to Kuala Lumpur on 5 August 1965 and summoned Lee Kuan Yew to present him with the separation agreement, which was signed on 7 August and passed through Parliament on 9 August, becoming effective immediately (Means 1970, 294–95; Chan 1971, 58–59). The Victoria Falls Conference that dissolved the federation of Rhodesia and Nyasaland took place in less than a week in June–July 1963: the federation was terminated formally in December of that same year. The Jamaican referendum in favor of secession took place in mid-September 1961, and the Federation of the West Indies was wound up in May 1962. The Karlstad Conference opened on 31 August 1905, and negotiations were completed on 22 September: then the Storting approved the arrangements on 30 September, the Riksdag legislated the abrogation of the Act of Union on 16 October, the king abdicated, and the Storting unanimously elected Prince Carl of Denmark as Haakon VII on 18 November.

The content of negotiations, of course, is primarily about the terms and conditions of disengagement. Even when it is not limited to this and the framework for future relationships is also established, events move quickly. In the Austria-Hungary case, an extremely complex set of institutions was established under the Ausgleich. These were patterned on the Hungarian proposal of 1866. But serious negotiations began only in January 1867. By mid-February the Hungarian constitution was restored along with a responsible ministry, and Hungary approved the Ausgleich on 29 May. In Austria, approval was delayed by an election and by the insistence that all financial arrangements be made final; nevertheless, the Reichstat enacted the Compromise on 21 December 1867.

The Settlement Involves a Relatively Short List of Items

In cases of peaceful secession, negotiations center on a few significant matters. This is not a sufficient condition for a quick resolution of the crisis, but it does appear to be a general feature of these secessions. The two parties settle the most pressing issues in framework agreements, leaving other matters and details to be worked out later.

The Singapore-Malaysia separation agreement, for instance, has only eight articles. It recognizes Singapore's sovereignty, commits the parties to a treaty on external defense and mutual assistance (spelling out four principles that primarily confer military rights upon Malaysia), establishes the principle of economic cooperation, repeals the economic union provisions of the 1963 constitution, and releases Malaysia from its guarantees of Singapore's debt. In the case of Norway and Sweden, the Swedes imposed the prenegotiation condition of a plebiscite to sound out Norwegian opinion. The actual negotiations concerned only the following items: first, Sweden's demand that Norwegian forts on the frontier be razed; second, the establishment of a ten-kilometer neutral zone along the border; third, guarantees for the unimpeded migration of the Lapps; fourth, equal rights for transit and access to transfrontier watercourses (for railroads and water for log drives); and fifth, an arbitration treaty to govern future disputes (Lindgren 1959, 145–51).

Finally, in the Austria-Hungary case, the negotiations concerned not only the principles of disengagement—the restoration of the Hungarian constitution, a fully responsible ministry, and the coronation of Franz Joseph as king of Hungary—but also the mechanisms for future coordination. These were complex, involving a small number of common ministers, decennial agreements about the common tariff schedule, each state's contributions to the common expenses, and a confederal system of "delegations" from each state to approve annual budgets. But much of this was left to be fleshed out in subsequent discussions and later practice. Hungary approved the arrangement even before the first tax contributions had been fixed. In any event, the complex institutional structure of what Lloyd George called this "ramshackle realm" was settled within a year's time.

Foreign Powers Play an Important Role

The dissolution of the new Commonwealth federations was crucially dependent on Great Britain's approval of terms and also on the probability of international recognition. In Malaysia-Singapore, the confrontation with Indonesia made precipitous action more likely (and more necessary, from Malaysia's standpoint). But Indonesia also offered potential new markets to Singapore, which quickly assumed a friendlier stance toward it; in fact, after Singapore withdrew from the Combined Defence Council in March 1966, Indonesia moved to establish normal relations with the new state (Boyce 1968, 24–25, 88–92). Despite Singapore's moves toward nonalignment and a new relationship with the United States, its partners in the existing Anglo-Malayan Defence Agreement tended to insist that it continue to cooperate with Malaysia in matters of defense (Vreeland et al. 1970, 358–59; Chan 1971, 41–47; Jenkins 1980, 26–28).

In Austria-Hungary, the threatened international position of the empire was an underlying cause of disengagement. In the longer term, relations with Germany (through the 1879 Dual Alliance against Russia) also helped maintain the confederal system of the Ausgleich. This mitigated the fear of absorption into Germany among the inhabitants of Cisleithania (especially the minorities) while diminishing the threat posed to the Magyars by the Southern Slavs (Mason 1985). More generally, the secession was peaceful and the new arrangement worked because outside powers—Germany, Turkey, and Russia—each could pose as an ally of some internal minorities, and therefore presented threats to others (hence Deák's remark, "For us Austria's existence is just as necessary as our existence is for Austria" [Tihany 1969, 118]).

Norway-Sweden provides further examples. As the consular crisis mounted, the Norwegians immediately understood how important international recognition of their new state would be. This underlay both a vigorous public relations campaign among the great powers and the decision to continue a monarchical system (with a Bernadotte as king, if necessary) (Lindren 1959, 112–14, 127–31). In addition, fear of outside intervention in Scandinavia certainly helped lead both sides toward compromise when, even during the Karlstad Conference, each country contemplated war (ibid., 182–86).

The Secession Is Accomplished Constitutionally

Peaceful secessions, without exception, are achieved through established legal processes. There is no legal rupture of the type associated with unilateral declarations of independence. This is a straightforward consequence of the predecessor state accepting the principle that secession will occur.

In Austria-Hungary, the restoration of the Hungarian constitution was effected through a royal letter, and the Ausgleich was properly passed by the Diet. Similarly, the Austrian Diet amended the 1861 constitution to bring it into conformity with the new arrangement, and these changes to fundamental laws were duly sanctioned by the emperor. In the Norway-Sweden case, established rules prevailed, as the Act of Union was abrogated by the two legislatures, the king abdicated his Norwegian throne, and the new king was properly elected and crowned. In the case of Singapore-Malaysia, the Malaysian Parliament took only three hours to pass the constitutional amendment that eliminated Singapore from the federation, by the required two-thirds majority (in fact, it passed unanimously, the PAP members having absented themselves by prior arrangement). The new colonial federations that broke up also did so constitutionally: each failure was "marked by a constitutional act, like federation itself" (Franck 1968, 170). Even in the case of Iceland's separation from Denmark in 1944, in the midst of war, when the Nazis controlled Denmark and the British were in Iceland, the matter was accomplished constitutionally. Iceland invoked a clause in the Act of Union that allowed for unilateral termination of the act, and the decision was confirmed as required by a national referendum (Andrén 1964, 97–98).

There Are No Other Substantial Constitutional Changes in Either the Seceding or the Predecessor State

One might anticipate that such a fundamental change as secession would either force or allow for other constitutional alterations. But this is not the case. The reason appears to be twofold. The predecessor state, and especially the seceding state, seek stability, the first for damage control and the second for international credibility. In addition, for the significant policy changes that each state generally does undertake, constitutional amendment is not a prerequisite.

In any event, there are some limited exceptions. In some short-lived colonial federations, the secession of one state—Jamaica or Nyasaland—led to the collapse of the rest of the federation. In Austria-Hungary, much of the drive for the new arrangements came from ethnic tension, not only between the two major ethnic groups but also between each of them and internal minorities. Hungary's Magyar majority was well served by their traditional constitution, and no postsecession change occurred there. In Austria, however, secession was accompanied by a vigorous debate about the degree of centralization that should obtain within the realm, with the non-Germanic minorities pressing the case for local autonomy. In the end, constitutional changes were enacted to confer the residual power upon the regional diets (May 1951, 37–38). Provincial legislation still required the emperor's approval, however, and the Crown also appointed the provincial governors and the presidents of the regional diets; moreover, in 1873, direct elections to the central parliament replaced indirect election by those diets, further weakening their power.

There were policy changes, however. In Hungary, separation allowed the continuance and heightening of social conservatism, including a firm policy of Magyar supremacy, which was pursued in the linguistic and educational fields. In Austria, by contrast, the German-speaking Liberal Party introduced important social and economic reforms (May 1951, 46–69; Mason 1985, 16–18).

In Malaysia, there were postsecession constitutional changes associated with ethnic issues, which had been made acute when Singapore joined and then left the Federation. In 1967, Malay became the sole official language, except in Sabah and Sarawak. But this was due to happen in any event under the 1957 constitution (Watts 1966, 234; Vreeland et al. 1970, 94; Ongkili 1985,

194–95). Further, in response to sectarian violence, discussion of racial issues was outlawed between 1969 and 1971, under constitutionally invoked emergency powers. For its part, Singapore established a constitutional commission in March 1966. But there was no change until 1969, and this was minor: the Presidential Council was established to examine legislation and advise on it.

Again, while there was no constitutional change directly associated with secession, there was considerable policy change. Malaysia moved to diminish internal economic barriers. Singapore did much more. Under the slogan "Survival," the government moved toward *dirigisme*, the construction of a "tightly organized society," with national service, new labor legislation attractive to investors, and a general stance favoring order and economic growth (Chan 1971, 48–51, 22–25; Bedlington 1978, 210–43).

In the Norway-Sweden case, policy changed in Sweden as the Liberals came to power in late 1905. But there was no constitutional change after secession. Norway provides a clear example of how secessionist states avoid unnecessary constitutional change: its leaders decided to retain the monarchy so as not to offend the European powers (a choice ratified by plebiscite) and even extended an invitation to a son of the very monarch whose abdication would be occasioned by secession. There was to be no change in the form of government, in order to avoid a constitutional crisis simultaneous with secession, to placate Swedish rage, and to attain quicker international recognition. Subsequently, Norway moved on several policy fronts to become one of the most liberal states in the world, but apart from an extension of the franchise, this did not involve internal constitutional restructuring.

Policies in the Two States Soon Begin to Diverge

In Austria-Hungary, secession produced two sovereign states. But, in contrast to the other cases, it was accompanied by new institutions for coordination. The keystone of the system was the monarch, Franz Joseph, emperor of Austria and king of Hungary, who chose separate ministries in each country, as well as special, common ministers for foreign relations, the military, and the joint finances to support these functions. This structure was successful in maintaining common defense, monetary, and tariff structure until the Dual Monarchy collapsed during World War I. But there was tremendous friction between the two states, and this grew over time. The tariff negotiations broke down in 1897, only Austrian tolerance permitted agreement on the level of financial contributions, and the Hungarians sought more influence over the National Bank and the army. Moreover, domestic policies on minorities and religious matters began to diverge shortly after the Ausgleich was enacted; indeed, secession had come about in part to allow autonomy in these matters.

In Norway-Sweden, domestic policies did diverge along broad ideological lines. But there was also some coordination within the Scandinavian framework. This was accomplished through informal mechanisms, like the Scandinavian Inter-Parliamentary Union, established in 1907, the Nordic Societies, established in 1919, and many voluntary associations (Lindgren 1959, 235, 245–46). In this, the common foreign policy of neutrality and isolation helped, as did the stabilizing presence of Denmark (and the later participation of Iceland and Finland). After the separation, the two (and three) countries sometimes passed parallel legislation, such as the Marriage Law of 1921–1925, but this continued a tradition dating back to the monetary convention of the 1870s and the Bank Drafts Act of 1880 (Leistikow 1950, 307–24, 311–18). Lindgren argues that "the union itself formed a barrier, and . . . its dissolution opened the way for an integration impossible under pre-1905 conditions" (1959, 7). But it would not do to overstate this case. The countries never signed a mutual defense treaty, Norway enjoyed a great power guarantee of its borders, and the kings did not meet until 1914. The development of genuinely integrative institutions awaited the formation of the Nordic Council in 1951 (Wendt 1981).

The countries of the colonial federations did not tend to harmonize policies upon dissolution. In Central Africa, economic integration had deepened considerably in the federation era, and existing trade patterns did continue, even with the renegade state of Southern Rhodesia (Spiro 1968, 80). But this was a consequence of the abject dependence of Zambia on Rhodesian coal and hydroelectric power for its copper industry. Apart from this, integration eroded, notably when Malawi and Zambia issued their own currencies in 1963. In East Africa there was an even longer history of cooperation among Tanganyika, Zanzibar, Kenya, and Uganda, with a postal union dating from 1911, a customs union from 1917, and a common currency from 1920. These arrangements deteriorated soon after the projected federation failed. By 1965 Tanzania was imposing quotas on Kenyan goods, and the currency union was fractured in 1966. Generally, economic policies came to diverge sharply, and there were also military tensions between the former partners (Franck 1968, 6–11, 17–18).

Singapore-Malaysia provides a striking instance of policy divergence. Article 6 of the separation agreement provided for cooperation in economic affairs and the establishment of joint committees and councils to promote it. But within a week of the secession, Singapore restricted imports of 187 manufactured goods from Malaysia. Malaysia retaliated. By October the governments had agreed to revert to the status quo ante; but when Malaysia announced it would work toward an internal common market within the federation, Singapore reimposed tariffs. It then established a work permit system for noncitizens, and Malaysia set up immigration controls (Chan 1971, 29–32). Despite some later relaxation of these measures, Singapore's policy on foreign labor was dictated exclusively by its domestic interests (Pang and Lim 1982).

In 1967 the currency union was ended. Singapore withdrew from the Combined Defence Council, and there was little cooperation in this area. There were no prime ministerial visits until the early 1970s (Bedlington 1978, 247–48). Singapore was even thrown out of the Associated Chinese Chambers of Commerce in Malaysia (Chan 1971, 39). As a consequence of nation-building policies on both sides, economic integration weakened. In 1964, Malay peninsula imports from or via Singapore were 37 percent of the total, and exports were 28 percent: this dropped to 9 percent and 20 percent by 1975 (ibid., 33, n. 48; Vreeland et al. 1970, 338). The federation itself was short-lived. But its breakup led to the erosion of an economy that had been integrating for decades.

Secession Is Irrevocable

There has never been a case of reunification after secession. This is because of two factors. First, the whole project of the seceding state is to acquire more autonomy. The exercise of these greater powers would be compromised by integrative arrangements. More important, however, are the effects of the transition itself. The process of secession marks both elites and the masses. It affects them profoundly. Not only is there the psychic break, with the recognition that the community is fractured, there is also the internal solidarity forged in the process of disengagement. Unity on each side develops through the crisis and is built by a collective concentration on the "Other." Hence each community is solidified through the transition process, and even where there is not great animosity between the two citizenries, the crisis forges separate identities and interests that cannot subsequently be subsumed under a larger unit. As Watts put it, "Whenever secession has occurred, it has inevitably been accompanied by sharp political controversies which are not easily forgotten. . . . The resentments aroused by the circumstances occurring at the time of separation have tended to persist and to discourage the subsequent creation of a looser form of association between the territories concerned" (Watts 1971, 69).

Systemic War in the Former Yugoslavia

Manus I. Midlarsky

I n 1991, Germany, newly reunified under Helmut Kohl, announced support for an independent Croatia emerging out of a disintegrating Yugoslavia; Germany dragged its allies in the EC after it and set the stage for ongoing communal strife in the Balkans. In 1878, a recently unified Germany led by Bismarck (the "honest broker") hosted the Berlin conference that ended the Russo-Turkish hostilities and, by establishing the new political entities of Serbia and Bulgaria, set the stage for communal strife lasting more than three decades. In the latter instance, a world war followed on these events; in the former, we have yet to see any signs of political violence beyond the confines of the former Yugoslavia.

Here we have two illustrations of intense communal violence, begun after the sovereignty of new political entities but with radically different international outcomes. What accounts for the difference? In particular, why, at the present time, has the extent of internationalization of the violence been minimized, while the extent of the violence itself, when compared to the late nineteenth- and early twentieth-century cases, has increased? Whereas there was serious communal violence in the earlier periods, it does not compare to the genocidal activities of the various actors in the recent communal strife in Bosnia-Herzegovina.

To understand the differences between the two cases, we need to turn to the earlier instances and consider their impact on the etiology of World War I. As it turns out, the concept of systemic war and a theoretical framework designed to explain it, initially useful in understanding the origins of World War I, will, with minor modifications, also be useful in understanding the extent of violence in the former Yugoslavia.

Let us turn first to the international system. By *stability* I mean the continuity of the system itself. Thus, I shall identify any communal violence that increases the probability of systemic war. *Systemic war* is a war entailing the breakdown of the international system as it existed prior to the outbreak. The scope of the war—the number of participating countries and the degree of civilian-military participation (with the resulting civilian casualties and battle deaths)—must be extensive to bring about a systemic breakdown. Essentially, the scope of the war and the widespread bloodshed (which also implies long duration) lead not only to the rise of new great powers and the decline of older ones, but also to extensive efforts to restructure the system in ways that will prevent the emergence of another widespread conflict of this type (for example, the agreements at Westphalia, Vienna, Versailles, or San Francisco).

There is, however, some ambiguity in the concept of communal strife. *Communal strife* can certainly be understood as the presence of conflict, including violence, between entire communities (towns, villages, rural environs), based on racial, religious, linguistic, or other differences. To a large extent, ethnicity is self-defining, in that the emphasis on social, linguistic, or religious identity tends to be a matter of group choice. The Flemings and Walloons in Belgium emphasize language differences, as do French-speaking and English-speaking Canadians. (The religious dimension appears to have been downplayed in recent years.) Often, external forces can sharpen ethnic distinctions; such was the case of Nazi policies toward the Jews before and during World War II. More recently, the loose association of urban Muslims in Bosnia, based on a shared religion, has probably been strengthened by the Serb and Croat attacks.

However, conflict between communities does not have to be based on such ascriptive criteria. These differences may be fused with other distinctions, such as class. Thus, a somewhat broader sense will prove useful in this context, for it will invoke theoretical bases for understanding the genesis of communal strife. For our purposes, then, strife between communities based on any one of the dimensions listed above will constitute a species of communal strife which, in addition, will include the possibility of conflict based on other criteria such as class. Unlike Chazan (1991) and Horowitz (1991), I do not distinguish between state formation, irredentism, and secession regarding the tendency toward internationalization. All three can be associated with communal violence and systemic war. The essential variable is the violence itself occurring at certain key points in the etiology of systemic war.

I shall adopt two strategies in this analysis. The first is principally historical. Here I ask the traditional question of origins. When we examine the events leading to the onset of World War I, do we find communal violence at some key originating point in the etiology of the conflict? And if we do discover communal violence, what are its precise dimensions? As it turns out, there are clear indications in this instance of the importance of communal violence at an early stage of the process leading to systemic war.[1]

The second strategy is more analytical. Given a theoretical framework for understanding how systemic wars begin, is there a role for communal violence as a causative agent? Are there any points within a causal sequence of variables at which communal strife plays a role in the onset of systemic war? If so, what is that role?

This chapter describes instances of communal strife in Bosnia-Herzegovina and Macedonia, including international consequences prior to World War I. I then detail the confluence of these instances of communal strife with a theoretical framework designed to explain the onset of systemic war (see Midlarsky 1992a). Finally, I examine the current strife in the former Yugoslavia as a regional systemic war, using the same theoretical framework, but with some modifications. This is a productive perspective for explaining the intensity of the recent strife, but also the absence of serious internationalization, in contrast to the period before World War I.

Origins of World War I

In two important instances, communal violence erupted into regional war and then had profound consequences for the onset of World War I. The first occurred at the very beginning of the period of concern here. The location of this strife, Bosnia-Herzegovina, is important because, after the first instances of communal strife, this region assumed critical importance in the policy conflicts among the eastern powers, culminating in the Bosnian crisis of 1908. This crisis, with its opposing coalitions, was to be a virtual dress rehearsal for the June crisis of 1914, precipitated by the assassination of Archduke Francis Ferdinand in Sarajevo, the Bosnian capital.

Bosnia-Herzegovina

The composition of the population of Bosnia-Herzegovina was at least 32 percent Muslim, 43 percent Serbian Orthodox, and 23 percent Croat Catholic. Jews made up less than 1 percent of the population. These figures are based on the first accurate population census of Bosnia undertaken by the Austrians in 1910 (Donia 1981, 1). We can infer from them that the Muslim population of Bosnia was probably higher in 1875, since the province was under Austrian administration after 1878, and some Muslims migrated to Ottoman-held territories after this date.

Muslims were Serbo-Croation ethnically, but had converted to Islam after the Ottoman Conquest (Donia 1981, 3; Schevill 1933, 393). The vast majority of landowners were Muslim, as were many of the peasants. Virtually all the Christians were peasants. As the agrarian situation worsened as the result of overpopulation and the limited possibility of emigration (Kinder and Hilgemann 1978, 81), hostilities between Christian peasants and Muslim landowners grew throughout the nineteenth century.

As the century waned, the Ottoman armed forces were increasingly called upon to protect the interests of Muslims. This was due to the increasing consciousness on the part of the Christian peasantry of their common identity in opposition to the Muslim elite. This condition was aggravated by Orthodox Pan-Slavists, who propagandized from Russia and Serbia, but also had indigenous roots.

The rural overpopulation in Bosnia-Herzegovina had several consequences. Landowners sought to take advantage of the surplus population, despite genuine efforts by the Ottoman administration to support certain rights of the peasantry. Reforms instituted in the late 1850s proved difficult to enforce, and the landowners continually attempted, with some success, to transform *agaliks* (landholdings to which the peasants had clear rights) into *begliks* (property that belonged fully to the landlord) (Jelavich 1983, 1:351). Rural overpopulation implied a high rate of subdivision of land owned or worked by peasants, thus rendering many of the holdings unusable as bases of sustenance (Midlarsky 1988b). Hence one would expect to find not only an increasingly land-poor peasantry but an increasing number of landowners, almost entirely Muslim, who benefited from the transformation of *agaliks* into *begliks*. And this is what we find, at least in data from around the turn of the century, which indicate a tripling of the number of Muslim landowners between 1885 and 1910 (Donia 1981, 39). This disproportionate increase occurred after the introduction of an Austrian administration that maintained almost intact the traditional legal system of landownership. Thus, earlier years probably witnessed a similar transformation; as Jelavich remarks, "The basic cause [of the revolt] was the agrarian situation and the strained relations between peasants and the landholders" (1983, 1:352).

These social conditions, however, were now to give rise directly to strife between communities. The hostility between Christian peasant and Muslim landowner, built up over a period of years, manifested itself in spontaneous uprisings against tax collection. The harvest of 1874 was especially poor in Bosnia and Herzegovina, and attempted tax collections in 1875 led to the initial uprising in Herzegovina (Shaw and Shaw 1977, 158). Attacks on the tax farmers ultimately spread to the Muslim villages themselves, especially after arms and ammunition had been obtained from neighboring Montenegro. The revolt quickly spread to all parts of Bosnia and Herzegovina.

International Consequences

After these uprisings, two small neighboring countries, Serbia and Montenegro, declared war on the Ottoman sultan in support of the rebels in Bosnia and Herzegovina. Russia saw this as an opportunity to dismember the Ottoman Empire once and for all. The Russo-Turkish War ensued in April 1877, and by the beginning of 1878 Russian forces were approaching Constantinople. Through the Treaty of San Stefano, sought by the Turks, vast gains were to be obtained for Bulgaria and Romania, including independence for Romania and penalties for the Turks. This inevitably aroused the interest if not the envy of concerned powers such as Austria-Hungary. In 1878, Bismarck called the Congress of Berlin to resolve these matters and especially to keep peace between his two allies in the Dreikaiserbund ('Three Emperors' League), Austria-Hungary and Russia.

Aside from the reduction of gains for Russia at Ottoman expense, a principal consequence of the Congress of Berlin was to reduce the size of Bulgaria (Crampton 1983, 22–23). Eastern Rumelia, which would have accrued to Bulgaria in the Treaty of San Stefano, was "returned" to the Ottoman Turks under the anomalous designation of "an autonomous province of the Turkish Empire" (Thompson 1966, 432). Here occurred the sequence of events that led directly to World War I.

A German, Prince Battenberg of the House of Hesse-Darmstadt, was elected to the Bulgarian throne with the consent of Tsar Alexander II (Kennan 1979, 104). Although Battenberg's relations with the Russian ruling house were strained at times, they became far worse after the assassination of Alexander II and the accession to the throne of Alexander III. At an early stage in his reign, sometime in 1883, the new tsar vowed to be rid of the Bulgarian monarch, largely because of the latter's intent to rule his country without undue Russian influence, including that of the two Russian generals sent by Alexander III to oversee matters.

After a period of intense diplomatic conflict between the two countries, matters came to a head in 1885 with a spontaneous uprising in Eastern Rumelia in favor of unification with Bulgaria. All the major powers were surprised by the event, and Battenberg rose to the occasion and assumed leadership of both halves of Bulgaria, even to the point of defending Bulgaria successfully against an invading Serbian army.

It was clear to the tsar, however, that the emergence of a united Bulgaria under a new national hero would not exactly wed the new country to any great power, not even to Russia. Indeed, Austrian power was being felt in the region, particularly in the ultimatum to Battenberg to cease his pursuit of the now defeated Serbian army. This was in addition to the already evident Austrian domination of Serbia, which had probably also been arrogated to the Russian sphere after the Congress of Berlin.

Thus, Russian policy in the Balkans was perceived to have been a grand failure. One of Russia's ostensible satellites in the region, gained as the result of the Congress of Berlin, was lost to Austria, and the other, Bulgaria, was moving in the same direction.

Here we see one of the consequences of the communal strife that occurred in 1875, culminating in the Russo-Turkish War of 1877–1878. As a settlement to that war, the Congress of Berlin had been called in part to keep peace between Bismarck's two allies, Austria-Hungary and Russia. Now, as the result of the events of 1885 in Bulgaria, the Dreikaiserbund seemed to be in more difficulty than ever. And this alliance was no mere political understanding among the three monarchies. It was Bismarck's creation, intended principally to keep Russia tied politically to Germany and hence removed from any French political moves that would seek *revanche* for the earlier cession of Alsace-Lorraine to Germany.

In December 1885, at the end of the brief Serbo-Bulgarian hostilities, the first open dissatisfaction over the Dreikaiserbund appeared in the conservative nationalist press. M. N. Katkov, the extremely influential editor of *Moskovskie Vyedomosti,* accused Battenberg and the three emperors' alliance of being a tool of England (Kennan 1979, 144). By the following summer, Katkov was ready for a fuller statement of this position. This was an editorial in *Moskovskie Vyedomosti,* published on 30 July 1886, in which he effectively urged the abandonment of the Dreikaiserbund (Kennan 1979). Although Austria-Hungary was perceived as the principal opponent, it was Bismarck and the German powers backing Austria that proved the real limitation on Russia's greatness. The German chancellor's machinations were squeezing Russia out of the Balkans. Russia could achieve its true stature as a great power only independently of the limitations of the Dreikaiserbund. In 1887, the tsar withdrew Russia from the Dreikaiserbund.

Thus, a direct line runs from the incidence of communal strife in 1875 through the Russo-Turkish and Serbo-Bulgarian Wars to the generation of a new alliance that was to transform the political landscape of Europe. This alliance was the outcome most dreaded by Bismarck. A Franco-Russian rapprochement was concluded in 1891 and strengthened in terms of defense in 1894; its target could only be Germany as the expression of French *revanche* and Russian resentment over past injury. The entire basis of Bismarck's eastern policy—the separation of France and Russia via the Dreikaiserbund—had collapsed.

Here, the influence of class-based divisions such as peasant and landlord intersected with communally derived divisions such as religion, leading to the onset of communal violence. The Franco-Russian alliance was facilitated by Montenegro and Serbia's declarations of war against the Ottoman Empire and the resulting Russo-Turkish and Serbo-Bulgarian wars. That laid the foundation for World War I. The path to the Balkan Wars later in this period entailed different but perhaps no less interesting dynamics.

Macedonia

The ethno-religious divisions of Macedonia, which lay at the origin of the Balkan Wars, were far more complex than those of Bosnia-Herzegovina. In addition to the 1,145,849 Muslims in 1906, there were 623,197 Greek Orthodox under the jurisdiction of the Patriarchate, 626,715 Bulgarian Orthodox who were members of the Exarchate (the Orthodox Church in Bulgaria), and a total of 59,564 "others"—Jews, Greek Catholics, and Vlachs (ethnic Romanians) (Shaw and Shaw 1977, 208). The Muslims, however, were not an ethnically distinct group, but consisted of Albanians, Turks, and Slavs, in addition to the mostly Slavic Muslim refugees from the earlier disorders in Bosnia, Herzegovina, and Bulgaria. Even the Christian Slavs were not a homogeneous group, but were either Bulgarian or Serbian.

This heterogeneous ethnic and religious mix lived in extreme poverty, as was the case in Bosnia and Herzegovina. The same sorts of Ottoman estates existed here too, but there was some tendency for the larger estates, the *chiftliks,* to be parceled out among the peasants. There were also very small peasant holdings. The land was in poor condition; virtually all arable land was under cultivation, with additional erosion of the topsoil as the result of massive deforestation.

In this mix of multiple communities and poverty, one would expect to find extreme competition if not violence. As of the late nineteenth century, four countries—Bulgaria, Greece, Serbia, and Romania—had put in claims for portions of Macedonia. The Albanians sought to incorporate sections of that territory into an autonomous region. Within this territory itself, several organizations were formed to represent specific ethnic, religious, or national interests.

Clearly, the varied goals pursued by these groups were incompatible and led to considerable communal violence.

> Starting in 1900 the different groups began their campaigns, ravaging the countryside, slaughtering officials as well as Muslim and Christian subjects who refused to accept their points of view. Trains and postal carriages were intercepted, foreigners and wealthy natives kidnapped for ransom, churches blown up. Macedonia became a common expression of horror in the foreign press particularly when incidents involved foreigners or Christians. (Shaw and Shaw 1977, 209)

A chaotic and violent situation developed, not dissimilar to that which recently existed in Lebanon; and the Ottomans found it increasingly difficult to control. By 1908, the Ottoman government had placed most of its army in this region. This concentration of force and the government's inability to control the situation precipitated the Young Turk revolution in that year (in Salonika, the Macedonian capital), with consequences that led directly to the two Balkan Wars. In an effort to consolidate its power among these various minorities, the government of the Young Turks (whose rebellion against Sultan Abdul-Hamid II originated in Macedonia) sought to impose a "common law, a national language and compulsory military service" on the province (Thompson 1966, 439).

International Consequences

Efforts by the government of the Young Turks to impose some uniform standards and to quell the revolts had a number of consequences. In 1910, a brigandage law was enacted, making parents responsible for the misdeeds of their children. Additionally, Bulgarian Christians felt discriminated against because of the forced closing of Exarchist schools, the shutting down of Bulgarian-language publications, and the suppression of Bulgarian clubs. Other groups, such as the Serbs, appeared not to receive the same sort of discriminatory treatment. Muslim refugees who were allowed to enter Macedonia from Bosnia and Herzegovina worsened the problem, since Bulgarian Christians were denied entry. During the summer of 1909, bands of insurgents were active once again. In 1910, meetings were held in Sofia to denounce the brigandage law and to protest the appointment of Serbian church officials, since corresponding Bulgarian Exarchate officials were not being appointed. Of course, with a Bulgarian population in Macedonia that was larger and politically more active than the Serbs, the Bulgars constituted a more serious threat to Turkish rule and received correspondingly harsher treatment. In December 1911, terrorists blew up railway installations and a mosque in Shtip (Crampton 1983).

Each of the surrounding Balkan powers saw some opportunity for national aggrandizement in these Macedonian troubles but awaited some concatenation of internal and external signals. The Macedonian reaction to the systematizing efforts of the Young Turks, combined with the external difficulties of the Ottoman Empire in Albania and Libya in 1910 and 1911, provided the signal for joint action in the form of the First Balkan War of 1912–1913. The victory over the Ottoman army was relatively easy. The Balkan forces numbered about 700,000, versus 320,000 for their opponent. Ottoman military power had been weakened by the domestic political conflicts and financial problems that left the army bereft of modern equipment. The Ottoman government had feared the outbreak of such a war and, in preparation, had reached settlements with the Albanians in September and with Italy in October. These involved major territorial cessions to the Italians, especially in North Africa. In previous years, the Ottoman armies had usually been able to defeat the Balkan forces, but the combination at this time was too strong. The Bulgarian army did the major fighting and was ultimately the principal force leading to the collapse of Ottoman rule.

After the Second Balkan War against a Bulgaria that had become territorially ambitious, the 1913 Treaty of Bucharest partitioned Macedonia and established an independent Albania. The great victors were Serbia and Greece (Jelavich 1983, 99).

The two Balkan Wars of 1912–1913 had consequences that included the near destruction of the Ottoman Empire and the considerable enlargement of Serbia. The near collapse of the Ottoman Empire in Europe during the First Balkan War was a frightening portent for Austria-Hungary, another multinational empire. The actual enlargement of Serbia to nearly twice its size prior to the Balkan Wars now had disastrous implications for Austria-Hungary. With the growing population within the empire and Serbian hostility toward the peremptory annexation of Bosnia-Herzegovina by Austria-Hungary in 1908, an enlarged Serbia could only mean trouble for the Hapsburg monarchy. With the assassination of Archduke Francis Ferdinand by a Serbian nationalist one year after the end of the Balkan Wars, the Austrians' determination to deal harshly with Serbia was reinforced, thus making war between the two countries far more likely.

There is an extremely close relationship between certain of the theoretical considerations advanced in this discussion of communal strife in Bosnia-Herzegovina, and later in Macedonia, and the sequence of variables that appear in the analytic framework I devised to explain the onset of systemic war.

Both instances of communal strife occurred under conditions of extreme scarcity. Land was not readily available and was of poor quality. The analytic framework predicts that under conditions of extreme scarcity, inequality will increase (Midlarsky 1988b). This was the case in Bosnia, with the increasing gulf between landlords and peasants. In a multipolar setting, the greater the scarcity, the greater the inequality between most and least favored actors. In fact, *multipolarity* is the first variable in the analytic sequence. Structurally, the situation in Bosnia was similar if not identical to the heterogeneous system of many actors existing in a state of poverty in Macedonia. The Macedonian situation also corresponds structurally to the multipolarity of the European system of 1914. Under such conditions, inequality is bound to increase and exacerbate relations among the actors in the system.

Convergence with an Analytical Framework

In earlier work (Midlarsky 1988a, 1989b), I put forward a theoretical framework for the analysis of systemic war. I did not intend it to be an exclusive explanation, since arms races, irredenta, nationalism, and failures of modernization (for example, in Russia and Turkey), among other factors, enter into the etiology of systemic war to varying degrees. Rather, I intended that this framework should detail the direct consequences of multipolarity and emerging inequality among the major powers. Through this framework, I generated a sequence of variables, which showed resource inequality occurring as a consequence of multipolarity, alliance formation following upon that inequality, and alliance memory, overlap in conflict structures, and changes in the balance of power leading to the occurrence of systemic war. Thus:

Multipolarity → Resource inequality → Alliance formation → Alliance memory → Overlap in conflict structures → Change in the balance of power → Systemic war

The first of these relationships was suggested by a probabilistic analysis that showed multipolarity to be associated with resource inequality but bipolarity to be associated with equality. The greater the scarcity of resources (such as in colonies or political satellites) in a multipolar setting, the greater the inequality of resource distribution between most and least favored actors. Such inequalities can lead less favored actors to seek allies as a way to redress the apparent inequality.

Envy and political intrigue can result in such a system, thus leading to the deterioration of interstate relations. This conclusion follows from the still widely accepted observation that equality is more conducive than inequality to political stability. Justice is virtually equated with equality in Aristotle's *Politics* and in John Rawls's second principle of justice, which demands equal access to all social and economic opportunities (Rawls 1971). Furthermore, entire theories of instability have been based on the premise of severe inequalities and have been confirmed empirically. These include theories based on relative deprivation, rapidly declining economic circumstances, and scarcity of valued commodities (e.g., Gurr 1970; Midlarsky 1988b). Given a particular society of states, equalities among the members are more likely than inequalities to yield stability in the long run. In the modern period the most stable societies by far are those with industrialized economies and their associated equalities; in contrast, severe inequalities are found in largely agrarian countries that are prone to instability.

Old conflicts can persist as the result of memory among alliances, especially the memory of conflicts with smaller powers, and these memories can have implications for major power wars. This memory, in turn, can lead to the overlap in conflict domains, specifically between disputes involving major powers only and disputes between major powers that also involve a lesser power. When these two sets of conflict behaviors overlap, nations are well on the way to systemic war.

Exactly this type of overlap existed in the period immediately preceding

World War I. Neither the pattern of great power disputes alone nor disputes also involving a smaller power were associated with instability during the period 1893–1914. Only when the two separate sets of disputes were combined did instability occur. During this period, the great power disputes were principally those occurring among France, Germany, and Great Britain. Disputes involving a smaller power were those between Austria-Hungary either alone or with a smaller Balkan ally on one side, and Russia with its own Balkan ally on the other. The 1908 Bosnian crisis and the early period of the June crisis of 1914 are cases in point. The dispute between Russia—in support of Serbia—and Austria-Hungary was the beginning of both crises. Only when Germany and France (in 1908), or Germany, France, and Britain (in 1914) were drawn into these crises did these Balkan-based disputes overlap with those of the great powers, endangering the system.

A perceived or actual change in the balance of power immediately preceded the onset of systemic wars. A principal actor in the conflict either gained significantly in power prior to the onset of the war or was perceived to have experienced such a gain. This change in the balance can be aggravated if another principal actor simultaneously appears to be losing power or if such a loss seems to be impending. Just such a scenario occurred prior to World War I. Not only did Serbia double in size as the result of the Balkan Wars, thus becoming a more substantial threat to Austria-Hungary, but the tottering great power also appeared to be disintegrating from within. The Slavic population was becoming restive and the central government was at pains to maintain internal unity. The size of Serbia magnified internal dissension, attracting the South Slavs, especially those in the province of Bosnia-Herzegovina, which had recently been annexed (1908). If Austria-Hungary were to disintegrate, Germany would be bereft of its only great power ally, whose forces were essential to oppose Russian forces in the East in the event of war. It was the actual change in the balance in Serbia's favor vis-à-vis Austria-Hungary, coupled with German fears for the future of its ally, that led directly to the onset of World War I.

In the first of our instances, communal strife had a direct impact on inequality in the distribution of scarce resources in the system, the second variable in our sequence. The Congress of Berlin, following the Russo-Turkish War and its role in Bosnian, Herzegovinan, and Macedonian communal strife, may have arrogated both Serbia and Bulgaria—fellow Slav countries—to the Russian sphere of influence. Prior to the Bulgarian *gâchis*, as Kennan calls it, Serbia was already lost to the Russian sphere and, as a result of the events of 1885, Bulgaria was moving in the same direction. Austria-Hungary and its ostensible great power ally, Germany, were the big winners, at Russian expense. We have already seen how Bismarck, the German chancellor, was blamed by Russian nationalists for having fomented the Austrian success. In fact, Bismarck continually urged the Austrians to respect Russian interests in the Balkans (Kennan 1979, 241). Yet the Russians felt so badly beaten by the Austrians in the competition for political satellites that they badly misperceived the German position. This "defeat" led to the rupture of one alliance, the Dreikaiserbund, and the beginning of another, the Franco-Russian alliance, which opposed the Dual Alliance of Austria-Hungary and Germany. Thus, the communal strife of 1875, via the subsequent Russo-Turkish and Serbo-Bulgarian hostilities, stimulated resource inequality and alliance formation. These are two of the variables in the theoretical framework I have presented to explain the onset of systemic war.

The second instance of communal strife leading to the Balkan Wars had strong direct and indirect effects on the propensity toward systemic war. The direct effect was the change in the balance of power (the next to last variable in our sequence) after the Balkan Wars. Serbia emerged at twice its initial size. This change favoring Serbia profoundly affected the June crisis of 1914, since the increased size of Serbia exerted a powerful influence on the already restive Slavic population within the empire. As early as 1908, after the de jure annexation of Bosnia-Herzegovina by Austria-Hungary, the Bosnian crisis set a virtual collision course between Austria-Hungary and Serbia. The largely Slavic population of those formerly Ottoman provinces vastly preferred incorporation into a Slavic state such as Serbia. At the time, the Serbs accounted for nearly half the population (43 percent) of Bosnia-Herzegovina and many Croats (23 percent of the population) also supported the principle of Slavic self-determination. The Austro-Hungarian annexation was bitterly opposed by Serbia. Indeed, this crisis was virtually a dress rehearsal for that of 1914. Russia, in support of its Serbian fellow Slav neighbor and in alliance with France, faced Austria-Hungary and Germany. The acceptance of a German ultimatum by a Russia weakened by the Russo-Japanese war prevented the onset of war but engendered extreme hostility in Serbia. A covert and sometimes overt propaganda campaign aimed at Slavic populations under Austro-Hungarian governance emanated from Serbia, right up to the time of the 1914 crisis. An enlarged Serbia was an intolerable magnet for this Slavic population now in a state of unrest, especially in the annexed provinces of Bosnia and Herzegovina. When the assassination of Archduke Francis Ferdinand occurred in Bosnia, with the apparent complicity of elements of Serbian right-wing government circles, the provocation was extreme and led to the ultimatum to the Serbs, precipitating the June crisis.

There is another sense in which the change in the balance of power was influenced by the communal strife leading to the Balkan Wars. It was during this period after the Bosnian crisis that the Dual Alliance between Austria-Hungary and Germany was strengthened. Bismarck's initial reluctance to fully support the Austrians ("He scattered promises so as not to carry them out"

[Taylor 1971, 278]) led to a transformation in the alliance. At Algeciras in 1906, when Austria-Hungary was the only great power supporting the Germans concerning the confrontation over Morocco, and during the Bosnian crisis, when German support of the Austrians was required, the two allies came closer together. German decision makers realized they needed the Austrians to defend against the large Russian forces to the east. Only a great power such as Austria-Hungary would be able to field armed forces large enough to oppose Russia in central Europe. The Schlieffen Plan, developed by the German general staff, required a strong move to the west at the early stages of a general war, followed by a strong move to the east, after the defeat of the western opponents. Clearly, large Austrian ground forces allied to Germany would be extremely beneficial in maintaining the integrity of the eastern front until German forces in the west could be transported east.

In this strengthened Dual Alliance lay the seeds of the coming systemic war. An alliance memory was formed, wherein the foreign policy concerns or "memories" of a smaller great power ally became the concerns of the stronger partner. In the future, the conflicts between the Austrians and the Balkan countries would become Germany's concerns as well, via the now strengthened Dual Alliance.

The rise of Serbia in 1913, initiated by the communal strife in Macedonia leading to the Balkan Wars, introduced several elements of the causal sequence that leads to systemic war. The alliance memory of Austro-Hungarian conflict with the Balkan countries became Germany's concern, which was far more serious now that Serbia was twice its initial size. This in turn led to the overlap of conflict structures, wherein what had been exclusively major power conflicts of Germany joined with the conflicts experienced by Austria-Hungary involving smaller powers.

Thus, a change in the balance of power between Austria-Hungary and Serbia at the end of the Balkan Wars had two major consequences. For Austria-Hungary, it meant an increased threat that had to be dealt with harshly in 1914. For Germany, it meant that an alliance memory and an overlap in conflict structures (two variables in our causal sequence) led to a perceived change in the balance of power in Germany's disfavor. Austria-Hungary was perceived to be an essential ally of Germany, and at the same time was threatened by the specter of internal disintegration because Serbia was attracting the Slavic population within the empire. Therefore, Austria-Hungary had to be supported at all costs; Germany even egged it on in the confrontation with Serbia (Fischer 1967; Nomikos and North 1976). If there was a threat to the internal integrity of the Dual Monarchy, Germany had to deal with it immediately and not wait for further dissolution to occur, since that might render Austria-Hungary useless as a great power ally. As it happens, the German calculation was correct, for despite the polyglot nature of their armies, the Austro-Hungarians fought reasonably well against the Russians and later, after they entered the war on the side of the Allies, against the Italians.

Bosnia-Herzegovina Today

With this understanding of the origins of World War I, let us turn to the recent situation in Bosnia and address the two questions indicated at the outset: Why has the extent of internationalization been low compared to the period preceding World War I; and why, at the same time, has the extent of violence apparently been greater? Consider first the recent history of the conflict. In reporting these events, I follow the account published in the *Economist* (1993, 23–26).

In June 1991 the federal Yugoslav army, increasingly dominated by Serbs, fought a ten-day war against local Slovene militiamen in Slovenia. This was a vain attempt by the federal government to prevent Slovene secession. There followed a seven-month war between Serbia and Croatia, ending in January 1992. Croatia lost approximately one-third of its territory (most of which was later regained), but achieved international recognition. In April 1992 the most destructive of all three wars began. This was the three-way struggle among Serbs, Croats, and Muslims for control of Bosnia-Herzegovina. Clearly, the Muslims were the major losers, with the Croats gaining some of Bosnia and the Serbs emerging as the winners of a large share of the territory. The scale of the killing is in dispute, but the savagery is not in doubt.

How did perhaps the most modern and open of all the Slavic eastern European countries descend to this level of barbarism? Warfare certainly does not have to be conducted with such savagery, and so we must seek other causes.

As of the last census, the republic of Bosnia and Herzegovina had 4.3 million citizens: 43.7 percent indicated in a census that they were Muslim, 31.3 percent said they were Serbs, and 17.3 percent identified themselves as Croats (Ramet 1992 [1992a, 259). The remainder, perhaps sick of the national stereotyping, claimed they were Yugoslavs, Turks, Jews, Gypsies, Eskimos, or Giraffes. Contrast this census result with that taken in 1910 (ibid., 106), for a province of approximately the same borders. The primary difference is the increase in the Muslim population relative to other groups and the corresponding decrease in the Serb population. This increase can probably be attributed to a greater Muslim birthrate compared to that of the Serbs. In 1948, the percentage of the Bosnian population was approximately the same as it had been in 1910, even though more Serbs than Muslims were killed in Yugoslavia. This is because the greater proportion of Serbs lost in the war died in Serbia and Croatia, with only about 32 percent of the total killed in Bosnia. Nevertheless, the memory of a larger number killed—some estimates were as high as 1 million, versus the actual number of 530,000 recently calculated (ibid., 181)—

probably had a major impact on the current Serbian perception that they had been victimized by Muslims, and especially by Croats during World War II. But from 1948 until 1981 the number of Muslims in Bosnia more than doubled, increasing from 788,403 to 1,630,037, while the Serb population increased by less than 200,000 (from 1,136,116 to 1,320,644). The number of Serbs in Bosnia actually declined from 1961 to 1981, probably due to migration to cities such as Belgrade as Yugoslavia industrialized. Migration was probably not as attractive to the rural Muslims (ibid.).

Economic strains also played a role. Yugoslavia's "self-management economy" instituted by Tito's government appeared to be combining the best of limited centralized planning with autonomous decision making at the factory level; but by the early 1970s it seemed to be a grand failure. Foreign debt, inflation, and—especially important here—the wealth gap between north and south grew. Slovenia and Croatia, the wealthier states, grew in wealth while Serbia and Montenegro tended to stagnate or in some respects actually declined economically relative to the average. When computed as a percentage of the average per capita product for Yugoslavia, Slovenia's wealth increased from 162 to 205 percent of the average between 1947 and 1948, Croatia's from 105 to 127 percent during the same period, but Serbia's declined from 101 to 98 and Montenegro's from 94 to 71 percent (ibid., 143). Interestingly, Bosnia's wealth also declined, from 86 to 64 percent during this period. (Note that I give increases and declines relative to a national average in order to emphasize the comparative aspect of nationalistic assessments. All the republics had absolute increases in economic growth during this period.)

The federal army, increasingly Serb-dominated, ate up approximately half the Yugoslav budget. The new constitution of 1974 gave the republics more power. These economic strains combined with nationalistic ones, which were always present beneath the surface, to shift power from the central government to the republics.

The Serbo-Croatian War might have been avoided if there had not been a string of Serbian villages just inside the Croatian border. This and other anomalies facilitated the onset of war. In turn, this war set the stage for the recent violence in Bosnia by destroying the delicate political balance among Muslim, Serb, and Croat politicians.

A seven-member executive council of sorts, consisting of three Muslims, two Croats, and two Serbs, presided over Bosnia. In the election of 1990, the Muslim party won eighty-six seats in the lower house of Parliament, the Serb party seventy-two, and the Croat party forty-four. Each nationality was supposed to have a veto over important issues.

Despite the veto rule, the Muslims and Croats voted for Bosnian sovereignty in October 1991. At the same time, the Serbs refused to accept Bosnian neutrality in the ongoing Serbo-Croatian War. Upon leaving Parliament, they established a "Serb Autonomous Region." In January 1992, a referendum was held on the independence issue; Muslims and Croats voted while the Serbs refused to participate. In March, the Serbs established their own assembly at Pale, not far from Sarajevo. By April, Sarajevo was under siege by former federal (Serb) troops, which were freed from duty in the Croatian War as a result of the peace of January 1992. In that same month, the EC, led by Germany and with a reluctant Britain and France in tow, recognized the independence of Croatia.

Explaining the Conflict

We begin to understand why, compared to the period preceding World War I, there has been both escalated violence and an absence of serious internationalization in the Bosnian crisis. The entire Yugoslav drama, from the Serbo-Croatian hostilities through the current strife, is a systemic war. Instead of the episodic communal violence found in Bosnia-Herzegovina at the turn of the century, there has been open warfare and virtual genocidal activity, or at least "ethnic cleansing," until very recently. The extent of overall destruction has been far greater in recent years. The framework used earlier to explain the outbreak of World War I can also explain in some measure the Yugoslav instance.

Multipolarity is the first variable that has a counterpart here, in that there are at least four active components of the former Yugoslavia—Serbia, Croatia, Slovenia, and Bosnia. As the economy deteriorated, scarcity set in. Theoretically, the consequence of scarcity is inequality. This condition manifested itself in the form of an emergent inequality between the richer north (Slovenia and Croatia) and the poorer south (Serbia and Montenegro). This inequality was exacerbated by the increasing reluctance of the richer republics to bankroll the Serb-dominated federal army, which absorbed roughly half the federal budget. Slovenia and Croatia also increasingly sought European (especially German) protection as the disintegration of Yugoslavia proceeded. Indeed, it was Germany, in the vanguard of the EC—possibly because of its earlier alliance with Croatia during World War II or because Croatia was for so long a province of the Austrian Empire—that hastened European recognition of independent Slovenia and Croatia and fostered increased Serbian hostility. Germans had long vacationed along the Dalmation Coast, which increased their affinity with the Croats. Another possible determinant of this hasty recognition of Serbia and Croatia may have been a desire to impose a fait accompli on the former Yugoslavia, in the mistaken hope that the existence of these newly recognized, sovereign entities would preclude the possibility of civil war. One consequence of such widespread warfare might be increased Balkan immigration into Germany at a time of increased ethnic tensions within Germany itself. Thus alliance formation, in an informal if not a formal sense, strongly influenced the Serbs to proceed as they did.

Croatia and Slovenia felt they had much more to gain economically from an association with Germany if they were independent states; Serbia now felt it could use its dominance of the federal army to gain territory as these new sovereign entities fell away.

It is probable that the renewed association between Germany and Croatia intensified the Serbian memories of the Fascist Croatian Ustase slaughter of Serbs (and Jews) during World War II. Some Muslims also participated in the killing. An intensification of memory could have resulted, making Serbs far more willing to fight, and to fight more brutally, than would otherwise have been the case.

The latent hostilities between Serbs and Muslims, always great, especially in rural environs, now overlapped with the ongoing Serbo-Croatian conflict. Hence, two conflict structures overlapped: enmity between Serbs and Croats and between Serbs and Muslims. This almost exactly parallels the overlap between Balkan conflicts involving Austria-Hungary on the one hand and European great power disputes on the other. The Serbo-Croatian War not only facilitated the Bosnian conflict, it raised issues of the balance of power in the Balkans, which led each of the protagonists, especially the Serbs, to seize as much territory as possible. (This is one possible reason for the willingness of the Serb-dominated Yugoslav federal army to withdraw from Slovenia after only ten days of war, and for the demonstration by the Slovenian militia of their willingness to fight. Given the geographic distance of Slovenia from Serbia, possibilities for the permanent conquest and annexation of territory were remote, especially when compared to Serbia's proximity to Croatia and Bosnia.) Calculations of the balance of power between Serbs and Croats appeared to strongly influence both groups to seize as much Bosnian territory as possible. Systemic conflict was the result. Thus, if we replace the term *alliance memory* with *intensification of alliance memory* and use the term *regional systemic war* instead of *systemic war,* the causal sequence detailed in the theoretical framework can just as easily explain the violence occurring in the former Yugoslavia.

Because this was a systemic war with great intensity, there was a reluctance on the part of other European powers and the United States to intervene. Systemic conflicts of great intensity but limited externalization potential—civil wars, for instance—tend to discourage direct intervention. The nineteenth-century experience of the United States, or more recently that of China and Nigeria, come to mind. External actors tend to avoid such involvement not only because of their own potential losses, but also because the self-absorption of the immediate protagonists in the war makes them appear less threatening internationally, at least in the short run.

There were other reasons for the absence of an immediate externalization of the conflict, however. The absence of a European multipolar system as it existed in the early twentieth century strongly diminished the probability of an immediate externalization. Great powers have much less incentive to intervene when they have few if any potential antagonists to be concerned about, lest their opponents gain from the conflict. Russia and Turkey have stakes in the conflict, but, in contrast to the period preceding World War I, they are more symbolic than driven by realpolitik. Russia extends its support to the Serbs partly as the result of a common Orthodox faith and historic national connections, but the outcome of the Bosnian conflict in no way affects a Balkan balance of power relevant to Russia, as was the case prior to 1914 in the Balkan disputes between Austria-Hungary and Russia. Turkey also no longer has a direct power interest in the Balkans; its borders now end well east of the recent Balkan violence, whatever religious affinities may exist between Turks and the Slavic Muslims in Bosnia. Resource inequality has been minimized by certain redistributive policies of the EC, and of course, the older styles of alliance formation endemic to Europe historically no longer apply to the EC (now EU) and NATO settings. As a result, conflict among the European powers has been minimized, and they have less desire to be involved in the violence that has occurred recently in the Balkans.

When did the Bosnian violence become virtually inevitable— that is, when was there no turning back from the path to systemic war within much of the former Yugoslavia? In prior research, I asked this question in regard to eight systemic wars, and the answer appeared to be clear-cut. The causal pathway to systemic war appeared to be irreversible only after the overlap in conflict structures occurred (Midlarsky 1988a, 204–06). Prior to that time, these wars could have been averted through strenuous efforts of diplomacy. Multipolarities and resource inequalities are found throughout the international arena, and even alliances differentially favoring one side, as Germany did in Slovenia and especially Croatia, do not necessarily lead to systemic war. But when alliance formation, even of the informal variety, facilitates the overlap in conflict structures, the conflict process enters the irreversible stage. When Germany openly tilted toward Croatia, thus encouraging independence, with the further (correct) implication that the remainder of the EC would be brought along, and with the promise of support from the recently unified economic giant of western Europe, this informal alliance obviously encouraged Croatian sovereignty. There was a further important implication for the Serbs. If Croatia and Slovenia were to be recognized by the EC, why should not Bosnia also be enveloped within the German embrace? Hence, when the EC officially recognized Croatian independence on 15 January 1992, the Serbs initiated the Bosnian conflict. Alliance formation facilitated both the Serbo-Croatian and the Muslim-Serb conflict, which overlapped in this now virtually unavoidable systemic war.

Why did this systemic war, though severe, avoid the truly horrendous loss of life involved in other systemic wars such as World Wars I and II? As in other regional conflicts of this type, the system in question simply did not have the autonomy required to persist unfettered on its path to massive destruction. There were few if any outside influences to limit the destruction in the two world wars, until one or another principal actor was defeated. Here, on the other hand, the Western powers and especially the United States took an active and ultimately successful role in limiting the extent of violence. Threats of intervention, even if only from the air, against exposed Serbian artillery positions were effective in reining in the most extreme ambitions of the Serb politicians, which could have included immediate action against the Albanians in Kosovo and against the Macedonians, as well as continued action against the relatively defenseless Muslims. Other systemic conflicts that could have proceeded much farther along the path of destruction, such as the Arab-Israeli War of 1967 and especially that of 1973, were limited by the active involvement of the superpowers, the United States and the USSR.

One finding of the earlier analysis has implications for the current Yugoslav situation. This is the almost certain occurrence of a mobilization war subsequent to the structural systemic war outlined in the causal sequence.[2] Indeed, I made this prediction in December 1993 at the first Tallahassee conference (a gathering of contributors to this volume), and the actual successful Croatian mobilization effort leading to the capture of the Serb-held Krajina region occurred in August 1995. Structural systemic wars follow a causal sequence of this type, as a result of the structural condition of multipolarity. After each conflict, such as the French revolutionary wars or World War I, there followed mobilization wars that entailed the strong mobilization efforts at conquest on the part of at least one protagonist in the earlier war. France in the Napoleonic Wars and Germany in World War II are cases in point. One reason for the occurrence of the later war is the relatively inconclusive outcome of the first, structural war. In the French revolutionary wars, a kind of stalemate resulted that could be overcome only by Napoleon's mobilization efforts against France's enemies. Germany was not so defeated in World War I that it could not rise again as a formidable great power after significant mobilization efforts leading up to World War II. Similarly, a new and heavy round in the fighting among Serbs, Croats, and Muslims became likely as a result of the residual anger among Croats and Muslims after the first war and in the absence of complete destruction of their communities, which would have ruled out a future mobilization. Alternatively, the Serbs could have mobilized more fully, as the French did in the first decade of the nineteenth century, and attempted a complete obliteration of the Muslim communities, also including as many Croats as possible.

Only the slow decay or "cleansing" of the remaining Muslim communities, or an internationally guaranteed settlement, could prevent the onset of a new mobilization effort on the part of the Croats, Muslims, or Serbs. The successful Croatian mobilization effort of August 1995 was the result in this instance.

Theoretically, the situation today in the former Yugoslavia resembles more closely the Macedonian situation leading to the two Balkan Wars than it does the situation in Bosnia at the end of the last century. And it is this theoretical resemblance that probably accounts for the increased violence today. Late nineteenth-century Bosnia demonstrated strong class and religious antagonisms emanating from the cleavage between Muslim landlords associated with the Ottoman government and Christian peasants. Much of the violence of that period in Bosnia was directed at least as much against the government and its tax farmers as against the Muslims themselves.

Recently, the violence in Bosnia has been less class-based and revolutionary and more wholly communal, and in this sense "primitive" (primordial, based on conceptions of blood, belief, kinship, or nation), as it was in Macedonia. Targets were identified not for their association with taxation and an oppressive government—essentially a mitigating factor in the intensity of the potential violence directed against individuals—but for their associations with a community, whatever their social class or connection to a government. Everyone was assigned a particular identity that was viewed either as wholly favorable or wholly unfavorable. Thus many people were assigned to the unfavorable category, with violence directed against all of them. This situation worsened somewhat with the 1974 constitution, which gave the republics more power and also declared "Muslim" to be a nationality. The situation was further exacerbated by the presence of three nationalities instead of the single dominant religious cleavage between Christian and Muslim that had existed earlier.

Theoretically, the existence of multiple communities under conditions of scarcity establishes a strong likelihood of inequality among them, and hence introduces more antagonism than that between only two such religious entities. The intense Macedonian communal conflict prior to the Balkan Wars and the recent "ethnic cleansing" in Bosnia illustrate this condition.

Conclusion

These findings have certain clear policy implications. First, if there is any hope of an early ending to the spiral toward systemic conflict, diplomatic intervention is required at an early stage, prior to the joining of two separate conflicts. Germany's hasty recognition of Slovenia and Croatia facilitated the joining of the Serbo-Croatian and Serbo-Muslim wars; hence, if that recognition had not been granted, war might have been averted. If that diplomatic effort had failed, an early military intervention in the hostilities, prior to the self-reinforcing hostilities inevitable in ethnic wars of this type, would have been necessary. Later, after the systemic conflict is well under way, only the credible threat of an effective external intervention can lead to a disengagement of the protagonists. Apparently, the NATO bombing of the Bosnian Serbs in 1995 constituted such a threat, thereby leading to the cease-fire and the Dayton, Ohio, peace talks.

Systems at Risk

VIOLENCE, DIFFUSION,
AND DISINTEGRATION
IN THE MIDDLE EAST

Monty G. Marshall

The term *ethnic conflict* has become a euphemism for substate conflicts we cannot explain or comprehend, especially those taking place in "low" cultures.[1] Ethnic conflict is the proverbial rug under which we sweep the dirt and debris of political relations in a world that continually defies and evades our understanding. Ethnic groupings seem to abound in the world, yet many consider them obsolete and inappropriate. Ethnic conflict has become the major challenge to the integrity and viability of the secular state. Ethnic violence threatens to drain the world community of its resources and human compassion, and to drag us all into its vortex of utter chaos. Yet we remain woefully unprepared to handle ethnicity as a political issue or as a conflict variable. Most recent inquiry into ethnic conflict has focused on ethnicity as a particular category in events analysis. The purpose of this chapter is to shift inquiry away from "ethnicity" as a category of analysis and toward *political ethnicity* as a consequence of systemic conflict processes.[2]

Ethnicity, the "condition of belonging to a particular ethnic group," is a conceptual umbrella under which anyone and everyone may hide from the relentless vicissitudes of life or may seek refuge during torrential storms. The term *ethnicity* covers all social identity groups organized on the basis of at least one ascriptive (physical or psychic) defining trait, such as genetics, religion, language, culture, or traditional residence (Rothschild 1981, 86–87; Bloom 1990). The implication is that any physical or psychic marker of social distinction, anything that appears to make one group of people different from others, may serve in the process of group formation and differentiation (and, possibly, division), based on a simple dichotomy between (1) those who have the specific trait (that is, "us") and (0), those who do not, "them" (GAP 1987).

On the positive side, ethnicity is the foundation of cultural diversity and pluralism on a global scale. Identification with an ethnic group can protect the individual ego from becoming lost and insignificant in the anonymity of mass secular society. The very quality that is defined as difference in relation to the exogenous macrosociety binds members of the endogenous microsociety together and provides them with a sense of commonality, community, and security. Difference is distinctiveness and often leads to mutual respect, tolerance, and appreciation.

On the negative side, ethnicity can lead to a preoccupation with self and social differences, an abiding distrust of others, and a nearly impenetrable barrier against social, economic, or political integration. The politicization of ethnicity presages the disintegration of complex societies into their constituent components; ethnicity can become parochial and thwart cosmopolitanism. Difference becomes division and that division leads to chauvinism and acrimony. Left unchecked, acrimony turns to hostility, and hostility to violence.

Mediating the difference between these polar extremes is the establishment and maintenance of myriad and fragile social ties and institutional linkages that crisscross group identity borders, a "web of group affiliations" (Simmel 1956). Such societal ties bind small groups into larger groups, making those larger organizations and societies viable and cohesive. Large social identity groupings and organizations are the foundation of industrial economies. The integration of many distinct social groups into a supraordinate organization is a requisite for development and modernity.

In this chapter, I am especially interested in the negative side of ethnicity because by definition, that is where the problems of ethnicity lie. This interest does not stem from a supposition that ethnicity itself is a cause of social disintegration and systemic underdevelopment; rather, I argue that politicized ethnicity is symptomatic of a troubled societal system, a system that needs immediate attention. I look at the "problem of ethnicity" from a systemic perspective: examine societal anomie and the loss of social control; explain political ethnicity and societal disintegration; and describe the transformation of aesthetic and progressive cultures into "cultures of violence."

Arendt provides the key to unlocking the relationship between violence and societal anomie. She makes a critical distinction between "power" and "violence." "*Power* corresponds to the human ability not just to act but to act in concert" (Arendt 1972, 143). "Power and violence are opposites; where one rules absolutely, the other is absent. Violence appears where power is in jeopardy, but left to its own course it ends in power's disappearance. . . . Violence can destroy power; it is utterly incapable of creating it" (ibid., 155). My theses in this chapter are theoretically and empirically informed by a larger, ongoing study, the Societal Development and Social Conflict (SDSC) project.

From a systemic perspective, the central issue of ethnic conflict is: Why ethnicity? That is, given the myriad ideologies, social and political identity groups, and functional and professional organizations available to the individual in our increasingly complex and interdependent world, why are ethnic identities in particular becoming the focal point for political mobilization and violence? One possible answer can be inferred from arguments advanced by many feminist critics of international relations theory. They argue that violence connotes the essential transformation of social relations (from amity to enmity) and that the incidence of violence in any form and at any level of association affects the general status of violence in social culture. "Feminist perspectives on security would assume that violence, whether it be international, national, or family violence, is interconnected" (Tickner 1992, 58). Ethnic violence may be somehow associated with or "connected" to other violence in the system, that is, it may merely be a part or a reflection of a pervasive, macrosystemic conflict process causing the transformation of all forms of societal relations and leading groups to engage in violence.

Feminist criticism also considers the categorical boundaries used in theory and questions the basic supposition that such (abstract) boundary distinctions actually provide operative closure in the real world.

> Realist models of international relations have been built on assumptions of rigid boundary distinctions between outside and inside, anarchy and order, and foreign and domestic. The outside is portrayed in terms of dangerous spaces where violence is unsanctioned. This threat of violence must be guarded against and controlled if security on the inside is to be achieved. (Ibid., 133)

The paradox of these perspectives is obvious. The act of guarding against the external threat is itself an example of the interconnectedness and transformative influence of violence; the threat transforms the peaceful society by eliciting an equivalent threat of violence (such as a "security dilemma"). Furthermore, the rationalization and glorification (or normative justification) of violence against the external "enemy other" (that is, in the *system's* public sphere) leads to an increasing toleration and eventual acceptance of violence within *society's* public sphere and spills over to saturate the *private* sphere as well. The strategic ideas of coercion, violence, and domination eventually pervade the societal system. Human culture is the medium and violence the noxious message; this is a "culture-of-violence" approach.

It has long been accepted wisdom that the perception of an external threat stimulates internal cohesion; this is often referred to as "diversionary theory" or a "rally round the flag" effect (see Coser 1956; Levy 1989; Lian and Oneal

1993). I agree with Russett and Graham (1989) when they argue that such a positive effect holds only in the short run, and that in the long run the opposite is more likely—that is, long-term rivalries tend to exacerbate internal tensions and social divisions. This negative effect can be assumed to increase markedly when such threats and rivalries involve actual violence, rather than simply the threat of violence. Gurr has been a staunch proponent of the "culture of violence" approach in political conflict theory (Gurr 1970, 1988; Eckstein 1980; Zimmermann 1983).

The main feminist argument, however, is that the individual is both the transmitter and the receiver of culture (and furthermore, that the roles of sender and receiver, especially in international relations, are strongly gender biased). As a transmitter of culture, the individual acts to create and re-create culture. However, the individual is first a receiver of culture and only later becomes a transmitter; the individual consciousness, then, must be considered a *social construct*. Yet, viewed from a systemic perspective, culture itself is primarily a social construct—that is, a construct of the physical environment and the sociopolitical context (or operational milieu).

Two research questions emerge from this discussion. First, does the example (or experience) of violence affect and alter the surrounding environment in ways that transform cultural norms from nonviolent to violent? Or more simply, does violence diffuse? Second, if we assume that a "culture of violence" does diffuse, what effects does the diffusion of violence have on societal relations?

There is a fundamental difference between a social group's political behavior when that group perceives its surrounding environment as threatening (or a social condition of insecurity) and when that environment seems nonthreatening (a condition of security). In a condition of general threat, groups operate in a "crisis mode" of decision making; this mode emphasizes exclusivity, enmity, and coercive or violent strategies of conflict management. When the environment seems less threatening, a "noncrisis" mode predominates; this mode emphasizes inclusiveness, amity, and cooperative strategies.

Since conflict is an inevitable condition of political relations, the main problem in political conflict theory is to understand why political relations move from nonviolent to violent. Some have argued that the existence of violence, and especially systematic violence (that is, protracted social conflict), creates or reinforces a social psychology of insecurity, which tends to diffuse through the network of social ties and alter the perceptions and policy priorities of the political actors most closely affected by the threat of violence (all actors in affective proximity, in this case, the protracted conflict region). The growing sense of insecurity leads to increasing exclusivity, enmity, and violence in political relations among all groups in proximity to the source of political violence.

While there has been increasing interest in diffusion processes in political research, these studies have looked primarily at temporal and spatial diffusion patterns of categorical events such as interstate war. In this study, I extend that inquiry to include *systemic diffusion*. The diffusion of insecurity approach focuses on the uses of violence in all political interactions (interstate, civil, and communal) and between all groups at any level of aggregation.

I have analyzed aggregate data on political relations in the Middle East during the period 1945–1990 in a series of tests of the systemic diffusion theory. I compiled the evidence from analyses of several global data sources: Correlates of War (for interstate and civil war and national material capabilities), Minorities at Risk (for communal conflict), United States Committee for Refugees (for refugee flows), and Polity II (for regime characteristics). The findings strongly support the diffusion hypotheses.

Background

In this chapter, I assume that ethnicity as cultural diversity is a collective good, both aesthetic and progressive; second, that politicized ethnicity (ethnic conflict) is an early warning of potential or progressive societal anomie; and third, that violent ethnicity (ethnic warfare) connotes social disintegration and systemic breakdown. In this view, the origins of ethnicity are irrelevant. The debate between primordial and instrumental approaches to the study of ethnicity overlooks the fact that ethnicity is a collective good. Even though ethnic identifications appear to be highly resilient and persistent over time (or static), they are also constantly adapting to changing circumstances (or dynamic). To adapt a popular phrase, if ethnic identifications did not exist, we would have to invent them. We can extend that proposition and assert that, where ethnic identifications do not already exist, or when their existing form is inadequate or inappropriate in reflecting current conditions, they are reinvented.

I reject the notion that ethnicity and ethnic conflict are important new categories of analysis. The "sudden explosion" of ethnic conflicts around the globe following the end of the cold war represents both a significant change in political relations and a mere artifact of the ways in which we *categorize* and *construct* our thinking on political behavior. The problems of ethnic conflict are not new, though they are certainly no better understood than they were at the turn of the twentieth century, when debates on the "nationality problem" raged in socialist party circles (Marshall 1992; Holdsworth 1967; Connor 1984b; Nahaylo and Swoboda 1990). Of course, the problems associated with the rise of Fascism, or radical nationalism, in the interwar period are better known. Clearly, during the "height" of cold war thinking, the subjective reality of political conflict (to use Martha Crenshaw's term [1988]—I refer specifically to the "two camps" or bipolar mentality) lent a false precision to our understanding of conflict dynamics and hence, to our perception of the degree of control the United States was able to exert over those events.

In recent years, critical inquiry in international relations theory has placed greater emphasis on challenging both the categories and the constructs of our thinking. Feminist and postmodernist writers especially have advanced extensive arguments concerning the effects of social constructions on the definitions of social roles and the outcomes of social and political interactions (Tickner 1992; Sylvester 1994). They especially criticize the division of the political world into public and private spheres. John A. Vasquez presents similar arguments in more traditional terms when he argues in *The War Puzzle* (1993) that the ways we think about power and war affect the probability of war's occurrence. He criticizes the conventional distinction between interstate and civil warfare; he also raises questions about what effects the way we categorize events have on our analysis and our ability to compare findings and build theory.

The essential question is not whether ethnic violence—or nationalist violence or communal violence or gang violence or state violence or domestic violence—is on the rise. The essential question is whether and to what degree the incidence of violence has increased (or decreased) in social and political interaction (that is, human society). Once the answer to that question has been determined, we can ask specifically where, and especially why, the use of violence has become the preferred method of conflict interaction and for what social groups.

This is not meant to imply that nothing can be learned from this kind of categorization of events. Once the essential problem has been identified and defined and the general context delineated, we can address the specifics and use them to gain clarity and insight. I have argued that ethnicity is a particularly amorphous concept. As a category for analysis, it poses few parameters for exclusion of cases from the analytic domain. However, its intrinsic ambiguity can be revealing.

The term *ethnic* implies communal minority status within an existing state. I use the term *communal minority* even though ethnic groups often form the communal majority of a state. Most often, however, these communal majorities (or nations), as political actors, are inseparable from the state itself. In those few cases where a communal majority group is deprived of state power by a powerful minority, the majority is relegated to minority status within political society. Such cases are rare and inherently unstable. Here, then, *minority* refers to the amount of influence a group exercises over the determination of state policy.

The main conceptual difference between *ethnicity* and *nationality* can be said to lie in the degree of access a communal identity group has to the institutions of state power. Political mobilization in terms of ethnic identity implies a rejection of broader association or integration (linkage) with the state, with other groups within the state, or with a wider or supraordinate identity grouping. The "subjective realities" of individuals within a condition of political ethnicity place great emphasis on parochialism and perceived differences. Ethnicity is a safe haven from the uncertainty and frustration of dealing with megasociety; politicized ethnicity is characterized by rapidly shrinking social horizons, the fragmentation of elaborate social networks into their smallest identity components, and the deterioration of social linkages until they are finally dissolved or abandoned. Political ethnicity, like nationalism, can quickly exacerbate social tensions, leading to a social psychosis of violent individuation (voice) and radical exclusivity (exit).[3]

In addition, the intrinsic ambiguity of ethnicity allows opportunistic elites great latitude in voicing grievances and making claims against established authorities and privileged social groups. The same ethnic identity can at different times be expansive or confined; the mobilized group expands and contracts according to the identity markers emphasized, the historical symbols invoked, and the collective memories and grievances evoked (Brass 1974). Political ethnicity claims a degree of group definitiveness that it cannot possibly support through objective criteria. This ambiguity of political ethnicity is especially problematic when it is coupled with perceptions of an inherent communal "nature" of group identity. Ambiguity of group identity in conjunction with the "natural" interspersion of peoples can and often does translate into ambiguity in the extent (or boundaries) of communal territory. This ambiguity can fuel competing claims to geographic space; these "border" disputes are the issues that most often lead to warfare (Mandel 1980; Vasquez 1993; Kirby and Ward 1987).

Even the claim that ethnic conflict and warfare are occurring is probably too optimistic, since it presumes a level of organization and coordination that is ephemeral at best. Ethnic groups themselves are not "unitary actors." Ethnic groups are the least institutionalized of political groups; that is, they have little formal organizational structure, standard procedures, or central coordination. Warfare involving ethnic groups is waged by informal, scattered militias in a process that is beyond effective control. Ethnic wars cannot be stopped by treaty because no one is granted authority to negotiate the group's sovereignty and no one is obligated by any social contract (either explicit or implicit) to accept a proposed settlement; the war must stop before its end can be negotiated.

There is no central authority, no chain of command, no hierarchy, and few rules in a condition of violent ethnicity. Ethnic leaders are simply voices; they cannot command nor can they devise or enforce generally acceptable solutions. Ethnic wars are wars of desperation and sheer survival; they are most accurately portrayed as "protracted social conflicts" and "cultures of violence." "It is only in the long run that they will 'end' by cooling off, transforming or withering away; one cannot expect these conflicts to be terminated by explicit decision" (Azar et al. 1978, 50). Ethnic wars stop when they can no longer be fought, because the issue of ethnicity itself is at once symbolic and ascriptive, nonnegotiable and fundamentally uncompromising. It is difficult to determine whether ethnic conflicts ever really end; they seem simply to become less salient under favorable circumstances.

Theory

Ethnic warfare is symptomatic of advanced systemic breakdown and societal disintegration. Arendt (1972) argues that all acts of violence are indicative of a loss (or lack) of effective control over human society. In this sense, ethnic violence is the most serious form of collective violence in that it presupposes a breakdown in the very authority structures that arc needed to impose whatever measure of control may be mustered against violence, even while the minimal organization and coordination necessary to invoke high levels of mechanized warfare are maintained. How might this condition come about?

Two critical elements in the control of violence are, first, the decision to use violence rather than a nonviolent strategy or remedy, and second, the availability of the means or instruments to pursue violence. (Many theorists, especially those from the realist school, would argue that these two elements are derivations of the relative capabilities of various actors to project power—that is, violence. I shall not enter into this "chicken-and-egg" debate here.) The second element is crucial, in that having access to the means of violence affects the "rational" calculus in considering the option of initiating violence to induce change in an interactive sequence. This option has become increasingly available to greater numbers of political actors.

The first element derives from the *psycho-milieu* and the second from the *operational milieu*; both derive from the *environmental milieu* (Sprout and Sprout 1965; see also Cioffi-Revilla and Starr 1995).

We can determine the context for our inquiry into the issue of ethnic violence by first examining the preconditions of such collective violence behavior within its relevant environmental milieu, broadly conceived to include both geopolitical and cultural aspects. We may then extend the inquiry by examining the special logistic factors pertaining to the conduct of such political violence within the specific operational milieu (that is, access to instruments such as weaponry). The human element, however difficult it may be to describe accurately and in detail, represents the ultimate object of research into political conflict behavior: understanding the social psychology of collective (or political) violence.

The primary agent of societal disintegration is *insecurity*. Insecurity is the psychic condition brought on by a perceived vital threat (actual or potential) to one's physical integrity. A corollary to the condition of insecurity is a distrust of certain associations (that is, with "them") and an unwillingness to pursue or maintain exogenous ties and linkages. This condition of insecurity is stimulated by the incidence of violence within reasoned proximity—that is, temporal, spatial, or systemic proximity. The condition of insecurity increases the individual's disposition to justify the use of coercion and violence in political interactions and broadens the acceptable range of discretionary applications of coercion and violence. As Gurr explains in setting out what has come to be known as the "culture-of-violence" hypothesis (1970, 170):

> If discontent is widespread in a society, anomie (normlessness) common, and political violence frequent, there is a tendency for attitudes of expectancy of violence to be converted into norms justifying violence. The process of violence-expectancy-justification-violence tends to perpetuate itself, contingent on the persistence of [the requisite functional conditions].

A condition of *crisis* is an acute sense of insecurity brought about by unexpected events that appear to pose an imminent threat to vital interests or integrity. In terms of conflict management, the condition of insecurity increases the propensity for political violence, while the condition of crisis increases the probability of political violence. The hypothetical mechanism of societal disintegration is thus the *diffusion* of insecurity through established networks of social relations in *protracted conflict regions*.[4]

Diffusion analysis has only recently been consistently applied to empirical security studies (Richardson 1960; Ross and Homer 1976; Most and Starr 1980, 1990; Bremer 1982; Faber, Houweling, and Siccama 1984; Houweling and Siccama 1985; Hill and Rothchild 1987; Kirby and Ward 1987; Most, Starr, and Siverson 1989; Siverson and Starr 1990, 1991). These "first generation" diffusion studies take a holistic or systemic approach to the study of interstate war and militarized dispute events.

This focus on interstate war and militarized disputes reflects the fact that the Correlates of War (COW) data bases are among the few, if not the only reasonably reliable aggregate data collections of conflict variables with a global scope available. Quantitative analysis in international relations (the questions asked and the ways in which those questions are investigated) is severely constrained by the a priori assumptions, methodologies, and interests of data-oriented researchers. Marshall (1993b) argues that much about the evidence of diffusion processes in the spread of violence and warfare is lost because of the ways we conceptualize, categorize, and codify political actors and events.

At least three findings in the diffusion literature are particularly pertinent to the present discussion. First, Most and Starr advance the plausible argument that *different* types of war may exist and that those varieties tend to result in different diffusion effects. More specifically, "It seems reasonable to surmise that large-scale international wars may not have tended toward diffusion during the 1945–1965 period, while small-scale civil, guerrilla, and colonial wars may have been much more inclined to diffuse" (Most, Starr, and Siverson 1989, 115). Second, they argue "that one should not reasonably expect war to diffuse throughout the international system as a whole, but rather that such diffusion will be constrained within sets of nations that interact significantly with each other" (ibid., 118). Third and finally,

> The pattern of international dispute initiation indicates that some positive form of contagion was present at the global level during the 1900 to 1976 period. The national level results suggest that this is not a process of addiction [or positive reinforcement], which in turn suggests that we are dealing with a process of infection or spatial diffusion. The inter-regional analysis indicates that this is not fundamentally a process whereby disputes spill-over from region to region, but rather, as the intra-regional analyses show, a process of infection [positive spatial diffusion] operating chiefly *within* regions. In short, coercion is regionally contagious. (Bremer 1982, 53)

From the diffusion literature we can distill three important points: first, theoretical postulations of diffusion processes relating to violence and coercion are supported by empirical research; second, different types of warfare should be included in diffusion research and analysis; and third, geographical regions defined in terms of significant networks of sociopolitical interactions are the proper context for studying diffusion processes.

The diffusion literature, however, severely limits itself by looking primarily at the temporal and spatial diffusion of *like events*. The concept of the "culture of violence" advanced by Gurr is more compatible with the idea of diffusion laid out here because it takes into account the idea of a *systemic diffusion* of a specifiable social process and related nonspecific, substitutable events and phenomena.[5]

In 1973 Arendt gave an early account of the possibility of substitutable group leadership. She argues that special social conditions favor the ascension of certain types of leaders, that such "leaders" cannot direct or alter, but can only give "voice" to the lead provided by the "will of the masses," and that, as conditions change, leaders are replaced and forgotten. Organizations can certainly pursue substitutable goals; for example, social organizations can form the mobilization nucleus for special political goals. What is here called "substitutable events or phenomena" incorporates the general idea in its many forms. In terms of the politics of identity, it refers to the idea that individuals may identify with multiple social groupings and may be mobilized by any one of a number of such identities depending on circumstances. For example, an individual may alternately be an active or inactive member of an interest group, political party, ethnic group, communal group, religious group, or polity (or may even latently identify with any number of groups). Which type of group organization is salient at any point in time is one distinct question for inquiry; what methods are employed by the group in political interaction is quite another question, because they are not directly explained by the choice of group organization.

In the simplest terms, *temporal diffusion* refers to the endogenous spread of the condition of insecurity over time, that is, incremental change in a particular political group or actor, the "already afflicted." *Spatial diffusion* refers to the spread of insecurity extensively—exogenously—outward from a source and across physical space, that is, to include others in the "affliction." *Systemic diffusion* denotes the spread of insecurity intensively, throughout the "web of group affiliations" until the condition of insecurity affects all social interactions and political relations within the system.

The development of a distinct "culture of violence," which will incrementally transform and eventually supersede the normative culture already in place in a social system, requires a substantial period of time. It is likely that, all other things being constant, the longer the period, the greater and thus more readily identifiable the indicators of cultural transformation and distinction will be. Although it should be assumed that the alterations resulting from the diffusion process will proceed as a function of the persistence of a particular source of insecurity, that relationship may not have a direct reinforcement effect. More likely, the actual violence exhibited at the source will be sporadic (but not random) and thereby will magnify the expected response due to a more powerful *partial reinforcement* effect.

Partial reinforcement, wherein a response is stimulated only part of the time, produces a much more insidious effect such that the "response will be much harder to extinguish if it was acquired during partial rather than continuous reinforcement" (Gleitman 1986, 110). In any case, because vital political processes cannot be studied through controlled experimentation, evidence of such a process must be located in prior experience. Ideally, the most compelling evidence will be found in relation to "constant" sources of political violence interactions. This ideal source is by definition a protracted social conflict. The partial-reinforcement effect is consistent with the definition of the *protracted social conflict:* "Protracted conflicts are hostile interactions which extend over long periods of time with sporadic outbreaks of open warfare fluctuating in frequency and intensity" (Azar et al. 1978, 50).

Several significant sources of theoretical insecurity can be identified; "constant" source violence does exist and this makes possible a "test" of the diffusion of insecurity theory.

The very existence of protracted (violent) conflicts and "enduring rivalries" gives credence to the fundamental claim of temporal diffusion; social learning, institutional momentum, and the empowerment of "conflict" elites over "cooperative" elites drive the "growth of the coercive state" (Gurr 1988; Goertz and Diehl 1993; Marshall 1995). It is important to recognize that the temporal diffusion effect lends transformational momentum to the general diffusion effect. In other words, impressions from experience on an actor within a system tend to remain for some time. These impressions also give impetus to the incremental transformation of that actor's special subjective rationality and political culture (and eventually that of the system in general).

Of greatest interest here is the spread of the problem of political violence to involve additional groups or actors. The principal effect of diffusion of insecurity should be a simple function of spatial proximity; I propose a serial model. "Serial diffusion typically takes place outward from the core toward the periphery or peripheries. . . . In the serial model the process of diffusion is continuous and decays across space; the further from the core, the weaker the influence of the core" (Wellhofer 1989, 320). The universe of analysis for the study of the culture of violence or diffusion of insecurity process, the protracted conflict region (PCR), may then be defined spatially by the extrapolation of the three elements of diffusion: time, space, and system.

This primary "spatial diffusion of insecurity" hypothesis is represented in figure 6.1. The spatial hypothesis proposes that the insecurity effect from a source of political violence will diffuse outward and decay as a function of distance; the intensity of insecurity will be a function of the intensity of the violence at the primary source, or core, and the general, functional receptivity of the region to the insecurity effect. Variation in strength of effect among recipients of the stimulus must be explained by endogenous variables affecting their receptivity. Such individual variations are not of interest to systemic analysis; once the general effect is specified, particulars can be identified by future research. In must be acknowledged, however, that both functional and diffusion explanations of equivalent conflict behavior among proximate actors are plausible.[6]

The temporal diffusion hypothesis proposes that the intensity of insecurity (and its consequent behavioral manifestations), as well as the spatial and systemic "reach" of the condition of insecurity, will increase over the duration of stimulation from the core/source. The systemic diffusion hypothesis proposes that the degree of penetration of the insecurity effect into the cultural and social systems in the region will increase over the duration of the protracted conflict experience. The systemic effect will have the greatest immediate influence on those actors that are the least institutionalized; it will have the greatest resilience (once in place) among those actors that have been the most institutionalized.

The source or core of the PCR is the protracted social conflict itself (in

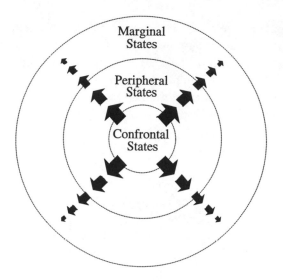

FIGURE 6.1
The Spatial Diffusion of
Insecurity: Protracted Conflict
Regions

this case, the Palestinian issue). Those states directly involved in the core conflict comprise the *confrontal states*. The states bordering on the confrontal states are termed the *peripheral states;* those bordering on the peripheral states are the *marginal states*.

The spatial diffusion model is applied to the Middle East region in figure 6.2; the states of the region and their classifications according to the proposed scheme appear in table 6.1. This geopolitical scheme of classification operationalizes PCR in the ensuing analysis of the diffusion of insecurity hypotheses. Although an "open systems" analytic approach is warranted by the spatial diffusion argument, it must be assumed that the diffusion effect is strongly conditioned by the "semiclosed" structure of the state system. State structures act as filters in the diffusion effect and provide the primary units of analysis in political systems theory. Even more important, all aggregate data are collected and codified according to state "bins" in international relations research.

Since the structure of the state system must be assumed to condition the diffusion treatment (i.e., the stimulus), secondary and tertiary processes of the diffusion of insecurity will occur. The primary, serial diffusion effects of insecurity will be manifested as alterations in the political priorities, policies, and actions of states (that is, toward greater militancy and increased conflict involvement). The main consequence of these primary diffusion effects will be an increase in the strength of the *security dilemma* affecting the PCR states. In general terms, as each state reacts to the perceived threat from the core violence, it acts to increase its own military security. As each state becomes militarily more powerful, it is seen as more of a potential threat to its increasingly insecure neighbors. Social integration is increasingly strained among states

TABLE 6.1 Middle East Protracted Conflict Region, 1946–1990

Confrontal States	Marginal States
Egypt (1946)	Chad (1960)
Israel (1948)	Ethiopia (1946)
Lebanon (1946)	Iran (1946)
Jordan (1946)	Kuwait (1961)
Syria (1946)	Oman (1971)
	Somalia (1960)
Peripheral States	Tunisia (1956)
Iraq (1946)	U.A.E. (1971)
Libya (1952)	Yemen AR (1946)
Saudi Arabia (1946)	Yemen PDR (1967)
Sudan (1956)	[Qatar][a]
Turkey (1946)	[Armenia][b]
[Cyprus][a]	[Azerbaijan][b]
	[Georgia][b]

Note: Year in parentheses indicates date of inclusion; if after 1946, date of independence.

a. These states do not meet the minimum population requirements of the SDSC study (1 million residents in 1990).

b. These states were not independent (or were only nominally independent) during the study period.

FIGURE 6.2
Middle East Protracted
Conflict Region

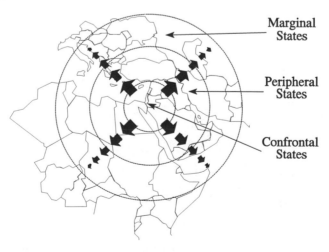

Marginal States

Peripheral States

Confrontal States

that may formerly have had friendly relations and common cause in the perceived threat posed by the violent core. New initiatives in all issue areas are hampered.

These secondary effects of the diffusion of insecurity are represented in figure 6.3. The model presented here is of an interlocking central place. This model takes into account the diffusion effects as they are conditioned by the structure of the system—that is, the structure of the primary nodes (states) and communication paths (social networks). "Here diffusion is not only multilinear, but may follow more than one path to each node" (Wellhofer 1989, 321–22). Each node will act as both an amplifier and a transmitter of the diffusion process. As each node is progressively affected and altered by the diffusion effects, it will contribute special impetus to the primary process dynamic. The general structural effect is systemic disintegration of the primary structural units, the states.

A second conditioning feature of the state system is the separation of interstate and domestic (or civil) relations: the qualitative separation of structure from infrastructure. The state acts as the node in the external system structure and the nucleus (or political focal point) of the internal system. The primary diffusion effect negates the assumption of statistical independence of political events; the main message here is that context matters in the analysis of social processes, security issues, and conflict management procedures. The secondary effect contributes to the "growth of the coercive state" through the generalization and dispersion of the diffusion dynamic. The perception of "pervasive insecurity" throughout the environmental milieu makes possible the creation of special normative justifications for militant attitudes, the denigra-

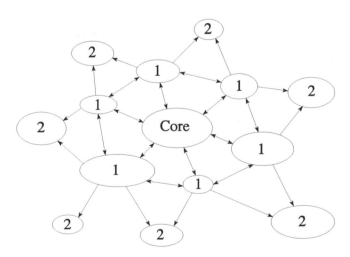

FIGURE 6.3 Interlocking Central Place Diffusion of Insecurity, with Secondary Insecurity/Diffusion Effects

tion of "out groups," and a greater acceptance or tolerance of the "efficacy of coercion" in securing "national interests."

This leads to the purposive construction of a special systemic rationale (via the mechanics of the security dilemma) that is consistent with these general perceptions. The subsequent, and increasing, diversion of crucial resources to support increased state militancy places greater pressures on domestic relations and internal systemic dynamics. In general, the interstate political processes of the diffusion of insecurity are systemically degenerative and debilitating and lead inexorably to what is best described as an *insecurity dilemma* (see Job 1992). Increased state militancy is accompanied by increasing societal tensions between the state actors and various substate actors. These increased domestic tensions are met with increased state coercion and repression. The normally progressive processes of integration and democratization are thwarted by increased civil tensions, social divisions, and political instability.

This proposed *tertiary* diffusion of insecurity effect is represented in figure 6.4. Insecurity is seen penetrating ever more deeply into the societal system (and social fabric) and leading to the societal disintegration of the structural nodes themselves. The tertiary effect may be thought to penetrate even more deeply into the social fabric to affect relations not only in the public sphere at the group level but also relations among individuals in the private sphere. This argument is consistent with feminist arguments of linkage in the incidence of violence between the public and private spheres.

Of course, over time such diffusion effects will transform the region and lead to the creation of protracted conflicts in addition to the core conflict.

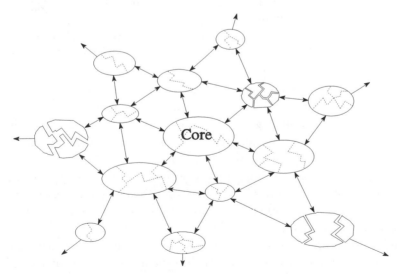

FIGURE 6.4 Interlocking Central Place Diffusion of Insecurity, with Secondary and Tertiary Insecurity/Diffusion Effects

These conflicts will contribute feedback effects to the general regional diffusion process. Such auxiliary protracted conflicts are most likely to break out in the marginal areas, that is, in the marginal states of the PCR's state structure and in the more marginal groups within the states themselves. This hypothesis can be explained by reference to "diversionary theory." Because the core conflict poses a real, external threat to the confrontal and peripheral states, these states will find it easier (and more credible) to rationalize their increasing militancy to their constituents. Internal dissent is less likely to be expressed because such expression will be seen as less socially acceptable and the state's repression of any such dissent more acceptable. In addition, the relative power disparity between the state and its substate actors will reach its highest level due to the concentration of power in the state to counter the external threat. The more marginal substate actors are likely to be ethnic minorities.

Evidence

Security studies have traditionally concentrated on events in the European core of the world system. Much is known about the conflict behavior of the world's major powers, primarily through the study of war, the most institutionalized form of violent conflict behavior. Little is known about the conflict behavior of the world's minor players. Models and theories developed from the study of major power experience do not appear to be appropriate or applicable to the minor powers.

The post–World War II global system presents a unique opportunity for the study of the hypothesized diffusion of insecurity process. The collapse of the great power (colonial) system after 1945 signified the entrance of the "Third World" societies into the analytic domain of security studies. These newly independent states are by definition less institutionalized than their European cohorts; they are also less "Europeanized" political cultures. Lesser institutionalization should translate into less systemic conditioning of fundamental conflict processes (that is, less control over events interactions and less procedural imposition, or channeling, of substitutable policies toward culturally preferred outcomes). Broader cultural variation in the sample population should allow a greater opportunity to control for the effects of cultural norms in the analysis of political behavior. In addition, the contemporary period has seen the number of state actors increase from 65 in 1930 to 107 in 1960; whereas just over 50 percent of the world population was "represented" in 1940, nearly 90 percent was so represented in 1950.[7]

The period for my study of the hypothesized "diffusion of insecurity" effect is 1946–1990; the focus is on Third World societies. A first-run analysis of the conflict data supports the claim that there are six regional clusters of violent conflict events in the study period.[8] Of these six regional clusters, I chose the Middle East for this analysis because it is the most "well-endowed" ex-ample of the hypothesized effect; this is because the conflict dynamics of the region have been especially exaggerated by global attention and natural re-source endowments.

Accurate and reliable data on conflict behavior that cover all the states in the global system have only recently been compiled and made generally acces-sible. Available data bases allow for tests of hypothesized diffusion of insecu-rity systemic effects, first, on major violent conflict events; second, on num-bers of military personnel; third, on state military expenditures; fourth, on indicators of state governance; fifth, on communal minority conflict; and sixth, on refugee flows. The basic test of each hypothesized consequence of the dif-fusion effect is covariation: "The typical statistical evidence to support a con-clusion that diffusion is occurring consists of covariation of the dependent phenomenon between units that are connected by the diffusion mechanism. In other words, if cases that are linked together display a greater degree of similarity than cases that are not linked together, this indicates that a process of diffusion may be occurring" (Frendreis 1989, 348).

I subjected each issue area to longitudinal analysis in order to look for changes over time. I augment the search for covariation by referring to changes in the relationships of variables; that is, there should be an increase in the magnitude of the hypothesized effects and the strength of the diffusion rela-tionship among "connected units" over the time span of the core protracted conflict (which, in the case of the Middle East PCR, is the entire 1946–1990 period). The time spans of the data sources vary and thus the time increments used in the longitudinal analyses also vary. The time increments are generally arbitrary and chosen mainly for convenience. Special attention should be paid to the inclusive years noted when cross-referencing the different tables and figures.

The diffusion of insecurity approach to the explanation of conflict behav-ior in the Third World competes with the *political development* approach ex-pounded by Huntington and others. For Huntington (1968), a too rapid pro-cess of modernization in the many newly independent Third World countries can contribute to political instability and increased conflict. However, accord-ing to this alternative approach, one would expect either a random distribu-tion of political instability throughout the Third World or, should there be a general cultural factor influencing a state's susceptibility to political decay or its drive toward modernization, uniformity in the growth of insecurity across cultural regions. The Middle East PCR is a primarily uniform cultural region; that is, it is primarily Arabic and Islamic. The diffusion of insecurity approach will find support if the dependent variables correlate with geographic posi-tioning within the PCR context and changes in those variables conform to the structure of serial diffusion.

Major War Episodes

The major war experiences of the states of the region appear in schematic form in table 6.2. Such war experiences include both interstate and civil warfare. Even though major wars are the most dramatic and "visible" violent conflict events, data on these events are meager and vary widely among data sources. I have subjected the most important information regarding the *magnitude* (total casualties, military and civilian, and population dislocations), *intensity* (destruction of property and consumption of resources), and *duration* (both of the experience itself and of its influence on behavior) to the greatest scrutiny, but it remains the least known and most problematic of conflict behavior data. One would expect that the confrontal states would experience the most such major wars and beginning at an earlier time; the peripheral states should experience fewer war episodes, beginning later than those in the confrontal states; the marginal states should experience even fewer episodes, beginning later than those in the peripheral states. The magnitude of any specific violent episode should be for the most part independent of the diffusion effect; magnitude is an indicator of the extent of loss of control over the conflict process (according to Arendt's view) and would thereby be dependent on factors endogenous to the actors involved.

Table 6.2 presents the major war episodes in the PCR, arranged according to geopolitical division. The low degree of accuracy and reliability of the data does not provide a solid basis for statistical inference, except in the grossest and most superficial terms (that is to say, these inferences are highly interpretive). The confrontal states have the highest level of violent conflicts, both in terms of the number of episodes and in their duration. The peripheral states enter the protracted conflict mode about ten to twenty years after the confrontal states. The marginal states enter the protracted mode about twenty to forty years after the core states and show a lower number of shocks. The data on major war episodes are consistent with the diffusion theory.

Military Capabilities

The primary instrument available to states for dealing with threats to their integrity is the military establishment. The main response of states to a condition or environment of insecurity is to increase military manpower and military expenditures. We would therefore expect the data on these variables to most clearly reflect the serial diffusion effect within the PCR. Tables 6.3 and 6.4 present the data on military personnel and expenditures, provided by the Correlates of War project and covering the period 1946–1985.

I first separated the data into four ten-year periods and indexed each of the variables per capita to control for variation in the size of states. Two reference groups are included for comparison: the group of highly industrialized

TABLE 6.2 Major War Episodes in the Middle East PCR Since 1948

Confrontal States

1948   4.0 Palestine War
1967   4.5 Israel-Arab War
1975   5.6 Lebanon Civil War

Israel 1946–1990+
   1948   1956   1967   1973   1978   1982   1988
Lebanon 1946–1990+
   1948   1958   1968   1975   1982
Syria 1948–1990+
   1948   1958   1967   1970   1973   1975   1982
[Palestine][a] 1948–1990+
   1948   1967   1988
Egypt 1948–1978
   1948   1952   1956   1967   1973
Jordan 1948–1980
   1948   1958   1967   1970

Peripheral States

1961   3.9 Iraq-Kurd War
1972   7.2 First Sudan Civil War
1980[b]   9.0 Iraq-Iran War
1986   10.1 Second Sudan Civil War
1990[b]   5.0 Iraq-Kuwait War

Iraq 1958–1990+
   [1948] 1958   1961   1974   1980   1990
Sudan 1963–1990+
   1963   1984   1986
Turkey 1974–1990+
   1974   1984   1990
[Cyprus][c] 1974–1990+
   1974   1986
Libya 1980–1988
   1980   1986
Saudi Arabia 1990
   1990

Marginal States

1980   7.8 Ethiopia Civil War
1980[b]   9.0 Iraq-Iran War
1988   4.5 Somalia Civil War
1990[b]   5.0 Iraq-Kuwait War

Somalia 1965–1990+
   1965   1977   1988
Ethiopia 1967–1990+
   1967   1978   1980   1984
Iran 1978–1990+
   1978   1980   1987
Chad 1980–1990+
   1980   1985
Yemen 1986–1989
   1986
Kuwait 1990
   1990

1990+[d]
   [5.1 Iraq-Kurd]
   [2.0 Iraq-Shi'a]
   [2.0 Iran-Kurd]
   [1.2 Turkey-Kurd]
   [3.8 Azerbaijan-Armenia]
   [3.4 Croatia]
   [1.9 Georgia]
   [6.5 Bosnia]
   [4.0 Ethiopia-Oromo]
   [3.2 Chad]

Sources: Sivard 1991; Brogan 1989; Small and Singer 1982; SIPRI 1991; Harff and Gurr 1988; Kaye, Grant, and Emond 1985; Tillema 1991; Singer and Small 1993; Gurr 1994, appendix.
Notes: The numbers before names of wars denote warfare magnitude score, following the method proposed by Gurr 1994, appendix 9. Scores are derived from the square root of the sum of (1) total deaths (in tens of thousands) and (2) the largest yearly total refugee population, including internally displaced (in hundreds of thousands). Inclusive dates denote years of protracted conflict episode for that state.

   a. Palestine is not an officially recognized state. It refers to the "occupied territories" of the West Bank and Gaza Strip.

   b. The Iraq-Iran War and the Iraq-Kuwait War were fought between a peripheral and a marginal state and are noted in both places.

   c. Cyprus does not meet the minimum population criterion for inclusion in the empirical analyses.

   d. 1990+ wars and magnitude scores are from Gurr 1994, appendix.

TABLE 6.3 Military Personnel and Expenditures, Middle East PCR, 1946–1985

	Highly Institutionalized States[a]	Confrontal States	Peripheral States	Marginal States	Non-PCR States[b]
1946–1955					
MILPER	718.7	36.8	185.0	50.1	42.4
MILPERC	.013	.015	.011	.004	.008
MILEX	3,307	36	119	60	108
MILEXC	47.5	11.1	9.9	3.6	17.0
1956–1965					
MILPER	597.3	64.3	115.2	44.3	36.2
MILPERC	.011	.015	.008	.003	.005
MILEX	5,119	114	130	46	94
MILEXC	57.8	26.2	12.1	8.8	11.9
1966–1975					
MILPER	635.0	116.1	135.6	39.1	36.2
MILPERC	.010	.018	.009	.006	.004
MILEX	10,007	770	556	253	188
MILEXC	117.3	130.0	69.6	56.9	18.2
1976–1985					
MILPER	630.9	183.1	208.8	73.3	45.1
MILPERC	.008	.022	.012	.011	.004
MILEX	23,127	2,257	6,173	1,676	641
MILEXC	286.1	366.4	651.8	417.7	51.9

Source: National Material Capabilities Data, 1816–1985. Correlates of War Project, University of Michigan; J. David Singer and Melvin Small, principal investigators, July 1990.

Key:
MILPER = Military personnel (in thousands).
MILPERC = Military personnel per capita.
MILEX   = Military expenditures (in millions of current year U.S. dollars).
MILEXC = Military expenditures per capita.

a. Western Europe, United States, and Canada.
b. Third World states not in any PRC cluster.

states (HIS) comprising most of the European states (western and eastern), the USSR, the United States, Canada, Australia, and China (a total of twenty-two) and the group of non-PCR states (NPCR) comprising all other Third World states not included in any of the six protracted conflict regions (totaling fifty-one). The Middle East PCR subsample has nineteen states (out of fifty-seven total PCR): five confrontal states (CS); five peripheral states (PS); and nine marginal states (MS).

The nineteen PCR states clearly distinguish themselves from the two reference groups. There is a fairly consistent buildup of military personnel

TABLE 6.4 Correlation Matrix for Military Personnel and Expenditures,
Middle East PCR, 1946–1985

	ncor[a]	MILPER	MILPERC	MILEX	MILEXC
1946–1950					
PCR	40/53	-.0826	.2124	-.3141	.2204
ETHNIND	.6104*	.0667	-.0618	.1204	-.1042
1951–1955					
PCR	45/59	-.0940	.3362#	-.2748	.2144
ETHNIND	.6043*	.1318	-.0950	.0204	-.4036#
1956–1960					
PCR	58/70	.0358	.5159*	.1102	.5508*
ETHNIND	.4543*	.0410	-.2622	-.1095	-.3921#
1961–1965					
PCR	83/85	.1194	.6214*	.3550*	.3566*
ETHNIND	.3940*	.0746	-.2359	-.0719	-.2846#
1966–1970					
PCR	89/89	.2184	.6378*	.4029*	.3748*
ETHNIND	.3278*	.0351	-.3024#	-.0564	-.2106
1971–1975					
PCR	100/100	.3683*	.5307*	.2885#	.2009
ETHNIND	.3290*	-.2172	.1118	-.1568	.0820
1976–1980					
PCR	100/100	.3417*	.4051*	.1627	.0138
ETHNIND	.3290*	-.2200	.3101*	-.1183	.4106*
1981–1985					
PCR	99/100	.3044*	.3662*	.0961	-.0144
ETHNIND	.3290*	-.2094	.3146*	-.0931	.5474*

Sources: See table 6.3; Taylor and Jodice 1983; *World Handbook of Political and Social Indicators III.*

Key:
MILPER   = Military personnel (in thousands).
MILPERC = Military personnel per capita.
MILEX   = Military expenditures (in millions of current year U.S. dollars).
MILEXC   = Military expenditures per capita.
PCR   = Confrontal (3); Peripheral (2); Marginal (1).
ETHNIND = Ethno-linguistic Fractionalization Index (0<—lesser; greater—> 1).

a. Top figure under "ncor" indicates *n* (total *n*/least *n*); lower figure indicates PCR-ETHNIND correlation.
* = Significant at .001 level.
# = Significant at .01 level.

(MILPER) and military personnel per capita (MILPERC) over the later three periods in the PCR states, in contrast to the maintenance of fairly steady levels over the entire temporal span in both the HIS and NPCR states. Military expenditures (MILEX) and military expenditures per capita (MILEXC) show increases throughout the four periods for all state groups (these figures are not indexed for inflation). However, the rate of increase in the PCR states is much greater than in the two reference groups. MILEXC in the HIS group increased by 22 percent in the second period, 102 percent in the third, and 144 percent in the final period. MILEXC in the NPCR states decreased by 30 percent in the second and then increased by 53 percent in the third and 185 percent in the fourth period. MILEXC in the CS group jumped 136 percent in the second, 396 percent in the third, and only 182 percent in the fourth. Increases in the PS group are 22 percent in the second, 475 percent in the third, and 836 percent in the fourth. Increases in the MS group are 144 percent in the second, 546 percent in the third, and 634 percent in the fourth periods.

There is quite obviously a strong push for greater military power in the PCR states over the span of the study period, with enormous increases in the latter half. Most of the increases in military spending in the peripheral and marginal states were financed through heightened oil revenues, but ability to pay is not the same as willingness to pay. The hypothesized spread of insecurity through the region and the increased magnitude of that insecurity over time are supported by the data. These data do not help us very much in differentiating between competing explanations of such changes in behavior, however. Both functional and diffusion theories can account for the increases, though according to Huntington's theory, one would assume that political decay and the resulting political instability would hinder the state's ability to increase its military power over the long term without substantial external assistance.

Table 6.4 presents an expanded analysis of the military capabilities data. I have shortened the time increments to eight five-year periods. Only the Middle East PCR states are included in the data analysis. The compilation of correlations among variables is designed to test the expected process of structural conformity to the serial diffusion model. Structural conformity of the dependent variables to the systemic diffusion process variable (PCR) would be indicated by a strong positive correlation. PCR scores range from 1 to 3, with a 3 denoting states closest to the PCR core.

Another possible explanation for change in systemic conflict behavior is the *ethnic fragmentation* argument (Gurr 1994, 5–8). This is a functional argument similar to Huntington's political development approach in that it assumes a process of systemic political decay and instability resulting from increasing competition among substate actors, in this case, ethnic groups. The placement of the role of ethnicity between the diffusion of insecurity theory—which proposes that political ethnicity is a consequence of systemic breakdown—and the ethnic fragmentation argument—which posits ethnic conflict as a cause of systemic breakdown—is useful. I added a control variable, an ethno-linguistic fractionalization index (ETHNIND), to test the explanatory power of an ethnic fragmentation argument in comparison to the diffusion of insecurity theory. ETHNIND scores for each state range from 0 to 1, with 0 indicating perfect ethnic homogeneity and 1 denoting perfect ethnic heterogeneity. The ethnic fragmentation explanation would find support in a positive correlation between ETHNIND and the dependent variables.

The data analysis reveals three distinct periods within the total time span: In the early period, about 1946–1955, there are mixed results, with no clear patterns in place but with some evidence of emerging patterns. Both the diffusion of insecurity theory and the ethnic fragmentation theory show some explanatory power, though the results are tainted somewhat by missing data and a smaller number of cases, due to the fact that some states are not yet independent actors. The PCR variable is gaining in salience (that is, positive correlation and significance) during this period. The ETHNIND variable shows a negative correlation, especially strong for the military expenditures per capita variable (MILEXC); this indicates that more ethnically homogeneous states are better able to devote large shares of state resources to the provision of military power. In the middle period, about 1956–1970, structural conformity to the PCR model is clearly indicated by very strong and consistent positive correlations in both military personnel and expenditures per capita (MILPERC and MILEXC). Again, in this period, it is the more ethnically homogeneous states that devote larger shares of state material and human resources to the provision of military power and security. In the most recent period, about 1970–1985, PCR conformity patterns show decreasing influence over the dependent variables, while ethnic heterogeneity shows increasing vigor as an explanation for differences in military policies. Now it is the most ethnically fragmented states that appear compelled to augment their military establishment (shown by the change from negative to positive correlations on the per capita variables). The significance of the PCR structure on the distribution of military expenditures is obliterated in the most recent environment of insecurity, which has brought uniformity to the entire region, in that all states have by now militarized to the same degree. Signs of advanced social disintegration become prominent during this period.

The analysis of military capabilities data shows that these indicators of the states' policy responses to the proposed "climate" of insecurity strongly support the systemic diffusion theory and are generally consistent with expectations regarding primary and secondary diffusion effects. The increasing salience of the ethnic fragmentation index in the most recent period supports the hypothesized tertiary diffusion effects. Figures 6.5 and 6.6 show the temporal changes in factor correlations presented in table 6.4: figure 6.5 shows

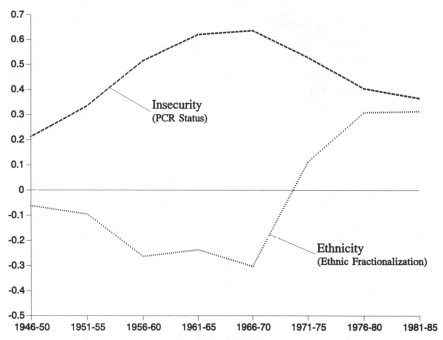

FIGURE 6.5 Insecurity, Ethnicity, and Militancy: Military Personnel per Capita

changes in the factor correlations of the insecurity (PCR) and ethnic fractionalization (ETHNIND) variables with the MILPERC (militancy—military
personnel per capita) variable; figure 6.6 shows the changes over time in the
PCR and ETHNIND correlations with the MILEXC (militancy—military expenditures per capita) variable.

Of special interest in the analysis is the observed characteristics of the
peripheral states. These states are "sandwiched" between the protracted violence at the PCR core (the confrontal states) and the increasingly insecure
marginal states. This *sandwich effect* might be explained by the special circumstances of the Middle East, in that those peripheral states have access to oil
revenues, which grant them license to divert larger absolute amounts of material resources to military expenditures. It is also likely that such behavior can
be explained within the diffusion model by the increasing strength of the security dilemmas of PCR states over time. Why this should affect the middle-
tier states more than others can be better explained by examining regime characteristics.

Proliferation of armaments throughout societies, and especially, the arming of substate groups, must also be taken into account. These unofficial arms
transfers are in general beyond quantification, so no "hard" evidence can be
mustered to specify the extent and magnitude of such proliferation or how the
arming of societies corresponds to the arming of states. We can assume that

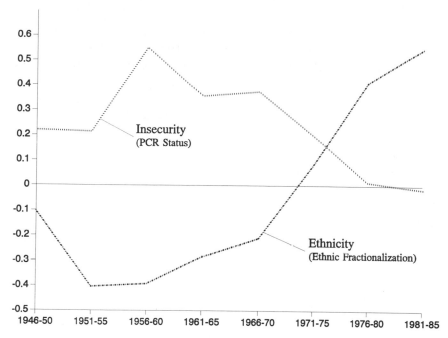

FIGURE 6.6 Insecurity, Ethnicity, and Militancy: Military Expenditures per Capita

increasing insecurity and the justifications of the evolving culture of violence create a strong demand for personal power and protection. Such strong demand will eventually be met, since that is the nature of our global free market system. The arming of societies is greatly enhanced when substate groups are armed directly by states. Of course, the availability of sufficient "firepower" figures strongly in the decision to resort to violence of any type (see Gurr 1970).

Regime Characteristics

How can we expect regimes to behave under conditions of systemic insecurity? I propose that, in general, the degree of regime coherence will increase as a function of its proximity to the source of systemic insecurity. This can be explained by means of *diversionary theory*. Under conditions of external threat, a society will cohere more strongly and be less tolerant of dissent from within, at least in the short term (Russett and Graham 1989). This means that the confrontal states can be expected to exhibit the greatest degree of internal cohesion and will thus be best able to afford the majority of their citizenry the highest degrees of democracy. Over the longer term, the internal cohesion of the confrontal states will tend to erode due to the seeming intractability of the external threat and the proven inability of the regimes to resolve the source of systemic insecurity.

The peripheral states, because they exist within a generalized environment of insecurity without an obvious source of external threat, can be expected to exhibit the greatest degree of regime rigidity; that is, the main source of threat for the peripheral states is their sense of the increasing security dilemma. These states' regimes can be expected to be strongly autocratic and coherent; internal dissent or other challenges to regime authority will be dealt with most severely. The marginal states, because they experience only a very vague sense of external threat and general insecurity, will exhibit the least cohesive societies and coherent regimes.

Table 6.5 presents an analysis of the Polity II data on four indicators of regime governance: institutionalized autocracy (AUTOC), institutionalized democracy (DEMOC), concentration of power (CONCEN), and regime coherence (COHERX) (Gurr, Jaggers, and Moore 1989, 1991). Again, I divided the data into four ten-year periods to show tendencies for change in the indicators over time. The non-PCR (NPCR) reference group data are provided for comparison.

The only regime variable that conforms to the PCR's structural characteristics is the indicator of institutionalized democracy (DEMOC). The correlations between the PCR and DEMOC variables are in the range of 0.300–0.350 across the entire time span and with noteworthy significance scores (i.e., less than 0.001). The confrontal states are the most democratic of the PCR states, but are less democratic than the non-PCR states, as expected; those scores on democracy fall over the long term, however. These states' regimes, after an initial increase, show signs of strain—that is, their coherence score falls. The peripheral states are the most rigid, and that rigidity increases over the time span of the data—that is, AUTOC increases, DEMOC decreases, CONCEN increases, and COHERX remains constant.

The marginal state regimes show no clear patterns except that institutionalized democracy is nearly nonexistent in these regimes; of greatest concern here is the extremely low coherence score in the most recent period. Returning to table 6.4, we see that there is a strong correlation in the Middle East PCR between the PCR and ETHNIND variables (.329). This means that the marginal states are generally more ethnically heterogeneous and the precipitous drop in the coherence scores for the marginal states in the most recent period may be seen to support the hypothesized tertiary diffusion effects. The regime coherence score is especially indicative of the propensity for political instability and, by inference, the probability of the occurrence of violent conflict. Eckstein asserted that polities with coherent (that is, internally consistent) authority patterns should outperform and outlast those with incoherent patterns (Gurr, Jaggers, and Moore 1989). Again, the peripheral states exhibit strong signs of the political effects of being situationally "sandwiched" between increasingly incoherent polities in the PCR.

TABLE 6.5 Autocracy, Democracy, Concentration, and Coherence in the
Middle East PCR, 1947–1986

	Non-PCR States[a]	Confrontal States	Peripheral States	Marginal States
1947–1956				
AUTOC	2.960	3.277	5.231	5.432
DEMOC	5.192	4.426	3.128	1.270
CONCEN	4.825	4.313	4.846	5.200
COHERX	.504	.458	.744	.450
1957–1966				
AUTOC	3.658	4.255	5.500	5.919
DEMOC	4.491	3.681	2.396	1.581
CONCEN	5.015	4.660	4.980	5.500
COHERX	.617	.620	.760	.766
1967–1976				
AUTOC	4.705	4.694	5.688	5.944
DEMOC	3.418	3.388	2.396	0.989
CONCEN	5.476	5.120	5.480	5.222
COHERX	.754	.580	.720	.611
1977–1986				
AUTOC	4.257	4.610	6.571	5.115
DEMOC	3.763	3.463	1.306	0.885
CONCEN	5.471	4.600	5.540	5.033
COHERX	.741	.400	.780	.222

Source: Polity II Data, 1800–1986; Polity II Project, Center for Comparative Politics, University of Colorado; Ted Robert Gurr, Keith Jaggers, and Will H. Moore, principal investigators, April 1989.

Key:
AUTOC   = Institutionalized autocracy mean (10-point scale).
DEMOC   = Institutionalized democracy mean (10-point scale).
CONCEN = Concentration of power mean (10-point scale).
COHERX = Coherent polities as proportion of total.

a. Excludes highly institutionalized states (Western Europe, United States, and Canada).

Communal Minorities

The evidence so far has been primarily on the conflict behavior of states in the Middle East PCR. The tertiary effects of the diffusion of insecurity model (see figure 6.5) posit that the ongoing diffusion process will penetrate societies intensively and affect the social and political relations between substate actors and the state and also between various substate actors. We would expect an increase over time of general societal tensions and in the incidence of civil violence, both public and private, involving both groups and individuals. Unfortunately, information on the conflict behavior of substate actors is sparse. The only systematic global data base that covers the conflict behavior of substate groups during the entire period under study is the Minorities at Risk project data base; I have used these data to analyze conflict involving communal minority groups.

The politicization and mobilization of communal identities can have serious consequences for the state's ability to govern and maintain a coordinated administrative system. Increasing social fragmentation can put the states governing those disintegrating societies at risk of becoming politically ineffective (losing social control) and administratively superfluous (losing legitimate authority—see Marshall 1993a). As a result, these states and societies become increasing vulnerable to external influence, interference, and intervention. If they are held together at all, it is through increasingly autocratic institutions and increasing state repression.

Table 6.6 shows the results of the analysis of the Minorities at Risk data (Gurr and Marshall 1990; Gurr 1993a, 1993c). Again, I analyzed the data by time increments: I coded the variables indicating group involvement in violent rebellion against the state (REBX) for each five-year period; I coded the variable indicating involvement and magnitude of intercommunal violence for each decade. All figures show increases over the full time span, with a substantial jump in violent activity in the late 1970s.

Not all minority groups can be expected to focus their conflict activity on confrontations with the state; some will see competition with other communal groups as a source of threat and as a target for violent acts. Other groups will stop short of displaying open rebellion, but will instead engage in political protest which, under the general conditions of insecurity, will tend to escalate to violent protest. When the additional information on intercommunal and protest violence for minority groups is included in the analysis, the number of groups involved in some form of violence is seen to increase. Violence scores increase over time, and again there is a substantial increase in the number of groups engaged in violence in the 1970s. This evidence supports the hypothesized tertiary effects of the diffusion of insecurity theory. It is probably safe to assume that, in the 1990s, *all* communal minority groups in the Middle East PCR are politicized; most are mobilized; and very many are actively engaged in serious acts of political violence.

There is no way to determine the magnitude of the effects that the increased systemic violence is having on the incidence of violence in the private domain. Public violence spills over into the private domain both directly, as when civilians are directly affected by military warfare, and indirectly, as individual and social psychology is transformed through the experience of violence and this change manifests itself in personal relations. Matthews touches on the idea of direct spillover when she points out that "the pattern of violence

TABLE 6.6 Rebellion, Violent Protest, and Intercommunal Violence
in the Middle East PCR, 1940–1989

	n/reb (n=31)	REBX	nviol (n=31)	VIOLX	VIOLM
1940–1944	n.a.	n.a.	6	38	6.33
1945–1949	4/0	0.533			
1950–1954	1/0	0.133	11	50	4.55
1955–1959	5/0	0.400			
1960–1964	7/0	0.733	13	87	6.69
1965–1969	11/1	1.133			
1970–1974	10/4	1.167	26	183	7.04
1975–1979	18/7	2.129			
1980–1984	21/7	2.419	26	222	8.54
1985–1989	22/8	2.484			

Source: Minorities at Risk Data, 1946–1990; Minorities at Risk Project, Center for International Development and Conflict Management, University of Maryland, College Park; Ted Robert Gurr and Monty G. Marshall, principal investigators, August 1992.

Key:
n/reb = No. of minorities engaged in acts of violent rebellion / No. engaged in protracted civil war.
REBX = Mean score on index of rebellion (5-point scale).
nviol = Number of minorities engaged in acts of violence (including rebellion, violent protest, and intercommunal violence).
VIOLX = Total summed score of rebellion, violent protest, and intercommunal violence scores for all groups.
VIOLM = Average total violence score for groups engaged in violence.

has changed. Civilian casualties accounted for 5 percent of the total in World War I, 50 percent in World War II and 80 to 90 percent in the conflicts of the past decade" (*Washington Post,* 8 March 1994, A19). The main indirect effects would be recorded as increases in violent crime, including domestic violence and rape.[9]

Resource Dislocations

At the individual level, insecurity and warfare lend impetus to mass population movements. In its less virulent form, a sense of general systemic insecurity can be expected to lend weight to the individual's rational choice of how and where to live (to the extent that such a choice is available). In a condition of increasing insecurity, there will be a discernible increase in the number of individuals migrating to what they think are more hospitable and secure areas. Societal elites especially will enjoy the liberty to choose their place of residence, their depository of monetary assets, and the placement of material re-

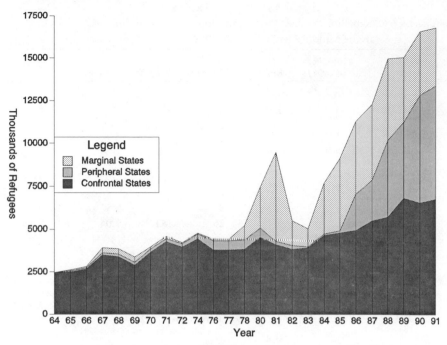

FIGURE 6.7 Dislocated Populations, Middle East Protracted Conflict Region

sources. Under conditions of systemic insecurity, the societal problems of "brain drain" and "capital flight" can be expected to increase over time. Under crisis conditions, these movements will increase dramatically. No systematic records on such resource movements are kept, however, and confirmation of these hypotheses is primarily a matter of observation and informal speculation (but see Askari 1990).

The common people are not afforded the luxury of optimal choice in residence and resource allocation. In the less intense conditions of systemic insecurity, we would expect pressure for increased population movements based on economic migration. Relocation away from the less secure areas is usually not an option for most people and especially for the indigent. Mass population movements can be expected to occur only under the most intense condition of insecurity, and especially, during crises of insecurity and warfare. Data on mass economic migrations are not generally kept, but data on mass refugee movements in the post-1945 era are compiled by the office of the UN High Commissioner for Refugees (UNHCR) and by the United States Committee for Refugees (USCR).

Figure 6.7 represents the total number of cross-border refugees (officially recognized by the UNHCR) and internally displaced persons (estimated by USCR) in the Middle East PCR for the years 1964–1991.[10] As the graph shows, the problem of mass population dislocations is persisting, fluctuating periodically, and increasing slightly (due primarily to population increases within the refugee camps) in the confrontal states through the entire period (and back to 1948). Such dislocations are small in the peripheral and marginal states, starting in the mid-1960s and continuing throughout the 1970s. (Population dislocations in the peripheral states are probably underreported due to the closed nature and institutional rigidity of those regimes; that is, such regimes exercise greater control over the dissemination of detrimental information about themselves.) There is a tremendous jump in the number of dislocated persons in the marginal states around 1980 and this condition persists throughout the 1980s. Mass population dislocations become a serious problem for the peripheral states in the mid-1980s and increase rapidly through the remainder of the period. The analysis of population dislocations generally supports the diffusion of insecurity theory and is consistent with the hypothesized tertiary effects. The analysis appears to further support the "sandwich" hypothesis, though this assessment must be qualified because of reporting inconsistencies; the data are certainly consistent with the proposed "sandwich" effect.

Conclusions

Human society is founded on the possibility of articulating an inclusive identity and on the existence of a critical mass of voluntary human associations. These associations are valued as the instruments of increasing mutual benefit. Since those instruments seem efficacious under prevailing conditions, they are institutionalized, that is, they become part of the physical structure, embedded in the psychological culture of society. The primarily *voluntary* nature of societal associations is essential because the construction, administration, regeneration, and extension of society require concerted effort; efficiency demands a minimal degree of dissension within the system. The occurrence of violence and the consequent sense of insecurity affect the essential, delicate relations of society and lead to the progressive disintegration of the elaborate network of social ties among individuals in affiliations and associations. Salient social identifications become biased toward ever smaller aggregations and more easily identifiable (or secure) distinctions between the inclusionary identity group (representing order and security) and the exclusionary environment (representing disorder and insecurity). It is probable, as many feminists have claimed, that even the relations within the "secured" identity group will experience increased strains and a greater incidence of criminal behavior and domestic violence. The extension of the diffusion of insecurity and the culture of violence arguments to the individual, family, and small group levels of aggregation await future research.

The evidence presented is generally consistent with the expectations and supports the basic premises of the diffusion of insecurity and culture of violence theories. The evidence supports four general conclusions: first, political violence in the post–World War II global system is concentrated in several specific regional clusters; second, analysis of the Middle East regional cluster, centered on the high-profile protracted conflict between Israel and the Palestinians, shows an increasing incidence of political violence in the region, and such violence tends to spread outward from the central core conflict over the duration of the conflict period; third, the increased incidence of violence and its pervasiveness within the regional environment affect all social group relations at all levels of group aggregation; and fourth, the disintegration of secular societies into political processes of increased contention among constituent "ethnic" components appears to be a later development in the general process of systemic militarization and societal disintegration.

The implications of the systemic diffusion approach in security studies are many and varied. In general, the resolution of protracted social conflicts and restraint from the use of violence and force are fundamental and immediate concerns for all peace-loving states, groups, and individuals in the global community, and especially in the regional community. Of equal concern is the problem of the proliferation of weaponry in regions at risk, which puts guns in the hands of those most likely to use them. The first step toward avoiding or resolving violent conflicts would be to deny the object of addiction to the addict (to the extent that the comparison is valid); the second step would be to isolate the condition while "inoculating" those likely to be exposed to the "infection" with measured doses of security. To extend the inoculation metaphor, prescriptions designed to enhance the natural "immune system" can counter the culture of violence. The world does not need a global policeman; it needs a world teacher. Future development is possible only within an environmental milieu dominated by peaceful conflict management.

The greatest implication of the diffusion of insecurity and the culture of violence theory lies in its application to the dynamics of the cold war. The irrational social psychology of nuclear annihilation is perhaps an even more subtly powerful brand of insecurity than is the rational fear of actual violence. The key to unraveling the extensive global culture of violence and its regional subcultures may lie in addressing the situation at the global systemic core: the protracted conflict relationship between the United States and the former USSR.

Disengagement in the Southeast Asian protracted conflict region may be a model for the transformation of cultures of violence into cultures of development. There, it seems that initial disengagement did not lead immediately to a decrease in the incidence of violence; it has taken nearly two decades for actual violence to abate in that situation. It is hoped that the current increase in the United States' external involvement in political violence abroad will begin to taper off, after making cultural adjustments in appropriate response to the ending of cold war hostilities. Likewise, the disengagement of the successor states of the USSR from the global culture of violence has raised the possibility that internal tensions will lead to violence. In the interim, the recourse to violence by the former antagonists remains fairly conspicuous at all levels, especially by the United States, since there is currently no external constraint on its use of force. The political leadership of each state prone to insecurity needs to apply extreme and conscious restraint on the preference for force in order to avoid perpetuating the "old world order" culture of violence.

The research in political diffusion processes is only just beginning. Understanding how the social system works and how it fails may provide needed insights into linkages among the most intractable contemporary social problems, such as substance abuse, rape, domestic violence, and criminality. The antidote for the toxic culture of violence is its antithesis: a culture of nonviolence, cooperation, and integration (Nye 1971; Keohane and Nye 1989).

Domestic Political Change and Strategic Response

THE IMPACT OF DOMESTIC CONFLICT ON STATE BEHAVIOR, 1816–1986

Zeev Maoz

How does ethnic conflict relate to global and regional change? What is the specific link between internal strife, domestic politics, and changes in the international environment?

One significant barrier to theoretical development in the international dimension of ethnic strife is the apparent lack of consensus regarding the assumed causal link between ethnic and interstate conflict. How does ethnic conflict become internationalized? Is it generated internally and then externalized, as some theories would suggest? Do ethnic conflicts weaken state structures, inviting external intervention? Or does the process involve a more subtle and complex series of interactions? A theory or set of theories should be capable of encompassing these potential linkages.

The disparate approaches, units, and levels of analysis used in the study of ethnic conflict present a second theoretical restriction. Usually, theories of international relations view ethnic conflict as an epiphenomenon—a by-product of interaction between the processes of state building and an anarchical system structure. A theory should allow for these processes and the impact they have on relations among states, but it should also be able to account for the potentially important role of domestic factors. Domestic variables are not meaningfully integrated into mainstream international relations research because of "paradigmatic blind spots" created by a systemic orientation. This problem becomes particularly acute when existing knowledge about domestically generated ethnic conflict is brought to bear on the study of interstate conflict, a relatively unexplored area for international relations.

It is time to explore some broader implications of the domestic sources of global change and in particular, the way that internal political transformations and challenges, including ethnic strife, affect a state's behavior in the international environment. In the first place, what kind of internal struggles, political and economic, affect the foreign policy of states? Second, how does a state react to changes in those characteristics? Third, are there systematic differences between states in terms of their reaction to environmental change and, if so, what factors account for these differences? Fourth, what can we learn from the mutual effects of domestic structures and environmental processes on the relationship between domestic politics and global change?

Ethnicity is a political factor with important implications for domestic and international ethnic conflict. Affect-laden behavior and structural arrangements (including institutions) can increase the salience of ethnic identity within elite decision making. I shall therefore consider the motivations of decision makers of individual states when they choose to become involved in an ethnic conflict within a state's arena of interaction.

Motivations and interests arise from political considerations as much as from the structural conditions associated with them. It is possible to assess the relative potency of these considerations even in a context that seems to be defined in such a manner as to give theoretical advantages to "top-down" logic.

The Politically Relevant International Environment (PRIE)

The concept of *international environment* has many synonyms in the professional jargon of world politics. For example, foreign policy scholars (e.g., Frankel 1963) make a distinction between the "psychological" and "operational" environment of decision makers. The operational environment is the set of objective circumstances in which decision makers operate. The psychological environment is these circumstances as perceived by the decision makers. Brecher et al. (1969) distinguish—in both types of environment—between the internal and external settings of decision making. For Brecher (1972, 2–8) and Brecher et al. (1969), the key aspects of the external international environment of states are the global, the subordinate, the subordinate other, the dominant bilateral, and the bilateral systems.

Theorists of the 1960s and 1970s assumed a high degree of homogeneity within a subsystem. This is clearly not the case in many instances, for example, in the Middle East or South and Southeast Asia. A regional subsystem is usually taken to be a geographical expanse that has several distinct characteristics: first, the political units (states) making up the subsystem are characterized by some degree of ethnic, cultural, religious, economic, or political homogeneity; second, the frequency and volume of interactions (both peaceful and conflictual) among indigenous political units in the regional subsystem are substantially greater than the interaction between indigenous units and political units external to the system; third, the interaction among indigenous units in the regional subsystem is characterized by a considerable degree of patterned regularity; and fourth, there exists some regional international organization that attempts to regulate the interactions among indigenous political units or otherwise serve as a regional problem-solving mechanism (this characteristic is not always present).

These criteria have served scholars in their efforts to delineate *international regions,* to use Russett's term (1967). And, despite some conceptual and empirical weaknesses, they have helped to define the boundaries of regional subsystems. However, a regional subsystem is not the same as the environment a state considers relevant when it contemplates its national security policy. Consider, for example, the Middle East subsystem. It is usually taken to consist of the region from Egypt in the west to Iran in the east and from Turkey in the north to the Emirates and Yemen in the south. If we want to use these boundaries to define the political environment of, say, Turkey, we may face several problems. First, since 1827 Greece and Russia—both nonregional actors—have occupied a more central role in the Turkish strategic calculus than all other Middle Eastern states taken together. This problem could be generalized to all states residing on the fringes of the regional subsystem. There is a high degree of ethnic heterogeneity in many subsystems.

There also exist numerous cases in which two political units from the same regional subsystem have little or no interaction with each other. Or, what is even more important for our purposes, the kind of interaction that does exist between states—however frequent and voluminous—may have little impact on their strategic calculus. Switzerland conducts extensive and voluminous interaction, primarily of a financial nature, with most other European states. However, very few states would consider Swiss foreign and security policy a key factor in their strategic calculus. Likewise, for states that share no common boundaries, the notion of regional subsystem may be relevant in terms of cultural, economic, or diplomatic interaction. However, the political or strategic changes in Chile may have little impact on the strategic policy of Costa Rica, and vice versa.

Yet the criteria established in the efforts to delineate regional subsystems are useful guides to the definition of the concept I wish to discuss. Buzan (1983) and Rosh (1988) use the concepts *Security Complex* or *Security Webs* to describe "the subsystem that policymakers in a given country take into account when formulating their security policies" (Rosh 1988, 672). Because their studies deal primarily with Third World states, they define these terms in a regional context. Since these terms are loaded, and since my approach to this issue is somewhat different, I offer an alternative but related concept for analysis. Each state has an environment that it considers significant for its planning, actions, and calculations. This is a state's politically relevant international environment (PRIE). The PRIE of a given state represents the set of political units (state and nonstate units) whose structure, behavior, and policies have a direct impact on the focal state's political and strategic calculus. This is the set of units upon which decision makers, intelligence agencies, the media, and the public focus their attention on an almost daily basis. These attract persistent and systematic attention whether or not important things or visible changes take place, because what happens in these units is perceived to have a direct, immediate, and profound impact on their own state. The need to react to developments in the units making up the politically relevant international environment of a state is far stronger than the need to react to developments of units outside the PRIE.

In addition, the threshold of a state's tolerance to developments in units within its PRIE is considerably lower than the threshold of the state's reaction to developments within units outside the PRIE. If a state within the PRIE increases its defense budget considerably, the tendency to react is far higher than the tendency to react to a substantial increase in the defense budget of states outside the PRIE. Likewise, an alliance between two states will be less likely to provoke a reaction if these two states are outside the PRIE than if at least one of the states is in the PRIE.

While the conceptual definition of the term is clear, the real question is, what is its operational meaning? Specifically, how do we know what the PRIE is when we look at a given state? There are two criteria I wish to offer to provide an operational definition of this concept. Both are grounded in basic maxims of international relations theory and are supported by substantial empirical evidence. These are contiguity and geopolitical status. In the first place, direct or indirect land connection or short cross-water distance between two political units make these units politically relevant to each other. Second, major powers have at least a regional reach, and most have global reach. Hence, all states in a region are part of the PRIE of those major powers that have a regional reach capacity. Likewise, the regional power is part of the PRIE of all states in the region. Following the same logic, we can conclude that the PRIE of major powers with global reach capacity consists of all states in the international system. Likewise, major powers with global reach capacity are part of the PRIE of each and every state in the international system.

The operational definition that follows from these criteria is thus that a state's politically relevant international environment includes all states that are directly or indirectly (that is, effectively) contiguous to it, all regional powers of its own geographic region, and all major powers with global reach capacity. Apart from the United States, regional and global powers are characterized by a high degree of ethnic homogeneity. The list of regional and global powers is given in table 7.1.

TABLE 7.1 Global and Regional Powers, 1816–1992

State	Years	Type of Reach Capacity	Region
United States	1823–1898	Regional	Americas
	1899–1992	Global	World
Great Britain	1816–1992	Global	World
France	1816–1940, 1944–1992	Global	World
Prussia-Germany	1816–1866	Regional	Europe
	1867–1918, 1925–1945	Global	World
Austria-Hungary	1816–1918	Regional	Europe
Italy	1861–1943	Regional	Europe, Africa
Russia–Soviet Union	1816–1917	Regional	Europe, Asia
	1922–1991	Global	World
	1992–	Regional	Europe, Asia
China	1949–1992	Regional	Asia
Japan	1895–1945	Regional	Asia

Source: Small and Singer 1982.
Note: Small and Singer define central and interstate systems and the major power on the basis of a "consensus of diplomatic historians." However, the distinction between global and regional powers is my own. There are other ways of conceiving of regional power, but given the difficulties of finding a precise definition, I stick to their original list. One reason is that virtually all other states that are considered regional powers fall with the population of PRIE of virtually all states in their region.

How do these criteria and the definition of a state's PRIE match the conceptual meaning of the term? First, virtually all authors who have focused on the sources and consequences of international conflict (Vasquez 1993; Goertz and Diehl 1992a; Siverson and Starr 1991; Holsti 1991) emphasize the importance of territorial contiguity as a source of conflict. This emerges also from a substantial body of evidence. As I have argued elsewhere (Maoz 1993b), territorial contiguity is not in itself a cause of conflict, but rather creates a context of relevance for states. This context may, and in many cases does, become a source of contention and disagreement between states over territorial issues. Territorial issues such as irredentas constitute the vast majority of interstate ethnic conflicts and wars (Holsti 1991; Vasquez 1993).

Second, the notion of global or regional reach covers a wide spectrum of strategically meaningful interactions between or among noncontiguous states. The question of whether global (or regional) reach is a result of global (or regional) interests of a state or the reverse is a chicken-and-egg issue. Be that as it may, reach capacity and span of strategic interests are generally strongly correlated. With respect to the PRIE concept, this correlation suggests that a state with global or regional reach capacity is interested in taking part in processes that occur within and between states that are not directly or indirectly contiguous, and has the capability of doing so. It also suggests that other states may be aware of the intent and capacity of noncontiguous states to intervene in their own internal or external affairs under certain circumstances.

A caveat is in order. Invariably, every definition of such a concept runs the risk of missing some of the importance of the term. The implication of this slippage between the abstract conceptual definition of PRIE and its empirical criteria is that glaring exceptions to the rule set down by the operational definition exist. In other words, we are likely to find very persuasive cases of states that should have been included in various PRIEs but are not. The opposite is also true. The criteria specified by the operational definition may identify states that should not be included in a given state's PRIE. For example, both Iraq and Iran should have always been part of Israel's PRIE, but the definition excludes them. Likewise, Israel should have been a part of the PRIE of Iran and Iraq but is not according to the definition. This is because Israel is not territorially contiguous to Iran and Iraq.

Nevertheless, this definition of PRIEs does have some key empirical facts going for it that make these few slippages negligible in relation to the empirical value of the concept. Because I use this concept to identify the states that are considered relevant to a state's political and strategic calculus, a key test of this definition is whether it captures some of the most important implications of such calculi. One of these implications is the initiation of, or involvement in, international conflict. If the states that are excluded from a given state's PRIE are not frequently involved in conflict against the focal state, then their omission is not unwarranted. The baseline population of states identified by the conditions set in the operational definition of PRIE is the population of politically relevant dyads. Consider the irredentist conflict between Iran and Iraq. If this population is engaged in most of the conflict and war behavior within any given period, then we can make a strong case for the validity of the operational definition.

Indeed, I have mentioned elsewhere (Maoz 1995, appendix to chaps. 3 and 4) that politically relevant dyads accounted for only 15.8 percent of all dyad-years for the period 1816–1986 (68,654 politically relevant dyad-years out of a total of 435,263 dyad-years). However, politically relevant dyads accounted for 87.3 percent of all militarized interstate dispute dyads (1,777 disputes between politically relevant dyads out of a total of 2,037 dispute dyads for the 1816–1986 period), and for 87.5 percent of all war dyads (217 war dyads out of a total of 248 war dyads). This is clearly strong evidence in support of the claim that, despite some important exceptions, the operational definition of PRIEs is essentially valid.

The focus on PRIEs is important because it reflects a relationship between external factors and states' foreign policies in terms that are both more concrete than in system-level models of national behavior and more general than in the case of dyadic or microlevel analyses of foreign policy decision. Systemic perspectives suggest that states are guided in their behavior by the principles and rules stemming from the structure of the international system.

The same can be said for the second most studied arms race, that which accompanied the Arab-Israeli irredentist conflict. Israel's calculus was always based on the assumption that it would have to fight simultaneously a coalition of several Arab states. Hence it had to respond to changes in the military allocations of Egypt, Syria, Jordan, Iraq, and—in some cases—Saudi Arabia and Iran. Likewise, Syria was primarily concerned with Israeli military power, but it could not and still cannot afford to ignore Turkey on its northern border and Iraq to the east. Obviously, dyadic analysis would miss or misrepresent this reality. The notion of PRIE is useful in that it defines the environment with which a state is concerned most directly and immediately.

PRIEs and Foreign Policy: Strategic and Political Factors

The political, strategic, and economic behavior of states depends to a large extent on the kind of environment surrounding them. When the characteristics of this environment change dramatically, states must adjust to meet the threats or respond to the opportunities created by these changes. Just which characteristics of the environment affect states' calculations, and what kind of foreign policy behavior follows from these calculations, depends to a large extent on which perspective of global change one has in mind.

Systemic and Regional Explanations

Systemic and regional approaches to change assert that changes in state behavior are to a large extent the result of states' readjustment to environmental shifts. According to these approaches, as long as the environment of states is relatively stable, we are apt to see fairly consistent behavior by a given state. Hence states' behavior can be quite predictable given reliable information on the attributes of their environment. Even if the state's international environment undergoes significant change, if we know something about how such changes affect states' calculations, we can predict—though perhaps less accurately—how states would react to such changes.

Systemic and regional approaches tell us also about the kind of changes that have a significant effect on state behavior. When we examine change and stability from such a general perspective, we must look at the distribution of capabilities, at the configuration of alliances, and at the spread of social movements and ideas.

Let us be more precise about how these approaches account for effects of environmental factors on state behavior. The point of departure of a systemic analysis is the notion of security dilemma (Herz 1957; Jervis 1978). In Posen's analysis of the international dimensions of ethnic conflict (1993), such conflict can become a regional security dilemma because it invites external intervention. From this perspective, ethnic conflict presents a security dilemma along two dimensions: states that pursue interventionist behavior because of the domestic opportunities that could be obtained from exploiting cleavages within other states, and states whose internal weakness leads to efforts toward self-defense against this external involvement. In either instance, the dilemma results from concerns that are domestically generated. In this context, ethnic cleavages and ethnic affinities are sources of insecurity for states. Leaders of states may be pressured by political opponents, or more directly, by the masses, to act on these linkages. The resulting foreign policy could lead to intensified interstate strife, in what Jervis (1976) calls the spiral model.

But herein lies the problem. Both processes are designed to increase states' security, thus contributing to international stability. Instead, they tend to make other states feel more, rather than less, threatened, thereby creating instability. When a state examines its environment and sees other states increasing their capabilities, either by higher defense spending or through alignment with other potential or actual enemies, the state feels increasingly threatened. Thus, the focal state does the same things, causing its neighbors to feel increasingly threatened as well.

The strategic repertoire of states in response to security dilemmas consists of several instruments of policy. Chief among those instruments are: conflict behavior, alliance formation, and military allocations (which include both human and material components). Hereafter, the term *strategic response* will designate these three types of behavior.

The implication is that two aspects of PRIEs invoke strategic responses of states. First, as the PRIE becomes increasingly militarized, a state feels increasingly threatened, thus more inclined to initiate conflict or to provoke others to initiate conflict against it, to form alliances, or to increase its military allocations. Second, as the state feels that it is being increasingly left out of strategic deals among units in its PRIE, or that units within its PRIE are aligning with external powers, the state's threat perception increases, thus provoking it to react.

Regional approaches that emphasize change as a function of cross-national social ideas, movements, and ideologies are similar to the systemic perspective's focus on alliances and military allocations. Ethnic ideologies and nationalism may be threatening in the abstract to states that are opposed to them. However, as much as a state is opposed to an idea or to a social movement, it cannot target its opposition in military terms, as long as these ideas or movements are not institutionalized within states. Even then, opposing ideologies, as hostile as they may appear to leaders of a given state, cannot justifiably constitute a threat unless there are real capabilities to back them up. Consider, for example, how Pan-Arabism has affected the behavior of states in the Middle

East. Pan-Arabism was a sweeping, cross-national movement that infiltrated many parts of the intelligentsia in several Arab states in the 1930s, 1940s, and 1950s. A crude characterization of this movement is embedded in the argument that the Arabs are one nation and that the union of all Arab states would heal all the social, economic, and political problems of the Arabs. As long as this was just an ideology, it led to concern among both moderate Arab states and Israel but it did not create a concrete and identifiable threat. However, when political leaders in key Arab states started to subscribe explicitly to this ideology, and when things they did suggested that they might have an intention of following and exporting Pan-Arabism, states began to react. Radical Islam may affect the strategic calculations of moderate states in the Middle East in much the same way. This implies that a state's PRIE is not perceived as strategically threatening if hostile ideologies merely settle in the government of the PRIE states. Rather, a regime or polity change in a state's PRIE becomes threatening only if this change is coupled with concrete strategic threats in the form of capabilities or alliances.

Both systemic and regional approaches make the following propositions. First, as a state's PRIE is increasingly militarized, the likelihood of strategic response—conflict involvement, alliance formation, and military allocations—by a state increases significantly. Second, as a state's PRIE is increasingly polarized in the alliance commitments of states that make up this PRIE, the likelihood of strategic response by a state increases significantly. Of course, a critical requirement is that the alliance commitments of states in the PRIE not include an alliance with the focal state. Otherwise, increased alliance commitments of fellow allies may actually increase, rather than decrease, a state's security.

Systemic and regional approaches do not require us to look at the political makeup of a state's environment as an important factor determining the state's sense of security or insecurity. Systemic and regional models of change tend to view domestic structures and processes as a function of external forces, or to view domestic and foreign policy as two independent processes that are affected by different things. Hence, they do not require us to examine how changes in the domestic political makeup of a state's PRIE affect its foreign policy behavior. Nor do these approaches lead us to examine the effect of the political regimes of states comprising a given PRIE on a state's behavior.

The reason for ignoring the domestic political makeup of states' PRIE is twofold. First, from a realist or neorealist perspective, a state with a political regime radically different from that of another state is not a threat to that state in and of itself. It may or may not become a threat if the other state has a capacity to convert the political differences in its domestic political system and ideology into an effective military threat. Thus, political differences that are not converted into effective military threats do not matter very much in a state's strategic calculus. Second, realist and neorealist approaches, especially in their systemic and regional guise, claim that political and ideological affinities have little or no impact on alliance behavior and strategic planning. A state constitutes a threat to another state to the extent that it is powerful, or when it is allied with powerful states. This applies whether or not the other state shares ideological ties or political or ethnic affinities. Likewise, if a state is aligned with another, differences in ideology, domestic structure, and religious, cultural, or ethnic affinities would not matter. Because domestic factors are secondary to strategic calculations in an anarchical international or regional system, ideological similarities are overshadowed by conflicting strategic considerations, just as ideological and political differences are overshadowed by common strategic interests.

We may therefore advance a third proposition, namely, that changes in the PRIE of states that are not converted into increased militarization or increased strategic polarization will have little or no effect on a state's strategic behavior. In other words, if changes take place in a state's PRIE that do not have strategic implications, they would not result in a reassessment of the strategic environment of the state. They may affect other aspects of a state's behavior (e.g., economic, diplomatic, or cultural aspects) but will not carry strategic consequences.

Another implication of this "black boxing" of states is that states that differ in their domestic political composition behave in much the same way under similar environmental conditions. Democracies that feel threatened by a militarized and polarized PRIE are going to behave in the same way as authoritarian states. Since states are not threatened merely because they face a more democratic or a less democratic PRIE, it does not matter if the state we examine is a democracy, an autocracy, or an "anocracy." (Generally speaking, an anocracy is a state that possesses either strong democratic and autocratic characteristics that cancel each other out, or that is in the process of political change with its political institutions having little concentration of power [Gurr 1974; Gurr, Moore, and Jaggers 1989; Maoz and Russett 1991, 1993].) Hence the fourth and final proposition of the systemic and regional explanation: there is little or no difference between democracies and nondemocracies in terms of their response to changes in their PRIEs. Both types of states would respond to changes in their PRIEs in the manner posited in first three propositions above.

National Explanations

Contrary to systemic and regional explanations, the national perspective on global change does not ignore the impact of the PRIE on a state's foreign policy. Rather, by focusing on the internal characteristics and processes of states in general, it argues that states do not plan and develop security policy and foreign policy only in terms of a situation defined solely on the basis of the distribution of capabilities and political commitments in their PRIE. Rather, states define their situation at any given time in terms of the political structure of their international political environment. Specifically, the key points of the national perspective are: first, that the more different the political makeup of a state's PRIE is, in terms of the regimes of states comprising it, the more affected that state will be; second, and as a result, democracies are more threatened than nondemocracies by a politically hostile PRIE; third, given that states' assessment of threat is affected by the political makeup of their PRIEs, changes in this political makeup will be more threatening if the new makeup is less politically similar to a state's own regime than if it is more similar. To be more precise, the national perspective on global change asserts that nondemocratic states will react unfavorably to any kind of change in the domestic political makeup of the PRIE, that is, they will tend to increase their rate of conflict involvement both when their PRIE becomes more democratic and when it becomes less democratic than in the past. On the other hand, democracies are likely to react favorably to democratization in their PRIE and unfavorably to a more authoritarian PRIE.

Recent empirical evidence suggests that the political characteristics of states' environment in terms of domestic political structures and political processes of relevant reference groups have a profound impact on states' behavior. First, revolutionary political change in a state has an effect on that state's environment (Maoz 1995, chaps. 3–4). The state undergoing revolutionary change becomes the target of disputes initiated against it. This finding, which is consistent at both the national level and the dyadic level, is of major significance. It implies that other states often react in a violent manner against a changing state. In addition, intuitive evidence (Walt 1992) clearly indicates that states are highly sensitive to changes in the political makeup of states in their PRIE.

Second, the consistent and strong evidence that democracies are unlikely to fight each other suggests that, for democracies, PRIEs made up of a large number of democratic states will elicit cooperative behavior. As the rate of democratic dyads increases for a state, the likelihood of conflict with states in the PRIE decreases. Maoz and Russett (1991, 1993) show that domestic political stability is strongly and consistently related to dyadic conflict. Politically relevant dyads made up of stable states are considerably less likely to engage in conflictual behavior than are politically relevant dyads in which at least one state is domestically unstable. Bueno de Mesquita and Lalman (1992) also suggest that the ability of states to signal intentions and to read such signals is significantly affected by regime structure.

This suggests that the domestic political makeup of a given PRIE plays an important role in the strategic calculus of states. But why is this the case, and—more important—why should this factor be so independent of the capabilities and alliance commitments of the states making up any given PRIE? The national perspective of global change suggests several factors to account for this evidence.

First, states make strategic plans based on both capabilities and intentions. No one would deny that a dramatic change in the military capabilities of members in a state's PRIE, or a technological breakthrough that has military applications, will be a cause of grave concern among strategic and political planners. However, it matters a great deal whether this change takes place in a state that is an ideological and political rival or in a state that is considered a friend, even if it is not a formal ally. Likewise, for any given level of capabilities and alliance commitment, a state that shares similar views, values, and concerns is less likely to invoke fear and hostility than a state that is seen to pursue contradictory goals, to espouse a different ideology, and to follow different norms of conduct than a neighboring state.

According to Maoz and Russett (1993), democratic states are inherently predisposed to externalize norms of international conduct that reflect their domestic political structures and codes of behavior. These norms promote compromise over violence as a means of resolving disputes, a vision of the political game as essentially cooperative, and the guarantee of fundamental rights to minorities or to losers of political competitions. The stakes of political games in democracies are important, but they very rarely involve life-and-death issues. Even if cooperative games are not a true characterization of democratic politics, zero-sum games are also certainly not a true characterization of them. At the very least, democratic politics is a mixed-motive game. To use Rapoport's terminology (1960), democratic politics are either games or debates; they are never fights. (The distinction focuses on the objectives of players. In debates, the objective is to persuade the opponent. In games, the objective is to outwit and outmaneuver the opponent. In fights, the objective is to destroy and eliminate the opponent.) In order to externalize such norms in international politics, democracies require an environment that is not only willing to play by these rules but is also committed not to exploit them. The more receptive the environment of democracies to such norms, the less likely conflict becomes.

Autocracies also externalize their own internal norms of political conduct, but the norms they externalize are just the opposite of what Maoz and Russett label "democratic norms." The games played in authoritarian political systems are essentially zero-sum. Not only is there a tendency to have a clear-cut winner and a clear-cut loser in each and every political competition that counts, but the winner is safe only if the loser has been eliminated. *Political compromise* is not in the lexicon of most authoritarian regimes. Because of the zero-sum nature of the game, the regime's tolerance of political opposition is very low. The regime is safest when all opposition has been eliminated. Violence is the most effective means for resolving social conflict.

These norms of conduct can be applied in any kind of international environment. When the environment is composed of other authoritarian states, the application of authoritarian norms is necessary. When the international environment is composed of democratic states that attempt to apply democratic norms of compromise and peaceful resolution of conflict, applying authoritarian norms is the smart thing to do. It provides authoritarian practice an advantage and allows exploitation of the opponent.

Knowing the tendency of authoritarian states to exploit moderation and compromise, democracies resort to the same rules when dealing with nondemocratic states. This is the reason, Maoz and Russett argue (1993), that democracies are simultaneously just as likely as nondemocracies to fight other states of a different political persuasion, and unlikely to fight one another. In the same vein, authoritarian states are as likely to fight nondemocratic states as they are to fight democratic states.

Hence, while democratic states, in applying their norms, are sensitive to the kind of environment that surrounds them, authoritarian states are clearly insensitive to the international environment in applying their norms. A useful analogy is provided by Axelrod (1984, 1986), who compares this logic to that which governs norms and cooperation among egoists. Axelrod's frame of reference is the infamous Prisoner's Dilemma game. This game is one of the most powerful models for social paradoxes because it shows that rational behavior yields irrational consequences, and that individual rationality contradicts group rationality. His question is a fundamental philosophical puzzle. Assuming that the Prisoner's Dilemma provides a meaningful model for numerous interpersonal, social, and international situations, how is it possible to reconcile two facts that seem to be diametrically opposed, namely, that players in such situations are rational actors out to maximize their utility and yet even the most bitter adversaries learn to cooperate with each other?

The answer Axelrod develops to this puzzle, through a series of computer simulations, mathematical models, and case studies, is quite simple. Cooperation emerges over time because actors know that, in the long run, if they do not hang together they are bound to hang separately. In other words, actors learn that cooperative reciprocity is the "best" rule to follow in such situations. This rule, which he calls TIT-FOR-TAT, after the program that won his computer tournaments, asserts that actors start by cooperating on the first move of the game and replicating their opponent's previous move thereafter. This rule appears quite simple and innocuous at first blush. However, its revolutionary significance lies in its evolutionary potential. It has a remarkable ability to induce cooperation in the long run even under quite hostile conditions.

The analysis is based essentially on an evolutionary or generational analysis of the Prisoner's Dilemma game. Players are assumed to be using a certain strategy in playing the game. If a player does well at a given round of the game, he or she is likely to repeat this strategy the next time around. If a player does not do well, he or she may change strategy in the next round or may do so poorly that the player disappears. This is a nice twist to the "survival of the fittest" notion of evolutionary biology, only here a player does well either if most other players are very stupid and allow themselves to be exploited, or if there are enough players who are willing to cooperate with the first player. Axelrod shows that, from this perspective, the reciprocating logic of TIT-FOR-TAT induces other exploitative strategies either to move toward cooperation with it or to disappear. In itself, TIT-FOR-TAT was immune to attempts by other strategies to exploit it in the long run.

The key point of Axlerod's analysis is that a cooperative strategy can do well, and thus survive and multiply in an environment of "meanies," only if there is a minimal number of other cooperative strategies with which it inter-acts. In such a case, its reciprocating logic leads it to defect when confronting a "meanie" not because it is in its nature, but rather because it replicates the behavior of the meanie. On the other hand, it can do well when playing against another program that is willing to cooperate or—at minimum—can learn to reciprocate cooperation for cooperation. (Axelrod [1984, 33] calls this *nice-ness*. A program is said to be *nice* if it is never the first to defect.) Provided there is a sufficiently large number of such strategies, they will do marginally better than other kinds of strategies. Hence, there is a chance that some other players will learn what works and adopt these strategies in the next generation. Now, as the number of *nice* strategies increases, there are more interaction opportunities between them. Thus, they will do even better in the second generation than the other strategies. Hence even more exploitative strategies will be abandoned in the transition to the third generation. And so forth.

In terms of our analysis, the analogy is very clear. If we assume that democracies apply *nice* strategies of international conduct, then they can feel more comfortable in a PRIE that is increasingly democratic. (I do not mean to imply any kind of normative connotation, beyond the definition of *niceness* offered by Axelrod. Rather, the assertion is that democracies will start with cooperation, but will be quite willing to reciprocate exploitation for exploita-tion, and will even be vengeful in some cases. The only point is that they are considered unlikely to be the *first* to exploit their opponents.) Hence, when their PRIE changes in a more democratic direction, their conflict involvement rates will decline. Likewise, when the PRIE of a democratic state becomes less democratic, its conflict involvement rates go up.

For a nondemocratic state, what matters most is change itself. Environ-mental change invokes threats and opportunities irrespective of its direction. If the PRIE of an authoritarian state becomes more democratic, there are more "suckers" to exploit. If the PRIE becomes less democratic, it must make sure that the other states do not exploit it. In either case, the conflict involvement, alliance formation, or military preparedness of a nondemocratic state can be expected to go up.

The national perspective of global change has a good explanation for why Maoz and Abdolali (1989) find no consistent correlation between the proportion of democratic-democratic dyads and the rate of systemic conflict. The reason is that a systemic generalization of the dyadic democratic peace result is logically impossible. Bremer (1993) and Maoz and Russett (1993) find that dyadic conflict is a function of a number of factors, and not only of the political makeup of the dyad. It is quite possible, therefore, that the relative frequency of democratic-democratic dyads is increasing in the system as a whole, but the democratic-democratic dyads are made up primarily of noncontiguous states. Hence, the increased democratization of the system would have little or no impact on the rate of conflict in it.

Consider a hypothetical example. Suppose the international system consists of thirty states divided into three regions. Let us assume that the size of the system is fixed over a certain short time span. Thus, over this time span, the system contains 435 nondirectional interaction opportunities (dyads). (This is obtained by the well-known formula $n(n-1)/2$.) Suppose now that out of these states there are seven democracies distributed over the regions, such that there are three democracies in region A and two democracies in each of the other regions. Hence there are a total of twenty-one democratic-democratic interaction opportunities in the system (that is, 5 percent of all interaction opportunities are democratic-democratic). However, if we assume that the regions are separated from each other, then politically relevant dyads can exist only inside the region but not across regions. Suppose now that three states, one in each region, change their regime type from autocracy to democracy. Assuming that the democratic peace proposition is valid for dyads, and that the likelihood of conflict between democracies is forty times less than that between either nondemocracies and other nondemocracies, or between democracies and nondemocracies, how would the conflict level in the system be affected by the increased democratization? Table 7.2 presents a summary of some of these changes.

In a systemic context, the number of politically relevant democratic-democratic dyads increases to twelve (about 4 percent of all dyads). This should have a very weak effect on the rate of conflict in the system. Although the proportion of politically relevant democratic-democratic dyads has more than doubled in each region, it is still so low that it makes only a marginal difference in the rate of conflict in the system as a whole. However, in the context of PRIEs of states, this is more significant. Consider, for example, the impact of democratization of a major power or a regional power on global and regional conflict. If a major power becomes democratic, that change would translate to

TABLE 7.2 Effects of Democratization on Systemic and Regional Conflict:
A Hypothetical International System

Before/After Democratization	Hypothetical Region	No. of States	No. of Dyads[a]	No. of Democracies	No. of Dem.-Dem. Dyads[b]	Proportion of Dem.-Dem. Dyads[b]
Before	A	10	45	3	3	0.07
After		10	45	4	6	0.13
Before	B	10	45	2	1	0.02
After		10	45	3	3	0.07
Before	C	10	45	2	1	0.02
After		10	45	3	3	0.07
Before	World	30	135	7	5	0.04
After		30	135	10	12	0.07

a. Politically relevant dyads only.
b. Democratic-democratic dyads.

all $n-1$ dyads involving the major power and other states in the system. Political change in regional powers translates into $k-1$ dyads involving the regional power and all other states in the region. On the other hand, democratization of a minor state would have only a local impact. That is, it would affect only the states with which it is contiguous. If a state has many neighbors, democratization will have a more pronounced impact than if it has few neighbors. Thus the impact of democratization, as seen from the vantage point of the national perspective of global change, is differential and depends on where this process takes place and which nation is involved.

In sum, the national perspective on global change posits the following hypotheses. First, states tend to react to changes in the domestic political makeup of their PRIEs. This reaction is independent of changes in the military capability or in the alliance commitments of members of the PRIE. Second, states tend to react differently to changes in PRIEs as a function of their political regime. Specifically, democracies are more sensitive to the nature of the change in their PRIE than are nondemocracies. Third, these differences consist of two behavioral tendencies. Democracies tend to reduce the rate of their strategic response (i.e., conflict involvement, alliance formation, and military allocation) as their PRIE becomes increasingly democratic, and to increase their strategic response rate as their PRIE becomes increasingly nondemocratic. On the other hand, nondemocracies increase their strategic response rates following changes in the domestic makeup of their PRIE, irrespective of the nature of this change. Fourth, democracies are less tolerant of unstable PRIEs than are nondemocratic states.

Empirical Analysis

Changes in the PRIE of states may also affect different strategic behaviors of states. In order to examine empirically the effects of strategic and domestic political changes in PRIEs on states' behavior, I conducted the following analysis. First, to assess the effects of environmental political factors on conflict behavior of states, I conducted a bivariate cross-tabulation in which I dichotomized the level of democratization in states' PRIEs. A PRIE is considered democratic when the average regime score is positive. A PRIE is considered nondemocratic when the average regime score of member states is negative. Likewise, a revolutionary changing PRIE is one in which more than two revolutionary changes have taken place over the last three years. Figures 7.1–7.4 show the differences between democracies and nondemocracies in terms of their reactions to domestic political attributes and changes in their PRIEs. Table 7.3 lists the statistical effects on conflict behavior of environmental regime and of revolutionary change in states' PRIE.

The results suggest a strong and consistent relationship between the political structure of states' PRIE and their conflict behavior. Specifically, as the environment becomes increasingly turbulent in terms of domestic political changes in relevant actors, states tend to increase their dispute and war involvement to a significant extent. Yet, as the PRIE becomes increasingly demo-

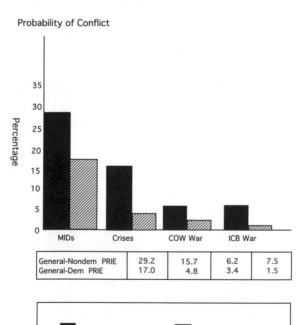

FIGURE 7.1
Effects of Demographic
PRIE on Conflict
Behavior of States,
1816 (1929)–1986

	MIDs	Crises	COW War	ICB War
General-Nondem PRIE	29.2	15.7	6.2	7.5
General-Dem PRIE	17.0	4.8	3.4	1.5

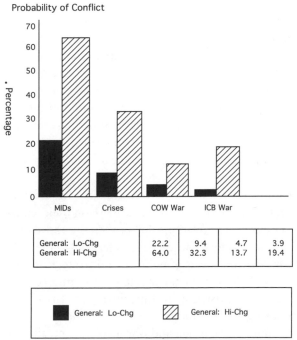

Probability of Conflict

FIGURE 7.2
Effects of Demographic
PRIE on Conflict
Behavior of States,
1816 (1929)–1986

DEM: DEM-PRIE	16.4	3.7	3.5	1.1
DEM: NONDEM-PRIE	43.5	17.4	8.4	8.7
Nondem: DEM-PRIE	27.8	9.8	5.1	3.2
Nondem: NONDEM-PRIE	28.6	16.2	6.0	7.7

DEM: DEM-PRIE   DEM: NONDEM-PRIE

Nondem: DEM-PRIE   Nondem: NONDEM-PRIE

Probability of Conflict

FIGURE 7.3
Effects of Revolutionary
Changes in States' PRIE
on Conflict Behavior
1816 (1929)–1986

General: Lo-Chg	22.2	9.4	4.7	3.9
General: Hi-Chg	64.0	32.3	13.7	19.4

General: Lo-Chg   General: Hi-Chg

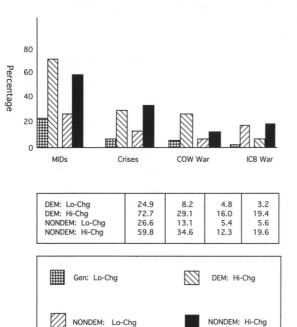

Probability of Conflict

FIGURE 7.4
Effects of Revolutionary
Changes in States' PRIE
on Conflict Behavior
1816 (1929)–1986

	MIDs	Crises	COW War	ICB War
DEM: Lo-Chg	24.9	8.2	4.8	3.2
DEM: Hi-Chg	72.7	29.1	16.0	19.4
NONDEM: Lo-Chg	26.6	13.1	5.4	5.6
NONDEM: Hi-Chg	59.8	34.6	12.3	19.6

Gen: Lo-Chg   DEM: Hi-Chg

NONDEM: Lo-Chg   NONDEM: Hi-Chg

cratic, states tend to reduce their conflict behavior substantially. The breakdown of the population into democratic and nondemocratic states suggests that—in accordance with our hypothesis—democracies are more sensitive to political upheaval in neighboring states and to their regime structure. We have been able to develop a modest generalization from the dyadic level to a minisystem level. Specifically, using the concept of PRIE, we find indications that regime structure in a state's PRIE has a substantial dampening effect on dispute and war behavior. This effect is particularly strong for democracies, but it does not always lead to the dampening of conflict behavior with nondemocracies.

However, for a more complete analysis, we need to consider the effect of domestic political change and regime structure of states' PRIE on their strategic behavior. Thus, we must examine the relationship between the above variables by controlling for other—primarily strategic—characteristics of the PRIE of states. We also need to consider the effects of political and strategic factors in states' PRIE on other forms of strategic behavior. Hence, I examined each state in the international system that existed at any time during the 1816–1986 period for each of the years during which it was independent. I examined three types of behaviors for this population: conflict and war involvement, alliance

TABLE 7.3 Regime Type, Revolutionary Change in PRIE, and Conflict Measures

	Average Regime Type			No. of Revolutionary Changes		
	General	Democracies	Nondemocracies	General	Democracies	Nondemocracies
Dispute involvement						
	215.55**	255.34**	0.41	574.13**	253.70**	180.12**
	$g = -0.33$**	$g = -0.59$**	$g = -0.02$	$g = 0.72$**	$g = 0.78$**	$g = 0.61$**
	$m_b = 0.56$	$m_b = 0.49$	$m_b = 0.54$	$m_b = 0.72$	$m_b = 0.67$	$m_b = 0.69$
Crisis involvement						
	195.97**	90.05**	23.47**	158.87**	54.49**	65.64**
	$g = -0.58$**	$g = -0.69$**	$g = -0.28$**	$g = 0.64$**	$g = 0.64$**	$g = 0.56$**
	$m_b = 0.52$	$m_b = 0.45$	$m_b = 0.64$	$m_b = 0.86$	$m_b = 0.84$	$m_b = 0.82$
War involvement						
	42.49**	30.99**	90.05**	102.37**	52.09**	28.38**
	$g = -0.30$**	$g = -0.43$	$g = -0.69$**	$g = 0.53$**	$g = 0.58$**	$g = 0.42$**
	$m_b = 0.59$	$m_b = 0.47$	$m_b = 0.45$	$m_b = 0.86$	$m_b = 0.87$	$m_b = 0.9$
ICB war involvement						
	121.24**	22.39**	22.39**	134.77**	62.07**	43.94**
	$g = -0.69$**	$g = -0.80$**	$g = -0.43$**	$g = 0.71$**	$g = 0.76$**	$g = 0.61$**
	$m_b = 0.51$	$m_b = 0.42$	$m_b = 0.66$	$m_b = 0.91$	$m_b = 0.89$	$m_b = 0.89$

Notes: Numbers in each cell represent: upper row: chi-square statistic (1DF); middle row: Yule's Q statistic; lower row: m_b statistic (see Maoz 1995, appendix). No. of cases are as follows: for disputes and war, 11,491 in the general case; 2,878 for democracies; and 6,563 for nondemocracies; for crises and ICB war: 6,197 for the general case, and N = 3,362 and 1,692 for nondemocracies and democracies, respectively. Missing cases are due to lack of regime data.

** = $p < .01$.

formation, and human and material military allocations (Maoz 1995, chap. 5 and appendix). I conducted the analysis, first, on the entire population of states, and then on democratic and nondemocratic subsets. The democratic-non-democratic breakdown was designed to allow us to test the hypothesis that democracies are more sensitive than nondemocratic states to changes in the domestic makeup of their PRIEs.

The general relationship between changes in the PRIE of states and various aspects of foreign policy behavior is presented in table 7.4. Overall, states are sensitive to both strategic and domestic political changes in their PRIEs. However, the effects of strategic factors on dispute involvement, alliance formation, and human and financial military allocations are not always consistent. In terms of dispute behavior, states do not react violently either to changes in the average military capabilities in their PRIE, or to changes in the alliance commitments among states in their PRIE. Nor is the dispute behavior of states affected by the democratization level in their PRIE. However, alliance formation and military allocations are indeed sensitive to the average regime level of states' PRIE. As the level of democracy in states' PRIE goes up, states seem to feel less threatened by their environment. Thus, they typically respond by reducing their drives to increase security either by forming alliances or by increasing human and material allocations for their military.

States do react to revolutionary changes in their PRIE. When the number of revolutionary changes in states' PRIE goes up, states tend to respond with greater levels of conflict involvement. States also react to changes in their own internal strategic and political situation: they increase their rate of dispute involvement following revolutionary political changes. This finding is in accordance with recent research (Maoz 1995). Dispute behavior is not affected by regime type: the level of democratization of a state has no apparent effect on its dispute behavior. Domestic political changes in states' PRIE also have a significant positive effect on their alliance formation and military allocation policies. States tend to increase their military personnel and military expenditures in response to such changes. They also tend to form alliances in response to political changes in their PRIE. In sum, important aspects of the strategic behavior of states are affected by changes in the political makeup of their PRIE. States respond not only to strategic developments but also to political developments in their environment, and this response appears consistent in different forms of response.

How do these strategic and political factors affect different political systems? Table 7.5 presents analyses based on different regime types. A logistic analysis of disputes, war, crises, and ICB war is provided in tables 7.6 and 7.7.

These analyses reveal some interesting differences between democracies and nondemocracies in terms of their reaction to internal and environmental changes. Let us begin with the effect of domestic and environmental factors on national dispute behavior. First, the conflict behavior of both democracies and nondemocracies is positively affected by internal revolutionary change.[1] This suggests that the effect of domestic political change on dispute behavior is maintained even when one controls for regime type of states. Second, changes in states' military capability also have a consistent effect on their dispute involvement. This effect is also fairly consistent and applies to democracies and nondemocracies alike.

The number of alliance commitments of states—democracies and nondemocracies—does not appear to have a significant effect on conflict behavior. However, in cases where the effect is statistically significant, the relationship is negative. This implies that to the extent that the alliance commitments of a state make it feel secure, it will have less of a tendency to become

TABLE 7.4 Effects of Strategic and Domestic Changes in States' PRIE on Foreign and Security Behavior, 1816–1986

Independent Variable	Dispute Involvement[a]	Alliance Commitments	Military Personnel	Military Expenditures
Constant	0.131**	0.004	0.024	0.076
	-0.438**	(0.001)**[b]	(0.002)**	0.003)**
Change in national material capability	4.116**	-0.689	-0.898[c]	0.766[c]
	4.942**	(0.185)**	(0.005)**	(0.007)**
Regime score	-0.001	0.001	0.000	0.000
	0.001*	(0.000)*	(0.000)	(0.000)**
Domestic political change in focal state	0.209**	-0.016	0.002	0.001
	0.430**	(0.004)**	(0.002)	(0.002)
Capability change in state's PRIE	-0.400	-0.241	0.083	0.091
	-6.867**	(0.210)	(0.018)**	(0.032)**
Lagged weighted alliance commitments of focal state	0.000	0.974	-0.000	-0.001
	-0.001	(0.003)**	(0.000)	(0.000)
Lagged dispute behavior	0.692**	-0.015	-0.001	-0.001
	0.156**	(0.004)**	(0.000)**	(0.001)**
Average regime score of state's PRIE	0.000	-0.000	-0.001	-0.001
	-0.002*	(0.000)	(0.000)**	(0.000)**
No. of domestic political changes in state's PRIE	0.067**	0.013	0.004	0.005
	0.053	(0.002)**	(0.001)**	(0.001)**
Lagged average alliance commitments of PRIE members	-0.011*	-0.001	-0.000	0.002
	-0.130**	(0.000)	(0.000)	(0.001)**
Adjusted R²	0.550	0.967	0.862	0.630
Durbin-Watson statistics	2.061	2.025	1.909	2.166
N	8,830	8,830	8,823	8,823

Notes: Analysis on war involvement, crisis involvement, and ICB war involvement are reported in Maoz 1995, appendix. Interpretations of results are based also on these variables.

a. Lagged values of dependent variables were introduced to reduce serial correlation. Durbin-Watson statistics are brought in here only as a check. Since this is a pooled design, it does not really provide an adequate test of autocorrelation.

b. Entries in parentheses are standard errors. For disputes, entries in the second rows are parameter estimates of poisson event-counts regression.

c. Lagged values of military expenditures and military personnel, respectively.

* $p < .05$; ** $p < .01$.

TABLE 7.5 Effects of Changes in PRIE on International Behavior of Democratic and Nondemocratic States, 1816–1986

	Dispute Involvement		Alliance Formation		Military Personnel		Military Expenditures	
	Democracies	Non-Democracies	Democracies	Non-Democracies	Democracies	Non-Democracies	Democracies	Non-Democracies
Constant	0.172** -0.568**	0.139** -0.419**	0.037 (0.057)a	0.056 (0.012)**	0.018 (0.003)**	0.029 (0.002)**	0.073 (0.006)**	0.091 (0.004)**
Change in national material capabilities	3.763** 5.783**	4.811** 5.630**	-1.510 (0.516)**	-0.265 (0.190)	0.930 (0.008)**	0.882 (0.007)**	0.802 (0.013)**	0.714 (0.010)**
Revolutionary political change in focal state	0.144 0.354**	0.215** 0.475**	-0.005 (0.017)	-0.018 (0.003)**	0.003 (0.004)	0.001 (0.002)	0.006 (0.007)	0.001 (0.003)
No. of alliance commitments of focal state	-0.001 -0.001	0.000 -0.001	0.968 (0.005)**	0.952 (0.004)**	-0.000 (0.000)	0.000 (0.000)	-0.001 (0.000)*	-0.001 (0.000)
Change in military capabilities in PRIE	-0.788 -6.632**	-0.354 -5.411**	0.347 (0.725)	-0.254 (0.188)	0.032 (0.031)	0.113 (0.024)**	-0.019 (0.062)	0.161 (0.041)**
Change in no. of alliance commitments in PRIE	-0.011 -0.114**	-0.012 -0.117**	-0.002 (0.000)**	0.000 (0.000)	-0.000 (0.000)	-0.000 (0.000)	0.001 (0.000)*	0.002 (0.000)**

Average regime score of states in PRIE	-0.003**	0.000	0.000	0.000	-0.001	-0.001	-0.003	-0.000
	-0.006**	0.002*	(0.000)	(0.000)	(0.000)**	(0.000)	(0.001)**	(0.000)
No. of revolutionary political changes in PRIE	0.063**	0.068**	0.042	0.009	0.004	0.003	0.005	0.003
	0.062**	0.002	(0.012)**	(0.002)**	(0.001)**	(0.001)**	(0.002)**	(0.001)*
Lagged dispute involvement	0.593**	0.706**	0.019	-0.025	-0.002	-0.000	-0.004	0.000
	0.144**	0.147**	(0.015)	(0.003)**	(0.000)**	(0.000)	(0.001)**	(0.000)
R^2 Durbin-Watson Statistic[c]	0.504	0.565	0.977	0.934	0.902	0.836	0.693	0.564
	2.086	2.041	1.846	2.214	1.872	1.924	2.263	2.075
N	1,933	6,899	1,933	6,899	1,932	6,893	1,932	6,893

Notes: Lagged values of dependent variables were introduced to reduce serial correlation.

a. Entries in parentheses are standard errors. For disputes, entries in the second rows are parameter estimates of poisson event-counts regression.

b. Durbin-Watson Statistics are brought in here only as a check. Since this is a pooled design, it does not really provide an adequate test of autocorrelation.

* p < .05; ** p < .01.

TABLE 7.6 Logistic Analysis of Dichotomized Dispute and Crisis Behavior of States

Independent Variable	Dispute Involvement	Crisis Involvement, 1946–1986	War Involvement	ICB War, 1946–1986
Constant	-1.746	-1.999	-2.903	-2.378
	(0.061)**	(0.275)**	(0.203)**	(0.501)**
Change in national material capability	8.292	11.288	4.399	-1.699
	(1.173)**	(3.101)**	(1.655)**	(6.255)
Regime score	-0.001	0.002	0.003	-0.002
	(0.001)	(0.002)	(0.001)	(0.004)
Domestic political change in focal state	0.556	0.461	0.894	0.540
	(0.117)**	(0.218)*	(0.195)**	(0.364)
Capability change in state's PRIE	-7.800	-11.159	0.694	-28.633
	(1.385)**	(4.043)**	(2.397)	(7.897)**
Lagged weighted alliance commitments of focal state	-0.004	0.008	0.009	-0.011
	(0.001)*	(0.003)**	(0.002)**	(0.005)*
Lagged dispute behavior	0.973	0.981	1.984	1.320
	(0.043)**	(0.120)**	(0.109)**	(0.233)**
Average regime score of state's PRIE	0.001	-0.014	-0.005	-0.008
	(0.002)	(0.005)**	(0.004)	(0.009)
No. of domestic political changes in state's PRIE	0.250	0.031	0.011	0.001
	(0.043)**	(0.061)	(0.058)	(0.012)
Lagged average alliance commitments of PRIE members	-0.039	0.010	-0.019	0.009
	(0.011)**	(0.038)	(0.028)	(0.070)
Model's gamma	0.609	0.520	0.771	0.672
-2 Log likelihood	1,500.98	199.49	829.023	101.97
N	6,106	2,482	6,107	2,296

a. ICB War refers to the International Crisis Behavior Project's coding for war as an event.

TABLE 7.7 Logistic Analysis of Dichotomized Dispute and Crisis Behavior of Democratic and Nondemocratic States, 1816–1986

Independent Variable	Dichot. Dispute Invol.[b]		War Involvement		Crisis Involvement		ICB War Involvement	
	Democracies	Non-Democracies	Democracies	Non-Democracies	Democracies	Non-Democracies	Democracies	Non-Democracies
Constant	-1.237[c] (0.219)**	-0.843 (0.125)**	-3.883 (0.488)**	-2.752 (0.266)**	-2.564 (0.755)**	-2.059 (0.356)**	-3.492 (1.970)	2.195 (0.623)**
Change in national capabilities (2.035)**	6.031 (1.633)**	5.151 (3.024)	3.780 (2.380)**	6.209 (9.846)	13.076 (4.395)**	15.231 (31.252)	17.363 (8.872)	-6.135
Revolutionary political change in focal state (0.286)**	0.733 (0.130)**	0.427 (0.447)**	1.214 (0.222)**	0.856 (0.702)	0.167 (0.232)*	0.462 (1.268)	0.001 (0.343)	0.542
No. of alliance commitments of focal state	-0.007 (0.003)**	-0.001 (0.002)	0.000 (0.004)	0.007 (0.004)	-0.008 (0.005)*	0.005 (0.003)	0.009 (0.013)	-0.017 (0.006)**
Change in military capabilities in PRIE	-6.675 (3.381)*	-6.221 (2.899)*	-1.842 (4.557)	-10.313 (5.242)*	12.003 (9.075)	8.992 (5.516)	35.713 (28.287)	-27.643 (8.443)**
Change in no. of alliance commitments in PRIE (0.022)	-0.029 (0.017)	-0.005 (0.046)	0.078 (0.039)	-0.028 (0.076)**	-0.216 (0.046)*	-0.103 (0.228)	-0.332 (0.078)	-0.079

continued

TABLE 7.7 continued

Independent Variable	Dichot. Dispute Invol.[b]		War Involvement		Crisis Involvement		ICB War Involvement	
	Democracies	Non-Democracies	Democracies	Non-Democracies	Democracies	Non-Democracies	Democracies	Non-Democracies
Average regime score of states in PRIE	-0.018	0.001	-0.007	-0.003	-0.046	-0.006	-0.087	0.007
(0.004)**	0.003	(0.008)	(0.005)	(0.019)**	(0.006)	(0.029)**	(0.010)	
No. of revolutionary political changes in PRIE	0.185	0.152	-0.111	-0.087	0.002	-0.060	0.364	0.131
(0.063)**	(0.066)**	(0.101)	(0.099)	(0.101)	(0.104)	(0.165)*	(0.180)	
Lagged dispute involvement	1.084	0.897	2.711	1.161	1.093	1.037	1.788	1.373
	(0.088)**	(0.050)**	(0.274)**	(0.123)**	(0.313)**	(0.137)**	(0.787)**	(0.256)**
Gamma	0.703	0.587	0.757	0.786	0.681	0.484	0.883	0.640
-2 Log likelihood	599.562	922.703	283.289	525.677	103.882	138.550	43.258	80.251

Notes: Lagged values of dependent variables were introduced to reduce serial correlation. Durbin-Watson statistics are brought in here only as a check. Since this is a pooled design, it does not really provide an adequate test of autocorrelation. Entries in parentheses are standard errors.

a. Dropped from the analysis due to colinearity with other variable.

* p < .05; ** p < .01.

involved in some types of conflicts. The inconsistent relationship between alliance commitments of a state and its conflict involvement prevents us from saying anything meaningful about the differences between democracies and nondemocracies on this score. Obviously, past conflict involvement affects present conflict involvement of both democracies and nondemocracies. We can say that, except for the domestic political change variable, which has a consistent effect on both types of systems, strategic factors that have to do with a state's own attributes do not permit consistent generalizations across regime types regarding the internal determinants of conflict involvement.

More meaningful and significant in this sense are the effects of strategic and political characteristics of states' PRIE on their conflict involvement patterns. First, the strategic attributes of states' PRIE do affect their conflict behavior, largely in the expected direction, but these effects are not robust and vary from one type of state to another. Both democracies and nondemocracies are affected by the capability structure and the alliance structure in their PRIE. As the capabilities and alliance commitments of states in their PRIE go up, states become increasingly deterred from entering disputes, wars, and crises. However, this relationship is far from consistent. The effect of increased capability on dispute involvement is more pronounced for nondemocracies than for democracies, and the same applies to strengthened alliance commitments in states' PRIE. (Recall that military capability is measured in proportionate terms. This means that as states increase their military capabilities compared to other states in the system, they tend increasingly to get involved in disputes.)

The differences are most pronounced in the effect of environmental domestic political factors on states. Democracies are affected by the political makeup of their environment, while nondemocracies are considerably less so. First, the average regime score of states in the PRIE of a democratic state has a negative impact on its dispute behavior: the more democratic the PRIE of a democracy, the less likely it is to get involved in disputes. This is in line with the democratic peace result.[2] This is not the case for nondemocratic states. The political makeup of their PRIEs has no apparent effect on their conflict behavior. Second, both democracies and nondemocracies are affected by the number of revolutionary political changes in their environment. However, the impact of revolutionary political change is stronger on democracies than on nondemocracies.

Regarding the analysis of alliance formation processes, a caveat is in order. As the saying goes, it takes two to tango. States must have common interests to form an alliance. Nevertheless, there are significant differences between democracies and nondemocracies in terms of their reaction to internal and external changes by alliance formation. For democracies, the key internal determinant of alliance formation is a change in relative military capability. As the state's military capability goes up, the state feels less inclined to give up its sovereignty by entering alliances. (Of course, past alliance commitments are a strong predictor of present alliance commitments for both democracies and nondemocracies.) The alliance formation behavior of nondemocracies is affected primarily by revolutionary political change. States undergoing revolutionary political change are likely to reduce their alliance commitments. When nondemocratic states undergo this political change (or when revolutionary political change converts a democracy into a nondemocracy), the "new" polity becomes less attractive as an alliance partner. It is apparently less inclined to enter alliances. This effect does not exist for states that become democracies.

The reduction in alliance commitments as a response to nondemocratic revolutionary political change in a given state is probably more a reaction of the environment than of the state itself. The change in political regime that often accompanies such revolutionary changes creates considerable uncertainty in the minds of surrounding states, regarding both the ability and willingness of the changing state to meet its international commitments. This is reflected in the fact that, for both democracies and nondemocracies, the number of political changes in their PRIE has a negative effect on their alliance formation behavior. The implication is that environmental political changes reduce the inclination of states to place their security in the hands of others. States feel that their partners need to be politically stable if they are to trust them.

Neither democracies nor nondemocracies are affected by the level of democratization in their PRIE in their alliance formation behavior. This adds some credence to the notion that the political makeup of states in the environment does not play an important role in the alliance-related calculus of a state. Yet both democracies and nondemocracies are affected by revolutionary political changes in states that form their PRIE. The effects of such changes on the alliance formation behavior of democracies are marginally stronger than those for nondemocracies. In both cases, political changes in states' PRIE generate incentives to form alliances. Finally, alliance behavior of democracies is not affected by their past dispute involvement. However, nondemocratic alliance formation is affected. Increased dispute involvement reduces the tendency of nondemocratic states to form alliances.

The analysis of military allocations suggests significant support for the hypotheses, both for military personnel and for military expenditures. First, strategic characteristics of PRIEs of states do not seem to have a consistent impact on military allocations, and this applies both to democracies and to nondemocracies. Second, political characteristics of PRIEs do seem to have a significant effect on the military allocation behavior of states, but significantly more so for democracies than for nondemocracies. Specifically, as the level of democratization in a state's environment goes up, the state tends to reduce its human and monetary defense burden. However, when the environment becomes less democratic, democracies tend to increase their allocations. In addition, both democracies and nondemocracies increase their military allocations in response to revolutionary changes in their PRIEs. However, the impact of revolutionary change in the PRIE on military allocations for democracies is higher than for nondemocracies. This conclusion is based on standardized parameter estimates (not reported in the table), and on the size of the T-statistics. Note that some methodologists (for example, King 1986; Achen 1983) warn against the use of standardized estimates to assess relative potency of statistical associations.

These analyses largely suggest that, contrary to what systemic and regional models would have us believe, states are consistently affected by the political makeup of their PRIE, in some instances more than by its strategic makeup. Moreover, democracies respond to strategic and political changes in their PRIE in ways that are in some cases substantially different from the reactions of nondemocracies. In particular, democracies tend to display higher levels of sensitivity to the political makeup of their PRIE than do nondemocracies.

Conclusion

Our findings consistently support the national approach toward global change in its account of the impact of environmental changes on state behavior. National strategy is consistently affected by the political makeup of the state's international environment. This indicates that democracies behave quite differently from nondemocratic regimes, and not only in that they are unlikely to fight one another.

Democracies do not fight one another, but they are nearly as likely to fight other states as are nondemocracies. Given that their rate of conflict with other democracies approaches zero, this means that their rate of conflict with certain nondemocratic states is higher than that of nondemocracies (see table 7.8).

Recall that, according to Gurr (1974), anocracies represent for the most part political systems in a state of transition. These states are most likely to be revolutionary emerging or revolutionary changing political systems. Clearly, democracies have more than their fair share of conflict with anocracies, and in some cases the probability of conflict between democracies and anocracies is higher than that between autocracies and anocracies (although anocracy-anocracy dyads are most frequently engaged in conflict). What we see, then, is that—as Maoz and Abdolali find (1989)—democracies tend to get entangled in conflict with unstable states. The difference between the low frequency of

TABLE 7.8 Regime Types and International Conflict: Politically Relevant Dyads, 1816–1986

Dyad Type	Probability of			
	MID^a	Crisis	COW War	ICB War
Democracy-Democracy	0.013	0.001	0.000	0.000
Democracy-Anocracy	0.052	0.015	0.012	0.006
Democracy-Autocracy	0.047	0.017	0.010	0.007
Anocracy-Anocracy	0.062	0.024	0.016	0.011
Anocracy-Autocracy	0.052	0.022	0.010	0.009
Autocracy-Autocracy	0.036	0.013	0.007	0.004
Avg. Dyad^b	0.046	0.015	0.010	0.006

Notes: Ns for this table include 55,810 politically relevant dyad years for the period 1816–1986 and the MID (and COW war) data. Of this population, there were 2,673 dispute dyad years and 556 war dyad years. For the ICB data (1929–1986), there were 35,217 politically relevant dyads, out of which there were 540 crisis dyad years and 217 ICB war dyad years.

a. Probabilities are the number of conflict cases for this category divided by the total number of dyads of this type.

b. Average dyadic conflict is the number of dyadic conflicts divided by the total number of dyads in the dataset.

conflict between democracies and the "normal" overall dispute involvement of democratic states is thus accounted for by exactly this kind of intervention in unstable regimes.

These findings also provide a good explanation for why previous studies of the democratic peace phenomenon (Maoz 1995) could not generalize from the dyadic to the systemic level for the relationship between regime types and international conflict. When we move from a dyadic to a systemic perspective, we tend to lump together things that do not fit, with the exception of major power relations. In other words, the lack of conflict between Israel and Costa Rica could not logically be considered democratic peace, but rather a reflection of the lack of opportunity for conflict. The risk of systemic aggregation of states that are strategically irrelevant to one another is precisely that findings valid at a lower level of aggregation will not be scientifically valid—let alone theoretically meaningful—at the global level of analysis.

The concept of PRIE suggests that such an aggregation should be based primarily on those external actors that concern a given state on a daily basis and to a considerable degree. It is those actors that the state monitors and it is to the behavior of those states, not necessarily to general trends in the system, that states react.

On a practical level, this analysis suggests that, as the political makeup of the system's members changes, both risks and opportunities present themselves. Changing states may constitute threats to their neighbors, depending on the form of government they develop. To the extent that the decomposition of old states into new brings about internal—most notably ethnic—conflict, and that new states are incapable of developing democratic institutions, the danger of war increases, because such states are taken to constitute threats to their environment. In such cases, a dangerous combination of an unstable regime and radical views is likely to provoke democracies to offset the danger through violent conflict, alignment, and military allocations. The last two factors are in themselves connected to warfare.

Ethnicity, Minorities, and International Conflict

David R. Davis, Keith Jaggers,
and Will H. Moore

While the resurgence of ethno-nationalism throughout Eastern Europe and the former Soviet Union has refocused the attention of international relations scholars on the ethnic dimensions of international conflict, a linkage between ethnicity and international conflict has yet to be generally accepted within the discipline. In this chapter, we examine the impact of ethnic conflict within states on the occurrence of conflict between states. Using a cross-sectional study of all geographically contiguous dyads in the international system (circa 1978), we examine foreign policy behavior to see if dyads in which there is a minority at risk exhibit different conflict patterns than the system norm. Further, we examine whether state-communal group ethnic affiliations across dyads influence the level of state-to-state conflict within the international system. Finally, we probe the impact that common ethnic ties within dyads have on dyadic interactions.

There are two bodies of literature germane to our inquiry. First, a number of studies have focused on the impact of ethnic conflicts on the behavior of other states. Most of these works are contributions to edited volumes and focus on the impact of a particular ethnic conflict on the foreign relations of the state (e.g., Suhrke and Noble 1977a; Shiels 1984a, Boucher et al. 1987; Chazan 1991). Some of these collections are more theoretical than empirical (such as Rosenau 1964), while others mix theory and evidence (for example, Midlarsky 1992b). Other work on the international relations of ethnic conflict focuses explicitly on the role of third parties as mediators (Halpern 1964; Modelski 1964; Luard 1972a; Suhrke and Noble 1977b; Touval and Zartman 1989;

Stedman 1992; Licklider 1993; McGarry and O'Leary 1993; Haglund and Pentland 1996; James 1996; Kaufman 1996; Ryan 1990a). Finally, some studies explicitly seek to test hypotheses concerning the relationship between ethnic conflict and foreign policy behavior (Heraclides 1990; Midlarsky 1992a; Carment 1993a; Carment et al. 1993a; Carment and James 1994b; Moore and Davis 1994). There is also a small body of literature on the impact of the international system on ethnic conflict within states (Nagel and Whorton 1992; Rasler 1992).

A second body of literature we consider directly relevant focuses on ethnic groups and their conflicts with nation-states (e.g., Young 1982; Horowitz 1985; Gurr 1993a, 1993c; Posen 1993). In these studies, no explicit effort is made to link the conflict with the behavior of other states in the international system, though linkages are often recognized. It is also interesting that many of the case study essays in the edited collections fail to make explicit reference to international linkages, though they often refer to the behavior of one or two key states in the international system that played a role in supporting one side or another in the case at issue.

Unfortunately, in both sets of literature, little effort has been devoted to specifying theoretical linkages between these two types of conflict. As one reviews the descriptive-historical case studies that dominate the literature on ethnic conflict, one cannot help but note that in every case the behavior of other states in the international system is relevant to the tale. From this observation, one might conclude that there is necessarily a linkage. And indeed, we believe it is precisely this conclusion that has led to the publication of some of the edited works. However, we find that Suhrke and Noble (1977c, 230–31) reject the contention that "internal ethnic conflict constitutes a major source of international conflict." Shiels (1984b, 263) describes the international system as relatively immune to the turmoil caused by ethnic strife, but notes that for the handful of states that are involved in a given case, "ethnic separatism can be a very persistent and thorny problem indeed." Assessing the ability of international bodies to regulate internal wars, Luard (1972b, 215) concludes that "the record of international organizations in dealing with civil-war situations so far has been very mixed. Some would even dismiss it." Nevertheless, Heraclides (1990) and Carment (1993a) begin their studies by arguing that the topic has not been given the attention it deserves. In this chapter, we attempt to rectify that neglect.

While it seems clear that in specific instances of ethnically driven domestic conflict, a small subset of international actors can play an important role, we wonder whether the conclusions drawn by Suhrke and Noble, Shiels, and Luard are generalizable. Put simply, no one will contest that a few states in the international system choose to support one side or another in a given ethnic conflict. However, can we take the larger step and argue that ethnic conflicts have a widespread and important effect on the behavior of states toward one another? In other words, states or domestic actors may support a particular rebel group; but are ethnic conflicts a significant driving force for the pursuit of conflictual foreign policies? More important, can we find such a relationship across a substantial sample of cases?

One can understand the issue in terms of the distinction between structural and behavioral explanations of foreign policy behavior. In explaining the foreign policy of states in the international system, are we better off focusing on the structural attributes of those states or on behavioral variables? Dina Zinnes (1980, 327) argues that "international violence is probably not the result of special conditions but rather the consequence of certain attributes of nations." Nevertheless, we anticipate that ethnic division will *not* drive international conflict patterns and that Suhrke and Noble, Shiels, and Luard drew the proper conclusions. We have designed a study to systematically explore this issue.

Few of the studies mentioned above consider the following question: What implications does this research have for general theories of international politics? While we focus explicitly on the effects of ethnic conflict within states on conflict patterns between states, at a more general level we are concerned with the question of how domestic authority patterns overlap and interact with international authority patterns. In raising this question, we hope to challenge realist assumptions that have traditionally guided the study of international cooperation and conflict. In particular, we seek to examine the realist assumption that sovereign states are the fundamental building blocks of international relations. If, as we suspect, they are not, then we must ask ourselves what the competing authority patterns are that cut across territorial boundaries and influence the interaction of states in the global arena. To answer this question we posit that ethnicity provides an alternative authority pattern to the territorial state which, at least potentially, can have an impact on the dynamics of interstate relations.

Central to the realist perspective on international relations is its treatment of the "state" as a unified actor. International relations theorists argue that since the signing of the Peace of Westphalia in 1648, the nation-state has represented the theoretical cornerstone to understanding the political dynamics of the international system. However, "to aver that humanity is divided into 'states,' though technically correct, is also trivial because it obscures the equally important fact that humanity is divided in many other ways as well" (Ferguson and Mansbach 1991, 381). Thus, while we accept the notion that the territorial state remains the central actor in the international environment, we also concur with Ferguson and Mansbach's observation that "at best, the state is a primary symbol of identity that competes with other symbols of identity for the loyalties of citizens. For this reason, it is . . . one of many 'polities' that compete for human loyalties and that form authority relations" in the international system (ibid., 369). As Robert Slater points out (1993), with the collapse of the territorial boundaries of the cold war era, the (re)emergence of nationalist rivalries, and the "New World Order's" revitalization of international and regional organizations, the political influence of the "state" and its analytical usefulness are under considerable challenge and stress.

Stephen Ryan (1990a, xxii–xxiv) points out that beginning in the late 1960s, the "state-centric" approach to international relations came under attack from a variety of quarters, even from scholars who began to make a case for ethnicity as one of what Ferguson and Mansbach call the primary symbols of identity. With a sense of renewed vigor, intellectual challengers to the realist paradigm have begun to create a new research agenda that seeks to elaborate on patterns of authority in the international environment, patterns that either replace (Ferguson and Mansbach 1991) or rival (Rosenau 1990) the state in its authority. Recognizing the influence of both vertical (e.g., territorially defined) and horizontal (e.g., ethnic, class, gender, etc.) authority patterns in global politics, Rosenau (1990, 39) argues that loyalties can be divided among numerous authorities and that humanity should be conceived "as congeries of authority relations."

If we accept Rosenau's contention that there are competing authority patterns in the international system, how does this belief affect the way we study international conflict behavior? Most significantly, this implication forces us to look beyond "national interests" as an explanatory variable of foreign policy behavior. In addition to serving as an instrument for the accumulation of national power, foreign policy actions may also reflect more affective motivations that stem from the commitment of citizens and rulers to authority patterns that transcend national boundaries. By examining the international dimensions of ethnic conflict, we hope to gain further insight into this puzzle.

The ethnic characteristic of a state can be understood as an attribute, in much the same way that the type of authority structure within the state (regime type) is an attribute. While the impact of ethnicity on international interactions has been relatively ignored, the impact of "regime type" has been the focus of considerable recent work. In particular, scholars have found that democracies, while just as war prone as other types of states, almost never fight one another and almost always win the wars they are involved in (see Chan 1984; Maoz and Abdolali 1989; Lake 1992; Maoz and Russett 1992, 1993; Russett 1993; Dixon 1994). This set of findings poses a considerable challenge to the realist conceptual framework and its assumption that all states act in the same manner.

Hypotheses

Several scholars have called for students of international politics to disaggregate ethnic conflict as a concept and perform more fine-grained analyses in an effort to locate linkages (for example, Heraclides 1990; Chazan 1991; Carment 1993a). While agreeing with the utility of that approach, we resist that effort in this study. We are interested in performing a broad-gauge, empirical "brush-clearing" exercise. That is, we contend that we are as yet unfamiliar with the empirical cross-national terrain. Thus it will be useful to establish what that terrain looks like before we do more fine-grained analyses.

Conceptually, then, we are first interested in whether the mere existence of a politicized communal group in a given state has an impact on the level of interstate conflict between that state and others in the international system. The concept of a "politicized communal group" was developed by Gurr for his Minorities at Risk project. According to Gurr (1993c, 163), politicized communal groups are identified by one or both of the following criteria: first, the group collectively suffers from systematic discriminatory treatment by the state or other groups in society; second, the group orchestrates political mobilization in defense of its self-defined interests. This concept is useful to us because it is broad-gauge: that is, it does not simply apply to ethnic groups that are actively engaged in armed conflict with the state that claims sovereignty over disputed territory. Yet it is not so fine-grained as to be meaningless (i.e., it applies not to ethnic groups as a whole, but rather to *politicized* ethnic groups). We recognize that this conceptualization provides a stiff test for the hypothesized linkage between ethnic conflict and international behavior and we are dubious about the presence of a linkage so broadly conceived.

Gurr (1993a) describes the data set in significant detail.[1] While the United Nations University (1987) indicates that there are more than 5,000 distinct ethnic groups in the world, Gurr's Minorities at Risk data set identifies 227 *ethnic groups at risk,* making up more than 17 percent of the world's population and affecting over 70 percent of the countries of the globe. The Minorities at Risk data set is made up of countries with a population of over 1 million and with ethnic groups that account for at least 1 percent of the country's population. Further, many distinct groups are treated as a single group in several countries to facilitate the collection of data (Gurr 1993a, 3–10). Table 8.1 presents a brief overview of the politicized communal groups by region in 1990.

The evolution of politicized communal groups throughout the world has been documented by Myron Weiner among others. Weiner suggests (1987, 36–37): "In country after country, a single ethnic group has taken control of the state and used its powers to exercise control over others. . . . In retrospect there has been far less 'nation-building' than many analysts had expected or

TABLE 8.1 Countries with Politicized Communal Groups in 1990

	No. of Countries in Region with Politicized Groups	Percent in Region	No. of Groups in Region
Advanced industrial democracies	12	57	23
Eastern Europe and the Soviet Union	5	55	32
East, Southeast, and South Asia	15	71	42
North Africa and the Middle East	11	58	29
Africa south of the Sahara	29	81	72
Latin America and the Caribbean	17	81	29
Totals	89	70	227

Source: Gurr 1993c, 165.
Notes: Gurr's Minorities at Risk data set is made up of countries with a population of over 1 million and with ethnic groups that account for at least 1 percent of the country's population.

hoped, for the process of state-building has rendered many ethnic groups devoid of power or influence." Moreover, the existence of politicized communal groups within the international system has produced a more perplexing and intractable form of conflict than that associated with the conflict of the cold war era. "They often appear intractable because the well-worn policy tools of economic reform and counterinsurgency neither satisfy nor suppress the underlying desires of the protagonists to protect and assert their group identities" (Gurr and Marshall 1990, 8). In fact, between 1945 and 1990, 51 (22 percent) of the politicized communal groups listed in table 8.1 have supported serious insurgency campaigns, while 142 (63 percent) have taken some kind of violent political action against the state (Gurr and Marshall 1990).

Well-worn historical anecdotes from World War I suggest that the existence of politicized communal groups and ethnic conflict within states have a tendency to spill over into the international arena. This assumption was key to Woodrow Wilson's "League philosophy," which posits that self-determination is essential to creating a stable and peaceful international environment. What Suhrke and Noble (1977b) dub "the Wilson proposition" challenges realist notions of international relations by contending that, in the postwar era, states formulate policy in an effort to guarantee the rights of self-determination to the peoples of the globe. This is similar to the theory of instrumental versus affective motivation for foreign policy advanced by Suhrke and Noble (ibid.) and echoed by Heraclides (1990), Carment (1993a), and Stack (this volume). Thus, we advance the hypothesis that states that have a minority at risk will have more conflictual relations with other states than those that do not, because other states value the right of people to engage in self-determination.

Hypothesis 1: Conflict levels, including war, between any two countries will be higher if there is a minority at risk in at least one of the countries.

Moreover, ethnic identities rarely coincide fully with the territorial boundaries of the modern state. According to Gurr and Marshall (1990), while most ethnic groups are concentrated in one of several adjacent regions, more than one-third of the groups have kindred distributions across three or more countries.

Given the significance of ethnic authority patterns in such cases, the relationships between states that share a common language, religion, or culture will tend to be imbued with a powerful affective component. In other words, these states can be said to be united by stronger horizontal authority patterns than those with fewer shared symbols of ethnic identity. Under these conditions, strong partisan alignments will be present between states with similar ethnic ties or between a state with a specific cultural affinity to a disadvantaged communal group in another country. Again, this is an affective motivation: states' foreign policy is determined not strictly by national interest, but by citizens' or elites' ethnic ties to kindred groups in other states. Shiels (1984a; 1984b, 11) generalizes Suhrke and Noble's (1977c) finding that affective involvement across borders increases the likelihood of partisan violence, and Vasquez (1992), Zartman (1992) and Moore and Davis (1994) argue that "ethnic alliances" may be one of the mechanisms by which ethnic conflict spills across borders. Both Shiels (1984b) and Suhrke and Noble (1977b) expect this relationship to exist because the neighboring states' support for their rebel group will increase the group's ability to wage violence. Rather than focus on the impact of this linkage on the internal conflict of a state, we anticipate that the existence of such an ethnic linkage will lead to conflict between the two states. Thus we offer the following hypothesis:

> *Hypothesis 2:* Conflict levels, including war, between any two countries will be higher if there is a minority at risk in one state and members of the same minority group are in power in the other state.

Finally, while we hypothesize that affective motivations are important determinants of the internationalization of ethnic conflict, instrumental motivations cannot be ignored. Even in situations where horizontal authority patterns are weak, states' foreign policy behavior may be affected by the presence of ethnic groups. Two scenarios present themselves. First, when two states face a conflict with a common minority group, they may cooperate and join forces in the face of a common enemy. This possibility is expressed in the following hypothesis:

> *Hypothesis 3:* When the same minority is at risk in two states, the intrastate conflict levels will be high and those states will exhibit more cooperative interaction patterns.

Second, states may involve themselves in foreign ethnic conflicts to bolster their political, economic, or military standing in the region. This is especially likely in situations where external actors can easily exploit ethnic conflict to their own benefit at little direct cost to themselves. According to Suhrke and Noble (1977b, 6), ethnic conflict "provides a tempting opportunity for outsiders to use it for their own ends. The temptation lies in the fact that a situation exists that can be exacerbated easily; a minimal intervention provides a proportionately greater effect." In other words, if one country has a national interest in the political disruption or demise of another, "the prospects of a relatively 'cheap' intervention will suggest cost-benefit calculations in favor of such action" (ibid.).

While domestic ethnic conflict can provide a convenient pretext for increases in bellicose foreign policy behavior, states are unlikely to involve themselves in the ethnic disputes of other states without first calculating the costs involved in such an action. If the affective argument made in H_2 holds, then the costs incurred in such actions are largely dependent on the magnitude of grievances experienced by the minority at risk. This is the case because the level of grievances experienced by the group helps determine their potential for collective action against the state (Gurr 1993c, 166–67). Therefore, the higher the levels of grievances experienced by the communal group, the higher their potential for collective action and the greater the marginal rate of return on involvement incurred by external actors. On the other hand, the lower the level of discrimination and magnitude of grievances, the weaker the group's prospect for effective collective action and the higher the costs entailed in external involvement. This discussion can be formalized in the following hypothesis:

> *Hypothesis 4:* The higher the magnitude of grievances experienced by the minority group, the higher the level of international conflict, including war, will be between any two countries.

Gurr's argument, which leads to H_4, follows a somewhat circuitous route between latent mobilization and intervention. While we anticipate that the hypothesized relationship will exist, a stronger linkage should be found between actual mobilization and higher conflict within a dyad. That is, states will not only monitor discrimination in an effort to assess latent mobilization potential, but will also monitor actual mobilization. This leads to the following hypothesis:

> *Hypothesis 5:* The higher the level of mobilization evidenced by the minority group, the higher the level of international conflict, including war, between any two countries.

Design, Data, and Methods

How can one determine whether the presence of ethnic groups at risk has an impact on international conflict? With respect to research design, we wish to determine whether knowing the status of ethnic groups at risk tells us anything about international interactions. We seek to evaluate this issue at the most general level that is possible. We also hope to determine whether the presence of ethnic groups is systematically related to international behavior.

While scholars have debated the position that interactions between two given states are best understood as a consequence of the behavior of the two states, rather than of the attributes of those states, we choose to treat ethnicity as an attribute in much the same manner as regime type in the context of international interactions. We focus on dyads because they serve well as a unit of analysis when one looks at the impact of attributes on states' conflict behavior. That is, if we want to know whether a state's behavior toward another state is affected by the presence of a given attribute, then we need to study dyads (Most and Starr 1989; Siverson and Starr 1991). If it can be shown that this linkage existed across a sample of all states (rather than a sample of a few states experiencing severe ethnic conflict), then we would become believers. However, it would be unreasonable to examine all dyads. Thus, we restrict ourselves to dyads in which conflict/cooperation is likely. Since we are particularly interested in conflict, we restrict ourselves to bordering dyads. Following Siverson and Starr (1991), we use a sample in this analysis consisting of all geographically adjoining dyads in the international system ($n = 282$) (land borders only; in creating their contiguous borders data set, Siverson and Starr also include water borders of less than two hundred miles). In the Siverson and Starr approach, borders are used to operationalize the *opportunity* concept and *alliances* are used to measure willingness. We are not interested in studying diffusion, but rather conflict and cooperation, so we replace alliances with ethnicity variables. Thus, our work builds on the *opportunity and willingness* approach advocated by Starr.

The data are from two sources: Azar's Conflict and Peace Databank (COPDAB, April 1982), which measures the international event interactions of all states in the international system from 1948 to 1979 on a fifteen-point scale ranging from *very cooperative* to *very conflictual*; and Gurr's Minorities at Risk project. Four measures of the broadly defined dependent variable (international interactions) are used in the analysis. These are: average conflict sent, average cooperation sent, net interactions, and war between the members of each dyad during the 1977–1978 period. *Average conflict* is a measure of the intensity of the conflict within the dyad, and is the sum total of weighted conflict within the dyad, with controls for the number of interactions. *Average coop-*

eration is a measure of the average level of cooperation within the dyad; it was constructed by taking the total cooperation and dividing it by the number of interactions. *Net interactions* is the average level of cooperation within the dyad, less the average level of conflict. *War* is a measure of the direct violent interactions within the dyad; it was constructed by adding up the weighted COPDAB events in which armed clashes took place between the members of the dyad (i.e., a score of 13, 14, or 15 on the COPDAB scale).

The independent variables in the analysis are all measures of the status of minorities within the dyad. All measures of the independent variables are from Gurr (1993a). *Minorities at risk* is a dummy variable indicating the existence of at least one minority at risk within the dyad. *Advantaged ethnic link* is an indicator of the position of the minority group within the other society in the dyad, with a value of 1 indicating that the minority in state A is incorporated into the power structure of state B, and 0 indicating that the minority at risk in state A is not incorporated into the power structure of state B. Our third independent variable, *same advantaged ethnic link,* is a dummy variable with a value of 1 when the same ethnic group is incorporated into the power structure in both states. Our fourth independent variable is a measure of the aggregate level of grievances experienced by the ethnic group (Lee 1993, 22). A final independent variable measures the extent of mobilization of the minority group. The Minorities at Risk data contain information on the amount of rebellion each minority group engaged in during the late 1970s. That variable is used as our measure of ethnic mobilization.

In all equations, we use a dummy variable to control for the democratic status of the dyad, with 1 indicating that *both states* are democracies and 0 indicating that is not the case. We use the Maoz and Russett (1992) measure for democracy, constructed from the Polity II data.

In the results presented below, we analyze the impact that the existence of minorities, their position within the political structure, and the level of discrimination/grievances they experience have on a number of measures of the level of conflict and cooperation within the dyad. Given the hypotheses outlined above, we would expect to find the following relationships:

H_1: We expect the existence of a minority at risk within the dyad to be negatively related to the average level of cooperation and positively related to the level of conflict. The variable net interactions will be negatively related to the existence of a minority group. Finally, we expect war, like conflict, to be positively influenced by the existence of a minority at risk.

H_2: We expect the advantaged ethnic link variable, which indicates whether the minority at risk in state A has political power in state B, to display the same type of linkages as the presence of a minority at risk. In particular, it will be positively related to conflict and war and negatively related to cooperation and net interactions.

H_3: We expect the same advantaged minority variable, a dummy variable indicating the existence of a common minority group within the dyad, to be positively associated with cooperation and negatively associated with conflict.

H_4: We expect the grievances indicator to be negatively related to net interactions and average cooperation, and positively related to war and average conflict.

H_5: We expect mobilization to be negatively related to net interactions and average cooperation, and positively related to war and average conflict.

Throughout the results, we expect that democratic dyads will exhibit different patterns of behavior. Specifically, we expect the democratic dyad variable to be positively related to the level of cooperation and net interactions, and negatively related to conflict and war.

Results

We examined the impact that ethnic ties and the status of minorities have on the four measures of our dependent variable (net conflict, average conflict, average cooperation, and violent hostilities). Table 8.2 presents the results of our analyses with parameter estimates, their associated t-ratios, and the F-ratio for the equation. Goodness of fit statistics are not reported because we anticipate that ethnic conflict has an impact on foreign policy behavior only at the margins. Hence, one would anticipate that our equations will not account for a substantial amount of the variance in foreign policy behavior. In fact, the R^2's for our equations were all less than .10. Coefficients for ethnic tie, mobilization, and grievances are significant at the .10 level or greater.

These results provide some support for our hypotheses. The first equation regressed net interactions on the independent variables and failed to produce any significant parameter estimates. This raises significant specification concerns, but is not surprising given that we only expect the structural and behavioral aspects of ethnicity to influence foreign policy behavior on the margins. The implication from this first run is that ethnicity does not influence overall international behavior within dyads.

A slightly modified picture emerges, however, when we consider the second equation, which concentrates on belligerent foreign policy behavior. These estimates indicate that the existence of an ethnic tie between a minority at risk and the same group in power across the border has a significant impact upon

TABLE 8.2 Impact of Ethnic Ties and Status of Minorities

Dependent Variable	Independent Variables	Coefficient	t-Ratio	F-Statistic
Net interactions (N = 279)				
	Democratic dyad	0.97	0.28	2.32
	Minority	-0.69	-0.25	
	Ethnic tie	-3.43	-1.33	
	Same minority at risk	0.21	0.07	
	Grievances	-0.18	-1.28	
	Mobilization	-0.28	-0.65	
	Constant	*6.53*		
War (N = 278)				
	Democratic dyad	1.67	0.02	3.58*
	Minority	33.97	0.36	
	Ethnic tie	278.11	3.20*	
	Same minority at risk	73.63	0.74	
	Grievances	-4.52	-0.98	
	Mobilization	35.88	2.44*	
	Constant	*-1.34*		
Average cooperation (N = 281)				
	Democratic dyad	2.71	1.73	1.82
	Minority	-1.04	-0.80	
	Ethnic tie	-1.77	-1.49	
	Same minority at risk	0.05	0.03	
	Grievances	0.03	0.54	
	Mobilization	-0.24	-1.18	
	Constant	*12.94*		
Average conflict (N = 279)				
	Democratic dyad	1.57	0.53	2.02
	Minority	-0.92	0.38	
	Ethnic tie	-1.90	0.85	
	Same minority at risk	-0.10	0.04	
	Grievances	0.24	2.04*	
	Mobilization	0.04	0.09	
	Constant	*6.20*		

* = significant at the .10 level or greater.

belligerent foreign policy behavior within a dyad. This serves as conditional support for H_2: ethnic ties have a positive impact upon warlike behavior in bordering dyads. The mobilization variable was also significant and in the expected direction, providing conditional support for H_5: ethnic groups that successfully mobilize for rebellion tend to exist in dyads characterized by higher levels of conflicts between the two states. This finding is consistent with Suhrke and Noble (1977a) and Heraclides (1990).

We also separated cooperative and conflictual behavior into two separate variables. Interestingly, democratic dyad—our control variable—was only significant with respect to cooperation (and then only at the .10 level): in none of the other three equations did it come close to statistical significance. None of the other variables had statistically significant parameter estimates, suggesting that the ethnic structure of states and the ethnic conflict within states does not influence cooperative foreign policy behavior.

Finally, the only variable that has a significant impact on average conflict is the level of grievances. This supports H_4, but counters H_5. To that extent, we are a bit puzzled. It would not have been too surprising had both grievances and mobilization been insignificant, but we did not expect that grievances would have an impact while mobilization did not. This finding undermines the instrumental argument we made concerning the hypotheses and is consistent with an affective interpretation. That is, if states are being instrumental, then they should respond to less ambiguous information (i.e., they would be more responsive to mobilization than to grievances, though they might respond to both). However, an instrumentally motivated state would not be responsive to information of poor quality in the presence of better information. The affective argument nevertheless suggests that states will be responsive to the plight of their brethren (such as grievances). Mobilization does not *necessarily* imply high levels of grievances (in fact, the two are not highly correlated). Thus, the finding that grievances drive dyadic conflict levels is not only inconsistent with the instrumental motivation of H_4 and H_5, but is consistent with an alternative affective motivation of those two hypotheses.

To recapitulate, the results of the analyses are mixed. We never locate strong, statistically significant support for the argument that the existence of a minority group within a dyad is associated with the foreign policy behavior of the states in that dyad. Thus, the argument advanced in H_1—that the ethnic makeup of a state has an influence on interdyadic behavior—must be rejected. We find conditional support (i.e., in the particular case of violent hostilities) for H_2, which argues that the across-dyad position of other members of the minority group makes an important difference in understanding interstate conflict behavior. We reject H_3, which anticipated that conflict would be lower and cooperation higher in dyads that shared the same minority group at risk within each state. Both H_4 and H_5 are supported to a limited degree by the results of our analysis. The argument that the conditions under which the minority lives act as a cue for states seeking to advance their interests is not supported in the case of average conflict—where grievances are positively related to the level of conflict within the dyad. However, when we examine war—where mobilization increases the level of conflict —we find support for the instrumental position.

We began this investigation with the assumption that ethnicity is unlikely to be systematically related to the international behavior of states, and as a consequence, we intentionally invoked a broad-gauged conceptualization of the ethnic factor. Our results indicate that, though the simple presence of a politicized communal group will not measurably influence foreign policy behavior, such behavior is affected by the presence of an advantaged majority in one state when the same minority is at risk in an adjacent state. Further, the extent to which they are either experiencing grievances or have mobilized against the state further influences foreign policy behavior. Finally, the presence of the same minority at risk across two states does not lead them to join common cause. Thus, we find support for our skepticism in that the most broad hypothesis must be rejected, but we must revise our beliefs in the face of support for hypotheses 2, 4, and 5.

Conclusion and Implications

Several recent studies (Heraclides 1990; Chazan 1991; Carment 1993a) attempt to designate more effective categories of ethnic conflict, which may be secessionist, irredentist, anticolonialist or other. We have ignored that call in this study and sought to determine whether we could find a linkage between ethnic conflict and international behavior, treated grossly. Whereas we anticipated that our null findings would lend greater credence to the recent calls by Heraclides and others, we find that we have unearthed just such evidence of that gross linkage. Nevertheless, as the Carment study demonstrates (1993a), it is useful to perform more discriminating analyses and to search for better specified patterns using less general conflict categories. This is a fruitful direction for future study and we urge others to join us in pursuing it.

An additional problem with our study concerns the temporal domain of the sample. It is quite possible that these results are an artifact of the international behavior of states in 1977–1978. To the extent that those are representative years, our results will stand. However, if those years were unusual, then these results will not hold for a more comprehensive temporal frame. We were constrained with respect to our domain by the data set. The Minorities at Risk data are from about 1985 and the latest years for which we could find interna-

TABLE 8.3 Neighboring States in Which Ethnic Groups Are in Power in One State and at Risk Across the Border

Status of Minority Group		Status of Minority Group	
Advantaged	At Risk	Advantaged	At Risk
Afghanistan	Pakistan	Lesotho	South Africa
Albania	Yugoslavia	Malaysia	Singapore
Angola	South Africa	Mauritania	Morocco
Belgium	United Kingdom	Mauritania	Algeria
Burkina Faso	Ghana	Mexico	United States
(Upper Volta)		Mozambique	South Africa
Cambodia	North Vietnam	North Vietnam	Cambodia
Chad	Sudan	Pakistan	India
China	North Vietnam	Romania	Bulgaria
Congo	Angola	Rwanda	Burundi
Egypt	Israel	Saudi Arabia	Israel
France	United Kingdom	Singapore	Indonesia
Haiti	Dominican Republic	Somalia	Ethiopia
Hungary	Romania	Somalia	Kenya
Hungary	Yugoslavia	South Korea	Japan
India	Bangladesh	Swaziland	South Africa
Ireland	United Kingdom	Syria	Lebanon
Jordan	Israel	Syria	Israel
Lebanon	Egypt	Turkey	Bulgaria
Lebanon	Israel	Zaire	Angola

tional events data were 1977–1978. We did not extend the events data further back (say, to 1975) because, although ethnic variables are sticky with respect to time, they are not constant.

Ideally, we would approach this study in a different manner. Because of data constraints, we use a cross-national study of a single time period using societal level measures of ethnicity. To draw conclusions about the existence and nature of ethnic/international conflict ties, we would prefer to have time-series data measuring both ethnically driven domestic political activity and international interactions. If such data were available, we would be able to tell something about the direction of this linkage and the process through which the two interact. Currently we are constrained in our ability to address this issue.

We close with a brief consideration of policy implications. We shall set aside the ethical and humanitarian imperatives that press states to intervene and mediate both ethnic and international conflicts and instead focus directly on security issues. First, a list of "high risk" states can be easily constructed in accord with hypothesis 2 (see table 8.3). That is, the international community would do well to monitor the relations between states where an ethnic group is in power in state A and at risk in state B across a border. Regional nongovernment organizations might play a role by offering good offices to mediate any conflicts that appear to be heating up.

Second, reports of human rights groups and intelligence reports that suggest that an ethnic group is being further persecuted should not be ignored on geopolitical grounds when members of that same ethnic group have power in a neighboring state. That is, simply because a given country does not fall within the strategic domain of others does not mean that instability in that country can be safely ignored. This study shows that ethnic instability has a relationship to international conflict when a cross-border ethnic linkage exists. Hence, not only should interactions between these "high risk" states be monitored, but the internal situation between the state and the ethnic groups should be monitored as well.

The Ethnic Dimension
of International Crises

Michael Brecher and Jonathan Wilkenfeld

A casual observer of the international system of about 1994 might conclude with some justification that the defining characteristic of the current decade is the prominence of conflicts with ethnic overtones, be they in Somalia, southern and central Africa, the former Yugoslavia, the former Soviet republics, or elsewhere. Yet ethnicity was until recently a neglected factor in world politics, linked to the struggle for self-determination in Africa, Asia, and the Middle East against the imperial powers of the West. It has acquired high visibility only since the end of the cold war.

The catalyst for much of the ethnic conflict in the spotlight today was the disintegration of the USSR and the withdrawal of Soviet power from eastern Europe in 1989–1991: this unleashed new forces that cast a fresh light on the role of ethnicity in interstate, as well as intrastate, politics. Minorities, long suppressed or dormant under Communist rule, emerged as sources of discontent: ethnic Hungarians in Romania, ethnic Turks in Bulgaria, ethnic Germans in Poland. A second dramatic expression of this new phenomenon was the minority status accorded to 25 million ethnic Russians in peripheries of the former USSR—in the Baltic states, Ukraine, Moldova, Tajikistan, and other former Muslim Central Asian Republics of the Soviet Union. What was unthinkable during most of the seventy years of Soviet power now became a reality.

In the post-Tito federation of Yugoslavia as well, ethno-politics emerged, at first in Slovenia and Slovakia in 1990 and later in Bosnia-Herzegovina. The renewed salience of ethnic identity and the demands for ethnic sovereignty shaped the debate and the violent conflict that ensued.

One indicator of ethnicity's newly recognized salience is the intense dramatic attention the media have devoted to several conflicts: the conflict between Armenia and Azerbaijan over the disputed enclave of Nagorno-Karabakh; the Yugoslav inferno; civil wars between Georgia and its Abkhazian minority; conflict in Sri Lanka with the secessionist wing of its Tamil minority; the struggle for power between the Tutsi and the Hutu in Rwanda; and the ongoing conflict among tribal groups in Somalia, among many others.

Another indicator of ethnicity's salience is the emergence of a critical mass of general literature on ethnicity and politics during the past few years, notable among them systematic work attempting to place this phenomenon in a broader analytic context (Gurr 1993a, 1993c; Horowitz 1985). Even more relevant to the present investigation is the increasing number of studies dealing with ethnic conflict and international politics in general, notably works by Rosenau (1964), Said and Simmons (1976), Suhrke and Noble (1977a), Ryan (1988), Heraclides (1990, 1991), de Silva and May (1991), Chazan (1991), Midlarsky (1992b), Schechterman and Slann (1993), Carment (1993a, 1993b), and Carment and James (1995).

Are these ethnic crises, which seem to dominate the international system today, uniquely associated with the conditions of the contemporary post–cold war system, or are we witnessing a variant on a phenomenon that has long characterized international politics? If the latter is the case, what have we learned from the historical record that will better equip us to anticipate and manage such occurrences in the future?

The relationship between ethnic or communal conflict and international system factors has been explored in a number of ways. Gurr, for example, proposes four general international dimensions to communal conflicts within states: first, conditions that facilitate the mobilization of communal groups by contributing to their sense of common identity, cohesion, organization, and capacity for political action; second, conditions that prompt regimes to adopt policies that exacerbate relations with communal minorities; third, logistic assistance and sanctuary for contenders; and fourth, facilitation of mediation, negotiation, and accommodation (Gurr 1992, 4–5).

Zartman also discusses the conditions under which internationalization of communal strife may occur. In his view, communities may overflow boundaries to encompass fellow members in neighboring states, seeking support or sanctuary. The neighbor may see the conflict as a security threat and may join the home state in suppressing the communal group. Or it may see the conflict as an opportunity to pursue its own interests against the home state. Finally, in some cases, it may prefer to serve as a mediator in the dispute (Zartman 1992; Heraclides 1990).

One aspect of ethno-politics that has not yet been explored to any great extent is the relationship between ethnicity and international crisis, one aspect of the oft-postulated linkage between domestic conditions and international behavior. Clearly, the most dangerous ethnic conflicts from the point of view of system stability are those that spill over into the international system as crises and become part of the existing rivalries among international actors.

Given the relatively low level of attention accorded ethnicity until recently, it is all the more surprising to discover that 35 percent of all international crises from the end of World War I through 1988, as identified by the International Crisis Behavior Project, had an ethno-political dimension (see Gurr 1993a, 1993c). The analyses reported are based on 303 international crises for the period 1918–1988. Brecher and Wilkenfeld et al. (1988) and Wilkenfeld and Brecher et al. (1988) also include summaries for the 278 crises between 1929 and 1979. A volume now in preparation (Brecher and Wilkenfeld 1997) will report on the data set and provide summaries for the entire 1918 to 1994 period. Excluded from this set are 70 cases classified as intrawar crises, which are defined as follows: first, the crisis is an integral part of an ongoing war; second, at least one of the principal adversaries is a continuing actor in that war; and third, it is an interstate war, not a civil or purely guerrilla war.

The focus of this study is the relationship between ethnicity and crisis, or more precisely, the effects of interstate ethnic conflict on the configuration of crises in the international system. To that end, we have developed a model of ethnicity and crisis, have framed a general proposition about the link, and have deduced a working set of hypotheses. These we test against the International Crisis Behavior (ICB) *system level* data set covering most of the twentieth century. In a later study we intend to extend the analysis to the *actor level* and to compare ethnic/nonethnic crises in the dominant (East/West) system and in two subsystems, the Middle East and South Asia, from 1945 to 1988, and in different regions across time.

Definitions

The concept of "interstate ethnic conflict" entails disputes deriving from both secessionist and irredentist pressures. According to Carment (1993b, 22–23), who introduced ethnicity into ICB research and generated the initial ICB ethnicity data set,

> An *interstate secessionist conflict* . . . in which one or more ethnic groups seek a reduction of control or autonomy from a central authority through political means . . . leads to an interstate crisis in four non-mutually exclusive instances: (1) when ethnic groups refuse to recognize the political authorities that can trigger a foreign policy crisis for the state in question (internal challenge . . .); (2) trigger foreign policy crises for the state's allies . . . ; (3) invite external involvement based on . . . one or more state

interlocutors supporting the secessionist group . . . ; and (4) invite external involvement of one or more states based on ethnic affinities supporting the state-centre triggering an international crisis. . . . An *irredentist conflict* is the claim to the territory of an entity—usually an independent state—wherein an ethnic ingroup is in a numerical minority. . . . The redeeming state can be an ethnic nation-state or a multi-ethnic plural state. The territory to be redeemed is sometimes regarded as part of a cultural homeland, as part of a historic state, or as an integral part of one state. The claim to territory . . . [and] an irredentist conflict leads to interstate ethnic crisis in three non-mutually exclusive ways: (1) by triggering a foreign policy crisis for one or more states . . . ; (2) external threats made by one or both states; [and] (1) and (2) can trigger (3) foreign policy crises for allies of the two states.

The analyses reported here combine the secessionist and irredentist cases into a single measure of interstate ethnic conflict. That is, we differentiate simply between interstate crises that are characterized by ethno-political conflict and those that are not.

As for "international crisis," the International Crisis Behavior Project has been guided by the following definition:

An international crisis is a situational change characterized by two necessary and sufficient conditions: (1) distortion in the type and an increase in the intensity of disruptive interactions between two or more adversaries, with an accompanying high probability of military hostilities; and (2) a challenge to the existing structure of an international system—global, dominant or subsystem—posed by the higher-than-normal conflictual interactions. (Brecher and Wilkenfeld et al. 1988, 3)

We applied this definition to all such interstate eruptions from the end of 1918 to the end of 1988, embracing all state actors across all regions, cultures, and political and economic systems in the contemporary era. In that manner, we identified 387 international crises, including 818 foreign policy crises,[1] that is, situations with three necessary and sufficient conditions deriving from a change in a state's external or internal environment. All three are perceptions held by the highest level decision makers of the actor concerned: a threat to basic values, along with the awareness of finite time for response to the external value threat, and a high probability of involvement in military hostilities (Brecher 1972, 1977).

The ICB Project focuses on military-security crises. We recognize—but have not systematically explored—political, economic, or cultural crises. While nonmilitary security crises may in fact include a higher proportion of ethnic conflicts, ICB's focus on crises with a major impact on system-level dynamics required they be excluded.

The Ethnicity Crisis Model

Some international crises have an interstate ethnic component. Others erupt outside that setting, that is, without the condition of intergroup conflict based upon separate identity. This distinction between ethnic and nonethnic conflict is central to the present analysis. The guiding research questions are as follows: Are there differences between international crises with and without ethnic differentiation and, if so, what are they?[2] Specifically, does the attribute of ethnicity affect any or all of the crucial dimensions of crisis, from onset to termination? Furthermore, are the effects of ethnicity upon crisis accentuated or moderated in a setting of protracted conflict, or are they impervious to it? (The concept of protracted conflict use here is not to be confused with Gurr's use of the term *protracted communal conflict,* which refers to the extent to which communal group members took part in antistate terrorism or rebellion over a sustained—at least fifteen-year— period [Gurr 1992].) Underlying these questions is a general proposition about ethnicity and crisis, and a set of hypotheses derived from it.

> *Proposition:* Ethnic international crises differ from nonethnic crises in a number of ways, including type of trigger, values at stake, role of violence in crisis management, extent of involvement by the major powers and the global organization, and type of crisis outcome, both in its content and its form. A setting of protracted conflict will sharpen the differences between ethnic and nonethnic crises.

The presence or absence of ethnicity generates a set of expectations about the process and management of crises. Specifically, we postulate that international crises with a pronounced ethnic element will be characterized by:

> *Hypothesis 1:* a greater likelihood of violence in crisis triggers;
>
> *Hypothesis 2:* higher stakes, that is, a perceived threat to more basic values;
>
> *Hypothesis 3:* a primary role for violence in crisis management;
>
> *Hypothesis 4:* more political than military activity on the part of the major powers;
>
> *Hypothesis 5:* more involvement and greater effectiveness of the global organization;
>
> *Hypothesis 6:* more ambiguous crisis outcomes, that is, stalemate or compromise; and
>
> *Hypothesis 7:* less formal agreements to mark the termination of crises.

In addition,

Hypothesis 8: A setting of protracted conflict between the crisis adversaries will accentuate each of these traits, resulting in three crisis configurations: ethnic crises within a protracted conflict; ethnic crises outside a protracted conflict; and nonethnic crises.

In other words, protracted conflict becomes an intervening variable in the analyses that follow. "Protracted conflict" refers to an environment of ongoing disputes among adversaries, with fluctuating interaction ranging from vio-lence to near tranquility, multiple issues and spillover effects on all aspects of their relations, and the absence of mutually recognized or anticipated termi-nation (Wilkenfeld and Brecher et al. 1988). Recently, the concept of *enduring rivalries* has received considerable attention in the international conflict lit-erature (Gocrtz and Diehl 1992b, Huth and Russett 1993). The concept of protracted conflict used here is closer in origin to that developed in Azar (1972) and in Azar, Jureidini, and McLaurin (1978).

The first attribute of the ethnicity crisis model to be explained is crisis *onset.* This refers to the act, event, or situational change that produces the ba-sic conditions for an interstate (international and foreign policy) crisis. The breaking point or trigger may be a verbal act (protest, accusation, demand, etc.), a political act (severance of relations, alliance formation, etc.), an eco-nomic act (embargo, dumping, etc.), a nonviolent military act (mobilization of reserves, shift to an offensive posture, etc.), an indirect violent act (directed at an ally or client state, etc.), or a direct violent act (military attack) (see Brecher and Wilkenfeld et al. 1988; Wilkenfeld and Brecher et al. 1988; Brecher and Wilkenfeld 1989a; Brecher 1993).

The postulate that ethnic crises are more likely than others to be *triggered* by violence (H_1) is derived from the effects of ethnic differentiation. One such effect is mutual mistrust. Another is the expectation of violence from an adversarial ethnic group. Ethnicity also generates several layers of disharmony and issues in dispute. Moreover, the values at stake are likely to be fundamen-tal in an ethnic conflict, creating a predisposition to initiate a crisis by violence lest the adversary do so first—the first law of state behavior in an international system of anarchy.

In nonethnic crises, by contrast, there is no logical reason to anticipate a violent rather than nonviolent trigger. The type of trigger will depend upon the specific configuration of a crisis—the attributes of the adversaries, the cen-trality of the issue(s) in dispute, the power balance, etc. However, the long-term effects of ethnicity—especially intense mistrust—which spill over to per-ceptions and behavior, are absent from these crises. Thus, while violence may be present in triggers to nonethnic crises, it is no more likely than nonvio-lence; and it is less probable than violence in ethnic crises.

The greater likelihood of a violent trigger to ethnic crises will also be influenced by the conflict setting in which an interstate crisis erupts (H_8). A protracted conflict (PC) between the same adversaries creates cumulative hostility, which accentuates the anticipated effects of ethnic differentiation. Moreover, the periodic recourse to violence in a protracted conflict—one of its defining characteristics—reinforces the belief by all adversaries that violence will recur; and this creates a further inducement to preemptive violence at the onset of an interstate crisis. This additional stimulus to violence is not present in ethnic—or nonethnic—crises outside a protracted conflict. In short, all other things being equal, we can postulate a hierarchy in the likelihood of violence in crisis onset: ethnic crises within a PC; ethnic crises outside a PC; and nonethnic crises.

The second crisis attribute to be explained is *value threat,* that is, the most serious threat during an international crisis perceived by any of the crisis actors. This may be a minor threat to population or property; it may be a threat to economic interests (trade restrictions, termination of aid, etc.), to the political system (overthrow of a regime, intervention in domestic politics), to territorial integrity (annexation of territory, partition, etc.), or to the actor's influence in the international system; it may be a threat of grave damage (large casualties in war); or finally, it may be a threat to the most basic value, existence (politicide).

The reason we anticipate a more basic value threat in ethnic crises (H_2) is that ethnic adversaries clash over core values—group identity, language, culture. Often this clash extends over a lengthy period, as part of a protracted conflict. By contrast, threatened values in nonethnic crises are specific to the issues in immediate dispute, without the hostile state of mind engendered by ethnic differentiation. The setting of protracted conflict also accentuates the value component: ethnic—and nonethnic—crises within a PC are shaped by the psychological legacy of ongoing and pervasive conflict. Basic values are more likely to be threatened in an environment of deep, abiding mistrust of, and hostility toward, the adversary as a consequence of earlier clashes or crises. As with triggers, value threats are less likely to take the most extreme form in crises outside a PC setting.

Hypothesis 3 focuses on *crisis management:* the primary techniques used by states to protect threatened values in a crisis, they range from negotiation to mediation to nonviolent pressure to violent military acts. The model postulates that ethnic crises, and even more so, ethnic crises within a protracted conflict, are more likely than other crises to be characterized by violence in the response of crisis actors. Why should this be so?

Violence is prevalent, perhaps inherent, in ethnic disputes. It is also a central and endemic attribute of a protracted conflict. As long as ethnic adversaries see no end to their glaring differences and disputes and view their conflict in zero-sum terms, the dynamics of their hostile relationship create a disposition to violence in crisis management, as in crisis onset. The persistence of competition over values and the deep-rooted expectation of violence generate a reliance on violent behavior in crises. This is especially so when an ethnic crisis erupts within a protracted conflict. In nonethnic and non-PC crises, by contrast, adversaries function in an environment of less frequent and less severe violence. Crisis actors are as likely to rely on negotiation, mediation, or some other peaceful technique of crisis management as on violence in coping with a crisis. In short, an environment of ethnic conflict is more conducive to violence in crisis management. The "lessons of history" strengthen that tendency. A nonethnic and, even more so, a non-PC setting does not.

Hypothesis 4 focuses on *major power activity* in crises. This may be no involvement, low-level (political, economic, and propaganda) involvement, semimilitary involvement (covert support, military aid, or advisors), or direct military activity (dispatch of armed forces). This hypothesis postulates more political than military activity by major powers in ethnic crises.

The rationale is that, despite their higher disposition to violence, ethnic crises are less likely to spill over beyond the territory of the adversarial actors and will therefore be less destabilizing for the dominant (major power) system. Major global powers have a vested interest in system stability, in order to ensure their continued status at the top of the system hierarchy. Since ethnic crises are less dangerous to that system's stability, major powers are more inclined to confine their activity in such crises to political intervention—if they intervene at all.

A protracted conflict setting for an ethnic crisis has a dual effect. It reinforces the preference of major powers for political activity; but it increases the likelihood of some kind of intervention by the powers. The reason is that such crises pose a greater challenge to dominant system stability than non-PC crises. Thus major powers, playing the role of system managers, are more inclined to attempt to reduce the intensity, scope, and duration of violence in such crises to prevent destabilizing escalation. Nonethnic crises, especially those outside a PC setting, are more likely to be managed by the adversarial actors through nonviolent techniques, thus reducing the pressure on major powers to become involved at all. In short, major powers can be expected to be most active in ethnic crises within a protracted conflict and least active in nonethnic crises; and their activity is more likely to be political rather than military.

Global organization involvement in crises may be low (fact-finding, good offices, etc.), medium (mediation, a call for action by adversaries, etc.), or high (observation, sanctions, emergency military force). Hypothesis 5 postulates that ethnic crises, especially those within a PC setting, will be characterized by more active and effective involvement on the part of the world body than will nonethnic cases.

The rationale is similar to that cited for expected great power activity.

Ethnic conflict accentuates mistrust and hostility between crisis adversaries. As such, it is an additional—and serious—obstacle to successful direct negotiation between the parties, and often even to the initiation of such negotiations. Mediation facilitates communication and concessions, with minimal "loss of face." And ethnic groups have less distrust of the global organization than of major powers or even the relevant regional organization in negotiating a mutually acceptable crisis termination. Thus, when victory is unattainable or the costs are perceived as excessive, an ethnic crisis actor is likely to turn to the world body to play a mediating role. Nonethnic crisis actors will tend to do the same in this situation, but the tendency will be less pronounced than in ethnically driven interstate crises.

As with major power activity, a protracted conflict setting will accentuate reliance on the global organization. For one thing, crises within a PC generally, and ethnic crises even more so, leave the parties dissatisfied and their tendency to violence undiminished. For another, the world body is perceived to have less self-interest in the outcome than other third parties. And since, like the major powers, the world body attempts to manage the global system to maximize stability and nonviolent change, it has a vested interest in mediation. In short, it is more highly disposed to intervene in ethnic crises to achieve accommodation, if not resolution, of the underlying conflict.

The last dimension of the ethnicity crisis model relates to *outcome*, in both its *content* and its *form*. We postulate that ethnic crises will terminate with more ambiguous outcomes (H_6) and less formal agreements (H_7) than nonethnic crises. Once more, the context of protracted conflict will accentuate these tendencies.

Ethnic crises tend to be eruptions in a continuing conflict over core values. Whatever value is at stake in a particular crisis, ethnic adversaries do not identify its outcome in decisive terms: regardless of the outcome, the underlying conflict remains. Indecisive results, like compromise or stalemate, symbolize an unresolved conflict. Subsequent crises are anticipated by both—or all—adversaries. In this respect, as in many others, the impact of ethnicity is similar to that of protracted conflict.

When the protracted conflict is the setting for an interstate crisis—and ethnicity and protractedness are often associated—this tendency toward ambiguous outcomes is even more pronounced, for crises within a PC are akin to phases in a multi-issue continuing dispute. The parties anticipate more crises—and violence—in the future. An end to their conflict is nowhere in sight or too distant and uncertain of attainment to serve as a reliable basis for choice and behavior in any crisis situation. They are prisoners of expectations rooted in the dynamics of a protracted conflict. Such conflicts are extremely difficult to resolve, even without the ethnic dimension. The ethnicity dimension only exacerbates the conflict and its periodic crisis eruptions between the same ad-

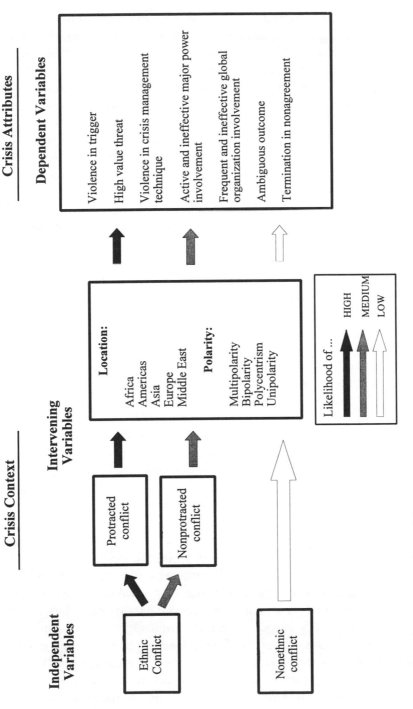

FIGURE 9.1 Ethnicity Crisis Model

versaries. By contrast, nonethnic crises—and non-PC crises—have more autonomous starting and termination points. They are usually less threatening than ethnic—and PC—crises. They are not affected by the legacy of an ongoing conflict sharpened by identity, an us-them syndrome. Actors can address the specific crisis. Outcomes will therefore be clearer and unlinked to other crises and outcomes. Victory and defeat can be more readily identified and accepted as such.

As for the *form* of outcome: because ethnic crises are viewed by the protagonists as interim stages, termination represents a decline in the intensity of threat perception and hostility, a pause between two phases of acute, ongoing conflictual interaction. An agreement to end a crisis is an acknowledgement by the parties that the specific source of the crisis has been overcome, but the ethnic conflict remains. Thus crisis termination is more likely to take the form of a tacit understanding that a crisis will fade, until the next outbreak of ethnic strife; or perhaps, an informal agreement will be reached. Formal agreement is least likely in an ethnic crisis. Once more, a PC environment increases the likelihood of less formal outcomes to ethnic crises. By contrast, a nonethnic crisis lends itself to a more formal agreement. It can be treated by the parties as an aberration from a normal relationship of cooperative interaction. In short, ethnicity—and protractedness—spill over into the mode of crisis termination, as with other crisis attributes. (Hypothesis 8, on the effects of protracted conflict, has been alluded to frequently in the presentation of the ethnicity crisis model. It does not require separate attention here.)

We tested our hypotheses on a large body of evidence drawn from the ICB data set for 387 international crises from the end of 1918 to the end of 1988. Figure 9.1 is a schematic representation of the ethnicity crisis model. What does the evidence from twentieth-century interstate crises indicate about these hypotheses?

Analysis

The empirical analyses aggregated the data at the system level. The cases evaluated here treat the international crisis, rather than the individual actors that participated in the crisis, as the unit of analysis. A number of system variables are in fact aggregated versions of actor-level variables. These include international crisis trigger (the trigger for the first actor to experience a foreign policy crisis in the crisis cluster), gravity of threat (the gravest threat experienced by any of the actors in the crisis), and crisis management technique (the most serious crisis management technique used by any actor in the crisis).

We consider intrawar crises to be special cases of international crises in general and exclude them from the analyses. Furthermore, when we examine polarity, we also exclude the 1939–1945 period, on the grounds that this world war international system does not conform to the general characteristics of polarity.

The data set being used to evaluate the model contains fewer ethnicity crises than that originally generated by Carment (1993a, 1993b). The essential difference between the two lies in the necessary condition for designating a case as an ethnicity crisis. For Carment, "The central question is: was ethnicity a salient aspect of any component or phase of the conflict?" Given the ubiquity of ethnic diversity in most states, this seems to us far too broad a criterion, leading to the inclusion of cases in which ethnicity is a marginal attribute of the crisis. The ICB project used a more narrow criterion: ethnicity has to be "the central" attribute of the international crisis and, at the actor level, in the behavior of a crisis actor. We asked ICB researchers on ethnicity and crisis to code a new variable, which identifies the degree to which ethnicity was *central* to the crisis. Findings for this variable are reported in Brecher and Wilkenfeld (1997).

The following analyses examine 303 international crises when all intrawar crises are excluded, and 296 international crises when World War II is also excluded. Of the 303 international crises, 105 (or 35 percent) were ethnic in origin.

Before turning to a general examination of the model, we need to examine ethnicity and crisis from the vantage point of two overarching perspectives: *polarity* and *region*. Figures 9.2 and 9.3 present these perspectives.

With regard to polarity, we focus on three systems. *Multipolarity* refers to a system of diffuse military power and political decisions among three or more units (for example, 1918–1939). *Bipolarity* indicates a concentration of power and decision in two relatively equal actors that limit the independent behavior of bloc members or unaffiliated actors (as was the case between 1945 and 1962). Finally, *polycentrism* identifies a hybrid structure, with two preeminent centers of military power and multiple centers of political decision (as in 1963–1988).[3]

Crises with ethno-political dimensions were proportionately more prominent under multipolarity than in either of the two later systems (figure 9.2). In fact, the difference between multipolarity and bipolarity in terms of the presence of ethnicity in crises is particularly sharp (45 percent of multipolarity crises, 29 percent of bipolarity crises, 34 percent of polycentrism crises). It seems that the two post–World War II international systems were somewhat more effective in managing ethnic conflicts, at least in terms of minimizing the extent to which they spilled over into the international system as full-blown international crises. This latter finding, of course, must be tempered with our knowledge that the post–cold war era, when fully analyzed, will undoubtedly yield results more closely resembling multipolarity—that is, once again the system will be shown to have had difficulty in coping with ethnic conflict.

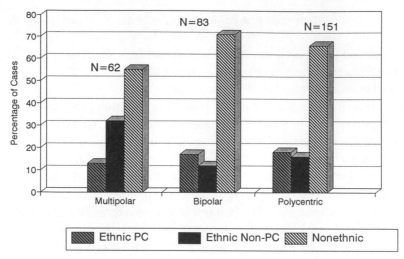

FIGURE 9.2 Ethno-Political Crises and Polarity

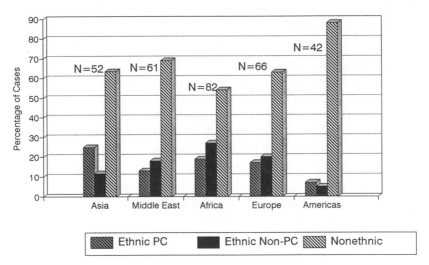

FIGURE 9.3 Ethno-Political Crises and Region

On the question of geographical location (figure 9.3), we note important distinctions among the five regions. Ethnic conflicts dominate Africa, accounting for 46 percent of its international crises. Since this is the region with the largest number of crises overall (eighty-two, virtually all in the post–World War II period, especially since 1960), this finding has important implications for crisis trends in the contemporary system, particularly since we can expect tribal (ethnic) identity to continue indefinitely as an important factor in most regions of Africa. The Americas, with only 12 percent ethnic crises, is notable for their low level. The findings for Asia reveal that the vast majority of ethnic crises occurred within protracted conflicts, whereas the opposite is true for the Middle East, Africa, and Europe.

We propose that certain tendencies, such as extent of violence, degree of threat, activity by third parties, definitiveness of outcome, etc., will be accentuated under the combined influence of ethnicity and protractedness, will be somewhat less prevalent in ethnic nonprotracted conflicts, and will be least in evidence among nonethnic conflicts.

Table 9.1 and figures 9.4 and 9.5 deal with *ethnicity* and *crisis trigger*. Overall, the data reveal no statistically significant pattern. Ethnic protracted conflicts are no more likely than ethnic nonprotracted conflicts or nonethnic conflicts to be triggered by violence.

Figures 9.4 and 9.5 include international crises that were characterized by ethnicity and that occurred within a protracted conflict setting. (World War II is excluded from the analysis of polarity in figure 9.5; thus, N = 48 for this and subsequent polarity analyses.) Earlier, we hypothesized that this group of crises would be most likely to exhibit violence in their triggers. A regional breakdown shows considerable diversity. For Africa, ethnic protracted crises are far

TABLE 9.1 Sources of Ethno-Political Crises

	Nonviolent Event(s)	Internal Challenge	Nonviolent Military Action	Violent Event(s)	Total
Ethnic protracted conflict	19	2	8	22	51
	(37)	(4)	(16)	(43)	(17)
Ethnic nonprotracted conflict	19	5	9	21	54
	(35)	(9)	(17)	(39)	(18)
Nonethnic conflict	62	19	32	85	198
	(31)	(10)	(16)	(43)	(65)
Total	100	26	49	128	303
	(33)	(9)	(16)	(42)	(100)

Notes: Percentages are read in the following way for tables 9.1<N>9.9: Percentages are summed across the categories in a row: for example, in table 9.1, the 19 nonviolent events in the first column represent 37% of the cases classified as ethnic protracted conflict. For the final column (row) of each table, the total number of cases in the row (column) appear and percentages are summed across (down): for example, the total of 198 nonethnic conflicts and 100 nonviolent events represent 65% and 33%, respectively, of the cases in the table.

$X^2 = 2.28$, p = .89

177

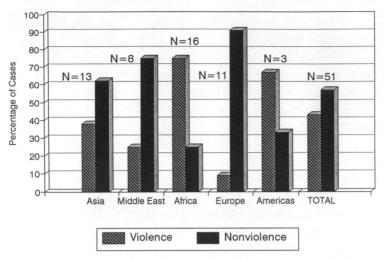

FIGURE 9.4 Violence as Trigger in Ethno-Political Protracted Conflicts, by Region

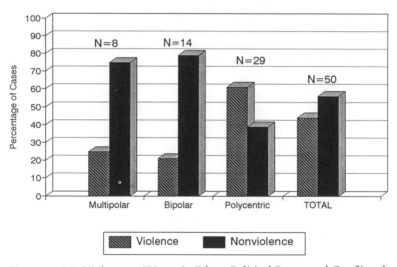

FIGURE 9.5 Violence as Trigger in Ethno-Political Protracted Conflicts, by Polarity

more likely to exhibit violent triggers than in other regions. (Since only two cases in the Americas were ethnic conflicts in the context of a protracted conflict, they will not be included in this and subsequent discussions of regional patterns.) With regard to polarity, violent triggers are considerably more likely to characterize ethno-political PCs for polycentrism than for bipolarity and multipolarity.

Combining these two findings, we note that eleven of the sixteen polycentric crises with violent triggers were African. These eleven African polycentric cases with violent triggers include Ogaden I 1964, Shaba I 1977, Ogaden II

1977, French Hostages (Algeria) 1977, Shaba II 1978, Raid on SWAPO 1979, Ogaden III 1982, Chad/Libya VI 1983, Chad/Libya VII 1986, Chad/Libya VIII 1986, Somalia-Ethiopia Border 1987. The preeminent association of African crises with violence conforms to the preeminence of ethnicity and ethnic conflict among the multitribal states of Africa, compared with other regions.

Table 9.2 presents the relationship between ethnicity and gravity of *threat to values*. Ethnicity-based crises differ from nonethnic crises in that two types of threats stand out. With regard to threats to existence and threat of grave damage (the most serious of all threats perceived by crisis actors), ethnic protracted conflicts show a 27 percent rate, compared to 7 percent for ethnic nonprotracted and 12 percent for nonethnic conflict cases. In addition, territorial threats account for 57 to 61 percent of all ethnic crises, regardless of whether the crisis occurred within a protracted conflict. This is twice the proportion of nonethnic crises (28 percent). Thus our findings generally point to higher threat among ethnic protracted conflicts, as hypothesized, and a preponderance of threats to the territory of the state.

Let us turn to a finer breakdown of the data, introducing controls for region and polarity. We focus here on *territorial threat*, since this threat appears to be uniquely associated with ethnic crises (52 percent of all crises involving perception of threat to territory were ethnic crises). In figure 9.6, Asia stands out as the region in which crises within ethnic protracted conflicts are

TABLE 9.2 Threats to Values in Ethno-Political Crises

	Low Threat	Threat to Territory	Loss of Influence	Threat of Grave Damage	Threat to Existence	Total
Ethnic protracted conflict	6	29	2	8	6	51
	(12)	(57)	(4)	(15)	(12)	(17)
Ethnic nonprotracted conflict	11	33	6	0	4	54
	(21)	(61)	(11)	(0)	(7)	(18)
Nonethnic conflict	90	56	30	13	9	198
	(46)	(28)	(15)	(7)	(5)	(65)
Total	107	118	38	21	19	303
	(35)	(39)	(13)	(7)	(6)	(100)

Note: See table 9.1, note.

$X^2 = 51.10$, $p = .00$

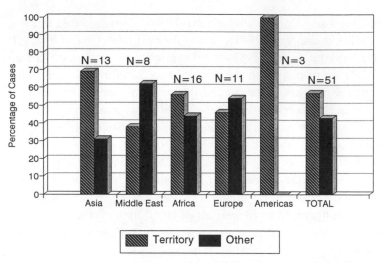

FIGURE 9.6 Territorial Threat in Ethno-Political Protracted Conflicts, by Region

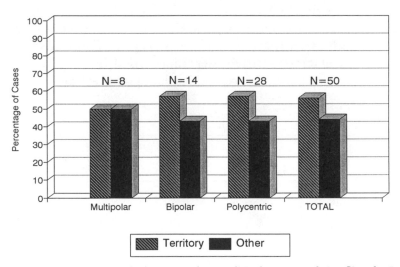

FIGURE 9.7 Territorial Threat in Ethno-Political Protracted Conflicts, by Polarity

most likely to involve a threat to territory (69 percent), followed by Africa with 50 percent. The nine Asia cases include eight in South Asia: Junadagh 1947, Kashmir I 1947, Pushtunistan I 1949, Pushtunistan II 1955, Pushtunistan III 1961, Rann of Kutch 1965, Kashmir II 1965, and Punjab War Scare II 1987 (the lone exception is West Irian II 1961—Southeast Asia). There are no significant differences among the three systems in terms of the effect of polarity on these distributions (figure 9.7).

Table 9.3 presents the relationship between ethnic conflict and *crisis management technique*. The data do not show any relationship between the extent

TABLE 9.3 Crisis Management Techniques in Ethno-Political Crises

	Peaceful	Nonviolent Military	Violent	Total
Ethnic protracted conflict	17	6	28	51
	(33)	(12)	(55)	(17)
Ethnic nonprotracted conflict	18	10	26	54
	(33)	(19)	(48)	(18)
Nonethnic conflict	71	41	86	198
	(36)	(21)	(43)	(65)
Total	106	57	140	303
	(35)	(19)	(46)	(100)

Note: See table 9.1, note.
$X^2 = 3.06$, p =.55

of ethnicity in crisis and the propensity to use violence in crisis management. Thus, we have found that both trigger and crisis management techniques fail to show any differences between crises with and without ethnic dimensions.

If we refine the examination of crisis management technique by focusing exclusively on ethnic protracted conflicts (figures 9.8 and 9.9), we note that all regions except Europe show a preponderance of crisis management by violent means—67 percent for Asia, 60 percent for the Middle East, and 75 percent for Africa. Interestingly, only Africa among these three regions showed a similar preponderance of violence in crisis triggers (see figure 9.4), indicating that for Asia and the Middle East, crises in ethnic protracted conflicts triggered by nonviolence, as well as those triggered by violence, tended to become violent in crisis management. Asian examples of nonviolent triggers and violence in crisis management include Indonesian Independence I 1945, Junagadh 1947, Pushtunistan I 1949, and Cambodia/Thailand 1958. Middle Eastern examples include Israel Independence 1948, Six Day War 1967, October–Yom Kippur War 1973. In terms of polarity (figure 9.9), the post–World War II international systems showed much higher rates of violence in crisis management than was the case for multipolarity. In fact, it is bipolarity that shows the greatest mismatch between violence in trigger and crisis management (57 percent). That is, protracted crises with ethnic dimensions, in the immediate aftermath of World War II, were particularly vulnerable to the use of force in crisis management, perhaps as a legacy of the war.

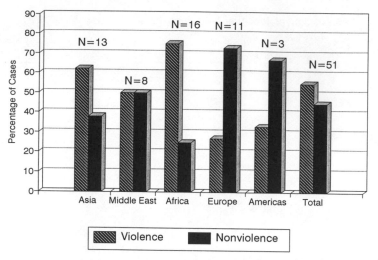

FIGURE 9.8 Crisis Management Technique in Ethno-Political Protracted Conflicts, by Region

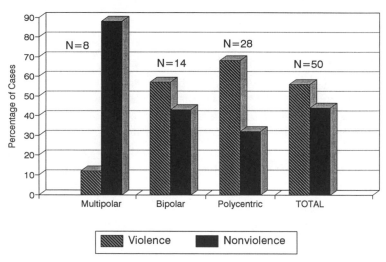

FIGURE 9.9 Crisis Management Technique in Ethno-Political Protracted Conflicts, by Polarity

With regard to major power activity in international crises and the effectiveness of such involvement in terms of crisis abatement (tables 9.4 and 9.5), we hypothesized that political rather than military activity would be more prevalent among ethnic crises, and protractedness would accentuate that trend. The results show that, as hypothesized, political activity is highest in ethnic PC crises and military activity is lowest for this group. It is interesting to note that major powers remained uninvolved in 44 percent of ethnic nonprotracted

TABLE 9.4 Major Power Activity in Ethno-Political Crises

	None	Political	Covert Semimilitary	Military	Total
Ethnic protracted conflict	8 (16)	20 (39)	17 (33)	6 (12)	51 (17)
Ethnic nonprotracted conflict	24 (44)	8 (15)	15 (28)	7 (13)	54 (18)
Nonethnic conflict	41 (21)	68 (34)	57 (29)	32 (16)	198 (65)
Total	73 (24)	96 (32)	89 (29)	45 (15)	303 (100)

Note: See table 9.1, note.
$X^2 = 18.95$, p = .00

TABLE 9.5 Effectiveness of Activity by Major Powers in Ethno-Political Crises

	None	Low	Marginal	Very Important or Most Important Factor	Total
Ethnic protracted conflict	9 (18)	17 (33)	6 (12)	19 (37)	51 (17)
Ethnic nonprotracted conflict	22 (41)	12 (22)	4 (7)	16 (30)	54 (18)
Nonethnic conflict	39 (20)	59 (30)	15 (7)	85 (43)	198 (65)
Total	70 (23)	88 (29)	25 (8)	120 (40)	303 (100)

Note: See table 9.1, note.
$X^2 = 13.05$, p = .04

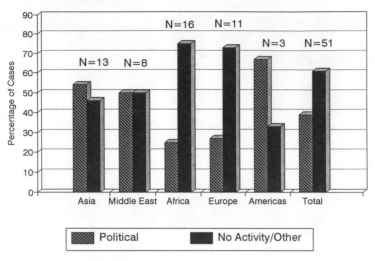

FIGURE 9.10 Activity by Major Powers in Ethno-Political Protracted Conflicts, by Region

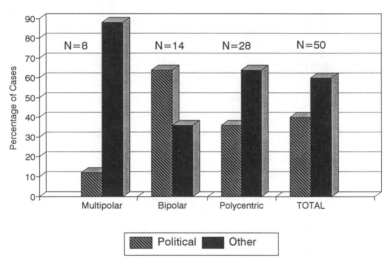

FIGURE 9.11 Activity by Major Powers in Ethno-Political Protracted Conflicts, by Polarity

conflicts, more than twice the uninvolvement rate for the other two types of conflicts.

Political activity on the part of the major powers in ethnic protracted conflicts is most typical of Asia and the Middle East (figure 9.10), and political activity on the part of major powers was most pronounced in bipolarity (figure 9.11). Eight international crises satisfied all these criteria: ethnic protracted conflict, Asia or Middle East region, bipolar international system, and political activity on the part of major powers. They were: for Asia, Indonesia Independence I 1945, Pushtunistan II 1955, West Irian I 1957, Cambodia/Thailand 1958, and Pushtunistan III 1961; and for the Middle East, Palestine Partition 1947, Israel Independence 1948, and Shatt al Arab I 1959.

There is no evidence to support the notion that the likelihood of effective major power activity is affected by the extent to which the crisis occurs in the context of an ethnic protracted conflict (table 9.5). And once again, ethnic nonprotracted conflicts are least likely to exhibit any sort of major power activity, regardless of its effectiveness. Ethnic protracted conflicts are most likely to exhibit effective major power activity when they occurred in Europe (68 percent), a not particularly surprising finding, given that most European crises occurred during multipolarity, and most major powers were in fact European powers (see figure 9.12). Only in multipolarity did major power activity have a reasonable chance of being effective (figure 9.13). European crises during multipolarity showing effective major power involvement include Albania Border 1921, Albania 1926, Remilitarization of the Rhineland 1936, Czech May Crisis 1938, Munich 1938.

Tables 9.6 and 9.7 provide comparable analyses for *global organization activity* and *effectiveness*. Global organizations (the League of Nations in the interwar period, then the United Nations) were considerably more likely to become involved through medium- or high-level activity in crises within ethnic PCs than in either ethnic non-PCs or nonethnic conflicts (table 9.6). It is at what we term the "medium" level of activity—condemnation, call for action by adversaries, mediation—that global organization activity is particularly strong—28 percent for ethnic protracted conflicts, compared to 11 percent for ethnic non-PCs and 19 percent for nonethnic conflict. The Middle East stands out as the region with the highest probability by far of activity on the part of the global organization (see figure 9.14), while the polycentric international system has the highest rate of global organization involvement (see figure 9.15). Combining these two sets, we arrive at the following list of international crises: Six Day War 1967, War of Attrition I 1969, October–Yom Kippur War 1973.

Global organizations are more likely to be *effective* in crises within ethnic protracted conflicts than in other cases (see table 9.7), particularly if we combine marginally effective with effective cases (36 percent effectiveness for ethnic protracted conflicts, 22 percent for nonethnic nonprotracted conflicts, and 13 percent for nonethnic conflicts). Global organization effectiveness was evident in international crises in Europe and the Middle East, and most notably for the polycentric system (figures 9.16–9.17). Early instances in which the League of Nations was particularly effective in crisis abatement included the

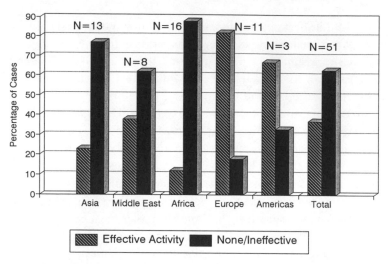

FIGURE 9.12 Major Power Involvement in Ethno-Political Protracted Conflicts,
by Region

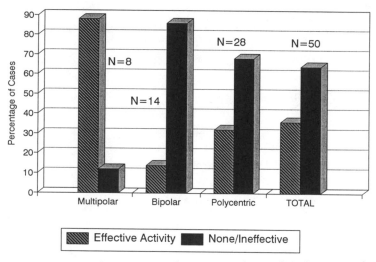

FIGURE 9.13 Major Power Involvement in Ethno-Political Protracted Conflicts,
by Polarity

Persian Border Crisis of 1920 and the Albanian Border Crisis of 1921. Polycentric crises in which United Nations activity was effective in crisis abatement included the three Cyprus Crises of 1963, 1967, and 1974, Kashmir II
1965, Rhodesia's UDI 1965, War of Attrition I 1969, Bangladesh 1971, October–Yom Kippur War 1973, Moroccan March 1975, Aegean Sea 1976, French
Hostages 1977, and Raid on SWAPO 1979. In combination, these findings sup-

TABLE 9.6 Activities of Global Organization (GO) in Ethno-Political Crises

	GO Nonexistent or No Activity	Low-Level	Medium-Level	High-Level	Total
Ethnic protracted conflict	19	15	14	3	51
	(37)	(29)	(28)	(6)	(17)
Ethnic nonprotracted conflict	33	11	6	4	54
	(61)	(21)	(11)	(7)	(18)
Nonethnic conflict	106	50	38	4	198
	(54)	(25)	(19)	(2)	(65)
Total	158	76	58	11	303
	(52)	(25)	(19)	(4)	(100)

Note: See table 9.1, note.
$X^2 = 11.84$, p = .06

TABLE 9.7 Effectiveness of Global Organization in Ethno-Political Crises

	None	Little	Marginal	Great	Total
Ethnic protracted conflict	19	14	7	11	51
	(37)	(27)	(14)	(22)	(17)
Ethnic nonprotracted conflict	33	9	4	8	54
	(61)	(17)	(7)	(15)	(18)
Nonethnic conflict	106	66	10	16	198
	(54)	(33)	(5)	(8)	(65)
Total	158	89	21	35	303
	(52)	(29)	(7)	(12)	(100)

Note: See table 9.1, note.
$X^2 = 18.58$, p = .00

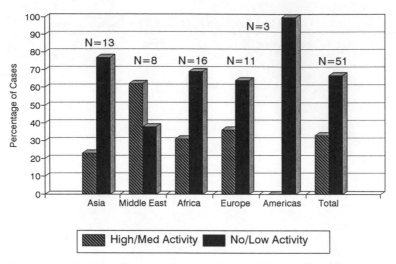

FIGURE 9.14 Global Organization Activities in Ethno-Political Protracted
Conflicts, by Region

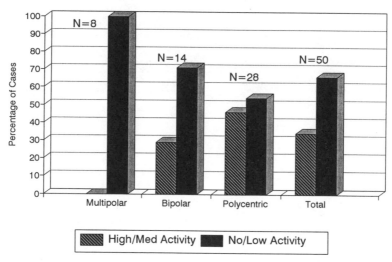

FIGURE 9.15 Global Organization Activities in Ethno-Political Protracted
Conflicts, by Polarity

port the hypothesis that global organizations are both more active and more
effective in crises within ethnic protracted conflicts. This is significant since
the record of major power activity and effectiveness in crisis abatement is at
best mixed.

We conclude with two assessments of the *outcome* of international crises
from the perspective of ethnicity, *substance* and *form*. In table 9.8, we note a

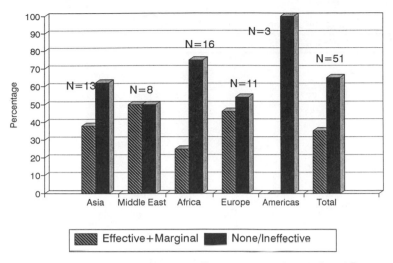

FIGURE 9.16 Global Organization Effectiveness in Ethno-Political Protracted
Conflicts, by Region

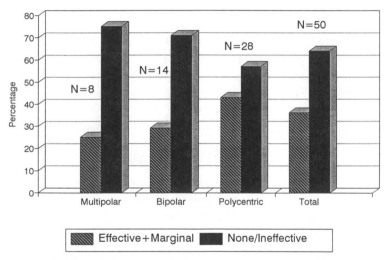

FIGURE 9.17 Global Organization Effectiveness in Ethno-Political Protracted
Conflicts, by Polarity

very sharp distinction between crises within ethnic protracted conflicts on the
one hand (65 percent rate of ambiguous outcomes), and the 33 percent rate
for ethnic non-PC cases and 48 percent for nonethnic crises. The high rate of
ambiguous outcomes for ethnic PC crises—that is, termination in stalemate
or compromise—attests to their inconclusive character, owing presumably to
the intractable nature of the underlying conflicts. Ambiguous outcomes in

TABLE 9.8   Substance of Outcomes of Ethno-Political Crises

	Ambiguous	Definitive	Total
Ethnic protracted conflict	33	18	51
	(65)	(35)	(17)
Ethnic nonprotracted conflict	18	36	54
	(33)	(67)	(18)
Nonethnic conflict	95	103	198
	(48)	(52)	(65)
Total	146	157	303
	(48)	(52)	(100)

Note: See table 9.1, note.
$X^2 = 10.35$, p = .00

ethnic PC crises were strongly evident in Asia (69 percent) and Africa (81 percent), while the Middle East and Europe showed reasonably strong tendencies toward definitive outcomes (see figure 9.18). While definitiveness was more visible in multipolarity crises, ambiguity typified the more contemporary bipolar and polycentric cases (see figure 9.19).

Finally, table 9.19 presents the relationship between ethnicity and form of outcome. Contrary to what we hypothesized, ethnic protracted conflicts are more likely to terminate in agreement (47 percent) than are either ethnic nonprotracted (38 percent) or nonethnic conflicts (28 percent). The tendency for ethnic protracted conflicts to terminate in agreement is most strongly present in Asia and Europe (figure 9.20), while bipolarity was the international system most conducive to agreement (figure 9.21).

Conclusion

Although only a portion of the hypothesized relationships were supported by the data, the findings point to an important interaction between ethnicity and protractedness, rendering the already seriously destabilizing consequences of protracted conflicts even more alarming. In particular, the presence of ethnicity in crises within protracted conflicts tended to accentuate violence in triggers for African crises and in responses in Africa and Asia, particularly during bipolarity; to heighten threat perception on the part of decision makers; to stimu-

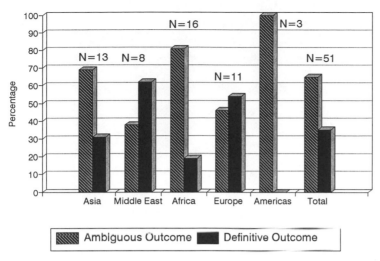

FIGURE 9.18 Substance of Outcome in Ethno-Political Protracted Conflicts, by Region

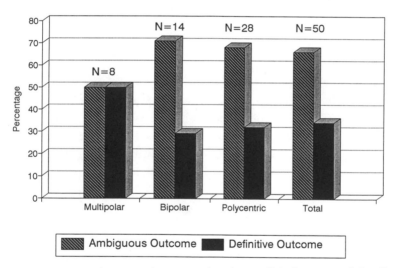

FIGURE 9.19 Substance of Outcome in Ethno-Political Protracted Conflicts, by Polarity

late the involvement of global organizations; and to lead to a higher rate of agreement among the parties, but also to a higher rate of ambiguous outcomes (the latter are the seeds for future conflict). While the major powers performed important mediating roles in crises during multipolarity, that role shifted in part to the United Nations during the polycentric system.

These are clearly warning signals as we move into an international system,

TABLE 9.9 Types of Outcomes of Ethno-Political Crises

	Agreement	Tacit	Unilateral	Imposed	Faded or Other	Total
Ethnic protracted conflict	21	3	10	5	6	45
	(47)	(7)	(22)	(11)	(13)	(17)
Ethnic nonprotracted conflict	18	2	16	7	4	47
	(38)	(4)	(34)	(15)	(9)	(18)
Nonethnic conflict	48	11	81	10	20	170
	(28)	(6)	(48)	(6)	(12)	(65)
Total	87	16	107	22	30	262
	(33)	(6)	(41)	(8)	(12)	(100)

Note: See table 9.1, note. There are 41 cases, virtually all from 1980<N>1988, for which data are not yet available.
$X^2 = 15.24$, p = .05

which appears to be characterized by an even higher rate of ethnicity in international crises, while many of the protracted conflicts of the previous system remain unresolved. There are important consequences for the international system from crises that arise in protracted conflicts with ethnic origins, and it is this concern that should guide future work on ethnicity, crises, and world politics.

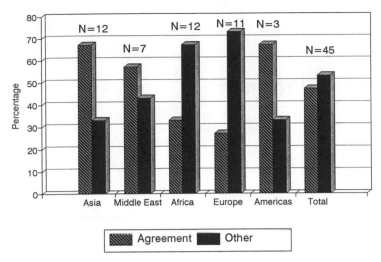

FIGURE 9.20 Form of Outcome in Ethno-Political Protracted Conflicts, by Region

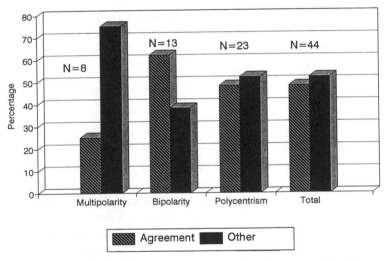

FIGURE 9.21 Form of Outcome in Ethno-Political Protracted Conflicts, by Polarity

Secession and Irredenta in World Politics

THE NEGLECTED INTERSTATE DIMENSION

David Carment and Patrick James

Nationalism, taken by itself, is both in logic and experience, a principle of disintegration and fragmentation which is prevented from issuing in anarchy not by its own logic but by . . . the configurations of interests and power between the rulers and the ruled and the competing nations.
—Hans Morgenthau, "The Paradoxes of Nationalism"

Ethnic strife, which includes secession and irredentism, is a challenging development for students of international relations. There is widespread belief, both popular and academic, that the political and economic interests of states, along with imperatives of the international system, can explain serious conflicts. This outlook, however, grossly underestimates the impact of certain kinds of *identity* and *community* (Ryan 1988; Rosenau 1990). It also fails to address the roots of "protracted" ethnic conflicts (Smith 1986a, 65). Since multiethnic environments have become common, both within and between sovereign states, the scarcity of related research is revealing: theory and policy have lagged behind emerging reality (Gurr 1992; Midlarsky 1992b; Smith 1993a, 1993b).

While studied primarily at the domestic level, ethnic conflict also frequently creates interstate "spillover" effects (Chazan 1991; Heraclides 1991). The implications of ethnic conflict for international relations, however, are not well understood (Smith 1986a; Ryan 1988; Azar 1990). The ongoing strife in Eastern Europe and throughout the Third World, for example, opens a range of possibilities that is difficult to comprehend (Moynihan 1993).

Both theoretical and practical objectives lie behind this study of the interstate dimensions of ethnic conflict. From a scholarly point of view, it is clear that the present neglect of ethnic strife within the field of international relations should be rectified. A more precise delineation of the *causal relationship* between ethnic and interstate conflict is needed. Thus, a primary objective of this inquiry is to develop a model that identifies the conditions under which ethnic strife is most likely to produce international conflict. A study of the interstate dimensions of irredentism and secession will also have broader relevance to theory and policy with respect to management and termination of conflict. The results of such policy-oriented research could be used to identify the international conditions and actions that affect the dynamics and resolution of ethnic conflict. From that perspective, the central goal of this inquiry is to lay the groundwork, in terms of theory and evidence, for *preventive peace-keeping.*

Attempts should be made to anticipate and prevent future ethnic conflicts through preventive diplomacy and peacekeeping. Preventive diplomacy entails discovering the conditions necessary for successful resolution of ethnic conflict through a focus on issue areas that are of common interest to the adversaries. Preventive peacekeeping, on the other hand, concentrates on identifying the conditions that trigger ethnic conflict. These may be domestic or international, and are necessary, but not sufficient, conditions for peacemaking. Preventive peacekeeping entails the development of early warning indicators of the transmission of ethnic conflict into the international sphere (Carment and James 1994b).

Conventional Wisdom and the Interstate Dimension of Ethnic Conflict

There is a lack of consensus about the causal link between ethnic and interstate conflict. Consider, for example, the conclusion of one of the earliest studies of ethnicity and interstate conflict. From their investigation of eight "diffusionist" ethnic conflicts, Suhrke and Noble (1977a) infer that these events do not constitute a significant source of interstate strife. But experiences in more recent years suggest that ethnic conflicts can produce violent—and often unmanageable—interstate conflict (Heraclides 1991; Carment 1993a).

Disparate approaches, units, and levels of analysis used in the study of ethnic conflict also hold back progress. Theories of international relations usually treat ethnic conflict as an epiphenomenon, that is, a by-product of the interaction between state building and anarchy (Weiner 1992). While a theory should allow for these factors, it must also consider the potential impact of domestic factors on interstate relations. Domestic variables have been integrated into mainstream research only in recent years because of the "paradigmatic blind spots" of international relations as a field (Stavenhagen 1987).

Orientation toward systems and states, as levels and units of analysis respectively, discouraged the exploration of domestically generated ethnic conflict.

Thus general theories of conflict, including those derived from *realism* and *neoliberalism,* are not well suited to explain the interstate dimensions of ethnic strife. A third paradigm, world systems theory, tends to overlook the military and geopolitical dimensions of ethnic conflict. It concentrates instead on the way that economic dependence engenders competition among ethnic groups within developing societies (Thompson 1989). World systems theory emphasizes class as the "central cleavage and source of conflict within and across states" and excludes "military and geopolitical competition" (Nagel and Whorton 1992, 3).

Given these problems, it is appropriate to reconsider the two dominant approaches: can either of them explain current changes, most notably those related to ethnicity, in the international system? How does ethnic conflict lead to interstate conflict? Is it generated internally and then externalized, as some theories (such as the diversionary theories cited in James 1987 and Levy 1989) would imply? Or do ethnic conflicts weaken state structures and invite external intervention? Or finally, does the process involve more subtle and complex interactions? A theory should be capable of addressing these potential linkages.

Neoliberalism and the Vulnerable State

Among the advocates of a neoliberal approach, Robert Jackson and Carl Rosberg (1982) develop the idea of the inhibited state to explain the maintenance of African boundaries. Their argument is that vulnerability to internal ethnic turmoil, along with weakness in general, restrains African states from supporting efforts to change boundaries. These factors bolster norms because recognized vulnerability creates a common interest in international rules and institutions. The concept of the inhibited state is similar to Keohane's (1986c) notion of specific reciprocity, in which the behavior of each state is contingent on that of the others.

Each state presumably cooperates because of a common fear—balkanization—where all Africa's boundaries might be challenged. To neoliberals, conditional cooperation of this kind emerges if future interests (extreme fear of balkanization, as in Africa) outweigh those of the present (intervention in other states). Horowitz offers a similar view (1985, 275): "Transborder ethnic affinities more often promote restraint in supporting separatists or intervention in behalf of a central government fighting to suppress separatism. Fear of contagion and domino effects is widespread." Internal cleavage is a signal of the incompleteness of the solidarity task and a threat to unity, hence the sensitivity with which such states frame their foreign policy objectives (Jenkins and Kposowa 1992).

Multiethnic states will be concerned if peers "defect" or do not cooperate. Neoliberal approaches attempt to explain the process of noncooperation among weak states, that is, their support for ethnic struggles elsewhere. Potential defection creates the need for verification and sanctions. Regimes and international institutions are regarded as the general means through which "cheaters" are monitored and punished as a way to encourage reciprocity.

The Organization of African Unity (OAU), and to some extent, the United Nations, have been promoted as institutions that can facilitate cooperation among multiethnic states. However, as documented by Haas (1983), the OAU's effectiveness as a regime is doubtful at best, and cooperative behavior among African states cannot be traced to its actions. Even Jackson and Rosberg (1982) concede that nonviolent interaction and cooperation among African states is linked more closely to tacit agreement among the major external actors not to become involved directly in ethnic strife.

Neoliberalism is useful in accounting for the absence of intervention by weak states in ethnic strife elsewhere. However, there are also several shortcomings to this explanation. First, the approach cannot explain the widely varying policies of individual states, both weak and strong, outside Africa (such as the Balkans or South and Southeast Asia) and even within that subsystem. For example, despite their presumed sensitivity to involvement in ethnic strife, the multiethnic Balkan states are engaged in intense and destructive conflict. To cite just a few African examples, the subsystem features recurrent Somali irredentism, conflicts between Chad and Libya, Sudanese turmoil, support for Islamic secessionist movements outside Africa, and (for decades) regional destabilization by South Africa.

Since neoliberalism assumes the inherent sensitivity of multiethnic states, it is difficult to explain why many become involved in ethnic conflicts. The inherent weakness in the neoliberal argument is the assumption that a state's foreign policy results primarily from relations with its peers. This view tends to underestimate the importance of domestic politics in relation to *transnational ethnic affinities*. For states experiencing ethnic strife and resultant disorder at home, foreign policy becomes an extension of domestic needs. Many states find themselves involved in an ethnic conflict precisely because of strong transnational affinities. In other instances, intervention in a weak, deeply divided state may arise out of opportunism, as implied by political realism.

Finally, the neoliberal explanation is not necessarily relevant to states that are less ethnically diverse. Will stable, ethnically homogeneous states—e.g., Japan or Germany—behave as predicted by neoliberalism? Perhaps states with internal harmony will be more adventurous in their foreign policies. Can international regimes work effectively in conflicts that involve ethnically homogeneous states? Neoliberalism is silent on these and other related issues.

Realism, Anarchy, and the Diffusion of Ethnic Conflict

Also at odds with the dynamics of ethnic strife is an exclusive focus on international anarchy as the cause for most wars and conflicts in the system. Mearsheimer's realist account (1990) suggests that the appeal to chauvinistic ethnic sentiment results from the need to mobilize the population in the face of a threatening international environment. Geopolitics is used in a similar way to account for state breakdown and ethnic mobilization. For example, in assessing the collapse of the Soviet Union, Waller argues that states seeking political legitimacy through conquest inevitably encounter resistance, which produces overextension or policy failure. The result is delegitimation and "an opening in the political process for opposing factions" (1992, 43). In either instance, ethnic conflict is viewed as an outcome that results from a state's search for security in the international environment. If a state loses its ability to regulate an ethnic conflict, the problem becomes a structural security dilemma (Posen 1993) because it could invite external intervention. Thus ethnic conflict poses a security dilemma for states in two ways: first, aggressive behavior is a consequence of internal cleavages and transnational ethnic affinities; and second, efforts to avoid external involvement are a product of internal weakness.

Within ethnic conflict settings the security dilemma is not an inherent factor, as suggested by realism. It results instead from specific sources of insecurity for states, namely, ethnic cleavages and affinities. Leaders of multiethnic societies may be pressured by political opponents (or more directly by the masses) to act on these linkages, which in some cases can be perceived as threatening by other states. In other instances, when cleavages and affinities are great enough to invite external involvement, the situation can become a real source of insecurity for all states. At best, this view is only half correct. Involvement in ethnic conflict also derives from concerns that transcend a state's external security. In both its collective and individual forms, involvement in ethnic strife also entails, to cite the most important examples, transnational ethnic affinities, domestic pressures, and humanitarian concerns (Heraclides 1991).

Assumptions that the state is rational *and* unitary are also troubling. Realism's emphasis on rational behavior in response to external, structural features of the international system understates the importance of domestic politics. Whether elected or not, national leaders must consider how their actions will play at home. This is true even if a foreign policy venture is expected ultimately to succeed (Bueno de Mesquita, Siverson, and Woller 1992; James 1993). Foreign policy must also satisfy ethnic constituencies that can threaten a regime's survival. Given the key role of appeals to ethnic sensibility in the political strategies of many national leaders, it is essential to assess the impact of this factor at the international level (Premdas 1991). Jurisdictional concerns of decision makers in the domestic arena should be integrated with the constraints imposed by the international system.

Interstate conflicts with an ethnic basis, in sum, may not be caused by the system structure, which establishes boundaries for action (Brecher 1993). What, how, and why states choose is determined by *internal* processes. The origins of ethnic conflict, manifested in dyads and further aggregations, lie in the interaction of domestic variables. Thus, it may be possible to prevent or discourage such strife by addressing its sources at that level.

A Model of Interstate Ethnic Conflict

Apart from a few exceptions (Suhrke and Noble 1977a; Heraclides 1991), existing treatments of interstate ethnic conflict fail to incorporate both domestic and transnational variables. In ethnic conflict settings, decision makers must consider the dispersion of preferences among the constituent interests within society as well as international opportunities (Bueno de Mesquita, Siverson, and Woller 1992). We shall argue that interactions between two domestic variables—ethnic composition and institutional makeup—can account for preferences about involvement in ethnic strife. Thus the state as a rational actor is constrained by both internal and external forces. In making choices, leaders are influenced by *affective* and *instrumental* motivations at the domestic and international levels (Heraclides 1991). This position is consistent with critiques of rational choice that emphasize the well-known limits to rationality. (Simon 1985 articulates the problem especially well in a discussion on bounded versus substantive rationality.) This kind of decision-making process is known as a two-level or "nested" game, because constraints and opportunities are important at both the domestic and international levels (Putnam 1988; Tsebelis 1990).

Both the choices of elites and masses, and their interaction effects, are significant at the domestic level. To the extent that they must consider the behavior of their own *and* other ethnic groups, elites become strategic actors. When the range of choices is extended into the international arena, elites must find strategies appropriate for additional constraints and opportunities. Variation in policies can be explained by differences in opportunities at both levels, rather than in terms of the norms and rules of domestic culture or individual personalities.

Any model of ethnic foreign policy must include two stages or levels of interaction. The first is the decision-making processes of elites; attention to this stage can explain the specific route to a preference ordering and the resulting decision. A state that is external to a conflict and supports either a state-center or minority group is said to have an ethnic foreign policy. The second stage of interaction occurs when two variables effectively create an interstate ethnic conflict: transnational ethnic affinities and ethnic cleavage. The conflict may be either secessionist or irredentist in nature.

With respect to irredenta, ethnic linkages are not theoretically necessary because claims can be based solely on territory. In reality, however, many irredenta are mixed and disputes about the nature of the claim usually involve mobilization of groups based on the principle of reuniting ethnic kin. For that reason, and because the focus of this investigation is on ethnic factors conducive to interstate conflict, we shall define irredenta as territorial *and* ethnic in nature. In other words, there must be an attempt to detach land and people from one state in order to incorporate them into another, like the recurrent rival claims to Kashmir by India and Pakistan. Irredentist conflicts can readily become internationalized, because these events involve two or more states in conflict over a specific territory.

"Interstate secessionist conflict" refers to formal and informal aspects of political alienation in which one or more ethnic groups pursue, through political means, reduced control by a central authority. Both the state-center and the secessionist group can be expected to seek and obtain external support. This competition exacerbates internal disruption and leads to interstate conflict. Such strife may involve politically mobilized, organized ethnic insurgency movements and the use of force (Heraclides 1989). We use "secession" as a synonym for separatism in the broader sense. Gurr (1993b, 21) uses the term in this sense "to signify any strong tendency within an identity group to attain greater political autonomy." This definition includes the anticolonial struggles (violent and nonviolent) of groups within a newly independent state (like Indonesia or Algeria) and more well-known insurgencies (such as Tamil separatism in Sri Lanka and Bangladesh; see also Heraclides 1989, 1991).

Ethnicity, Domination, and Diversity

When ethnicity is salient, an "affective" constraint is said to exist (Heraclides 1990; Chazan 1991). As described by Heraclides (1990) and others, ethnicity is a means available for political mobilization. A common, but erroneous, assumption is that the emotional roots of ethnicity make it irrational (Horowitz 1985, 132–35). The presence of affect in decision making does not mean that elite action must be irrational. Although it is difficult to reconcile identity-based behavior that contains an affective component with instrumental theories of interstate conflict, two points are worth noting: First, affect can provide either a constraint or an opportunity for leaders, and second, it is not a primordial drive only within elites but is distributed among the masses (Meadwell 1991).

Elites are positional players who seek to optimize their power relative to the leaders of other ethnic groups. In pursuing outcomes favorable to their ethnic group, elites also act from instrumental motivations. Thus the most important question facing a decision maker is: "If I make a foreign policy decision considered favorable to my ethnic group, what are the long- and short-term ramifications for my political standing *vis à vis* my ethnic group, the other ethnic groups within the state, and relations with other states?" Decision makers are strategic in looking for answers to this multifaceted question. They would prefer to appease ethnic groups whose backing is crucial over the long term. To find out when (and if) affect will be salient in influencing elite decision making it is necessary to examine the ethnic structure of the state in relative rather than absolute terms. Mass support is crucial when inter-elite competition is intense. As Tsebelis observes (1990, 163), while short-term differences between elite behavior and mass aspirations are not infrequent, such discrepancies cannot persist, especially if issues are considered important.

When leaders can improve standing in their group without depending on others (through force or democratic means), that ethnic group is said to be dominant within the state. Outcomes will be optimal for that group. In the foreign policy domain (assuming that decision makers act rationally), elite-mass interaction will be a two-way street. Elites prefer to formulate foreign policies that appeal to their ethnic constituency, even at the expense of other groups, in order to mobilize followers and increase power. In dominant settings an ethnic group claims control over the decision process even on issues that primarily concern others. Institutional mechanisms for conflict management between groups are underdeveloped and foreign policy issues of an ethnic character take on special significance in the domestic arena. When inter-elite competition within a dominant ethnic group is extensive, leaders may introduce new issues that discredit opponents and create avenues for securing power. In other instances, popular opinion may prevent elites from pursuing conciliatory or accommodating strategies with rival ethnic groups (Tsebelis 1990). Carried to an extreme, of course, the elite's policies could stimulate outside interference.

When the setting is ethnically diverse, *intra-ethnic*, elite-mass configurations become more important. Processes similar to the case of group dominance are likely to take place, but the results will be different. In a diverse setting, elites who face ethnic competition may rely extensively on support from other groups. Compromise becomes more likely. In such cases, elites depend on the backing of more than one ethnic group and in turn pursue mobilization based on ethnic *and* cross-cutting identities. Elite-mass arrangements within these societies are relatively efficient, because an attempt is made to improve the condition of virtually every group (for example, Ivory Coast). In contrast, states dominated by a single ethnic group produce redistributive policies that aim to enhance the position of one faction at the expense of the others (e.g. Turkey).

Institutions, Leadership, and Control

Political institutions constrain elites. For the purposes of this inquiry, "institutional constraint" refers not to the government in power (that is, the members of the elite who make authoritative decisions), but to the much broader, underlying patterns of political authority and constitutional structure.

"Institutional constraint" is not synonymous with "democracy." Instead, there are three dimensions that relate to the executive, the legislature, and the general public: first, executive constraint (ranging from seizure of power to competitive elections); second, executive regulation (from unlimited authority to legislative parity); and third, regulation of participation (from no formal arrangements to formal institutionalization) (Gurr 1974, 1990; Morgan and Campbell 1991).

Democratic election means that institutional constraints are high and the elite depends on a specific constituency for support, as in India. The elite is constrained in that decision making is highly institutionalized. There is a great deal of variation; in many instances, political constraints evolve through coups, political collapse, and controlled political transition. Unlike domestic policy, foreign policy should be more resistant to the vagaries of public opinion, especially during periods of interstate conflict and war. But if elites must play in the electoral arena as constituted by federal or consociational arrangements, for example, then the masses will be influential in the decision-making process, regardless of the area: "Visible politics—that is politics designed to be watched (and approved) by the masses has an ideological and polarized character" (Tsebelis 1990, 167).

Institutional constraint is low in some states by virtue of elites not being elected to office by popular vote or having seized power through force or coercion (for example, Nigeria). In a state with little or no experience in managing ethnic tensions, and with low constraints, hegemonial exchange, and its more coercive variant, the "control" model, is not unusual (Lustick 1979; Rothchild and Chazan 1988). Hegemonial exchange is a statist response intended to manage the overt aspects of intergroup ethnic conflict. Elites bargain over the distribution of resources and control the population through patron-client relations. When present, electoral politics have less influence over elite conduct.

Where constraints are institutionalized, the relationship between elite and masses is a nested game, involving parliamentary and electoral politics. The same cannot be said of low-constraint states, because the masses play a less direct role. Elite-generated conflict is concentrated within the military regime itself, rather than between the masses and the rulers. For obvious reasons, elites with a monopoly on power in low-constraint situations can be expected to rely on noninstitutional devices for the control and management of conflict between groups (Lustick 1979).

Interaction Effects: Shaping Foreign Policy Preferences

How do political constraints and opportunities interact with ethnic composition in the formation of foreign policy? Since elites play politics at two different levels—domestic and international—the payoff structures of both must be considered (Putnam 1988, 434). We shall assume that a state is represented by a single leader with independent policy preferences, in search of a foreign policy that will be attractive to constituents. Depending on the interaction effects between variables, certain leaders may prefer policies that lead to confrontation because of anticipated domestic payoffs. In other instances, the configuration of domestic variables will inhibit such tactics and shift the elite toward more peaceful measures.

Certain principles govern interaction effects at the first stage. These principles are acted on in accordance with what Putnam (1988) calls "win-sets." A win-set at stage one consists of all the successful foreign policy strategies that would "win," that is, be considered successful by the masses. Interaction effects at this stage have important implications for whether an ethnically oriented foreign policy will be pursued and deemed successful. Simply put, stage one win-sets influence a state's calculation of the cost-benefit ratio for involvement in an ethnic conflict.

Figure 10.1 presents variations in win-sets based on interaction effects. The win-set is minimal for high-constraint, ethnically diverse states, and maximal for low-constraint, ethnically dominant states.

		Ethnic Composition	
		Dominant	Mixed
Institutional Constraints	Low	I_a Maximum	I_b Moderate
	High	II_a Moderate	II_b Minimum

FIGURE 10.1 Interaction Effects: Comparing the Size of Win-Sets

Consider first the interaction effects involving low institutional constraints in dominant and diverse settings, or Types I_a and I_b, respectively. (The analysis begins with these arrangements because of the presumed simplicity of the relationship between elite and masses.) In cases where constraints are low, first stage win-sets are large because eschewing involvement is not costly. The only formal constraint on elites in these cases is the bureaucracy or military. If the elite comes to power through force (as in Libya, Somalia) it will depend on a narrow band of support from groups (that is, the military or bureaucracy) that are comparatively free from domestic pressures. The relationship between the military and the elite is therefore an important, but not enervating, limitation.

Leaders in a setting of low constraint can manipulate the size of the stage one win-set. For example, in a Type I_a case, a dominant faction will control an ethnically homogeneous military that can manipulate group symbols to mobilize the population. Consensual procedures in the development of foreign policy, if present, are likely to be "rubber stamp" operations. Power tends to be concentrated and the elite relatively immune to domestic pressures.

Type I_a settings essentially mean that the elite leads and the masses follow. Ethnic issues, including those related to foreign policy, are redistributive (meaning that any benefits accrue to the dominant ethnic group), but not in a way that could threaten the power base of the elite. This occurs primarily because interactions with the masses are used to promote elite interests. Leaders in a low-constraint situation would not pursue an ethnic foreign policy if it constituted a threat to their status. When constraints are low and ethnic composition uniform, an elite is unlikely to face legitimate and significant criticism at home as a result of external confrontation. Thus, pursuit of an ethnically oriented foreign policy is attractive for the elite and the win-set at stage one is at the maximum.

Elites in Type I_a cases are constrained, however, at the international level. While heavily imbued with an ideology, the resulting foreign policy need not be inherently aggressive. A rational elite will take into account a number of factors, including absolute and relative capabilities, alliance structure, and so forth. In other words, for a Type I_a state the main factor influencing the decision to become involved in ethnic strife is the international cost/benefit ratio.

There is little uncertainty about domestic politics, which can strengthen an elite's resolve in the international arena. Involuntary defection is less likely because domestic political outcomes are under control. However, the elite may defect "voluntarily" because political costs are low. In other words, leaders can be expected to behave as rational, maximizing egoists, as represented in the game of Prisoner's Dilemma (Axelrod 1977, 1984). This result approximates realist accounts of state behavior.

Within Type I$_b$ (diversity and low constraint), issues important to a specific ethnic group are unlikely to generate interest, because the payoffs are small. If the military is of a different group from the majority, or the elite represents more than one ethnic group, then it is normally impolitic to pursue a confrontational, ethnic foreign policy. The exception occurs when both international *and* domestic benefits can be expected. The size of the stage one win-set will be smaller, with suboptimal outcomes. Granting ethnicity a central place in foreign policy is dangerous because it may incite potential enemies within the state to seek support from neighbors. If no such risks are present, an ethnic foreign policy is more likely. Type I$_b$ states are not immune from involuntary defection; ethnic diversity increases the chance that leaders of a group cannot or will not cooperate on certain policies. Thus these states can be expected to support means to monitor and control defection. This would include international rules and institutions that derive from an acknowledged vulnerability; therefore, the resulting behavior approximates that of Jackson and Rosberg's inhibited state (1982).

Strategies in high-constraint situations and the potential size of stage one win-sets can be explained through more extensive interaction effects. Leaders are simultaneously constrained by the ethnic affinities of their constituency (that is, the supporting coalition) *and* by formal, institutional arrangements. Decisions about secession or irredentism are particularly acute in democratic societies, where internal constraint is expressed in terms of party formation, electoral politics, and cabinet composition (Bueno de Mesquita and Lalman 1992). Thus, the stage one win-set is small from the outset. Preferences for belligerence are modest because, to be considered successful, an ethnically oriented foreign policy must satisfy several conditions. According to Morgan and Campbell (1991, 191), constraints are greatest "when competition is highly institutionalized. Well organized permanent parties that compete in a systematic fashion provide a ready outlet for opposition to a leader and constitute a focal point around which opposition can form."

Type II$_a$ cases include high institutional constraints and a dominant, "like-minded" ethnic group. The elite can be expected to go along with the ethnically oriented sentiments of the masses, because replacement is quite possible. The main problem is to manage the discrepancy between the expectations of political friends and enemies on one hand and the outcome on the other. A leader must be ready for opposition tactics that are influenced heavily by ideology, a sense of historical injustice, perceived grievance, or a threat to values that justify a future society. Concerns about involuntary defection will be paramount. In contrast to both Type I$_a$ and I$_b$, the elite does not lead. "Like-minded" refers to those cases in which even political opponents offer "all-purpose" backing for an ethnic foreign policy. This support is crucial in expanding the stage one win-set. Indeed, if domestic payoffs have been promised to all elites, leaders may adopt an ethnic foreign policy even if it appears to be costly (below a certain threshold) in the international arena (Putnam 1988).

Type II$_a$ states are uncommon. States with at least some institutional constraints are rarely dominated by a single ethnic group that supports most policies. (Japan, Iceland, and Germany are notable exceptions.) However, the implications for newly democratizing states controlled by a single and like-minded ethnic group are clear: pressure for ethnic warfare will be intense. The experiences of the Commonwealth of Independent States and the Balkans confirm that suspicion.

Type II$_b$ settings, in which the constituency is composed of different ethnic groups, create different incentives and constraints. The constituency is diverse. An ethnic foreign policy will be unlikely if and only if leaders can withstand the pressures of "outbidding." The size of the stage one win-set will be the minimum among the four types examined, especially if force is used against an adversary with which some members of the constituency have an ethnic affinity. Institutional constraints will reduce the opportunities for pursuing risky foreign policies even further. Elites can be expected to promote self-policing policies that downplay ethnicity as a source of foreign policy.

Variants of Types II$_a$ and II$_b$ arise when a leader is faced by a constituency composed of one part of a single ethnic group. Intense political competition may take the form of multiparty ethnic factionalism. An ethnic foreign policy becomes "heterogeneous" as factional conflict increases.

Multiparty systems strive to accentuate ideological "product differentiation" (Downs 1957, 141). Factions that stress an aggressive, ethnically oriented foreign policy may emerge when there is a great deal of similarity between two leading moderate parties. All other things being equal, multiparty systems should facilitate involvement in ethnic strife. In Type II$_b$, for example, the initial stage one win-set is small because of institutional constraints, but leaders will often seek to increase its size by initiating inter-elite confrontation (Horowitz 1985).

Type II$_a$ outbidding may result in a shift to a one-party state. This can occur, for example, when a democratically elected, multiethnic party succumbs to adversaries on one or both sides (e.g., Zambia, Kenya). The single-ethnic parties make it possible that the original, multiethnic party, unable to satisfy either extreme, will be left with a diminished base. To maintain support, leaders may strive to represent a single ethnic group (Horowitz 1985). Such competition, in Type II$_a$ and II$_b$ cases, could lead to a more aggressive foreign policy than would otherwise be expected. In general, the political party with the greatest interest in an ethnic foreign policy will also have the most extreme position on that issue. If other parties (including those in power) are in a position to oppose fanaticism, then an ethnic foreign policy can be prevented. In other words, the more autonomous the state, the greater its ability to oppose—or impose—an extreme ethnic foreign policy.

Preferences for involvement in an interstate ethnic conflict are reflected in the win-set's size. Since states of Type I_a can choose from a broad range of options that would be satisfactory to the masses, belligerence may be preferred. Differences between Types I_b and II_a are difficult to predict; each can be expected to fit between extremes. Type I_b states are inhibited because of diversity, while II_a states are constrained by institutions. Both are moderate, although outbidding can increase II_a's propensity for an ethnic foreign policy. Options contract as the interactions between ethnic composition and institutional constraints take full effect, so that a Type II_b state, under normal conditions, is least likely to find an outcome that is acceptable to its constituents. An ethnic foreign policy venture will not be attractive.

Identifying states that use force requires greater understanding of the types of interaction. Ethnic conflicts operate according to the following basic principles.

1. States have mechanisms available to them that allow enforcement of foreign policies. For example, states can manipulate the ethnic divisions of rivals and reinforce transnational affinities through material and diplomatic support.

2. The leaders of a state will be penalized if they fail to protect their ethnic groups (i.e., domestic constraints) or if they pursue objects beyond their means (i.e., international constraints).

3. Ethnic affinities and cleavages create a security dilemma for states that, under certain conditions, can escalate tensions.

4. States can anticipate what others will do, based on a "reading" of their opponent's constraints and commensurate win-set size.

5. Low-constraint states can choose not to initiate interaction since the domestic costs of that decision are low.

6. Given the knowledge that the players might meet again, states will attempt to behave in ways that manipulate each other's stage one win-set.

7. For a multiethnic, institutionally constrained state, the best strategy depends on the strategy of the other player, and in particular, on whether there is room for development of cooperation.

8. An effective strategy for maintaining security, in both domestic and foreign terms, depends on the characteristics of a state, but also on the nature of the other strategies with which it must interact.

Differences between elite and mass preferences determine whether a state will use force. Sometimes elite action is decisive in causing conflicts to become violent. The elite of a low-constraint state faces the widest range of choices in seeking involvement in the ethnic affairs of its peers. Given that the size of the stage one win-set shapes the probability of force in interstate ethnic conflict, that becomes most and least probable for interactions involving I_a low-constraint (dominant) and II_b high-constraint (diverse) states respectively, with I_b and II_a in the middle range.

Since behavior is inhibited primarily by foreign rather than domestic constraints, confrontations involving Type I_a states will depend on the international benefits expected from an ethnic conflict. Anticipation of minor constraints in both environments can create intransigent policies and reduce the aversion to a use of force. These states would be expected to behave according to realist accounts, that is, to pursue interests with international payoffs, such as reclaiming territory. If the international payoffs are commensurate, interstate ethnic crises that involve these states could be the most violent.

From a different perspective, the causal mechanism linking domestic structure to conflict behavior for unconstrained and diverse states relies almost entirely on the various ethnic segments that impinge on an elite's power. Thus, for a leader in I_b, the only relevant constraints follow from perceptions of how the decision may affect retention of power (presumably of interest to all but the most entrenched dictators) and the state's security. However, short of the use of force, ethnic groups will find it very difficult to mobilize against leaders in the absence of institutions. Since military regimes enjoy a comparative advantage in using force, ethnic opposition will be relatively weak (at least in comparison to high-constraint states) unless external military support is forthcoming.

Relative to unconstrained elites in dominant settings, a low-constraint elite faced with diversity must worry about the implications of an aggressive ethnic foreign policy for its internal groups. This might explain why so few low-level crises in African interstate politics escalate to open warfare. John N. Collins (1973) suggests that fear of ethnic disorder is a sufficient condition for inhibiting conflict between African states. When conflict does arise, it is because these states experience greater instability or sensitivity to disorder (Jenkins and Kposowa 1992). For African state elites, foreign policy is an extension of domestic policy. Fear of repercussions at home inhibits overt aggressive behavior. Thus the ramifications of domestic disorder produce nonviolent conflict among these states (Collins 1973).

Conflicts that involve high-constraint states create the potential for contagion, which affects the strategies and tactics of elites in both states. For example, the elites of two constrained, multiethnic states have an interest in minimizing each other's win-set, to ensure that the rival does not formulate an aggressive foreign policy. With respect to its own win-set, however, the elite's motives are mixed. Ethnicity becomes a double-edged sword when politicized. On the one hand, the larger the win-set, the more able a state is to carry out its foreign policy objectives (ethnic or otherwise). On the other hand, under certain conditions, enlarging the win-set could weaken its position. For a Type II$_a$ state, enlarging the win-set through outbidding may lead to dangerous, potentially irreversible aggressive behavior and even domestic political calamity. This is because regime type and ethnic composition are highly visible characteristics of states. The elite of another state will seek to exploit opportunities created by these traits, which include transnational ethnic affinities and political divisions.

Highly constrained states are more vulnerable to domestic political threats. Add the compounding effects of ethnic composition and it becomes clear why counteraggression may be inhibited. It can be expected that doubly constrained states will be cautious in confrontations with each other. If ethnicity does become a salient issue, the two sides will either try to maintain the status quo or negotiate. This may be especially difficult if cleavages and affinities are strong. Since elites are strategic players, the ramifications of their decisions must be considered for both the domestic and international arenas.

Elites must also consider the long-term ramifications that hostile policies engender, including unanticipated reverberations. Selection and adjustment of a strategy is therefore determined by their preference orderings. How do substantial domestic constraints influence preferences? Large, domestic political costs discourage selection of strategies that involve the use of force (Bueno de Mesquita and Lalman 1992). This is because an elite's best strategy is not independent of those used by others. Elites engage in "safety" strategies that minimize domestic costs (Maoz 1990a). Therefore, for fear of repercussions at home, a constrained, multiethnic state rarely uses violence against a neighbor. Support instead may be low-level (i.e., diplomacy) or covert rather than open and militaristic (Heraclides 1990). Outbidding, of course, will change the preference structure and decrease the probability of peaceful interactions. Confrontation and violence become more likely.

From the preceding discussion it is possible to derive a general hypothesis, which bears some relation to the neo-Kantian proposition of democratic peace (Doyle 1986; Ray 1993) but includes interaction effects:

Hypothesis 1: The use of force in interstate ethnic conflicts varies with the type of state involved: Type I$_a$ (low constraint–ethnically dominant) states have the highest disposition toward force (realist variant); Types I$_b$ (low constraint–diverse) and II$_a$ (high constraint–dominant) states are moderately disposed (neoliberal variant); and II$_b$ (high constraint–diverse) states have the lowest disposition.

Propensity for Protractedness

When an ethnic group in a secessionist conflict is receptive to external support and intervention seems likely, some states may still be inhibited in using force. For a state of Type II_a or II_b, perhaps already seriously divided, military coercion of another state may not be possible. The size of the stage one win-set for those less immune to domestic pressures (i.e., I_a) increases dramatically if the ethnic conflict can be limited. If that is the case, then less constrained, ethnically homogeneous states may not be interested in conflict resolution. Since it creates specific benefits and few domestic costs for these elites, they may prefer to prolong and even escalate a dispute. Protracted conflict and future escalation therefore become more likely for Type I_a states. (Azar, Jareidini, and McLaurin 1978, 41–60, define protracted conflicts as "hostile interactions which extend over long periods of time with sporadic outbreaks of open warfare fluctuating in frequency and intensity. These are conflict situations in which the stakes are very high—the conflicts involve whole societies and act as agents for defining the scope of national identity and social solidarity.")

For irredentist cases the logic is similar. An irredentist group that is to be "retrieved" by an intervening state also faces two options. The elite may express great apprehension about annexation. Even if ethnic affinities are strong, the retrieving state may contain a composite of ethnic groups, so a decision in favor of irredentism will not necessarily result in ethnic self-determination for the new state (Horowitz 1991). Secession might be the preferred alternative for most ethnic leaders in separatist regions. For an irredentist claim to be translated into action, there must be an ethnic group that is receptive and elites who see their interests as being best served in the newly incorporated state. Such conflicts can become protracted by their very nature, especially if the intervening state faces few domestic costs, as is the case of Type I_a.

For a state to become involved in secessionist strife there must also be a minimal level of openness among the elites being courted. This implies a reasonable level of consensus among decision makers—something that may be difficult to obtain in Type II_b states. Of course, the nature and tangibility of this support may vary across several dimensions.

Either way, there is a great deal of resistance to external involvement from the state-center among ethnically diverse states. For obvious reasons of security, highly diverse states may be less likely to become involved in a protracted irredentist or secessionist conflict, because another state may want to press its claim continually to bolster support at home.

This line of reasoning produces a second general hypothesis:

Hypothesis 2: Interstate ethnic conflicts present constraints and opportunities such that protracted conflict is most likely for Type I_a (low constraint–ethnically dominant) states; less likely for Type I_b (low constraint–diverse) and II$_a$ (high constraint–dominant) states; and least likely for Type II$_b$ (high constraint–diverse) states.

Conditions Aggravating Interstate Ethnic Conflict: Affinity and Cleavage

Are there mediating variables that either increase the chances of a state initiating an interstate conflict or invite intervention? What factors affect the size of the stage one win-set? These and other related questions lead naturally to a discussion of ethnic affinity and cleavage, which create opportunities for politically motivated exploitation and therefore increase the probability of involvement in irredentist and secessionist conflict. For low-constraint states, international opportunities are more important than domestic ones. If there are domestic implications, affinity and cleavage will influence heavily the strategies of highly constrained elites. After all, these elites must be sensitive to the interests of constituents—even those beyond the state's borders.

Ethnic affinities relate directly to the problem of sovereignty, that is, the ability of states to implement authoritative claims. Efforts to control the flow of people, culture, and resources are significant in interstate ethnic conflicts. Quite often, authority is not defined solely in terms of territory; partial sovereignty exists and will shape the size of a state's win-set. Within ethnic conflict settings, transnational affinities are important to understanding relationships between states. Not only do elites view ethnic affinity as an opportunity to be exploited, but groups targeted for support also perceive these international linkages as potentially useful.

Transnational ethnic affinities exist among most groups in the international system, especially those that have undergone diaspora. Russians living in the Ukraine and the Baltic, the Tamils of South India, and the Chinese of Southeast Asia are a few prominent examples (Taylor and Jodice 1983; Neilsson 1985; Gurr 1992). Interventions by the United States in both World War I and World War II may be traced, at least in part, to an affinity for the UK, the point of origin for the overwhelming majority of immigrants until more recent years. Defining transnational affinity is difficult, however, because there is more than one way to establish ethnic identity (Rothschild 1981; Horowitz 1985; Smith 1993a, 1993b). Racial, religious, tribal (kinship), and linguistic cleavages may not coincide, and thus affinity in one area (linguistic) may be at odds with another area (kinship) (Chazan 1991). Moreover, elites can attempt to mobilize other transnational identities (Pan-Arabism as opposed to Islam, for example) or cultural subsystems at the expense of ethnic affinities. In sum, ethnic linkage with a group in another state does not guarantee mutual interest.

When more affinities (language, race, religion) exist between an ethnic group in two or more states, the anticipated connection is stronger, and it is more likely that an ethnic group will seek external support. Both the state-center and a minority adversary within a state will try to take advantage of these linkages. In some of these cases, elites may be carried along by mass ethnic fervor (Chazan 1991). Moreover, mutual interests are strongest for groups that experience high international ethnic affinities *and* perceive the "other" group as an enemy of the supporting state. The other or "out" group in this instance is the state-center or an ethnic minority. If affinities do not converge, then a state is less likely to pursue an ethnically oriented foreign policy. The state (or group) in question is also unlikely to seek ethnically based support. The size of a state's win-set cannot be enlarged by playing the ethnic card, and conflict becomes less probable.

Ethnic cleavage is a concept closely linked to transnational ethnic affinity (Gurr 1992). The term refers to the degree of divided political loyalties among ethnic groups within a state. For example, groups that aspire to self-determination, but are willing to work through existing political institutions and procedures, exhibit a relatively low level of cleavage. The degree of division is comparatively high for those who seek to transform the political status quo through force and/or external assistance. For intervening states, cleavage provides an opportunity to be exploited by others. It is an obvious domestic constraint. Loyalties will be divided when a state has underdeveloped system maintenance functions, weak institutions, and political parties based on ethnic groups. In such instances, the elites of the state-center and a secessionist ethnic group will actively seek external support. By contrast, cleavage is low when a state has strong institutions, political capacities for the management of ethnic tensions, and cross-cutting cleavages that weaken the capacity for mobilization on the basis of ethnicity.

This analysis points toward a third general hypothesis:

Hypothesis 3: Ethnic affinities and cleavage aggravate interstate ethnic conflicts such that the effects are minimal for Type I_a (low constraint–ethnically dominant) states; moderate for Type I_b (low constraint–diverse) and II_a (high constraint–dominant) states; and maximal for Type II_b (high constraint–diverse) states.

Testing the Hypotheses

Gathering the Data

We have relied on data about national attributes and events from the Minorities at Risk Project and Polity II. For several reasons, the International Crisis Behavior (ICB) Project is the obvious source on interstate conflict. The ICB case profiles, which describe in detail the actors involved, the circumstances and nature of the conflict, and its outcome, are ideal for coding purposes. Both system- and actor-level data are included. The data set permits comprehensive coverage of significant international conflict in the post-1945 era.

Although crises are by definition conflicts, many crises are managed successfully without recourse to violence, so the data set encompasses a wide range of interstate behavior. Among other important indicators, the ICB data include the number of states involved, the nature of the threat, and the issues over which the conflict arose. Such information is vital in determining whether the basis of the conflict is ethnic.

Furthermore, the ICB data focus specifically on conflicts that take place at the *interstate* level. Conflicts that have not yet produced international crises are excluded. (This choice is not without its drawbacks; some prominent ethnic conflicts are by definition excluded, as with Irish and Quebecois separatism.) Thus the ICB data set is not an exhaustive list of ethnic conflicts with an international dimension, but it does cover interstate ethnic crises over a substantial period.

Case Selection: The Characteristics of Interstate Ethnic Strife

For each crisis, we conduct a two-stage content analysis with the working definition of ethnicity and typology of interstate ethnic crises provided in this study. We initially coded each crisis on the basis of whether ethnicity is deemed a salient factor. Crises not considered to be ethnic conflicts are placed in a separate category. We based coding of the remaining cases as either secessionist or irredentist on the following criteria.

Interstate secessionist conflict refers to the formal *and* informal aspects of political alienation in which one or more ethnic groups seek a reduction of control or autonomy from a central authority through political means. The state-center or secessionist group will seek out and obtain external support, thereby enhancing internal cleavage and disruption leading to interstate conflict. Such conflicts may or may not involve the use of force and politically mobilized, well-organized, ethnic insurgency movements.

When ethnic groups refuse to recognize existing political authorities they can:

> 1. trigger a foreign policy crisis for the state in question (i.e., an internal challenge leading to external involvement);

> 2. trigger foreign policy crises for the state's allies, which collectively produce an international crisis;

> 3. invite external involvement based on transnational ethnic affinities (including threats of involvement) of one or more states that support the secessionist group, which triggers an international crisis;

> 4. invite external involvement, based on ethnic affinities, by one or more states that support the state-center, which triggers an international crisis.

Irredentist conflicts are by definition already interstate ethnic conflicts. Irredentism is a claim to territory by an entity—usually an independent state— in which an ethnic in-group is a minority. The original term *terra irredenta* means territory to be redeemed. It presumes a redeeming state and also such territory. The redeeming state can be an ethnic nation-state or a multiethnic, plural state. The territory to be redeemed is sometimes regarded as part of a cultural homeland or a historic state, or as an integral part of one state. The claim to territory is based on transnational ethnic affinities and is conditioned by the presence of cleavage between the minority in-group and its state-center.

An irredentist conflict leads to interstate ethnic crisis in three nonmutually exclusive ways:

1. It triggers a foreign policy crisis for one or more states through an internal challenge supported by the redeeming state.

2. It elicits external threats from one or both states.

3. Actions (1) and (2) trigger foreign policy crises for allies of the two states.

When there was doubt or ambiguity about face validity, we coded the case as a nonethnic conflict. We coded cases that exhibit both secessionist and irredentist characteristics based on the highest value threatened, in consultation with a colleague familiar with research on ethnicity. To ensure intersubjective agreement, a second individual recoded a random sample of seventy-five cases. This coding scored 80 percent agreement *prior* to consultation.

Two conditions characterize the interstate ethnic crises listed in table 10.1. First, at least one state must experience a foreign policy crisis, defined as a situation with three individually and collectively sufficient conditions deriving from changes in a state's internal or external environment. The highest-level decision makers of the actor concerned perceive all three of these conditions: a threat to basic values, awareness of finite time for response to the value threat, and a high probability of involvement in military hostilities (Brecher and Wilkenfeld et al. 1988). By definition, any foreign policy crisis falls within the boundaries of an international crisis, which disrupts the processes and challenges the structure of the system (Brecher and Wilkenfeld et al. 1988). Thus the unit of analysis is the crisis actor, and we have arranged these cases in sets that correspond to international crises. The second condition for inclusion is that each case meet the working definition of either an interstate secessionist or an irredentist conflict.

TABLE 10.1 Secessionist and Irredentist Crises, 1945–1988

International Crisis[a]	Ethnic Aspect: Secessionist (S), Irredentist (1)	Crisis Actor	Trigger Date[b]	Termination Date
Junagadh	I	India	17/08/47	09/11/47
	I	Pakistan	01/11/47	24/02/48
Palestine Partition	I	Syria	29/11/47	17/12/47
	I	Egypt	29/11/47	17/12/47
	I	Iraq	29/11/47	17/12/47
	I	Lebanon	29/11/47	17/12/47
Pushtunistan I	S	Afghanistan	*/03/49	31/07/49
	S	Pakistan	30/09/50	05/10/50
Punjab War	I	India	07/07/51	*/08/51
	I	Pakistan	10/07/51	*/08/51
Trieste II	I	Italy	10/10/53	05/12/53
	I	Yugoslavia	08/10/53	05/12/53
Pushtunistan II	S	Afghanistan	27/03/55	*/11/55
	S	Pakistan	29/03/55	14/10/55
Goa I	I	Portugal	10/08/55	06/09/55
Ifni	S	Spain	23/11/57	*/*/*
West Irian I	S	Netherlands	01/12/57	*/*/*
Sudan-Egypt border	I	Sudan	09/02/58	25/02/58
Tunisia-France I	S	Tunisia	31/05/57	27/06/57
Tunisia-France II	S	Tunisia	08/02/58	17/02/58
	S	Tunisia	24/05/58	17/06/58
Cambodia-Thailand	I	Cambodia	01/09/58	06/02/59
	I	Thailand	24/07/58	06/02/59
Shatt-al-Arab I	I	Iraq	28/11/59	04/01/60
	I	Iran	02/12/59	04/01/60
Ghana/Togo Border	I	Ghana	*/03/60	01/04/60
Ethiopia/Somalia	I	Ethiopia	26/12/60	*/*/*
Congo I — Katanga	S	Belgium	05/07/60	15/07/60
	S	Congo	11/07/60	15/02/62
	S	Congo	10/07/60	15/07/60
Mali Federation	S	Senegal	20/08/60	22/09/60
	S	Mali	20/08/60	22/09/60

continued

Table 10.1 *Continued*

International Crisis[a]	Ethnic Aspect: Secessionist (S), Irredentist (1)	Crisis Actor	Trigger Date[b]	Termination Date
Kuwait Independence	I	Kuwait	25/06/61	13/07/61
Pushtunistan III	S	Pakistan	19/05/61	*/06/61
	S	Pakistan	30/08/61	29/01/62
	S	Afghanistan	23/08/61	29/01/62
West Irian II	S	Indonesia	26/09/61	15/08/62
	S	Netherlands	19/12/61	15/08/62
Goa II	S	Portugal	11/12/61	19/12/61
Mauritania/Mali	I	Mauritania	29/03/62	18/02/63
Malaysia Federation	I	Malaysia	11/02/63	05/08/65
	I	Malaysia	15/09/63	09/08/65
	I	Indonesia	09/07/63	05/08/63
	I	Indonesia	14/09/63	09/08/65
Rwanda/Burundi	S	Rwanda	21/12/63	*/04/64
	S	Burundi	22/01/64	*/04/64
Morocco/Algeria	I	Algeria	01/10/63	04/11/63
	I	Morocco	08/10/63	04/11/63
Niger/Dahomey	I	Dahomey	22/12/63	04/01/64
	I	Niger	21/12/63	04/01/64
Kenya/Somalia	I	Kenya	13/11/63	04/03/64
Cyprus I	I	Cyprus	06/12/63	10/08/64
	I	Greece	06/12/63	27/03/64
	I	Turkey	30/11/63	29/12/63
	I	Turkey	04/08/64	10/08/64
	I	Greece	07/08/64	10/08/64
	I	Turkey	27/05/64	05/06/64
Ogaden I	I	Ethiopia	07/02/64	30/03/64
	I	Somalia	08/02/64	30/03/64
Congo II	S	Belgium	26/09/64	29/11/64
	S	Congo	04/08/64	30/12/64
Rann of Kutch	I	India	08/04/65	30/06/65
	I	Pakistan	08/04/65	30/06/65
Rhodesia's UDI	S	Zambia	05/11/65	27/04/66
Guinea Regime	S	Guinea	09/10/65	*/12/65

TABLE 10.1 *Continued*

International Crisis[a]	Ethnic Aspect: Secessionist (S), Irredentist (1)	Crisis Actor	Trigger Date[b]	Termination Date
Cyprus II	I	Cyprus	17/11/67	04/12/67
	I	Greece	17/11/67	01/12/67
	I	Turkey	15/11/67	01/12/67
Shatt-al-Arab II	I	Iraq	19/04/69	30/10/69
	I	Iran	15/04/69	30/10/69
Portuguese-Guinea	S	Guinea	22/11/70	11/12/70
Chad-Libya I	I	Libya	24/05/71	17/04/72
	I	Chad	27/08/71	28/08/71
Iraq Invasion - Kuwait	I	Kuwait	20/03/73	08/06/73
S. Yemen/Oman	S	Oman	18/11/73	11/03/76
Cyprus III	I	Greece	20/07/74	24/02/75
Moroccan March	S	Spain	16/10/75	14/11/75
	S	Morocco	02/11/75	14/11/75
East Timor	S	Indonesia	28/11/75	17/07/76
Lebanon Civil War I	S	Syria	18/01/76	30/09/76
Uganda Claims	I	Kenya	15/02/76	24/02/76
Aegean Sea	I	Greece	07/08/76	25/09/76
Shaba I	S	Zaire	08/03/77	26/05/77
	S	Angola	08/03/77	25/05/77
Lebanon Civil War II	S	Syria	07/02/78	20/02/78
Shaba II	S	Belgium	14/05/78	22/05/78
Raids on SWAPO	S	Angola	06/03/79	28/03/79
Onset Iran-Iraq War	I	Iran	17/09/80	*/11/80
E. Africa Confrontation	I	Somalia	05/12/80	29/06/81
Peru/Ecuador	I	Ecuador	22/01/81	02/02/81
Lebanon War	S	Lebanon	05/06/82	17/05/83
	S	Syria	07/06/82	01/09/82
	S	Israel	09/06/82	01/09/82
Ogaden III	I	Somalia	30/06/82	*/08/82
Threat to Sudan	I	Sudan	11/02/83	22/02/83
	I	Egypt	11/02/83	22/02/83
	I	Libya	17/02/83	22/02/83

continued

TABLE 10.1 *Continued*

International Crisis[a]	Ethnic Aspect: Secessionist (S), Irredentist (1)	Crisis Actor	Trigger Date[b]	Termination Date
Sudan/Ethiopia	I	Sudan	20/11/83	20/02/84
Chad/Libya VII	I	Chad	10/02/86	*/05/86
	I	Libya	16/02/86	*/05/86
Rebel Attack-Uganda	S	Uganda	19/08/86	20/09/86
Chad/Libya VIII	I	Chad	12/12/86	11/09/87
	I	Libya	02/01/87	11/09/87
Punjab War Scare II	I	India	15/01/87	19/02/87
	I	Pakistan	23/01/87	19/02/87
Somalia-Ethiopia	I	Somalia	12/02/87	*/04/87
Western Sahara	I	Morocco	25/02/87	*/*/*
	I	Algeria	16/04/87	04/05/87
	I	Mauritania	16/04/87	04/05/87
Nigeria-Cameroun	I	Nigeria	02/05/87	26/09/87
India Intervention-	S	India	03/06/87	30/07/87
Sri Lanka	S	Sri Lanka	04/06/87	30/07/87

Sources: Brecher and Wilkenfeld et al. 1988; Wilkenfeld and Brecher et al. 1988.
Notes: Total no. of crises = 112, excluding intrawar crises.
  * = Exact date unknown.

Operationalizing the Variables

In this study we rely on ordinal measures designed to capture both the breadth and depth of institutionalization. *Institutional constraint* measures the extent to which the political system enables the masses to influence political elites. That process can occur in multiple ways; therefore, more than one indicator is used. Data for the political system of each individual state are taken from Polity II, assembled by Gurr, Jaggers, and Moore (1989; see also Gurr 1990). The cases correspond to "polities," defined as the basic political arrangements by which national communities govern their affairs (Gurr 1974, 1990). A polity persists as long as there are no significant changes in these traits.

We assign each crisis actor the value for a variable that it had at the time of the crisis. In the event of a change in polity between onset and termination, we coded the case for the polity prior to (or at the onset of) the crisis. Others have used the mean of the onset and termination values for this variable (Maoz and Abdolali 1989). Although that is also a legitimate strategy, we are concerned primarily with the behavior of polities during a crisis, so values at the onset are most relevant. Since three scores are being used in some cases, a small error in one of the variables should have little or no effect on overall measurement. In some instances a polity change or interruption took place (that is, codes 88, 77, 66 in Polity II), and in those cases we use the value that most closely approximated the polity at the onset of the crisis. In other instances, data are not available due to lack of recognition for a state (Cyprus I) or other reasons (Dahomey). In these cases we obtained information from other sources, including Brecher and Wilkenfeld et al. (1988) and Wilkenfeld and Brecher et al. (1988).

Each variable directly measures differences in political constraint. *Degree of decisional constraints* is designed to measure the independence of executive authority. *Executive constraint* appears as XCONST in the Polity II data set. Each category of constraint appears in the data set with an example: (1) unlimited authority—no regular limitations on the executive's actions (Dahomey, 1963); (2) intermediate category (Syria, 1967); (3) slight to moderate limitations on executive authority—some real but limited restraints on the executive (Indonesia, 1963); (4) intermediate category (Pakistan, 1951); (5) substantial limitations on executive authority—the executive has more effective authority than any accountability group but is subject to substantial constraints (Mauritania, 1962); (6) intermediate category (Cyprus, 1974); and (7) executive parity or subordination—accountability groups have effective authority equal to or greater than the executive in most areas of activity (United Kingdom, 1961).

Regulation of the chief executive is designed to measure executive recruitment. *Executive regulation* appears as XPREG in the Polity II data set. Each category appears with an example: (1) unregulated—changes in executive occur though forceful seizures of power (Yemen, 1962); (2) designational/transitional—chief executives are chosen by designation within the political elite, without formal competition (i.e., one-party systems or rigged multiparty systems) (Indonesia, 1962); and (3) regulated—chief executives are determined by hereditary succession (Saudi Arabia, 1966) or competitive elections (India, 1971).

Regulation of participation is designed to measure the extent of political competition and opposition. Participation regulation (PARREG in Polity II) includes the following categories: (1) unregulated participation—political participation is fluid and there are no enduring national political organizations (Pakistan, 1956); (2) factional or transitional—relatively stable and enduring political groups compete for political influence at the national level (Bangladesh, 1971); (3) factional/restricted—polities that oscillate more or less regularly between intense factionalism and restriction (Turkey, 1974); (4) restricted—some organized political participation without intense factionalism, but significant groups, issues, or types of conventional participation are regularly excluded from the political process (Sudan, 1983); and (5) regulated—

relatively stable and enduring political groups regularly compete for political influence and positions with little use of coercion (India, 1981).

Regime type and political constraints are *not* synonymous. For example, the pre-1989 Soviet Union would score high on at least two of the variables measuring constraints on executives (executive regulation and regulation of participation), but the regime was clearly not a democracy. Similarly, an autocratic regime characterized by familial executive selection shows higher levels of constraint than the concept *authoritarian* would imply. Thus the three variables tap into institutional and political constraints in a different way than does a dichotomous treatment by regime type. External validation, using the ICB variable for regime type, produces a measure of association of 0.60 with executive constraint.

We have combined these three indicators to create an index of political constraint (P). A fifteen-point ordinal scale provides an overall measurement of political constraint, divided at the median to give each actor a score of either 1 (low) or 2 (high) constraint.

We constructed an index that measures the ethnic composition of a state to tap the demographic and ethnic characteristics of each crisis actor. Variations in ethnic composition, in conjunction with institutional constraints, are associated with differences in behavior between states in ethnic conflict settings. In operational terms, the relationship between institutional constraints and interstate conflict is contingent on ethnic composition. Under this definition, a contingency factor is *not* a mediator or covariate. Ethnic composition does not mediate the relationship between domestic political constraints and foreign policy preferences; it moderates that relationship (Babbie 1979). The preference for a certain kind of ethnic foreign policy is a result of the interactive effects of ethnic composition and institutional constraints.

A state can contain a number of ethnic groups and also exhibit the characteristics of cleavage (India). Similarly, some states may feature only a few ethnic groups but divisions may be fractionalized (Sri Lanka). Here, we intend to tap into these two constructs separately. Whether diverse or homogeneous, a state's ethnic composition is not the same as its level of cleavage, though they may be related. Composition is a structural characteristic of a state. Thus the index of ethnic composition measures the diversity of ethnic groups in terms of the size of each group within a state, compared to the total population of the state.

The categories for ethnic composition are: (1) dominant—a homogenous state characterized by the dominance of a single ethnic group (e.g., Japan, Iceland, Sweden, Poland, or Kuwait); (2) moderate-dominant—a relatively homogeneous state characterized by the dominance of one ethnic group along with one or more small minorities with less than 10 percent of the total population (Libya); (3) moderate—a state characterized by the balancing of a large group against slightly smaller groups totaling less than 20 percent of the population (Sri Lanka); (4) moderate-diverse—a state characterized by the balancing of one or more large groups against several slightly smaller groups that together exceed 20 percent of the population (Zaire); and (5) diverse—a heterogenous, ethnically mixed state in which no ethnic group is numerically dominant and in which there are multiple linguistic and religious divisions. This occurs when many groups of relatively equal size are balanced against one another (Uganda).

The critical features of an ethnic group are that it is ascriptive and exclusive: its continuity depends on the maintenance of a boundary based on values and identity (Barth 1969, 14). We identify each ethnic group within a state on the basis of the following criteria: (1) race, (2) kinship, (3) religion, (4) language, (5) customary mode of livelihood, and (6) regionalism (Rothschild 1981, 86–87; Carment and James 1994a). Singular measures designed to tap ethno-linguistic or religious heterogeneity have been developed by Taylor and Jodice (1983), Banks and Texter (1963), Haug (1967), Grove (1974), Neilsson (1985), Gurr (1992), and Hill and Rothchild (1992). However, for the purposes of this chapter, there are two components: ethno-linguistic (consisting of criteria 1, 2, 4, 5, and 6) and religious groups (criterion 3).

Measuring diversity by simply counting the number of ethnic groups entails one deficiency: It does not reveal the relative size of each ethnic group. If raw measurements of ethnic diversity were to be used, it might be assumed (erroneously) that states with the same number of groups have the same degree of ethnic diversity. More precisely, a state with four ethnic groups of the same size possesses greater diversity than a state with one dominant ethnic group and three smaller ones (Shih 1991). For example, if the proportions of the groups in state A are .25, .25, .25 and .25, and in state B they are .05, .05, .05, and .85, the latter should score lower on a scale of diversity. If these two different types of diversity are to be distinguished, both the number of ethnic groups and their size must be counted (Shih 1991).

We measure diversity by combining the formulae for diversity (D) developed by Shih (1991) and Taylor and Hudson (1972): $D = (D_1 + D_2)/2$. D_1 is the measurement for religious groups:

$$(1) \quad D_1 = 1 - \sum_{i=1-3}^{n} \frac{ni^2}{N^2}$$

where
n_i = size of the ith religious group.
N = total population of the state.

D_2 assesses ethno-linguistic fractionalization (see Taylor and Hudson 1972; Taylor and Jodice 1983, 72; CIA 1990, 1991, 1992):

$$(2) \quad D_2 = 1 - \sum_{i=1}^{n} \frac{(ni)}{N} \times \frac{(ni-1)}{(N-1)}$$

where

N = total population of the state.

n_i = size of its ith ethno-linguistic group.

Additional data are drawn from Shih (1991), Barret (1982), and Taylor and Hudson (1972).

We then created an interval score for each state and cross-referenced it with scores developed by Shih (1991). We adopted this procedure to account for cases that appear to lack face validity or pose an operational dilemma. For example, Somalia has many kin-based ethnic groups at the domestic level, but in terms of the components provided, it looks very homogeneous. We code Somalia as an ethnically dominant state (1), which corresponds with Shih (1991).

We then converted the interval data into ordinal data. There are two reasons for this procedure. First, developments in population occur much more slowly than polity changes. Shih (1991), among others, demonstrates empirically that relative changes are fairly balanced, and that therefore a state's ethnic composition in 1970 will be similar to its ethnic composition in 1990, for example. Second, it is very possible that some ethnic groups undergo slower or more rapid change relative to others and to the total population of the state. Interval data, because of their precision, are useful only for making comparisons over a specific period (Babbie 1979). For the purposes of this study, relative population changes apply only to those states that have been crisis actors over the period in question (United States, United Kingdom, Soviet Union, France, Turkey, and Iran), because demographic changes in these states have not altered rankings on an ordinal scale of ethnic composition.

To create the four "ideal" types of state (figure 10.1), we combine the indices for institutional constraint and diversity in the following way. If P is 1 and D is less than or equal to 3, then the state is coded as I_a. If P is 1 and D is greater than or equal to 4, then the state is coded as I_b. If P is 2 and D is less than or equal to 3, then the coding is II_a. Finally, if P is 2 and D is greater than or equal to 4, then that state is coded as II_b.

Internal ethnic cleavage and affinities increase the possibility of the outbreak of conflict between states by creating the perception of a security dilemma. Elites may act to bolster their support at home or they may be pressured to act by other elites and by their ethnic constituencies. We argue that ethnic affinity and cleavage are *mediators* or *covariates* because they influence foreign policy choices leading to interstate ethnic conflict.

Recall that the index of composition, D, does not take into account the degree of perceived difference among ethnic groups. Measurements of cleavage, however, build in this important element. For example, Gastil devised ordinal scales to measure the national consciousness, political inequality, and individual repression of ethnic groups throughout the world (1979). Similarly, Terrel (1971) created an index of social cleavage, and Hill (1978) an index of ethno-linguistic fragmentation. All these studies were designed to tap the phenomenon of linguistic and cultural heterogeneity and the degree to which groups consider themselves to be a single people. In other words, an index of cleavage is different from an index of composition to the extent that it measures a sociopolitical structural characteristic including national consciousness, rather than an internal demographic characteristic. The underlying idea is that the higher the degree of ethnic consciousness, the greater the possibility of internal ethnic cleavage (Rosh 1987). As the degree of repression directed toward these minority groups increases, the degree of ethnic cleavage also increases (Gurr 1992). Conceivably the variable also taps into the intensity of potential separatism. For example, Neilsson and Jones (1988) provide a list of ethnic groups according to the degree of mobilization: unmobilized, latent, early phase of political mobilization, mobilized as insurgent movements, and mobilized as political movements.

The index is an ordinal scale in which low levels of cleavage reflect relative harmony between ethnic groups and high levels mean open conflict, repression, and ethnic consciousness (see also Hill and Rothchild 1992).

Rosh (1987) develops an index of ethnic cleavage on the basis of data from Gastil (1978) for states with more than two ethnic groups. The categories of ethnic cleavage and examples are as follows: (1) no cleavage—low or no ethnic minority consciousness, ethnic political inequality, and individual repression (Guinea); (2) low cleavage—individual repression, ethnic inequality, and minority consciousness occur only among a few small groups (France); (3) moderate cleavage—repression, inequalities and ethnic consciousness in evidence, occasional societal unrest and politicized ethnic rivalries likely (Tanzania); (4) moderate-high cleavage—high levels of repression and ethnic consciousness against more than one minority, occasional societal unrest leading to interethnic violence (Iraq); and (5) high cleavage—mass violence likely, repression widespread, ethnicity is highly politicized, interethnic struggle leading to collapse of state imminent (Sri Lanka).

Gastil assesses the minorities within each state for three dimensions, each measured on a ten-point scale: ethnic consciousness, political inequality, and individual repression. He first devises a weighted average of the individual measurements of ethnic minority consciousness, political inequality, and individual repression for each ethnic group within a state. The weighted average for each minority is obtained from the group's size relative to the total population. Weights are assigned on the basis of the percentage of the total population that each individual group constitutes. For example, a state with an ethnic group making up 40 percent of the population but scoring 10 on the individual repression scale would be assigned a score of 12, based on the weighting scheme from Rosh (1987). Similar weighting procedures are carried out for all the ethnic groups in each state for the other two dimensions. For example, Sri Lanka scores high on the cleavage scale (5) even though it has only three main ethnic groups. According to Gastil, this is because the Tamils, about 20 percent of Sri Lanka's population, score very high on the composite scale.

Gastil then devises a composite index for each state by adding together the interval scores for national consciousness, political inequality, and individual repression. This index ranges in value from 10 to 35 (Gastil 1979). Since the index developed by Rosh accounts for only forty of the states in the data set, we have developed similar indices for the remaining states by using information provided in Gastil (1979) and Shih (1991). For ease of comparability with the other measurements in the data set, we have converted the interval data to a rank order from 1 to 5.

To ensure validity of the ordinal measurement over time (since consciousness and repression vary within a given state), we link each ordinal score for cleavage to a combination of three ICB variables: mass violence, social unrest, and government repression. These variables specify whether significant forms of behavior are at low, normal or high levels within a state during a crisis. If a state experienced higher than normal levels of unrest, mass violence *and* regime repression, then the score is increased by one point to a maximum of 5.

In brief, a cleavage score of 3, for example, could be increased to 4 if all three ICB measurements are higher than normal, but no score could exceed the maximum of 5. By taking into account levels of turmoil within a society during a crisis, we develop a more accurate measurement of cleavage in a state. Finally, to ensure that the measurement is valid, we carried out a correlational analysis for a random sample of states (N = 30) with variables developed by Gurr (1992). These variables measure political and economic discrimination against ethnic minorities. Cross-indexing—an external validation procedure—showed 75 percent agreement in coding, which provides support for the index.

We have argued that the greater the number of affinities (linguistic, tribal, and religious, for example) between an ethnic group in two or more states, the stronger the proposed linkage. The more linguistic, religious, and tribal identities converge, the greater the potential transnational ethnic affinity and thus the greater potential that an ethnic group will seek external support on the basis of such connections. Elites on both sides within the state (state-center or minority group) will use the linkages to their advantage and may perceive that their state's insecurity stems from these affinities. In some cases, elites may be carried along by the fervor of mass ethnic sentiment entailed by these links (Chazan 1991). Somalia, for example, has a low level of affinity with its neighboring states because the majority of its ethnic group resides in Somalia itself. Thus Somalia approximates a "nation-state." Ethiopia, by contrast, is characterized by higher levels of affinity because many of its ethnic groups are dispersed among neighboring states (including the Somalis of the Ogaden).

Anderson et al. (1967), Gastil (1979), and Neilsson (1985) developed measurements for separated ethnic groups. For example, Anderson's analysis of irredentism identifies the location and number of ethnic groups relative to the state making the irredentist claim. Neilsson places 614 political units in five categories, according to how ethnic groups are dispersed. States with dispersed ethnic groups sharing several common characteristics (language and religion, for example) are said to be high on the affinity scale (Lebanon). Those with a small number of dispersed ethnic groups sharing few characteristics are lower (Japan). Categories of ethnic affinity and examples are as follows: (0) none— no (or very low levels of) ethnic dispersion among states (Japan); (1) low dispersal—a small number of the majority ethnic group are dispersed among a few states but the majority reside in a single state (Albania); (2) moderate dispersal—a state that is composed of ethnic groups not dispersed among other states and other ethnic groups dispersed among a few states (Ivory Coast); (3) moderate-high dispersal—a state in which the majority is dispersed among a few states and the minority ethnic groups are dispersed among many states (Malaysia); and (4) high dispersal—a state where all ethnic groups are dispersed among many states (Lebanon).

The Neilsson typology covers the range of states in this analysis. We use it to create affinity as a variable. To ensure validity, we cross-indexed the affinity variable with the variable concerning segments from the Minorities at Risk Project. This variable is designed to measure the number of adjoining countries in which there are other segments of an ethnic group. It is also measured on a five-point scale: (0) no adjoining countries, (1) one adjoining country; (2) two adjoining countries; (3) three adjoining countries; and (4) four or more adjoining countries. This cross-indexing procedure, based on a random sample of thirty cases, provides 65 percent agreement, meaning that states characterized by high or low levels of affinity generally had commensurate levels of ethnic group segmentation. It should be acknowledged that the number of borders might have an independent effect that cannot be distinguished on the basis of this measurement.

We selected two dependent variables for testing H_1. The first is *crisis management technique,* which refers to the most intense method used by an actor, along a scale from pacific techniques to violence. The variable is dichotomous:

nonviolent versus violent management. We combined the original ICB categories in the following manner: Nonviolent management includes (1) military nonviolent behavior; (2) negotiation; (3) adjudication; (4) mediation; (5) nonmilitary pressure; and (6) multiple nonviolence. Violent management includes (1) military violence and (2) multiple including violence.

The second dependent variable, *severity of violence* (for crises in which violence was used as a primary crisis management technique), identifies the level of violence as a primary crisis technique by any of the actors. This variable is also dichotomous: no violence or low violence versus serious clashes and warfare.

For the purposes of testing H_2, protracted conflict as a variable refers to crises that occur within, versus outside, such settings. Finally, our testing of H_3 focuses on inclusion of cleavage and affinity. For testing purposes, these variables are dichotomized as close as possible to the median.

The Findings

In our data analysis, we probed for differences among Types I_a through II_b with respect to crisis management techniques, severity of violence, and protracted conflict. For the purposes of testing, we excluded all the Intra-War Crises (N = 68) identified by the ICB project from the analysis. These cases, such as the 1973 October War and the 1967 Six-Day War, could enhance artificially the results related to violence. We excluded the following crisis actors from the analysis because each is considered to be a nonethnic actor within any given crisis: France, UK, the United States, and the USSR.

Measurements of association are provided in each table. When one works with a population of cases, characteristics do not need to be inferred (as they would be from a sample). In particular, Buchanan (1988, 188–89) notes Gamma > 0.2 and Somers' d > 0.1 as the commonly accepted thresholds for inferring a relationship.

The percentage of each type of actor using force as a crisis management technique is given in table 10.2. Conflicts leading to negotiation are not included, but their results can be inferred on the basis of the percentages. Likewise, the results for the control variables include only the high measurement categories in each instance. The relationship in this case is the reverse of that hypothesized. For example, there is a difference of 12 percent between the two extremes, but rather than reducing the propensity for using force as a crisis management technique, high diversity and institutional constraint appear to *increase* it. Inclusion of the two mediating variables (cleavage and affinity respectively) appears to strengthen the results for all types of states, especially for those more constrained (II_a and II_b), as anticipated. The results suggest a more complex relationship than hypothesized. On the basis of these preliminary results, there is no support for H_1. However, H_3—the expectation of a hierarchy of differences from I_a to II_b based on affinities and cleavage—fares somewhat better.

Why is the relationship shown in table 10.2 reversed from that hypothesized? One possible answer is that highly diverse and institutionally constrained states respond in kind. In other words, these states will use force depending on the kinds of states with which they interact. Making room for cooperation is an interactive process. Thus the use of force by ethnically diverse and constrained states is contingent on the strategy of the other state. Thus, for example, if a state of Type II_b provides support for a secessionist movement in another state, whether the former uses force to achieve this goal will depend

TABLE 10.2 States Using Force as a Crisis Management Technique (in percent)

Crisis Management Technique	I_a	I_b	II_a	II_b	Total
Force[a]					
(N = 112)	43	58	61	55	53
	(17)	(11)	(20)	(11)	(59)
Use of force by states with high ethnic cleavage[b]					
(N = 71)	50	53	67	59	56
	(11)	(9)	(10)	(10)	(40)
Use of force by states with high ethnic affinity[c]					
(N = 66)	35	50	70	64	53
	(8)	(6)	(14)	(7)	(35)

Key:
Type I_a = low constraint–ethnically dominant states.
Type I_b = low constraint–diverse states.
Type II_a = high constraint–dominant states.
Type II_b = high constraint–diverse states.

Sources: Table 10.2–10.4 are based on Gurr, Jaggers, and Moore 1989; see also Gurr 1990, Brecher and Wilkenfeld et al. 1988; Wilkenfeld and Brecher et al. 1988.

Notes: Statistics for each row in table 10.2–10.4 are based on the 2*4 (first row) and 2*4*2 (second and third rows) tables in which the cases appear. Figures represent percentages and frequencies, respectively: for example, 43% (or 17) of the Type I_a states used force in response to a crisis. We excluded all the intrawar crises (N = 68) identified by the ICB project from the analysis.
    a. Gamma -.18; Tau b -.11; Somers' d -.11.
    b. Gamma -.14; Tau b -.08; Somers' d -.08.
    c. Gamma -.40; Tau b -.25; Somers' d -.24.

TABLE 10.3 States Involved in War or Major Clashes
(in percent)

Severity of Violence	I_a	I_b	II_a	II_b	Total
War or major clashes [a]	43	21	18	25	29
(N = 112)	(17)	(4)	(6)	(5)	(32)
War or major clashes for states with high ethnic cleavage [b]	46	24	20	24	30
(N = 71)	(10)	(4)	(20)	(4)	(21)
War or major clashes for states with high ethnic affinity [c]	48	25	10	27	29
(N = 66)	(11)	(3)	(2)	(3)	(19)

Note: See table 10.2, note.
  a. Gamma .31; Tau b .17; Somers' d .17.
  b. Gamma .31; Tau b .18; Somers' d .17.
  c. Gamma .42; Tau b .24; Somers' d .23.

TABLE 10.4 States in Protracted Conflicts
(in percent)

Severity of Violence	I_a	I_b	II_a	II_b	Total
Protracted conflict [a]					
(N = 112)	68	26	58	30	51
	(27)	(5)	(19)	(6)	(57)
Protracted conflict for states with high ethnic cleavage [b]					
(N = 71)	72	29	87	29	55
	(16)	(5)	(13)	(5)	(32)
Protracted conflict for states with high ethnic affinity [c]					
(N = 66)	52	33	65	46	52
	(12)	(4)	(13)	(5)	(34)

Note: See table 10.2, note.
  a. Gamma .31; Tau b .19; Somers' d .19.
  b. Gamma .28; Tau b .18; Somers' d .18.
  c. Gamma .05; Tau b .03; Somers' d .03.

on how the latter responds, which in turn depends on its internal characteristics. Of course, if force is not used, these states can be expected to find alternative means to achieve foreign policy objectives that address the source of their insecurity.

The findings presented in table 10.3 confirm H_1. All measures of association are in the anticipated direction. In this instance, Type I_a states are more likely than any other type of state to become involved in ethnic strife leading to war or major clashes (an increase of almost 20 percent in comparison to II_b). The inclusion of high affinity appears to have only a modest impact on the original relationship. All results show strong measurements of association.

Table 10.4 presents the results for protracted conflict, which support H_2. As predicted, Type I_a states are most susceptible to involvement in such conflicts, especially when compared to the highly diverse states (I_b and II_b), but less so when compared to their politically constrained counterparts (II_a). The inclusion of high affinities and high cleavage appears to enhance the potential for involvement in protracted conflict for all states, especially those that are institutionally constrained. On the basis of these preliminary results, H_3 finds general support.

Conclusions

Judging from the mixed results, we would be presumptuous to offer any kind of general conclusion at this stage. More intricate analyses of the variables and their interaction effects must be made before moving on to any recommendations about policy. However, some preliminary observations, which build on the principles of state interaction, can be made on the basis of the model and testing thus far:

1. While strengthening decision makers at home, institutional arrangements can combine with multiethnic constituencies to weaken a state's international position.

2. Transnational ethnic affinities, cleavage, and outbidding have reverberations within the domestic arena.

3. High levels of cleavage and affinity provide opportunities for intervening states.

4. The interests of institutionally constrained and unconstrained elites diverge in ethnically diverse and dominant settings.

5. Elites facing dual constraints are likely to be more cautious in confrontations with other states.

Some of the evidence indicates that internal diversity, in combination with institutional constraints, could reduce overt interstate ethnic conflict in certain instances. Both conditions lead to mutual vulnerability among states, so the potential for belligerence is diminished. Furthermore, the concentration of power among elites is reduced, meaning that direct involvement in secessionist and irredentist strife will be less appealing. Associated with this conclusion, however, are several qualifications.

First, high cleavages and affinities appear to *magnify* differences in tensions by an appreciable degree. The evidence suggests that interstate conflicts with high affinities or cleavages may be by far the least manageable. When transnational affinities become salient, multiple cross-border connections between ethnic groups can make conflict resolution a very complicated task.

Second, both affinities and cleavages have the potential to drag states into conflict by providing additional opportunities to act. The problem becomes more acute when there are many states with strong ethnic affinities. As a consequence, institutionally constrained states may pursue more covert means to achieve their goals. Consider, for example, the dissolution of the Soviet Union, which transformed the 25 million ethnic Russians living outside the Russian Federation into a new diaspora. This situation represents a potential threat to stability *among and within* the Soviet successor states. Right-wing political groups in Russia pose as defenders of the national rights of the diaspora and may pressure the Russian government to act on these linkages (Kolsto 1993).

Third, ethnic diversity does not mean that conflicts involving these states will be more easily resolved; rather, conflict reduction is a more practical goal. The implication is that, while politically astute at the domestic level, ethnically dominant societies with redistributive policies stand a greater chance of becoming involved in interstate ethnic conflict (Moynihan 1993). International instruments, including preventive peacekeeping, should be developed to anticipate and deter potential interstate ethnic conflicts promulgated by these states.

A fourth and related issue is the management of political transition (Huntington 1991). The Yugoslavian case indicates that states undergoing political transition are most susceptible to overt conflict. The priority here is to encourage alignments based on interests other than ethnicity and reduce disparities between groups so that dissatisfaction declines. However, for a new state, a multiethnic character, compounded by internal cleavage and transnational affinities, may overwhelm fragile institutions. When political parties reflect ethnic interests, diverse and institutionally constrained developing states are prone to outbidding. This can enhance the potential for interstate conflict. On other occasions, new states experience levels of domestic disorder that divide the elites, which complicates decision making and prolongs the crisis or plunges the country into protracted conflict that encourages external intervention.

There are at least four areas in which the model could be developed further. First, it is possible that using a state's ethnic composition as an indicator of the link between elites and masses may be too indirect. Variables that measure the direct relationship of an elite to its political constituency should be derived. For example, in some instances, elites represent a dominant ethnic group that is highly divided between two or more constituencies. This relationship will affect the political process, especially if institutional constraints are high and ethnicity is *the* basis for political mobilization. Second, it might be useful to measure interactions between elite and mass preferences. For example, in some societies, cross-cutting cleavages are important in counteracting the effects of internal division. In these societies, ethnicity may be less of a basis for political mobilization, and hence, an ethnically based foreign policy becomes less likely. It might be possible to measure, perhaps through surveys, differences between elite and mass preferences. If feasible, such measures would determine whether there is a convergence on certain foreign policy issues. Third, affinity and cleavage appear to have important explanatory power in their own right. For example, the impact of these variables on the propensity for violent interstate ethnic conflict could be tested. These variables could be treated as structural conditions that presumably influence a state's security dilemma and behavior. Fourth, one might focus on where the model is most incomplete, that is, on determining the impact of ethnic conflict on the international system. The concern so far is primarily with the impact of certain variables on interstate ethnic conflicts. Comparing the cases selected for this study with nonethnic crises would provide additional insights with regard to basic differences between types of interstate conflict.

Preventing and Resolving Destructive Communal Conflicts

Louis Kriesberg

Interest in early warning systems and preventive diplomacy is currently very high. It might appear that if governments, international government and nongovernment organizations, and private citizens could only know in advance which conflicts will destructively escalate, they would act effectively to prevent that development. Actually, that is not likely for at least three reasons. First, it is difficult to mobilize support for costly action unless the consequences of inaction are obviously appalling. Second, often it is not evident what early action would be effective. Third, it is likely that little credit would be earned even if effective action were undertaken, since the claims of success would probably not be recognized.

As a means for overcoming these difficulties, I discuss a variety of policies that may prevent communal conflicts from deteriorating, many of which have been effectively used. Noting successes, not just failures, may embolden a variety of actors to attempt early preventive actions and to do so effectively. Success does not mean achieving utopian perfection, but rather averting or limiting what might otherwise be highly destructive and intractable struggles.

I examine communal conflicts, based on ethnic, religious, linguistic, and regional differences. The term "communal" refers to identities shared by people who believe they are or who actually are treated as if they were members of a nationality, ethnicity, religious community, or even locality (Agnew 1989; Anderson 1991; Horowitz 1985; Thompson 1990; Smith 1971; Connor 1994).

These identities are often acquired at birth, ascribed by others, and not to be denied. Some identities, however, are acquired by choice and actions later in life. Furthermore, there are possible discrepancies between self-identities and the identities others try to impose. Consequently, identities are generally negotiated by individuals and collectivities, and by persons who do and do not share them. These communal identities, even ethnic ones, do not have a fixed primordial character (Comaroff 1991; Gordon 1978; Brass 1991). It is true that, growing up in a family, each person is socialized to form some communal identities; but that identity is socially constructed. Moreover, everyone is socialized into several identities, often including a family, a kinship group or clan, a particular language, a religion, a social class, as well as a specific country and locality. These multiple identities, insofar as they do not coincide, inhibit conflict escalation and foster reconciliation when the fighting ends.

As used here, the term "communal conflict" is not limited to contending communal groups within a single country. Since the existence of a particular state may be one of the issues in contention, the term includes conflicts between states representing to a significant degree different communal identities, *and* conflicts between a state and a communally based social movement organization struggling to become a state or striving for greater autonomy.

Mass media, official, and academic attention is most frequently given to conflicts when they erupt in violence. Relatively little attention is given to relationships that are peaceful or nonviolently contentious. Attention, however, should be given to such cases so that we might learn what prevented them from becoming bloody and protracted struggles, and so that they might serve as models for what human beings can and do achieve.

Even now, looking around the world, we see many candidates for large-scale violent struggles that are quiescent, are being managed, or are in the process of settlement and perhaps resolution. Although their circumstances are not wholly satisfactory to all parties, they are better than the continuing violence and horrors of some communal conflicts. I cite several current and recent historical cases of not so bad achievements: first, the Franco-German enmity went on for generations, but the policies instituted at the end of World War II resulted in a level of integration that makes war between Germany and France virtually unthinkable; second, the Russian and Ukrainian republics, despite fundamental issues about borders and the control of the elements of the Red Fleet stationed in the Crimea, are generally cooperative; third, in Spain, the people of Catalonia have reached a mutually acceptable accommodation with the central government; fourth, in Belgium, the peoples in the French-speaking (Wallonia) and Flemish-speaking regions have developed a mutually acceptable process of accommodation; fifth, in South Africa, despite dire predictions for decades of large-scale fighting between blacks and whites, a fundamental and largely nonviolent transition to majority rule was accomplished; sixth, in Canada, despite some violence years ago and the failure so far to reach a widely shared mutual accommodation between French-speaking Quebec and the rest of Canada, the disputants continue to seek a solution through the existing political system; seventh, Czechoslovakia peacefully separated into the Czech and Slovak Republics; eighth, in many countries, even with significant communal differences, conflicts are much more significantly grounded in class, ideology, or ties to particular leaders.

Since the term *conflict* refers to a wide range of phenomena, *prevention* also designates a wide range of actions. Typically, communal conflicts are eruptions of intense, direct, physical violence, but they may also be organized or unorganized resistance to the dominant group's discrimination, exploitation, indoctrination, or other kinds of felt oppression. Prevention, then, may mean avoiding eruptions of violence, or it may mean limiting it and preventing its escalation; but it may also mean reaching a settlement of the conflict or remedying the conditions underlying the possible eruption of violence.

Preventing violence, however, is not the only goal officials or citizens seek. For example, they often strive for justice or freedom for their own people. If violence avoidance were the only goal, it could be achieved at any time by one party's surrender or acquiescence to its oppression. Many conflicts are ended and the fighting stopped by the unilateral imposition of a settlement by one side, or even the annihilation or expulsion of a people. Consequently, the kind of relationship to which the conflict de-escalation contributes must also be considered.

In this chapter, I discuss the kinds of relations that communal groups have with each other. I also outline other conditions that affect the likelihood that one or another means of preventing destructive conflict escalation will be effective. I then map out possible policies to prevent destructive conflicts. Finally, I examine several cases.

Kinds of Communal Relations

At any given period, communal groups are living together in a relationship that is the result of past struggles and accommodations. Those relationships may be relatively stable, but more often are in contention and transition. For purposes of this paper, I will focus on two dimensions of the relationship: the degree of interdependence of the communal groups and the degree to which the form of the relationship is imposed by one of the groups (Shibutani and Kwan 1965; Nordlinger 1972; McGarry and O'Leary 1993). This focus will provide a basis for discussing the circumstances from which communal conflicts emerge and the conditions for an at least temporary settlement.

Communal relations vary in the degree to which communities are interdependent; interdependence may become so great that one of the parties is assimilated into the other or they merge together; or interdependence may be so minimal and indirect that one party is excluded by expulsion or genocide. Furthermore, some relationships are largely imposed by one party, others are facilitated or even imposed by external powers, while still others are the result of mutual accommodation and acceptance.

Table 11.1 presents the kinds of communal relations in terms of their degree of interdependence and degree of unilateral imposition. The distinctions between the categories are not rigid and many gradations exist—partly because communal groups are not monolithic and members pursue various strategies. Moreover, how the relations are seen to be shaped varies with the perspective adopted, since relations exist in various settings. For example, more than two peoples may be living in the same territory and that territory may be governed or dominated by still another people, as is the case under colonial rule or in empires. The dominating group may establish an overall structure, accepting or modifying the ranking among the subordinated groups, who had previously contended with each other. From the perspective of the ruling people, the relationship among the subordinated peoples may be regarded as of the subordinates' own making. From the perspective of the dominated groups, the structure of the relationship among them may seem to be externally imposed.

I give most attention in this chapter to ways of preventing destructive

TABLE 11.1 Intercommunal Relationships

Actions Shaping Interdependence	Integration	Coexistence	Separation
Unilateral imposition	Forced assimilation	Slavery; settlement reservations; apartheid; discrimination	Genocide; expulsion; secession; population transfer
Unilateral direction	Encouraged assimilation	Empire and indirect rule; autonomy; federation; discrimination	Encouraged migration
External imposition	Imperial rules	Protection of minority	Population transfer
External facilitation	Desegregation	Protection of human rights; power sharing	Border shift
Mutual accommodation	Voluntary assimilation; pluralism; mosaic	Power sharing; egalitarian federation; self-segregation; cantonization	Agreed-upon self-determination

conflicts that also promote relatively integrated relations between the communal groups. That is, the emphasis is on integration resulting from mutual accommodation. Imposed separations are understandably often viewed as immoral, since they are often accompanied by large-scale atrocities. Furthermore, they provide the basis for later efforts to redeem the losses and often to exact revenge.

The high frequency of unilaterally imposed outcomes must be recognized. Members of one community often have enforced their claims on another, denying the others' claims. This has often been done brutally, most notably by attempting genocide, or settling one community on land occupied by another people, or forcibly removing members of communities from where they once lived. For example, between 1939 and 1945, the Nazi German government transferred hundreds of thousands of Germans to areas incorporated into the expanded German Reich from areas of Eastern Europe where they had been living; it also moved Hungarians from Yugoslavia to Hungary; and within Yugoslavia, it removed Serbs from Croatia to Serbia. After World War II, immense numbers of many ethnic groups fled or were removed; for example, ethnic Germans were moved by the millions into the reduced territory that was now Germany. The Soviet government during Stalin's rule harshly transported many peoples from one region to another within the Soviet Union, while Russians moved into the areas from which the other peoples had been removed. The brutal treatment of ethnic groups related to these expulsions contributed to the recent dissolution of Yugoslavia and the former Soviet Union, and to the communal violence among and within some of the states arising from their ruins.

Such forced migrations have sometimes produced the separation of communal groups into discrete territories, but in other cases produced a forced integration, as when one community moved into territory long held by others and thereafter dominated them politically, economically, and socially through systems of discrimination. This occurred, for example, within states dominated by settlers who moved into the area, as in South Africa under apartheid.

Frequently, several communal groups have coexisted in the same political, social, and economic system under the dominating rule of one community or ruling group. In many of these systems the rule has been indirect, allowing considerable autonomy or even local political leadership to survive as long as taxes were paid and obedience was shown to the ruling emperor or king. This was the case, for example, in the Ottoman and the British empires.

Relations among the several subordinated communal groups within such systems may be hierarchical or involve discrimination against some communities and favoritism toward others. Ruling groups have often been viewed as playing one community against the other to maintain their rule; sometimes they have given particular opportunities in the military or educational system to a minority group, which was then greatly dependent on the rulers of the empire. When colonial rule ended, the minorities became vulnerable and were sometimes subjected to repression by the majority people.

Members of a subordinated community may respond in different ways to their position. Some members may seek assimilation within the dominant group, others may seek collective autonomy elsewhere, yet others may seek to transform the system so that communal differences become irrelevant, and still others may individually seek to escape by emigrating. For example, during the last century of tsarist rule of the Russian empire, many Jews took various routes to counter the anti-Semitism they suffered: some strove to assimilate and be Russian, some became Zionists and strove to establish a national homeland in Palestine, some joined socialist and communist parties to change the Russia system, and some emigrated to the United States or other countries of refuge.

External actors often try to intervene and establish new arrangements that structure intercommunal relations. This was done massively after World War I, when the victors established new borders in Europe. To some extent, the borders were drawn along ethnic territorial lines, as the Austrian-Hungarian, Ottoman, and Russian empires were broken up or reduced. But ethnic lines could not be clearly drawn. In some cases, large-scale population transfers were executed to bring ethnicity into better correspondence with the newly drawn state borders, for example, between Greece and Turkey. In other cases, new multiethnic states were created, as was the case for Yugoslavia and Czechoslovakia.

Finally, communal groups themselves sometimes reach an agreement about their relationship that reflects their acceptance of each other. These arrangements may involve separation in the form of independent states as, for example, with the independence of Norway from Sweden in 1905. Or, they may entail cooperation for particular purposes, as, for example, with French-German relations in the European Coal and Steel Community. They may also take the form of amalgamated political unions, but with institutionalized power sharing among the communal groups in the polity, or communal cantonization, or egalitarian federation with considerable regional autonomy (note the political structures in Switzerland, Belgium, and Spain, for example). Mutual understandings may be less formally structured and may allow for a high degree of integration, characterized by mutual acceptance of communal differences without discrimination; this is generally true of European ethnic groups in the United States.

Conditions Affecting Resolutions

Specific conditions set the parameters for establishing one kind of communal relationship rather than another. In order to determine which policies might be employed to reach desired outcomes, we must recognize the basic conditions that shape the course and outcomes of communal conflicts. Three sets of conditions merit notice: those pertaining to features of each communal group, those pertaining to the relationship between communal groups, and those pertaining to the context in which they are related.

Internal Features of Communal Groups

An important feature of a communal group that affects its relations with others is the extent to which membership in the group tends to be ambiguous and open or clearly bounded and ascriptively closed. That is, some groups allow or even welcome entry, for example by assimilation, conversion, or some other process. Other groups set up firm, impervious categories, where membership is determined unalterably at birth. Membership determined at birth is ascriptive, and includes kinship and to varying degrees ethnicity and "race" (Parsons 1951). Of course, the ascribed groups, including racial groups, are social constructs. In many societies, people select some genetically related characteristics to distinguish one "race" from another. But all individuals cannot be unambiguously placed in one or another "racial" category. Social, cultural, and other features are used to help locate people, and the categories vary from culture to culture and over time (Winant 1994; Gregory and Sanjek 1994). For example, in the United States, a clear social distinction is made between whites (primarily of European origin) and blacks (anyone raised in the United States who has some African ancestry). However, in many other countries, clear dichotomous lines are not drawn; rather, many mixtures are recognized but are not treated as fixed and absolute; for example, in Mexico, "mestizo" is a broad, vague category and persons can be more or less "mestizo" or "Indian," depending on the clothes they wear and the language they speak.

The nature of the beliefs held by various members of each group about themselves and others, about their preferred sociopolitical arrangements, and about the appropriate ways to attain and sustain those arrangements also shape their relations with other groups. Communities vary in the content and strength of their ethnocentrism and in their norms about tolerance. They vary in the degree of separation and integration they want with others with whom they live (Levine and Campbell 1972; Gurr 1993a).

Relative Position of Groups

The relative size, economic well-being, and political influence between each pair or among the entire set of communal groups within a political entity, geographic territory, or economic market are critical in shaping their relationship. Note that their relative position depends on the system boundaries in which they relate to one another; each can be a minority in one setting while a majority in another. For example, Israeli Jews have seen themselves as a minority in an immense Arab-Islamic region while Palestinian Arabs have seen themselves as vulnerable and weak in the face of Israel's strength as part of the West. Tamils in Sri Lanka see themselves as a vulnerable minority in a Sinhalese-dominated country, while the Sinhalese see themselves as threatened by the Hindu Tamils of Southern India and Sri Lanka.

The relative standing of communal groups also is affected by the multiplicity of identities everyone has. A person has an ethnic, religious, linguistic, local, and occupational identity, among many others. Some of these identities are neatly nested within each other and generally reinforce each other, for example, identification with a city, a province, and a nation. Others generally cut across one another, for example, professional and ethnic identities. How consistent or inconsistent these identities are perceived to be depends on the content of the identities and particularly on their exclusivity. Some identities include expectations of multiple identities, but others involve the denial of the appropriateness of dual loyalties, as for example nationality, when exclusively defined. Their relative salience varies over time, in different social settings, and in the way others relate to the individual. All identities do not neatly coincide and the way they overlap helps form cross-cutting ties among various communal groups. The multiplicity of communal memberships also means that in some contexts people share interests and even identities, though in other contexts they do not.

Political leaders may try to reduce communal conflicts among their constituencies by stressing shared identities, sometimes in opposition to outside adversaries. For example, the government officials of many new nations strive to emphasize their state identity and the external threats to it. The emphasis on national identity is more likely to supersede communal antagonism if the nation is defined in civic and territorial terms rather than in ethnic or other communal terms (see Smith 1991).

System Context of Groups

The social context within which the communal groups function profoundly shapes their relations. The context includes the structure of governance within which the groups interact, the cultural understandings they share, and the relations each has with external allies and supporters. The governance structure may embody recognition of communal differences with various forms of autonomy and power sharing, or it may deny such differences.

The social system to which antagonistic parties belong often has some procedures for managing conflicts and ways to redress grievances. These pro-

TABLE 11.2 Policies to Prevent Destructive Conflicts

	Phase of Conflict			
Goal	Emergence	Threat or Isolated Destructive Acts	Extensive Destructive Acts	Protracted and Extensive Destructive Acts
To correct underlying conditions	Economic growth; dialogue; reduced inequality; integration; shared identity	—	—	—
To prevent destructive acts	Use of legitimate institutions; dialogue conflict resolution training	Deterrence; reassurance; external mediation or intervention; crisis management; precise policies; nonviolent action; peacekeeping	—	—
To prevent escalation	Cross-cutting ties; nonviolent training; unofficial exchange	Nonviolent action; noninflammatory information; mediation; limiting arms; tit-for-tat; humanitarian assistance; peacekeeping	Changing expectations of victory or defeat; intervention; constituency opposition; limiting arms	—
To end fighting	—	Negotiation; reframing conflicts; confidence-building measures; mediation	Mediation; external intervention; limiting arms; negotiation	GRIT: problem-solving workshops; unofficial exchanges; step-by-step negotiation; constituency opposition
To move toward resolution	—	Negotiation; mutual reassurance; unofficial exchanges; super-ordinate goals; problem-solving workshops	Superordinate goals; interdependence; confidence-building measures; problem-solving workshops	Superordinate goals; acknowledgement of hurts; no humiliation; recogniton of an external enemy; mutual recognition; shared identity

cedures may be highly institutionalized, with official agencies to protect minority rights and active civil organizations to defend and advance minority concerns.

Possible Policies

If we are to decide what kinds of methods to use to prevent conflicts from becoming destructive, we must consider the goals being sought. Table 11.2 presents five sets of goals and four phases. Most of the preventive policies in the table overlap, but I have usually identified each policy with the goal to which it is especially relevant. Some policies are relatively long-term or would require intervening phases; these are not given in the table.

Not all strategies can be carried out by everyone. Some policies are usually conducted by one of the adversaries in the conflict and others by actors not directly engaged in the conflict as partisans. Some tend to be conducted by official representatives of one of the major antagonists in the conflict and some by officials of other governments or international organizations acting as intermediaries. Still other policies tend to be carried out by private persons belonging to one of the adversary camps or to an intermediary body, such as a religious organization, a university, or a humanitarian nongovernment organization.

I shall not discuss every policy identified in table 11.2. Rather, I discuss several major ways a conflict might be prevented from deteriorating into greater violence. Finally, I consider two cases in which such policies were pursued successfully and one case in which they were not. In the latter case the situation deteriorated.

Reducing Conflict-Generating Conditions

A number of conditions are frequently mentioned as sources of destructive communal conflicts. Among these are, first, increasing inequalities in power, wealth, and status; second, deteriorating economic conditions; third, reduced intercommunal interaction and communication; and fourth, dissolving shared institutions and identities (Paige 1975; Hechter 1975; Tiryakan and Rogowski 1985; Neuberger 1986; Zamir 1990; Snyder 1982; Peretz 1990; Clark 1984).

Policies to correct those conditions would therefore include reducing inequalities, improving economic and social conditions, integrating immigrants, improving dialogue among different peoples, and enhancing shared identities. For example, the success of the West German government in absorbing and integrating the German refugees from areas of Czechoslovakia, Poland, and East Germany undercut the risks of irredentist policies; on the other hand, the resistance in nearly all Arab countries to absorbing Palestinian refugees exacerbated the Israeli-Palestinian conflict (Kriesberg 1989).

Pursuing some of the policies has its own set of risks, as does not doing so. Reducing inequalities may raise unfulfilled expectations among the relatively deprived and may threaten the relatively advantaged, thus increasing mutual animosities. These effects can be controlled if the general social and economic conditions are improving, if communication among the peoples is enhanced, and if shared identities are made more salient. Stressing shared identities, however, can be experienced by some society members as forced assimilation into the dominant group's identity. The shared identity must be open to all citizens and must not require the abandonment of subdominant groups' basic self-identities. In actuality, these conditions are rarely if ever fully met.

Another set of policies affecting general social conditions may be directed at preventing violence, even apart from ameliorating the underlying conditions generating conflict. These include developing official and unofficial mechanisms for managing disputes. Within a country, this ranges from having elected governing organs ensure each community's representation to establishing local centers that foster intercommunal conciliation. This policy may be fostered by organizations in other countries introducing such approaches. For example, with the end of Soviet domination of Eastern Europe, many organizations based in the United States have assisted in conflict resolution training and in developing local institutions providing conflict resolution services.

In international affairs, strengthening regional and global institutions and collective security measures are ways to prevent violence. Within and among countries, developing ongoing ties among leaders and the rank and file from diverse communities can be helpful. Finally, widespread familiarity with nonviolent means of pursuing and resolving conflicts can foster their use and so prevent violence, but without the disadvantaged group acquiescing to oppression.

Other policies affecting general social conditions may be directed toward preventing conflicts from escalating into high levels of violence. These may include promoting norms against the use of violence and successfully encouraging nonviolent means of struggle. They also include developing cross-cutting ties of association and interest so that divisions, based, for example, on region, religion, and ethnicity do not correspond and reinforce each other (Dahrendorf 1959; Kriesberg 1982).

Limiting Threats or Isolated Destructive Acts

Once conflicts have emerged and at least one communal group or country has begun to threaten another with violence, additional policies may be necessary to avert the eruption of violence, which can become self-sustaining. The recourse to threats of violence usually reflects the sense that alternative ways of redressing grievances are not available or are ineffective. They may also be derived from widespread feelings of resentment, shame, and profound anger or from beliefs by leaders that such feelings can be aroused and drawn on to gain support for themselves in fighting against an enemy people.

The traditional policy for dealing with threats from an enemy is to issue counterthreats, presumably with the intention of deterring the foe. Of course, the risk here is that the other side interprets the supposedly deterring counterthreat as confirmation of the dangers it believes are posed by the enemy, requiring even greater threats. A destructive spiral is then under way.

More constructive policies include carefully calibrated, limited responses. This is best coupled with reassurances that recognize the other side's essential interests. Such reassurances may prevent the conflict from deteriorating destructively. Reassurance to the other party that its interests and values are not endangered may be conveyed through unilateral statements and actions or through the negotiation of mutual confidence-building agreements (CBMs). External intervenors, or government officials in the case of a country, may serve to facilitate negotiations and agreements to settle a dispute or may provide alternative ways to reach an accommodation. The Organization of Security and Cooperation in Europe (OSCE) is developing mechanisms to perform such services. External intervention, especially by a legitimate government within a country, may be able to impose a cease-fire.

To prevent an escalation of violence, other, longer-term policies may be effective. These include an adversary using self-limiting means of struggle such as nonviolent action. External agencies might make sure that noninflammatory information is provided. To stop escalation, one party may pursue a tit-for-tat strategy, initiating a conciliatory measure and then reciprocating the other side's actions at about the same level, cooperative for cooperative and confrontational for confrontational (Axelrod 1984; Goldstein and Freeman 1990).

Outside intermediaries may use several policies to help prevent further escalation. They may provide a variety of mediating services, including persons or organizations acting in unofficial capacities who explore with the adversaries the possibility of entering de-escalating negotiations. Governments and international organizations may also engage in mediation, using their resources to encourage settlement of matters of dispute. In addition, other governments or international government organizations may intervene and provide peacekeeping forces, when the antagonistic communal groups agree to them.

Several additional ways can help to stop violent fighting later on. One fundamental policy is to reframe or reconceptualize the conflict so that it appears to be a shared problem, or a problem less significant than other conflicts, or a block to the achievement of mutual positive goals. Such reframing can be fostered by external intermediaries and also by dissident groups within one or more of the adversary parties. Ultimately, the leadership—perhaps new—of one or more of the adversaries adopts this new conception of the conflict or begins to act in accordance with it. For example, when Anwar Sadat became president of Egypt after Gamal Nasser died, he undertook a different strategic approach, believing that the previous approach had failed. He shifted the relative importance of the issues dividing the Arabs and Israel and the means to attain the highest priority matters. He reduced the primacy of leadership of the Arab nation and believed Egyptian goals would be better achieved through Washington than through Moscow (Kriesberg 1992).

In terms of resolving the conflict, we can identify such policies as developing superordinate goals for the adversaries. This sometimes means finding a common enemy against whom they can unite. If the conflict has not escalated very far, mutual reassurances by the adversaries that they do not seek each other's destruction or that they seek only to protect what they have may help resolve the conflict. At least they provide the bases for negotiating a settlement that can lead to further agreements and ultimately a resolution. Unofficial as well as official intermediaries can be helpful in undertaking these policies; this may be done by organized exchanges between members of the different communal groups.

Halting Extensive Destructive Acts

Once intense and large-scale violence has developed, the prevention of further escalation, leading to the suppression of one side by the other, is extremely difficult. The dynamic of escalation takes over. To the adversaries the choice seems to be simply between victory and defeat. For extremists, this means the destruction of the enemy; the moderate position is to hurt the other side only enough to prove that it cannot win and then negotiate a settlement.

In a sense, prevention is no longer the goal. But prevention as used here includes measures to stop and reduce violence; continuing violence often means its institutionalization and an increased intractability. Preventing such developments can result from a variety of policies. One policy, more effective if pursued by external actors than by one of the adversaries, is to make it evident that the defeat of one side by the other will not be possible if the victor threatens the loser's existence. If a stalemate seems certain, the adversaries may well settle sooner rather than later. A quite different policy is to make it clear that defeat is certain for one of the adversaries, unless it accepts what is acceptable to the other side. Finally, resistance within one of the camps to the conflict's continuation may also inhibit its escalation and perhaps hasten its end.

Certain policies may lead to an end to the fighting. Intermediaries, official and unofficial, may identify and suggest options that allow adversaries to envision a satisfactory way out. One method is to change the mixture of parties involved in the settlement. For example, in the 1980s, several Central American countries were racked by internal conflicts, based on ideological and class differences as well as ethnic differences. These long-lasting and interlocking conflicts made it difficult to settle any one of them in isolation. A large move toward resolution was made in the accord reached among the presidents of the five Central American countries, who met in Esquipulas, Guatemala (Hopmann 1988; Wehr and Lederach 1991). Sometimes called the "Arias Plan," the accord included three components to be implemented simultaneously and according to a fixed time schedule. The formula included ending the violent conflicts, promoting democracy, and fostering economic integration.

Long-term resolution of the conflict is likely to require additional policies. These include confidence-building measures and using unofficial problem-solving workshops. Furthermore, increasing integration and developing superordinate goals can be useful as former adversaries see the possibility of shared benefits through cooperative endeavors.

Transforming Protracted and Extensive Destructive Acts

Some conflicts persist for many years, even generations. In such protracted struggles, even periods of relative quiescence are viewed as interludes in an ongoing struggle. Transforming such intractable conflicts is extremely difficult. They need to be halted and the underlying conditions perpetuating and sustaining the conflicts corrected.

A few policies may stress conflict resolution ideas and experiences that move parties out of the intractability in which they have become mired. These actions can interrupt and resolve such conflicts.

Much depends on the protagonists themselves. For example, constituency weariness with a protracted conflict may become the basis for resistance to continuing a costly struggle. The destructive means themselves may undermine the legitimacy of the struggle. Some leaders may respond to such changes, particularly if there have also been informal contacts with the opposing side indicating that an acceptable way out may exist. One way to communicate convincingly to the opponent that a mutual accommodation may be possible is to announce and make a conciliatory move, then persist in unilateral conciliatory moves, anticipating reciprocation. This is the graduated reciprocation in tension reduction (GRIT) strategy. Osgood (1962) discusses the strategy in relation to the cold war, and it has been analyzed largely in relationship to international conflicts (Goldstein and Freeman 1990).

One matter that tends to perpetuate a communal conflict is the apparent denial of the other side's right to exist. The mutual recognition of that right is an essential step in settling such conflicts, as occurred with the 1993 mutual recognition of Palestinians and Jews by the Palestine Liberation Organization and the State of Israel. To resolve a conflict so that it does not recur, one side must not humiliate or shame the other and provide fuel for later acts of revenge.

External changes are important here, and these depend on the actions of parties who are not among the conflict's primary adversaries. As other conflicts increase in salience for one or more adversaries, they tend to reduce the over-whelming prominence of the conflict they have with each other; thus, internal conflicts may lessen in the face of threats from a shared external enemy (Simmel 1956; Coser 1956).

The involvement of intermediaries can also foster mutual recognition and reassurances. This includes activities such as problem-solving workshops, extended dialogue groups, educational programs, participation in ritual acts of reconciliation, and investigations and trials of individuals who have perpetrated gross human rights violations.

Illustrative Cases

Let us consider three cases of successful and unsuccessful attempts at preventing destructive conflict escalation. We shall focus on the prevention of such destructive conflicts before they reach high levels of direct violence.

Canada

The conflict between French-speaking Quebec and the rest of Canada is of long standing, exacerbated by the economic dominance of English speakers over French speakers in Quebec (McRoberts 1988; Breton 1972). The political context, however, has provided legitimate channels for pursuing the conflict and moderating it; for example, the federal system allows for significant provincial authority and the party system has generally been dominated by national parties, often with leadership by someone from Quebec (for example, Pierre Trudeau of the Liberal Party). Furthermore, official and unofficial policies were directed toward building and sustaining a Canadian identity that incorporated and extolled the ethnic mosaic.

In the 1960s, the Quebec separatist movement grew rapidly and the Front de Libération du Quebec (FLQ), a tiny Maoist organization, conducted bombings and robberies. This culminated in October 1970 with the kidnapping of two officials, one of whom was killed. Prime Minister Trudeau invoked the War Measures Act and the FLQ was made illegal; the government's actions were forceful but not indiscriminate. Violence as a means of gaining independence was generally repudiated, even by advocates of independence.

Even earlier, some of the underlying social, political, and economic inequalities between French- and English-speaking Canadians were addressed through the modernization efforts of the Liberal Party of Quebec, known as the Quiet Revolution, which began in 1960. Some concerns related to protecting French speakers, particularly outside Quebec, were addressed by the Official Languages Act passed in 1969. The Parti Québécois, upon attaining power in

1976 in Quebec, strengthened the act and introduced other measures to enhance the role of French speakers in Quebec.

Many agreements have been proposed to find a new formula for the relations between Quebec and the other provinces of Canada, including the especially prominent Meech Lake Accord of 1987. None of the many efforts to reach a resolution of the conflict between Quebec and the rest of Canada has yet been accepted by majorities of all the required parties, whether for confederation or for separation, and dissatisfaction is widespread. Nevertheless, the conflict has been pursued using institutions generally regarded as legitimate. On the whole, the parties to the conflict continue to seek a negotiated settlement that will be acceptable to the adversaries and will enable them to work together in the future. Interdependence is evident and the search for a formula to satisfy the interests and preferences of most people within each camp continues, even though some groups would be willing to abandon that effort. In any case, despite considerable frustration and the failure up to now to reach a stable resolution, violence and compulsion have been disavowed and the process does not seem awful, especially when compared to that in places where ethnic or other communal differences have escalated into very destructive conflicts.

South Africa

South Africa, after decades of predictions that a very long and bloody violent struggle would convulse the country, has moved toward a political resolution of the conflict between the dominant white communities and the subordinated black and colored communities (van der Merwe 1989; Kane-Berman 1990; Adam and Moodley 1993; Giliomee and Gagiano 1991). In the transition, there was considerable violence, but it was not organized in a large-scale continuing manner, nor was it primarily between the white and black communities.

The actions that many people within South Africa and outside it have taken over the last few decades have modified the underlying conditions. This has helped to prevent both massively violent suppression by the government and large-scale armed revolution from below. Despite apartheid, there had been growing economic integration and mutual dependence among blacks and whites. The economy had grown well for many years, but in the 1980s its growth was hampered by apartheid and the sanctions imposed by much of the rest of the world.

The legitimacy of the apartheid system was undermined by the moral opprobrium with which it was viewed by people outside South Africa and even by increasing numbers of the more educated white South Africans. For example, the Dutch Reformed Church passed a resolution in October 1986 that the forced separation of peoples could not be considered a biblical imperative. Moreover, in the 1980s the resistance of blacks in the form of consumer and renter boycotts made it clear to most whites that apartheid could not be sustained without economic and social costs that were unacceptable. Repression had failed. Yet, at the same time, the armed struggle strategy of the African National Congress (ANC) was also failing during the 1980s. Bases to conduct the struggle, in Mozambique and other neighboring countries, were lost under extreme pressure from the South African government.

Significantly, new strategies pursued by the adversaries became increasingly reassuring to each other, as they turned to find nonviolent alternatives to settle their conflict. The ANC, though it had sanctioned armed struggle in the early 1960s, avoided terrorism.[1] Instead, in recent years, rent strikes and trade union action were actively pursued.

The ANC and the trade unions consistently stressed their nonracist goals. In 1984, white business leaders began to meet with ANC leaders, unofficially and outside South Africa, prior to the official negotiations. The shared identity of being South Africans was important to many, at least among the elites of the major communities.

Direct, mediated, and indirect conversations were held between South African government and ANC leaders to explore formulae for possible resolutions. After Nelson Mandela was unconditionally released from prison in 1990, he and President Frederik W. De Klerk cooperated in staging events and meetings to reassure each other's constituencies, as well as their own. These included recognition of the importance of moving toward healing and reconciliation, including expressions of guilt and understanding. The establishment of the Commission on Truth and Reconciliation was an important part of such movement.

Yugoslavia

Yugoslavia is an example of a horrible failure to prevent terrible violence. There had been warnings that this disaster might occur, and yet the actions and inactions of many parties propelled movement toward escalating violence rather than preventing it. Even in retrospect, it seems hard to say what might have been done by intermediaries to prevent what happened (Glenny 1992; Cohen 1995; Kuzmanic and Truger 1992). The intractability of the conflict was in place once the leaders of Serbia, Croatia, and Slovenia had mobilized their constituents into positions that threatened the other communities. To be effective, external intervention would have had to be extraordinarily well timed, threatening and reassuring at the same time (Kaufman 1994–95; Owen 1996).

Many conventional explanations stress long-standing mutual hatreds among the ethnic communities of the former Yugoslavia and the loss of central authority to keep the enemies from each other's throats. Such explanations miss important components that could have been modified with policies of early prevention.

Certain actions might have been taken to correct the underlying conditions. Thus, direct acknowledgment of the communal hurts of the past might have been helpful; for example, if after World War II trials had been held of persons alleged to have committed atrocities during the war, some of the desire for revenge that was available for mobilization might have been reduced.

Reducing economic and political inequalities related to region and ethnicity was difficult since the regions of the country differed greatly in their economic conditions. Fostering equality became even more difficult when economic conditions deteriorated in the 1980s.

Policies to increase the salience and significance of the Yugoslavian identity would have been helpful. In the past, many Yugoslavs felt pride for having stood up to the Soviets in 1948 and for having created a new and effective economic system, namely, publicly owned and worker-managed firms operated in a market system. As pride in such matters dissipated, new reasons for pride in Yugoslavia would have been useful. Perhaps its successful multiethnic character could have been touted. Another, less attractive option would have been to find a new external enemy.

Other policies might have helped contain the conflicts and fostered their pursuit by nonviolent means. More organizations might usefully have been established to directly address ethnic-related grievances and promote individual and collective human and social rights. Furthermore, if Yugoslavia had developed countrywide political parties in addition to the League of Communists of Yugoslavia (LCY), the collapse of the LCY would not have led so easily to ethnically based parties. The Yugoslav army might have remained a countrywide institution. As it happened, it failed to remain so and came to act as the Serbian army.

Long-term policies that would have reduced the scale of and emphasis upon armed force might have been helpful in preventing the rush to violence. Through socialization and training, alternatives to the reliance on guns and other tools of violence might have been promoted, for example, education about and training in conflict resolution and nonviolent action.

Contrary to these policies, the political leaders often pursued policies that undermined Yugoslav identity and institutions. Slobodan Milosevic and other leaders resorted to appeals, provocations, and manipulations to garner support on ethnic grounds. The public, in many cases, was resistant to the policies, but unable to stop the step-by-step deterioration.

Once the conflicts had moved to the threat of armed force and violent actions had been committed, additional policies might have prevented the escalation of the violence. The new government of Croatia, headed by President Franjo Tudjman, could have reassured ethnic Serbs living in Croatia that their communal rights would be recognized and protected.

External actors, such as the European governments, the OCSE, and UN mediators, might have striven to manage the conflict in a more comprehensive and coherent fashion. Instead, they dealt with each conflict as merely between two or three parties at one time. They might have given more reassurances to threatened parties and offered more opportunities for trade-offs. Some efforts were made, but the governments often pursued different policies, supporting different groups in what had been Yugoslavia. They could not themselves assure people that their rights would be protected and they did not effectively threaten those who endangered others' rights.

Conclusions

There are six conclusions to be drawn from this analysis. First, it is important to examine policies that successfully prevent conflicts from deteriorating destructively. Studying how matters go badly does not automatically inform analysts and policy makers about what might make matters go well. Of course, success is never total; therefore, we should examine conflicts that did not go as badly as they might have. Attention should be given to averting a disaster and doing well under the prevailing circumstances.

Second, the concept of prevention should be extended in time. Attention should be given to long-term policies to block the emergence of destructive conflicts. Public understanding of prevention needs to be increased so that government and nongovernment policies that take a long time will have added support. This includes developing norms and institutions that foster mutual respect of different communal groups, and developing interpersonal networks and bonds across communal divides. International nongovernment organizations are often able to sustain long-term policies, since they focus on specific matters with a committed constituency. This is illustrated in their persistent efforts in regard to human rights and humanitarian assistance.

Third, attention should be given to policies that have long-term peacebuilding consequences. Policies aimed only at halting the killing may freeze a conflict, but it may easily erupt again later. This means that a multitrack strategy should be planned. For example, economic development projects may be undertaken in ways that foster cooperation across communal lines. In addition, policies should be pursued that encourage forming an identity that is held in common by contending communal groups.

Fourth, preventing a conflict from becoming destructive depends most strongly on the protagonists in the conflict. Intermediaries from the outside can usually have only a limited effect. Third parties can, however, play useful, even critical roles at crucial junctures in the conflict. Under certain circumstances, an intermediary may powerfully channel the conflict. For example, a legitimate government not closely identified with either of the contenders in a communal struggle may intervene in the conflict between them.

Fifth, no single policy is likely to be adequate to reach any of the goals set forth here. Preventing conflicts from deteriorating and becoming increasingly destructive requires that various actors pursue many policies. Combinations that are mutually supportive need to be chosen, involving nongovernment as well as government players. The efforts of various intermediaries, both sequential and simultaneous, should be coordinated. That coordination may mean that different intermediaries clearly take the lead role at particular times.

Finally, we should recognize that, inevitably, policies are significantly shaped and selected on the basis of values and preferences, and not only on beliefs about the course of any given conflict or about conflicts in general. Thus, the decision to take an action to deter an adversary rests on beliefs about the consequences of such efforts, but also on the reluctance or readiness to resort to violence. This needs to be emphasized since avoiding violence is rarely the only goal of partisans or observers. But the frequent failure to avoid mutual losses in destructive conflicts should spur us all to discover and create constructive ways of managing conflicts.

Ethnic Conflict at the International Level

AN APPRAISAL OF THEORIES
AND EVIDENCE

David Carment and Patrick James

M ultiethnic environments have emerged rapidly as a permanent and important feature of politics within and between sovereign states. On the verge of the third millennium the causes of violent conflict are being redefined. No longer can potential or ongoing strife be subsumed within the ideological competition between East and West, which has shaped perceptions for almost half a century. Previously repressed by authoritarianism, dormant conflicts have come to the fore. Without an ideological framework, new and emerging issues take on an increasingly ethnic character because political leaders find it relatively easy to mobilize populations by stimulating a sense of collective identity (Maoz; Stack).[1]

These appeals to ethnicity have often been crucial in the ousting of entrenched elites. In other cases the rallying cry of "democratization" results in something other than effective pluralism; by-products include upsurges in rampant ethno-populism, the replacement of elites, or the shattering of fragile democratic institutions. The geopolitical map revealed the possibility that ethnic politics would become more pervasive even before the transformation of eastern Europe (Brecher and Wilkenfeld); today, there are more than 180 states in the international system and only a small number are ethnically homogeneous. Many newly emerging states, which struggle to solve an array of deep-seated problems, are prone to international conflict, crisis, and war (Maoz).

Given the need for better theory and evidence, the authors of the preceding chapters have addressed a wide range of issues related to the international politics of ethnic conflict. In this chapter we summarize the volume's contributions to greater understanding in three areas: international relations theory, cause and effect, and conflict management. We also offer a few general conclusions.

International Relations Theory and Ethnic Conflict

Prior to this decade the study of ethnicity could not have been further removed from international relations as a field of inquiry. From a "primordial" perspective, however, states are secondary to the intricate web of human relations, which are based on real and perceived ties of kinship (Stack). An individual belongs to a group, in the deepest and most literal sense, if for no other reason than to escape isolation. Thus primordialism indirectly draws attention to important reasons why that mainstream international relations theory largely ignores ethnicity (Stack): The failure to examine ethnicity as a meaningful force goes hand in hand with a preference for the study of material conditions and the relegation of domestic factors to a secondary role (Carment and James). Elements such as power or class receive primary attention as determinants of individual or group behavior within states and the anarchical global system.

Given that the term *ethnicity* suggests a romanticization—even mystification—of individual and collective behavior, the primordial interpretation is not attractive to social scientists. There is also great reluctance to view ethnicity in terms of primordialism because of the danger of embracing cultural determinism and therefore (albeit unintentionally), a form of racism. A further problem is that primordial arguments are reductionist, which may prevent rigorous assessment of ethnicity in terms of cause and effect.

One international pattern, however, is clear. As a consequence of internal changes induced by ethnically mobilized groups, states—as the primary actors in the system—are undergoing transformation (Ferguson and Mansbach 1989; Keohane and Nye 1989; Rosenau 1990). This conclusion finds support from diverse areas of research (Alfred and Wilmer; Marshall). Concurrently, the international political agenda has been altered as a result of changes in the system. Both processes have led to rule transformation, in an attempt to redefine the norms that states are expected to follow in mutual relations.

While it is difficult to fault political realism for a state-centered interpretation when the focus is on the global balance of power, prospects for nuclear warfare, or the potential collapse of the world's economic system, ethnicity is now increasingly relevant even to those issues. It is important to recognize that power, status, and capabilities are distributed unevenly among states, which means that conflict will be a continuing reality for any international system. Major powers are involved intrinsically in that process and "problem" states will continue to possess the military but not the political and economic means needed to control rebellion and contain ethnic strife. It is unlikely that the international community will intervene in conflicts where the state possesses the capacity for outright coercion of its minorities (e.g., India, Russia, China), though actions by individual major powers cannot be ruled out. Paradoxically, weak states riven by internal dissent attract the most third-party attention, yet these cases are least likely to produce diffusion and escalation in the system.

International relations theory must find a way to account for ethnically based interstate conflict that arises from third-party intervention (Davis, Jaggers, and Moore). Furthermore, the impact of domestic, ethno-political imperatives on international politics and the formation of foreign policies remain little understood. Each of these processes suggests that internal ethnic conflicts are unlikely to remain isolated, domestic problems. There is always the potential for "spillover" into the international arena. Recent examples include India's 1987 intervention in Sri Lanka's protracted conflict (as a "self-appointed peacekeeper"), Russia's similar involvement in Georgia, Indo-Pakistani confrontation over Kashmir and, depending on how state autonomy is measured, Serbian intervention in Bosnia, Croatia, and Slovenia at different junctures in the Yugoslav imbroglio.

Perhaps current concerns with ethnic conflict at the end of the cold war (and especially with the transformation of the Soviet Union and Yugoslavia) are obscured by an obsession with, and assumptions about, change in the international system. Indeed, anxiety is an artifact of an established way of thinking. What appears to be new in reality reflects ongoing uncertainties about the future (Marshall; Midlarsky). While current norms and institutions and even theory have not kept pace with developments in the international system, the real issue is that state-level changes, which include ethnic and indigenous struggles, have been in progress for some time. The difference now is that these events occur against the backdrop of larger systemic change, accompanied by calls for the politicization of indigenous issues (Alfred and Wilmer). Thus there is a great deal of uncertainty about exactly what all these conflicts mean for state interactions and international relations theory. From a policy perspective, inaction leads to the perception of loss of control and, as a consequence, the legitimacy and authority of the present system may be in transition. Perhaps international institutions will be less effective over the short term because of the perceived failure to respond to new demands placed upon them (Midlarsky; Brecher and Wilkenfeld).

Understanding Ethnic Conflict: Cause and Effect

Determining the necessary and sufficient conditions for ethnic conflict is a complex task. No two scholars seem to agree on the exact causes of ethnic strife. Extend these conflicts into the international domain, where there are spillover effects and interstate strife, and the presumed causes multiply.

Ethnic identity in international politics constitutes a paradox that has yet to be resolved, which in turn affects the interpretation of cause and effect. Congruities of kinship, speech, custom, and so on appear to have an ineffable and at times overpowering cohesiveness. In other instances, leaders of ethnic groups seem to be particularly skilled at manipulating these linkages to their advantage. Hence both subjective and objective definitions of the term become relevant (Kasfir 1979). According to a wide range of sources, the critical features of an ethnic group are that it is ascriptive and exclusive: its continuity depends on the maintenance of a boundary based on values and identity (Stack). For purposes of political mobilization, however, ethnicity also possesses objective markers.

Ethnic identification can attach itself to one or more of six different criteria, including (1) race—shared phenotypical features such as pigmentation, stature, and facial or hair type; (2) kinship—assumed blood ties and alleged ancestry such as generally is claimed by clans, tribes, and occasionally entire nations; (3) religion—as a leaven of social allegiances, not as a formal belief system about ultimate essences; (4) language—as a vehicle of communication and symbol of ethnic and cultural identity; (5) customary mode of livelihood—examples include the Javanese and Bengali who preen themselves as the bearers of customs and cultures superior to those of their neighbors; and (6) regionalism—in which groups of people are united because of a distinct geographic region (Rothschild 1981, 86–87).

Whether ethnic conflict is a short-term response to the processes of state and nation building is widely debated. Some argue instead that ethnic conflict is a psychological result of primordial identities, which are more permanent than those based on class and political orientation (Stack). Still others draw attention to the relevance of "situational" identities, which are evoked in certain structural circumstances to advance the material and political interests of actors whose primary allegiances and purposes are not ethnic (Carment and James; Marshall). Ethnic identities are assumed to persist because of shared historical and cultural experiences, but their salience is variable for both individuals and the group.

Interpretation of ethnicity's meaning largely determines the hierarchy (to the extent that one can be identified) among causal factors. Most theorists in this volume consider a combination of economic, political, symbolic, and psychological factors as essential to the development of animosity between groups. The background conditions to a conflict, however, can vary across cases. Reciprocity and interactions are also important factors to consider. Changes experienced at one level, such as dehumanization (a psychological factor), stimulate cohesiveness and eventually increase polarization between groups. Symbols are important group markers in this process of mobilization.

One argument is that antecedents to a conflict are usually structural in nature. For example, ethnic conflicts can arise when groups are geographically concentrated in backward or advanced regions. Ethnic conflict becomes probable only when certain international and domestic structural elements are present, such as a core-periphery differential that coincides with regional disparities and intense nationalism among ethnic groups (Midlarsky). Another possibility is that ethnic conflict within a state will intensify and project outward in response to changes in the international environment, most notably with respect to neighboring political systems (Maoz).

Consider, as a more specific example of how structure may affect the propensity for interstate ethnic conflict, the conditions prior to the onset of World War I and the current crisis in Yugoslavia. A multipolar system is associated with a more unstable environment (Midlarsky). In contrast to the reigning powers in 1914, the United States and the European powers have recently taken on the role (albeit imperfectly) of limiting the extent and spread of violence. This behavior is most likely an artifact of the cold war. During that period, conflicts central to the broader patterns of competitive international relations had the greatest potential for expansion (e.g., Turkish and Greek confrontation over Cyprus, Arab-Israeli strife). Accordingly, the international community devoted a great deal of energy to managing such conflicts. An important implication is that, during this period of superpower rivalry, some ethnic conflicts spread because bipolarity and the presence of nuclear weapons limited direct conflict between the superpowers but not among client states. In sum, both sides of the cold war may have supported (or suppressed) ethnic struggles to achieve broader foreign policy objectives (Midlarsky; Brecher and Wilkenfeld).

Aside from structure, political balancing between ethnic groups is seen as crucial to the outbreak of international conflict (Davis, Jaggers, and Moore). There is considerable debate about whether large or small ethnic minorities are at greater risk. For example, the case of Yugoslavia suggests that when the size and number of groups within states is relatively equal, conflict is more likely. An ethnic minority that is small in size but geographically concentrated, like those of the Baltics, India, or Sri Lanka, may predispose the state toward the most coercive of policies. By contrast, if the minority is large and territorially concentrated, as in the Sudan, it not only constitutes a greater threat but also possesses superior resources for its own defense. While the state may be ill disposed toward large and concentrated minorities, the capacity for coercion is reduced. Indeed, it may be easier to mobilize an entire population when there are both fewer opponents and structural elements that limit violent strategies. This combination of factors could push elites toward more peaceful measures in the pursuit of group definition and cohesion.

Ethnicity is a political factor with important implications for domestic and international ethnic conflict. Affect-laden behavior and structural arrangements (including institutions) can increase the salience of ethnic identity in elite decision making (Marshall). For the state-center, reactive behavior—to defend the entitlements of the state, such as rights and resources—is probable. For rebellious ethnic communities, proactive behavior, even including violence, is a likely instrument for mobilization (Marshall). These actions are intended to appropriate new entitlements for the group. To the extent that both sides seek outside support, such actions will include an international dimension. Through an emphasis on mechanisms common to both new and old states, a synthetic approach, which accounts for the interplay between affect and structure, may be able to explain the international orientations of multiethnic societies (Carment and James).

Transnational linkages between ethnic groups (i.e., affinities) can play an important role in eliciting international support, though it is debatable whether these factors are sufficient to bring about interstate violence. For example, linkages between groups in adjacent states are a vital source of material, ideological, and political support for ethnic minority claims, though the impact they have on externally generated strife is minimal (Davis, Jaggers, and Moore). Ethnic affinities relate directly to the problem of sovereignty, that is, the ability of states to implement authoritative claims. Efforts to control the flow of people, culture, and resources are most significant in interstate ethnic conflicts, such as the Ethiopia-Somalia crises, but also have implications for domestically generated strife (e.g., Russian support for the Serbs). Quite often, authority is not defined strictly in terms of territory; partial sovereignty exists. Within ethnic conflict settings, transnational affinities are important to understanding relationships between states. Not only do elites view ethnic affinity as an opportunity to be exploited, but specific groups on whom elites rely for support also perceive these international linkages as potentially useful.

From the perspective of rational choice, ethnic identification is often created or maintained as a basis for collective action when there are clear competitive advantages attached to such an identity (Carment and James). The advantages accrue primarily to urban elites, who can mobilize support through media, unions, and organizations. This suggests processes of state building that are associated primarily with urban and ethnic political development; allocation of positions within the civil service, universities, and other sites of employment would be determined on an ethnic basis.

This argument can be extended to the international arena. Conflict among ethnic groups within and between states may result from historical or demographic processes that trigger latent animosities and have distinct payoffs for elites. Other cases will reflect economic and political processes that provide the rationale for ethnic mobilization. Interethnic conflict promotes mobilization, which results in the formation of ethnic organizations, enhancement of identity, and subsequent escalation of conflict. An important implication of this argument is that external threats and conflicts between states can activate latent group identities and interests and prompt ethnic groups to mobilize in self-defense and self-interest (Davis, Jaggers, and Moore).

Equally important is how states respond to ethnic conflict. The main issue is how states develop and maintain stable political systems in a threatening international environment. For example, states involved in recurring episodes of violent ethnic conflict tend to maintain institutions specialized in the exercise of coercion (Carment and James). These states also develop elite political cultures that sanction the use of violence. To the extent that coercion produces outcomes favorable for the political elite, a future preference for those strategies is reinforced.

Success in the use of organized violence for national consolidation and suppression of internal challenges encourages the development of a police state. At times, protracted conflict and violence can extend this phase indefinitely, and viable states are extremely slow to emerge. Pervasive insecurity may produce relatively frequent interstate and civil warfare (Midlarsky). Postrevolutionary states, such as those that replaced the Soviet Union, face internal resistance in the immediate aftermath and may end up with closed regimes. Alternatively, when the results of coercion are unfavorable, more pacific strategies will characterize future conflicts (Marshall). If there is frequent success in the use of reforms, concessions, and displacement to manage internal challenges, institutions and norms of democratic rule will probably develop. Democratic states are unlikely to rely primarily on coercion in response to internal challenges; therefore, there is an interaction effect to consider.

Finally, there is a difference between factors that lead to conflict as opposed to an escalation to violence (Young; Davis, Jaggers, and Moore). Indeed, the label "ethnic conflict" itself reveals very little about what underlies intercommunal tensions and the sources of secession. On an abstract level these problems may be about human rights, participation, and justice. The manifestation of these issues becomes ethnic because that is the basis for exclusion or repression. However, as observed in several cases, secession need not be violent (Young) and much can be learned from instances of successful prevention of destructive communal conflict (Kriesberg). Furthermore, conflict itself has some positive attributes that should not be overlooked. *Conflict* refers to a situation of discord between two or more parties, which can be resolved peacefully. The term designates a perceived divergence of interest or a belief that the current aspirations of the antagonists cannot be achieved simultaneously.

Toward the Management of Ethnic Conflict

In this volume we have provided compelling reasons for reexamining the ways in which ethnic strife is viewed and managed by the international community. Conceptual and theoretical tools for preventive diplomacy and preventive peacekeeping are badly in need of attention. When the dominant factors are recognized, it becomes apparent that the ability to anticipate, understand, and mediate conflicts before they become violent needs improvement (Kriesberg).

Unlike most conflicts, which are not completely zero-sum, ethnic strife unfolds against a backdrop of fear, the fear that it will be resolved through the destruction or assimilation of a group. The search for a balance between minority and state interests occurs at various points in a state's development. Unfortunately, many ethnically divided states attempting to make the simultaneous transition to more open political and economic systems face extreme danger (Maoz). If the political system is arranged along ethnic lines and one group manages to become dominant, it will gravitate toward intransigence, confrontation, hypernationalism, and conflict. Over the short term, leaders of ethnically based political parties will lack the capacity to widen the policy agenda to encompass nonethnic issues. When other bases of mobilization are weak, ethnic elites depend on direct support from their constituency. Elites in turn seek to control and influence ethnic groups.

Related to this expectation is the experience of ethnic groups with peaceful cohabitation. Highly diverse states, while perhaps restrained from pursuing adventurous foreign policies, are still likely to succumb to internal strife. If one group becomes dominant and is incapable of withstanding the pressures of outbidding, then a more belligerent foreign policy is likely. Vital interests will probably be threatened and perceived in the context of incompatible and incontrovertible demands. For elites who play on these fears, the benefits are obvious. Conflict serves an important functional and potentially positive role for the elite and its followers (Marshall). When group cohesion is relatively low, performance expectations may be the only way to ensure mobilization, cohesion, and stronger support. This argument is a radical departure from the assumption that conflict can be resolved; instead, it is transformed or escalated. New issues become salient, the conflict spreads, and a pernicious cycle begins.

Cultural issues are certainly important in understanding the roots of violent ethnic conflict, but it is also essential to understand the interactions that take place between state and ethnic group, and ethnic group and international society respectively (Alfred and Wilmer). These interactions reflect assumptions embedded in both realist and idealist theories of international security. There is no reason that both theories cannot be partially accurate and consistent worldviews. From the realist perspective, reality consists of the continuing process of state building within a threatening international environment. From the idealist viewpoint, it is the very process of state building that elicits responses from ethnic minorities with different visions of the future. Self-determination is the central expression of the idealist position on ethnic minority struggle against state building.

Paradoxically, the idea of self-determination—a basic tenet of the United Nations Charter—also serves to undermine multiethnic societies, whose very creation is idealized in the "melting pot" phenomenon, experienced to some extent in the United States but rarely emulated elsewhere. The double-edged nature of ethnic nationalism is important to recognize in the context of conflict management. These struggles involve competing ethnic identities that operate within the domestic political sphere and spill over into the international arena, which can create seemingly insurmountable problems. Mutually incompatible dreams of national self-determination make resolution by the United Nations (and regional organizations) even more difficult, if not impossible. Thus it should come as no surprise that the UN system is seen by many as an insufficient instrument for resolution of ethnic strife.

Traditional processes of power-oriented bargaining and mediation create additional reasons for conflicts to become protracted. Power-based conflict management techniques produce temporary settlements but do not tackle the underlying issues. This interpretation implies that the main sources of ethnic conflict are questions of identity, effective participation, security, and other basic needs—social goals that, unlike material resources, are not in short supply (Stack).

Perhaps the primary distinction in this regard is between values that are not negotiable and interests that can be traded. The roots of ethnic strife lie in the fabrication of new identities and the triggering of old identities that belie state boundaries. Several factors contribute to this process. The coincidence of nation building and state building is a crucial turning point in the transition from a nation-state to an ethnic state construct: There are no prominent modes of political integration which do not involve either warfare (empire-building) or assimilation (state-building) (Marshall). The presumably consolidating process of nation building rests on self-determination, the same ideological base that serves as a launching pad for ethnic mobilization. The capacity of current international institutions to cope with such difficulties is questionable; resolution of ethnic conflicts becomes feasible only when underlying causal mechanisms, which focus on problems related to values and identity, are identified.

A number of conditions, procedures, and approaches would be useful in future ethnic conflict management. These approaches focus on the situations that arise before, during, and after violence. It almost goes without saying that the number and diversity of items related to each phase reflect both the range of knowledge gathered from the preceding chapters and the complexity of contemporary ethnic strife.

In phase one of ethnic conflict, before interstate violence breaks out, one might:

1. create proliferating points of power that reduce the salience of ethnic affinities at the interstate level;

2. raise the salience of cooperation based on nonethnic or intraethnic conflict;

3. raise the salience of the long-term implications of interstate ethnic conflict (regional disruption) over short-term (domestic) concerns;

4. encourage alignments between states based on interests other than ethnicity;

5. reduce internal cleavages within states through the reduction of disparities by means of international incentives (trade and aid);

6. develop policies of preventive diplomacy, which entails identifying the conditions necessary for the successful resolution of ethnic conflicts by focusing on issue areas that are of common interest to the adversaries;

7. encourage transition to systems in which institutional constraints are durable and which encourage mobilization on the basis of cross-cutting cleavages (this need not be equated with democratization);

8. identify those states and regions that are most susceptible to involvement in violent interstate ethnic conflict;

9. develop early warning systems for objective third-party mediators. These systems recognize that the most propitious and cost-effective time for managing ethnic differences is before violent interstate ethnic conflict breaks out;

10. promote and improve human rights monitoring systems that will reduce the salience of affinities as a basis for supporting armed minority struggle;

11. improve existing international laws and regulations on sanctions for states that pursue involvement in interstate ethnic strife.

In phase two, after violence breaks out, one might:

1. provide guidelines for the international community to follow regarding the recognition of secessionist minorities and irredentist struggles, and sanction states that do not follow these guidelines;

2. provide international incentives for the peaceful secession of ethnic groups based on mutual gain for the state-center and the minority (based on the assumption that secession will result in the destruction of a state through violence);

3. develop objective criteria for the international community to follow on issues of third-party mediation and violent interstate ethnic conflict in both secessionist and irredentist settings;

4. include all participants in the conflict in the negotiation process;

5. provide an internationally organized peacekeeping force as a legitimate deterrent for the reduction of violent interstate ethnic conflict.

In phase three, after violence has subsided, one might:

1. use resolution techniques operating outside external state interference, and allow the main antagonists to arrive at solutions at their own pace (assuming that the conflict has not resulted in the destruction of one or more states);

2. examine alternative bases of alignments that involve concessions by the state pursuing external involvement;

3. use mediating structures that focus on functional collaboration to promote cooperation and shared interests over time;

4. make security issues salient to both elites and masses as the basis for cooperation between states.

General Conclusions

Based on the diverse chapters in this volume, we can offer one general conclusion about ethnic conflict—whether it results in cooperation or a crisis that leads to war—namely, that it is not a culture-specific phenomenon. Interstate aggression cannot be wholly explained by ethnic group norms about violence. Hypernationalism, "ethnic cleansing," forced assimilation, genocide, and divide and rule all may be at the root of the most vicious disputes within states. However, even these conditions do not ensure that domestic ethnic strife will become an object of international concern and a source of interstate conflict and diffusion.

The arguments in this volume support a second basic conclusion: Conflicts with an ethnic foundation are not caused by system structure alone. Rather, interstate ethnic strife is related to variations in the constellation of political and ethnic constraints that impinge on elite and mass choices. Ethnic cleavages and affinities also appear to shape the kinds of choices available to the international community by presenting the state with additional internal and external sources of insecurity (Carment and James). A further implication is that domestic ethnic politics is very important to the generation of interstate conflict. It may be possible to prevent or discourage the international aspects of ethnic strife by addressing its sources at the domestic level and by reducing the salience of affinities and cleavages. The importance of transnational ethnic affinities in this process is fundamental. They can be used beneficially (through aid and trade) or can become sources of insecurity (support for insurgencies). The key priority is to provide incentives that reduce the salience of the ill effects while promoting the beneficial ones. Attention should be given to policies that have long-term peace-building consequences (Kriesberg).

Third and finally, extraregional actors are extremely important as sources of support in a conflict. The evidence indicates that such support imposes a constraint on efforts to manage ethnic strife that is not easily overcome. International backing for rebellious ethnic minorities is related directly to changes in the leadership pools and the strategies of minority groups. These may be evolving at a much faster pace than the coping mechanisms of the state-center and third-party efforts at mediation.

Future scenarios will likely involve ethnically divided states that attempt to make the transition to a more open political economy. These system members, of which the Soviet successor states are prime examples, are potential objects for renewed and vigorous collective efforts at conflict management. However, the policies implemented in past ethnic conflicts may be less effective in future international management of such strife. The key is to find incentives for interethnic cooperation that do not entail the involvement of extraregional actors. Sanctions, mediation, and international condemnation may be necessary but not sufficient conditions for the management of ethnic strife. Thus it is essential to augment these traditional approaches with those suited to the particularities of ethnic conflict.

NOTES

Chapter 3. Indigenous Peoples, States, and Conflict

1. Depending on, among other things, the length of time a particular indigenous community has been subjected to policies of coerced assimilation, many—particularly those in the First World and those who were the first to be "contacted" and subsequently marginalized politically and economically—are today experiencing a profound fragmentation arising from dissension about identity and values. This conflict, internal to indigenous communities, is not the subject of this chapter. Rather, we refer to the dimension of ethnic conflict in which indigenous peoples perceive themselves to be culturally distinct from the "dominant" culture of the nation-state that now surrounds them, and to the statements that leaders of such communities have made in a variety of public forums. For a discussion of the political problems associated with fragmented identity and values in an indigenous political community see Alfred 1991.

2. To be accurate, we cannot say whether the tendency toward incorporation was ever present. However, there are some histories among the Iroquois suggesting that the mysterious "mound builders" represent an era of indigenous history in North America when hierarchical and centralized social systems were the predominant form of social order on the continent. The mounds are said to be the ruins of the cities built during that period (Jennings 1993). Studies of the Maya, Inca, and Aztec expansions suggest that the relationship between the expanding hegemon and local cultures was quite different than that which underlies both the Roman conquest and the process of state building in Europe. Davies, for instance, reports the Aztec inclination to "leave original rulers in charge of newly conquered territory and rule indirectly through *tlatoani*" (1987, 204). Stern reports that the Inca "tried to operate within the cultural idioms appreciated by Andean peoples" (1982, 19).

3. The concept of *tribe* is laden with political assumptions about "more" and "less" evolved, complex, or developed forms of social and political order. Because the term originates in Western anthropology, however, it is often presented as an objective, universal, and scientific categorization. The term *nation* is similarly political, and while nations are viewed as moral (and evolutionary) equals, the nation is also frequently and implicitly cast as a form of organization that is morally, legally, and politically superior to the tribe. The idea of *community,* on the other hand, is much more neutral and descriptive of the locus of political life in most if not all nonindustrialized societies. Indigenous societies always constitute communities, though some think of themselves as nations, some as tribes, and some as affiliated confederacies. In all cases these communities

should be viewed as moral equals to nations, though their claims to legal and political equality are the central subject of many ethnic conflicts that involve indigenous peoples and nation-states.

4. We use the term *statehood* because it is entirely unclear that nation building— whatever that is—has anything to do with exercising the internationally recognized right of self-government, whereas statehood is unquestionably the basis for the international allocation of sovereignty.

5. Some of the numerical advantage must also be attributed to the toll taken by the introduction of alien diseases (against which the carrier population had developed immunities) into indigenous populations, usually, but not always, unintentionally.

Chapter 5. Systemic War in the Former Yugoslavia

1. During the post–World War II period, the cold war erected barriers to the sorts of violence found recently in Bosnia, barriers that were clearly absent prior to World War I. At that time, the presence of empires, especially in Ottoman Turkey and Austria-Hungary, set limits on interethnic strife. As Ottoman Turkey disintegrated, especially in Europe, and Austria-Hungary was increasingly threatened internally, these limits gradually eroded. In that sense, the probability of such strife occurring was about the same at the two historical junctures, but other variables were to have a differential impact on the intensity of strife when it occurred.

2. Structural wars are defined as those dependent on a particular structural condition (e.g., multipolarity) and on the subsequent causes delineated in the sequence of variables outlined above. Mobilization wars are far less dependent on international structure and the resulting set of variables, and more dependent on the internal dynamics of the polity that is mobilizing for war (e.g., Germany in World War II). Mobilization systemic wars occur after structural systemic wars, because the latter frequently have no definitive resolution (e.g., World War I) and allow for the possibility of a resurgent mobilization by a polity that had either been defeated during the earlier structural war or had not achieved a victory sufficiently decisive to satisfy its foreign policy goals. For additional material relevant to this distinction, see Midlarsky 1988a, chap. 7.

Chapter 6. Systems at Risk

1. It has become commonplace in the literature to see the political domain as divided into "high" (military security) and "low" (economic and social) politics. Such "hierarchical binary oppositions" (to use the feminist phrase—e.g., Tickner 1992, 7–8) are inherently biased and represent prejudicial thinking. Within "high" politics, there is a distinction made between "major" (or "great" or "super") powers and "minor" powers. Powers are considered "minor" if they cannot reasonably threaten a major power (in a conventional conflict "event"); therefore they are assumed to be of little consequence, of little interest to the paragons of security analysis. Security studies give little attention to conflict trends outside the "advanced" core of states, and as a result, that discipline remains ill-equipped to understand violent conflict processes in exactly those areas where they are most likely to occur. When attention is shifted from an "events" to "systemic process," the minor powers may be seen to wield a great measure of influence on the policies and actions transpiring within the system. In this context, a subjective distinction between "high" (Europeanized) and "low" (Third World) culture hides an important distinction between *highly institutionalized* social structures and *less institutionalized*

social practices. Interactive events taking place in a variable context of formal institution-alization are important analytically, since a comparison may reveal effects of *structural determination* (institutional conditioning) on the course of events.

2. I apologize for the license I have taken in describing certain uses of the term *ethnicity* in recent scholarship. Some scholars have diligently and rigorously examined and applied the special qualities of ethnic identification in their analyses. See especially the seminal work of Gurr and the Minorities at Risk Project, to which I am indebted for a large part of my understanding and insights into the issues of political ethnicity.

3. Until massive proliferation of advanced weaponry throughout the world under the auspices of cold war competition was finally accomplished, ethnicity could not compare to nationalism in the degree of virulence because ethnic groups did not usually have access to the means of mechanized, militarized violence (whereas nations, according to Max Weber's definition, had access to the state's "monopoly of legitimate force"). The "great powers" of the colonial system did selectively arm minor ethnic groups in their foreign "possessions" as a means to enhance their ability to control the subjugated populations, but seldom were these groups armed to the extent that they could pose a threat to the colonial power. See Laurance 1992 for an overview of global arms prolifera-tion in the post–World War II era.

4. Empirical analysis shows that the overwhelming majority of recorded episodes of political violence since 1946 have taken place in regional clusters: that includes 86 percent of interstate wars; 67 percent of extrasystemic wars; 74 percent of civil wars; and over 85 percent of the world's refugee flows. These regional clusters, or protracted conflict regions, center on six core conflicts: (1) Palestine; (2) South Africa; (3) Vietnam; (4) Korea; (5) Cuba/United States; and (6) India/Pakistan. The sheer magnitude and extent of the patterned, militarized violence in the less institutionalized political system characterizing the Third World clearly qualifies the "Third World War" as the third great systemic war of the twentieth century (Marshall 1995). See also Väyrynen 1984; Kelly 1986; Hensel and Diehl 1992; Buzan 1991; Maoz 1993a.

5. See Most and Starr 1989, 97–132, for an effective discussion of the idea of *foreign policy substitutability*, which refers to variability of policy response to a certain type of stimuli (i.e., there is no strict causal connection between a certain action and a certain reaction: one of a number of substitutable policies may be chosen as the reaction to a given stimulus and, conversely, a number of substitutable stimuli may evoke a given policy response). Gurr 1988, 58, also incorporates the idea of substitution of function in reference to institutions of coercion: "The personnel and agencies of warfare and internal security are interchangeable, though functional specialization between them develops more or less quickly."

6. Ross and Homer, for example, state that their research shows that "both diffusion and functional processes are needed to account for political instability" (1976, 22). Klingman warns that "no rote statistical method can ever with certainty distinguish between functional and diffusional explanations of a given cross-sectional distribution of traits" (1980, 310). Ross and Homer explain this analytical dilemma: identification of a correlation as resulting from diffusion when that is not the case "is most likely to occur when the variables under study are systematically related to ecological or environmental conditions which do in fact cluster throughout the world" (1972, 26). Klingman reveals a possible way out of this seeming paradox through an explanation of process differentia-tion: "The diffusion of traits only to societies capable of sustaining them is referred to in the literature on Galton's problem as 'semi-diffusion,' whereas pure diffusion with no functional basis is referred to as 'hyper-diffusion'" (Klingman 1980, 127; see also Ross

and Homer 1976). The systemic-relevant process is, then, *hyperdiffusion;* variations among analytic units within the system are the subject of semidiffusion. We can assume that a time-series analysis of the proposed diffusion effect from the systemic perspective will reveal an incremental process that could not be attributed to a strictly functional explanation.

7. The basic criteria for inclusion of a state in the following analyses are: (1) its recognition by the world community as an independent state and (2) a population of 1 million or more in 1990. The global number of states was 130 in 1990. The use of the state as the unit of analysis is especially problematic because these "equal units" vary in population size from 1 million to over 1 billion. The fact that aggregate data are only collected on the basis of these state units precludes any digression from such unit analysis. When possible and appropriate, I have standardized the data and subsequent empirical tests on a per capita basis in response to the unit comparability problem.

8. Prior to 1946, most violent conflict events were clustered in the European region; thus, the European region must be considered the "zero-th" PCR and the cold war the extension of that protracted conflict into the post–World War II global system. Whereas the "zero-th" PCR has been relatively nonviolent (under the ever present threat of nuclear annihilation), it has had an enormous influence on the conduct of political relations throughout the world. Any test of diffusion in regional subsystems is also a test of a generalized diffusion process at the global systemic level with Europe as the core. Cf. analyses of the "world system" (Wallerstein 1974) and of the "world order" (Falk 1966).

9. See Reardon 1993 for an overview of how warfare affects women in the private domain.

10. Information and estimates on refugee flows in the earlier period, 1946–1964, are given in Schechtman 1963 and Hakovirta 1986, but the data in these sources are not systematically compiled. They do point out the magnitude of initial refugee movements for the core PCR conflict. Many of these mass population dislocations from PCR cores persisted for a long time. The Palestinian refugee situation is certainly a case in point.

Chapter 7. Domestic Political Change and Strategic Response

1. Although OLS results are given for disputes in table 7.4 and table 7.5, they are less reliable than the poisson regression and logistic results for some aspects (Maoz 1995, chap. 5 and appendix). However, the OLS results suggest that the inclusion of lagged dependent variables eliminates autocorrelation biases in the case of disputes and military allocations variables. In cases where the Durbin-Watson statistic is outside the range of 1.90–2.10, the results of the analysis should be regarded as highly tentative due to potentially biased estimates.

2. It also confirms the hypothesis that a global analysis of the impact of democratization on dispute behavior is likely to be misleading. However, the analysis based on the concept and definition of PRIEs provides a consistent linkage between a dyadic and a relevant systemic formulation of the democratic peace result.

Chapter 8. Ethnicity, Minorities, and International Conflict

1. The data can by ordered by writing to Ted Robert Gurr at the Center for International Development and Conflict Management, Mill Building, University of Maryland, College Park MD, 20742. A small fee defrays the costs of duplication and distribution.

Chapter 9. The Ethnic Dimension of International Crises

1. Readers might recall that the ICB's data set normally has listed 390 international crises and 826 foreign policy crises. We are in the process of revising the ICB data set as we prepare Brecher and Wilkenfeld 1997, and this has led us to combine several cases and to eliminate several crisis actors.

2. Corollary questions, which are outside the scope of the present study, include the following: Has the impact of these crises on the international system been different from non-ethno-political crises? And have international systemic characteristics and dynamics had an impact on the nature of ethno-political crises?

3. Data collection is now under way for the years 1989–1994, to be incorporated into future analyses (Brecher and Wilkenfeld 1997). With this expansion of the data set beyond the end of the cold war, we anticipate a modification in the concept of polycentrism. That is, we will propose that the years 1963–1989 fall under "Polycentrism: Bipolar," i.e., the concentration of military power in two superpowers, and decision multipolarity, or the diffusion of decisional authority among many actors. For the years since 1990, we propose the designation "Polycentrism: Unipolar," i.e., the concentration of military power in one superpower, with continued diffusion of decisional authority.

Chapter 11. Preventing and Resolving Destructive Communal Conflicts

1. Nelson Mandela discusses the ANC decision in the early 1960s to sanction the establishment of MK, the Spear of the Nation, to conduct an armed struggle. He explains the choice of form of armed struggle: "For a small fledgling army, open revolution was inconceivable. Terrorism inevitably reflected poorly on those who used it. . . . Guerrilla warfare was a possibility, but since the ANC had been reluctant to embrace violence at all, it made sense to start with the form of violence that inflicted the least harm against individuals: sabotage. Because it did not involve the loss of life, it offered the best hope for reconciliation among the races afterward" (1994, 530).

Chapter 12. Ethnic Conflict at the International Level

1. Parenthetical citations giving only the author's name refer to chapters in this volume.

REFERENCES

Adam, Heribert, and Kogila Moodley. 1993. *The Negotiated Revolution.* Johannesberg: Jonathan Ball.

Agnew, John. 1989. "Beyond Reason: Spatial and Temporal Sources of Ethnic Conflicts." In *Intractable Conflicts and Their Resolution,* edited by Louis Kriesberg, Terrell A. Northrup, and Stuart J. Thorson. Syracuse, N.Y.: Syracuse University Press.

Agresti, Alan. 1990. *Categorical Data Analysis.* New York: Wiley.

Akwesasne Notes. 1978. *Basic Call to Consciousness.* Rooseveltown, N.Y.: Akwesasne Notes.

Alfred, Gerald R. 1991. "From Bad to Worse: Internal Politics in the 1990 Crisis at Kahnawake." *Northeast Indian Quarterly* 7:23–31.

Alger, Chadwick F. 1984. "Bridging the Micro and the Macro in International Relations Research." *Alternatives* 10:319–44.

Almond, Gabriel, and G. Bingham Powell. 1966. *Comparative Politics: A Developmental Approach.* Boston: Little, Brown.

Almond, Gabriel, and Sidney Verba. 1963. *The Civic Culture.* Boston: Little, Brown.

Anderson, Benedict. [1983] 1991. *Imagined Communities: Reflections on the Origin and Spread of Nationalism.* London: Verso.

Anderson, Charles W., Fred R. van der Mohden, and Crawford Young. 1967. *Issues of Political Development.* Englewood Cliffs, N.J.: Prentice-Hall.

Andrén, Nils. 1964. *Government and Politics in the Nordic Countries.* Stockholm: Almqvist and Wiksell.

Apter, David. 1965. *The Politics of Modernization.* Chicago: University of Chicago Press.

Arendt, Hannah. 1972. "On Violence." In *Crises of the Republic.* San Diego: Harvest/ Harcourt Brace Jovanovich.

———. 1973. *The Origins of Totalitarianism.* New edition. New York and London: Harcourt Brace Jovanovich.

Ashley, Richard K. 1986. "The Poverty of Neorealism." In *Neorealism and Its Critics,* edited by Robert O. Keohane. New York: Columbia University Press.

Askari, Hossein. 1990. *Saudi Arabia's Economy: Oil and the Search for Economic Development.* Greenwich, Conn.: Jai.

Axelrod, Robert. 1977. "Argumentation in Foreign Policy Settings." *Journal of Conflict Resolution* 24:3–25.

———. 1984. *The Evolution of Cooperation.* New York: Basic Books.

———. 1986. "An Evolutionary Approach to Norms." *American Political Science Review* 80:1095–1112.

Azar, Edward E. 1972. "Conflict Escalation and Conflict Reduction in an International Crisis: Suez, 1956." *Journal of Conflict Resolution* 16:183–201.

———. 1990. *The Management of Protracted Social Conflict.* Aldershot: Dartmouth Publishing.

Azar, Edward, and Chung-in Moon. 1988. *National Security in the Third World: The Management of Internal and External Threats.* Aldershot, England: Edward Elgar.

Azar, Edward E., and John Burton, eds. 1986. *International Conflict Resolution.* Boulder: Lynne Rienner.

Azar, Edward E., Paul Jureidini, and Ronald McLaurin. 1978. "Protracted Social Conflict: Theory as Practice in the Middle East." *Journal of Palestinian Studies* 8:41–60.

Azar, Edward E., and Thomas J. Sloan. 1975. "Dimensions of Interaction." *International Studies Association.* Occasional Paper No. 8.

Babbie, Earl, R. 1979. *The Practice of Social Research.* 2d ed. Belmont, Calif.: Wadsworth.

Banks, Arthur, S., and Robert B. Texter. 1963. *A Cross-Polity Survey.* Cambridge: MIT Press.

Barret, David, B. 1982. *World Christian Encyclopedia.* Oxford: Oxford University Press.

Barsh, Russel Lawrence. 1986. "Indigenous Peoples: An Emerging Object of International Law." *American Journal of International Law* 80:369–85.

Barth, Fredrik. 1969. *Ethnic Groups and Boundaries.* Boston: Little, Brown.

Bedlington, Stanley S. 1978. *Malaysia and Singapore: The Building of New States.* Ithaca: Cornell University Press.

Bell, Daniel. 1975. "Ethnicity and Social Change." In *Ethnicity: Theory and Experience,* edited by Nathan Glazer and Daniel P. Moynihan. Cambridge: Harvard University Press.

Blechman, Barry M., and Stephen S. Kaplan. 1978. *Force Without War: U.S. Armed Forces as a Political Instrument.* Washington, D.C.: Brookings Institution.

Bloom, William. 1990. *Personal Identity, National Identity and International Relations.* Cambridge: Cambridge University Press.

Bookman, Milica Zarcovic. 1993. *The Economics of Secession.* New York: St. Martin's.

Boucher, Jerry, Dan Landis, and Karen Arnold Clark, eds. 1987. *Ethnic Conflict: International Perspectives.* London: Sage.

Boyce, Peter. 1968. *Malaysia and Singapore in International Diplomacy.* Sydney: Sydney University Press.

Brass, Paul R. 1974. *Language, Religion, and Politics in North India.* London: Cambridge University Press.

———. 1991. *Ethnicity and Nationalism: Theory and Comparison.* New Delhi, Newbury Park, and London: Sage.

Brecher, Michael. 1972. *The Foreign Policy System of Israel.* London: Oxford University Press.

———. 1977. "Toward a Theory of International Crisis Behavior." *International Studies Quarterly* 21:39–74.

———. 1993. *Crises in World Politics.* Oxford: Pergamon.

Brecher, Michael, and Jonathan Wilkenfeld. 1989. *Crisis, Conflict and Instability.* Oxford: Pergamon.

Brecher, Michael, and Jonathan Wilkenfeld. 1991. *International Crisis Behaviour Project Code Book.* McGill University and University of Maryland.

Brecher, Michael, and Jonathan Wilkenfeld. 1997. *A Study of Crisis.* Ann Arbor: University of Michigan Press.

Brecher, Michael, Blema Steinberg, and Janice Stein. 1969. "A Framework for Research on Foreign Policy Behavior." *Journal of Conflict Resolution* 13:75–101.

Brecher, Michael, Jonathan Wilkenfeld, and Sheila Moser. 1988. *Handbook of International Crises.* Oxford: Pergamon.

Brecher, Michael, Patrick James, and Jonathan Wilkenfeld. 1990. "Polarity and Stability: New Concepts, Indicators and Evidence." *International Interactions* 16:49–80.

Brecher, Michael, Jonathan Wilkenfeld et al. 1988. *Crises in the Twentieth Century.* Vols. 1 and 2. Oxford: Pergamon.

Bremer, Stuart A. 1982. "The Contagiousness of Coercion: The Spread of Serious International Disputes, 1900–1976." *International Interactions* 9:29–55.

———. 1992. "Dangerous Dyads: Conditions Affecting the Likelihood of Interstate War, 1816–1965." *Journal of Conflict Resolution* 36:309–41.

———. 1993. "Democracy and Militarized Interstate Conflict, 1816–1965." *International Interactions* 18:231–49.

Breton, Raymond. 1972. "The Socio-Political Dynamics of the October Events." *Canadian Review of Sociology and Anthropology* 9: 33–56.

Brito, Dagobert L., and Michael D. Intrilligator. 1985. "Conflict, War, and Redistribution." *American Political Science Review* 79:943–57.

Brogan, Patrick. 1989. *World Conflicts: Why and Where They Are Happening.* London: Bloomsbury.

Buchanan, Allen. 1991. *Secession: The Morality of Political Divorce from Fort Sumter to Lithuania and Quebec.* Boulder: Westview.

Buchanan, James M., and Roger L. Faith. 1987. "Secession and the Limits of Taxation: Toward a Theory of Internal Exit." *American Economic Review* 77:1023–31.

Buchanan, William. 1988. *Understanding Political Variables.* 4th ed. New York: Macmillan.

Bueno de Mesquita, Bruce. 1985. "Toward a Scientific Understanding of International Conflict." *International Studies Quarterly* 29:121–136.

Bueno de Mesquita, Bruce, and David Lalman. 1992. *War and Reason.* New Haven: Yale University Press.

Bueno de Mesquita, Bruce, Randy Siverson, and Gary Woller. 1992. "War and the Fate of Regimes: A Comparative Analysis." *American Political Science Review* 86:638–46.

Bull, Hedley. 1977. *The Anarchical Society: A Study of Order in World Politics.* New York: Columbia University Press.

Burton, John. 1986. "The History of International Conflict Resolution." In *International Conflict Resolution,* edited by Edward E. Azar and John W. Burton. Boulder: Lynne Rienner.

———. 1987. "The International Conflict Resolution Priorities." *Forum Peace Institute Reporter* (June): 5–12.

———. 1990. *Conflict: Human Needs Theory.* New York: St. Martin's.

Burton, John W., and Frank Dukes. 1990a. *Conflict: Practices in Management, Settlement and Resolution.* New York: St. Martin's.

———. 1990b. *Conflict: Readings in Management and Resolution.* New York: St. Martin's.

Buzan, Barry. 1983. *People, States, and Fear.* Chapel Hill: University of North Carolina Press.

———. 1991. *People, States and Fear: An Agenda for International Security Studies in the Post Cold-War Era.* 2d ed. Boulder: Lynne Rienner.

Carment, David B. 1992. "Les dimensions internes des comportements en temps de crise: Etude de cas entre l'Inde et le Sri Lanka, 1983–1990." *Etudes Internationales* 23: 253–76.

———. 1993a. "The International Dimensions of Ethnic Conflict: Concepts, Indicators, and Theory." *Journal of Peace Research* 30:137–50.

———. 1993b. "The International Politics of Ethnic Conflict: The Interstate Dimensions of Secession and Irredenta in the Twentieth Century, A Crisis-Based Approach." Ph.D. diss., McGill University.

———. 1994a. A Summary of References and Readings for Participants in a Workshop on "The International Dimensions of Ethnic Conflict: Theory and Policy." Unpublished manuscript.

———. 1994b. "Canada, the United Nations and Peacemaking: The Management and Resolution of Ethnic Conflict, 1945–1988." *Canada in the Changing International Arena.* Waterloo: University of Waterloo Press.

Carment, David B., and Patrick James. 1994a. "The International Politics of Irredenta and Secession." Manuscript.

———. 1994b. "The International Politics of Ethnic Conflict: Peacekeeping and Policy." Manuscript.

———. 1995. "Internal Constraints and Interstate Ethnic Conflict." *Journal of Conflict Resolution* 39:82–109.

———. 1996. *The International Politics of Ethnic Conflict.* Columbia: University of South Carolina Press.

Carment, David, Athanasios Hristoulas, and Patrick James. 1993a. "The International Dimensions of Ethnic Conflict: Toward a Crisis-based Assessment." Paper presented at the annual meeting of the International Studies Association, Acapulco, Mexico.

———. 1993b. "Internal Constraints and Interstate Ethnic Conflict: Toward a Crisis-based Assessment of Irredentism." Paper presented at the annual meeting of the International Studies Association, Acapulco, Mexico.

Carr, E. H. 1939. *The Twenty Year's Crisis.* London: Macmillan.

CIA, Central Intelligence Agency World Factbook. 1990, 1991, 1992.

Chan, Heng Chee. 1971. *Singapore: The Politics of Survival 1965–1967.* Singapore: Oxford University Press.

Chan, Steve. 1984. "Mirror, Mirror on the Wall . . . Are the Freer Countries More Pacific?" *Journal of Conflict Resolution* 28:617–48.

Chaiwat, Satha-anand. 1993. "Kru-ze: A Theatre for Renegotiating Muslim Identity." *Sojourn* 8:195–218.

Chatterjee, Partha. 1975. *Arms, Alliances, and Stability: The Development of the Structure of International Politics.* Delhi: Macmillan of India.

Chazan, Naomi, ed. 1991. *Irredentism and International Politics.* Boulder: Lynne Rienner.

Christie, Clive, J. 1992. "Partition, Separatism and National Identity: A Reassessment." *Comparative Politics* 63:68–78.

Cioffi-Revilla, Claudio, and Harvey Starr. 1995. "Opportunity, Willingness and Political Uncertainty: Theoretical Foundations of Politics." *Journal of Theoretical Politics* 7:447–76.

Clark, Robert P. 1984. *The Basque Insurgents, ETA, 1952–1980.* Madison: University of Wisconsin Press.

Coakley, John. 1992. "The Resolution of Ethnic Conflict: Towards a Typology." *International Political Science Review* 13:343–58.

Cohen, Felix. 1960. *The Legal Conscience: Selected Papers,* edited by Lucy Kramer Cohen. Hamden, Conn.: Archon.

Cohen, Leonard J. 1995. *Broken Bones: Yugoslavia's Disintegration and Balkan Politics in Transition.* Boulder: Westview.

Collins, John N. 1973. "Foreign Conflict Behavior and Domestic Disorder in Africa." In *Conflict Behavior and Linkage Politics,* edited by Jonathan Wilkenfeld. New York: David McKay.

Comaroff, John L. 1991. "Humanity, Ethnicity, Nationality: Conceptual and Comparative Perspectives on the U.S.S.R." *Theory and Society* 20: 661–87.

Condren, Mary. 1989. *The Serpent and the Goddess: Women, Religion and Power in Celtic Ireland.* San Francisco: Harper.

Connor, Walker. 1972. "Nation-building or Nation-destroying?" *World Politics* 24:319–55.

———. 1978. "A Nation Is a Nation, Is a State, Is an Ethnic Group Is a . . ." *Ethnic and Racial Studies* 1:377–400.

——— . 1984a. "Eco-or Ethno Nationalism?" *Ethnic and Racial Studies* 7:342–59.

——— 1984b. *The National Question in Marxist-Leninist Theory and Strategy.* Princeton: Princeton University Press.

———. 1990. "When Is a Nation?" *Ethnic and Racial Studies* 13:99.

———. 1991. "From Tribe to Nation." *History of European Ideas* 13:5–18.

———. 1994. *Ethnonationalism: The Quest for Understanding.* Princeton: Princeton University Press.

Cooper, Robert, and Robert Berdal. 1993. "Outside Intervention in Ethnic Conflict." *Survival* 35:118–42.

Coser, Lewis A. 1956. *The Functions of Social Conflict.* New York: Free Press.

Coulter, Robert T. 1992. Presentation During Native American Awareness Week, Montana State University, Bozeman, 1 April 1992.

Cox, Robert W. 1986. "Social Forces, States and World Orders: Beyond International Relations Theory." In *Neorealism and Its Critics,* edited by Robert O. Keohane. New York: Columbia University Press.

Crampton, Richard J. 1983. *Bulgaria 1878–1978: A History.* Boulder: East European Monographs.

Crenshaw, Martha. 1988. "The Subjective Reality of the Terrorist: Ideological and Psychological Factors in Terrorism." In *Current Perspectives on International Terrorism,* edited by Robert O. Slater and Michael Stohl. New York: St. Martin's.

Dahrendorf, Ralf. 1959. *Class and Class Conflict in Industrial Society.* Stanford, Calif.: Stanford University Press.

Darling, Juanita, Tracy Wilkinson, William R. Long, and Stan Yarbo. 1993. "A New Call for Indian Activists." *Los Angeles Times,* 9 February, H1, H5.

Davies, Nigel. 1987. *The Aztec Empure: The Toltec Resurgence.* Norman: University of Oklahoma Press.

De Silva, K. M., and S. W. R. de A. Samarasinghe, eds. 1993. *Peace Accords and Ethnic Conflict.* New York: Pinter.

De Silva, K. M., and Ronald J. May, eds. 1991. *Internationalization of Ethnic Conflict.* London: Pinter.

Deloria, Vine, Jr. 1993a. "If You Think About It You Will See That It Is True," *Noetic Sciences Review* :62–71.

———. 1993b. *The Metaphysics of Modern Existence.* San Francisco: Harper and Row.

———. 1994. *God Is Red: A Native View of Religion.* Golden, Colo.: Fulcrum Publishers.

Deutsch, Karl W. 1966. *Nationalism and Social Communication: An Inquiry into the Foundations of Nationality.* 2d ed. Cambridge: MIT Press.

———. 1970. *Politics and Government: How People Decide Their Fate.* Boston: Houghton Mifflin.

Diehl, Paul F. 1983. "Arms Races and Escalation: A Closer Look." *Journal of Peace Research* 20:205–12.

———. 1991. "Geography and War: A Review and Assessment of the Empirical Literature." *International Interactions* 17:11–27.

Dion, Stephane. 1993. *Why Is Secession Rare? Lessons from Quebec.* Manuscript.

Dixon, William J. 1989. "Political Democracy and War." Paper presented at the annual meeting of the International Studies Association, London.

———. 1994. "Democracy and the Peaceful Settlement of International Conflict." *American Political Science Review* 88:14–32.

Donia, Robert J. 1981. *Islam Under the Double Eagle: The Muslims of Bosnia and Herzegovina, 1878–1914.* Boulder: East European Monographs.

Downs, Anthony. 1957. *An Economic Theory of Democracy.* New York: Harper-Collins.

Doyle, Michael W. 1986. "Liberalism in World Politics." *American Political Science Review* 80:1151–69.

Drake, P. J. 1966. "Singapore and Malaysia: The Monetary Consequences." *Australian Outlook* 20:28–35.

Dreisziger, Nandor, ed. 1990. *Ethnic Armies: Polyethnic Armies from the Time of the Hapsburgs to the Age of the Superpowers.* Waterloo, Ontario: Wilfred Laurier University.

Duchacek, Ivo, D. 1986. *The Territorial Dimensions of Politics Within, Among and Across Nations.* Boulder: Westview.

Easton, David. 1959, 1971. *The Political System.* New York: Alfred Knopf.

———. 1966. *Varieties of Political Theory.* Englewood Cliffs, N.J.: Prentice-Hall.

Eckstein, Harry. 1980. "Theoretical Approaches to Explaining Collective Political Violence." In *Handbook of Political Conflict,* edited by Ted Robert Gurr. New York: Free Press.

The Economist. 1993. "Bosnia: The Road to Ruin," 327 (May 29):23–26.

Ellina, Maro, and Will H. Moore. 1990. "Discrimination and Political Violence." *Western Political Quarterly* 43:267–78.

Emerson, Rupert. 1967. *From Empire to Nation: The Rise of Self-Assertion of Asian and African Peoples.* Cambridge: Harvard University Press.

Enloe, Cynthia H. 1973. *Ethnic Conflict and Political Development.* Boston: Little, Brown.

———. 1980. *Police, Military, and Ethnicity Foundations of State Power.* New Brunswick, N.J.: Transaction Books.

Esman, Milton. 1977. *Ethnic Conflict in the First World.* London: Cornell University Press.

Etzioni, Amatai. 1992. "The Evils of Self-Determination." *Foreign Policy* 89:21–35.

Faber, Jan, Henk W. Houweling, and Jan G. Siccama. 1984. "Diffusion of War: Some Theoretical Considerations and Empirical Evidence." *Journal of Peace Research* 21:277–88.

Falk, Richard A. 1966. *The Strategy of World Order.* New York: World Law Fund.

Feierabend, Ivo K., Rosalind L. Feierabend, and Rose M. Kelly. N.d. *Data Bank of Minority Group Conflict.* ICPSR Study No. 5209. Ann Arbor: Inter-University Consortium for Political Research.

Ferguson, Yale, and Richard Mansbach. 1989. *The State, Conceptual Chaos, and the Future of International Relations Theory.* Boulder and London: University of Denver.

———. 1991. "Between Celebration and Despair: Constructive Suggestions for Future International Theory." *International Studies Quarterly* 35:363–86.

Fischer, Fritz. 1967. *Germany's Aims in the First World War*. New York: Norton.

Fleras, Augie. 1991. "Aboriginal Electoral Districts for Canada: Lessons from New Zealand." In *Aboriginal Peoples and Electoral Reform*, edited by Robert A. Milen. Toronto: Dundurn.

Fletcher, Nancy McHenry. 1969. *The Separation of Singapore from Malaysia*. Data Paper No. 73. Ithaca: Cornell University Southeast Asia Program.

Franck, Thomas M., ed. 1968. *Why Federations Fail*. New York: New York University Press.

Frankel, J. 1963. *The Making of Foreign Policy: An Analysis of Decision Making*. London: Oxford University Press.

Frendreis, John P. 1989. "Modeling Spatial Diffusion: Reaction to Wellhofer." *Comparative Political Studies* 22:343–52.

Freud, Sigmund. 1930. *Civilization and Its Discontents*. London: Hogarth.

GAP (Group for the Advancement of Psychiatry). 1987. *Us and Them: The Psychology of Ethnonationalism*. Formulated by the Committee on International Relations, report no. 123. New York: Brunner/Mazel.

Gastil, Raymond. 1978. *Freedom in the World: Political Rights and Civil Liberties*. New York: Freedom House.

Gawitrha'. 1991. *Dwanoha=Our Mother: One Earth, One Mind, One Path*. Six Nations-Grand River, Ontario: Pine Tree.

Geertz, Clifford. 1973. *The Interpretation of Cultures: Selected Essays*. New York: Basic Books.

Giliomee, Hermann, and Jannie Gagiano, eds. 1991. *The Elusive Search for Peace: South Africa, Northern Ireland, and Israel*. New York: Oxford University Press.

Gilpin, Robert. 1981. *War and Change in World Politics*. Cambridge: Cambridge University Press.

Gimbutas, Marija. 1982. *The Goddesses and Gods of Old Europe: 6500–3500 B.C. Myths and Cult Images*. Berkeley: University of California Press.

Glazer, Nathan. 1981. "The Universalization of Ethnicity." In *At Issue, Politics in the World Arena*, edited by Stephen L. Spiegel. New York: St. Martin's Press.

Glazer, Nathan, and Daniel P. Moynihan. 1975. Introduction to *Ethnicity: Theory and Experience*, edited by Nathan Glazer and Daniel P. Moynihan. Cambridge: Harvard University Press.

Gleitman, Henry. 1992. *Psychology*. 2d ed. New York: W. W. Norton.

Glenny, Misha. 1986. *The Fall of Yugoslavia*. New York: Penguin.

Gochman, Charles S. 1991. "Interstate Metrics: Conceptualizing, Operationalizing, and Measuring the Geographic Proximity of States since the Congress of Vienna." *International Interactions* 17:93–112.

Goertz, Gary, and Paul F. Diehl. 1992a. *Territorial Changes and International Politics*. London: Routledge.

———. 1992b. "The Empirical Importance of Enduring Rivalries." *International Interactions* 18:151–63.

———. 1993. "Enduring International Rivalries: Theoretical Constructs and Empirical Patterns." *International Studies Quarterly* 37:147–71.

Goldmann, Robert B., and A. J. Wilson, eds. 1984. *From Independence to Statehood: Managing Ethnic Conflict in Five African and Asian States*. London: Pinter.

Goldstein, Joshua S., and John R. Freeman. 1990. *Three Way Street: Strategic Reciprocity in World Politics*. Chicago: University of Chicago Press.

Gordon, Milton M. 1975. "Toward a General Theory of Racial and Ethnic Group Relations." In *Ethnicity: Theory and Experience,* edited by Nathan Glazer and Daniel P. Moynihan. Cambridge: Harvard University Press.

———. 1978. *Human Nature, Class, and Ethnicity.* New York: Oxford University Press.

Greeley, Andrew M. 1977. *The American Catholic: A Social Portrait.* New York: Basic Books.

Greenfeld, Liah. 1992. *Nationalism: Five Roads to Modernity.* Cambridge: Harvard University Press.

Gregory, Steven, and Roger Sanjek, eds. 1994. *Race.* New Brunswick, N.J.: Rutgers University Press.

Grove, John D. 1974. "Different Political and Economic Patterns of Ethnic and Race Relations: A Cross-National Analysis." *Race* 15: 303–28.

Gunnell, John G. 1988. "American Political Science, Liberalism, and the Invention of Political Theory." *American Political Science Review* 82:71–88.

Gurr, Ted Robert. 1970. *Why Men Rebel.* Princeton: Princeton University Press.

———. 1974. "Persistence and Change in Political Systems." *American Political Science Review* 68:1482–1504.

———. 1978, 1990. *Polity II Handbook.* Ann Arbor: Inter-University Consortium for Political and Social Research.

———. 1988. "War, Revolution, and the Growth of the Coercive State." *Comparative Political Studies* 21:45–65.

———. 1990. "Ethnic Warfare and the Changing Priorities of Global Security." *Mediterranean Quarterly* 1:82–98.

———. 1991. "Minorities at Risk: The Dynamics of Ethnopolitical Mobilization and Conflict, 1945–1990." Paper presented at the annual meeting of the International Studies Association, Vancouver, Canada.

———. 1992. "The Internationalization of Protracted Communal Conflicts since 1945: Which Groups, Where and How." In *The Internationalization of Communal Strife,* edited by Manus I. Midlarsky. London: Routledge.

———. 1993a. *Minorities at Risk: A Global View of Ethnopolitical Conflicts.* Washington, D.C.: United States Institute of Peace.

———. 1993b. "Resolving Ethnopolitical Conflict: Exit, Autonomy, or Access." In *Minorities at Risk,* edited by Ted Robert Gurr. Washington, D.C.: United States Institute of Peace.

———. 1993c. "Why Minorities Rebel: A Global Analysis of Communal Mobilization and Conflict since 1945." *International Political Science Review* 14:171–201.

———. 1994. "Peoples Against States: Ethnopolitical Conflict and the Changing World System." Presidential address to the annual meeting of the International Studies Association, Washington, D.C., 1 April.

Gurr, Ted Robert, and James R. Scarritt. 1989. "Minorities Rights at Risk: A Global Survey." *Human Rights Quarterly* 11:375–405.

Gurr, Ted Robert, Keith Jaggers, and Will H. Moore. 1989. *Polity II Codebook.* University of Colorado: Center for Comparative Politics.

———. 1991. "The Transformation of the Western State: The Growth of Democracy, Autocracy, and State Power since 1800." In *On Measuring Democracy,* edited by Alex Inkeles. New Brunswick, N.J.: Transaction.

Gurr, Ted Robert, and Monty G. Marshall. 1990. *Ethnopolitical Conflicts since 1945: Report of a Global Survey.* Technical Report to the Academic Research Support Program, United States Department of Defense.

Haas, Ernst. 1983. "Regime Decay: Conflict Management and International Organizations, 1945–1981." *International Organization* 37: 189–256.

Haglund, David G., and Charles C. Pentland. 1996. "Ethnic Conflict and European Security: What Role for NATO and the EC?" In *The International Politics of Ethnic Conflict*, edited by David Carment and Patrick James.

Hakovirta, Harto. 1986. *Third World Conflicts and Refugeeism: Dimensions, Dynamics and Trends of the World Refugee Problem.* Commentationes Scientiarum Socialium 32. Helsinki: Finnish Society of Sciences and Letters.

Halpern, Manfred. 1964. "The Morality and Politics of Intervention." In *International Aspects of Civil Strife*, edited by James Rosenau. Princeton: Princeton University Press.

Harff, Barbara, and Ted Robert Gurr. 1988. "Toward Empirical Theory of Genocides and Politicides: Identification and Measurement of Cases since 1945." *International Studies Quarterly* 32:359–71.

Haug, Marie R. 1967. "Social and Cultural Pluralism as a Concept in Social Systems Analysis." *American Journal of Sociology* 73: 294–304.

Hechter, Michael. 1975. *Internal Colonialism.* London: Routledge and Kegan Paul.

———. 1992. "The Dynamics of Secession." *Acta Sociologica* 35, 4:267–83.

Heisler, Martin O., ed. 1977. *Ethnic Conflict in the World Today.* Philadelphia: American Academy of Political and Social Science.

Heizer, Robert Fleming, and Alan F. Almquist. 1971. *The Other Californians: Prejudice and Discrimination Under Spain, Mexico, and the United States to 1920.* Berkeley: University of California Press.

Hensel, Paul R., and Paul F. Diehl. 1992. "Testing Empirical Propositions about Shatterbelts, 1945–1976." Paper presented at the annual meeting of the International Studies Association-Midwest, East Lansing, Michigan, 20–21 November.

Heraclides, Alexis. 1989. "Conflict Resolution, Ethnonationalism and the Middle-East Impasse." *Journal of Peace Research* 26·197–212.

———. 1990. "Secessionist Minorities and External Involvement." *International Organization* 44:341–78.

———. 1991. *The Self-Determination of Minorities in International Politics.* Portland, Ore.: Frank Cass.

———. 1992. "Secession, Self-Determination and Nonintervention: In Quest of a Normative Synthesis." *Journal of International Affairs* 45:399–420.

Herz, John. 1957. "The Rise and Demise of the Modern State." *World Politics* 9:473–93.

Hess, Franke S. 1990. "Explaining International Movements: A Study of Global Activism Among the World's Indigenous Peoples." Ph.D. diss., University of Maryland at College Park.

Higham, John. 1974. *Strangers in the Land, Patterns of American Nativism 1860–1925.* New York: Atheneum.

Hill, Ken. 1978. "Domestic Politics, International Linkages and Military Expenditures." *Studies of Comparative International Development* 13:35–39.

Hill, Stuart, and Donald Rothchild. 1987. "The Contagion of Political Conflict in Africa and the World." *Journal of Conflict Resolution* 30:716–35.

———. 1992. "The Impact of Regime on the Diffusion of Political Conflict." In *The Internationalization of Communal Strife*, edited by Manus I. Midlarsky. London: Routledge.

Hoffmann, Stanley. 1977. "An American Social Science: International Relations." *Daedalus* 106:41–60.

Holdsworth, Mary. 1967. "Lenin and the Nationalities Question." In *Lenin: The Man, the Theorist, the Leader; A Reappraisal,* edited by L. Schapiro and P. Reddaway. New York: Praeger.

Holsti, Kalevi J. 1991. *Peace and War: Armed Conflict and International Order, 1648–1989.* Cambridge: Cambridge University Press.

———. 1993. "Armed Conflicts in the Third World: Assessing Analytical Approaches and Anomalies." Unpublished manuscript.

Hopmann, P. Terrence. 1988. "Negotiating Peace in Central America." *Negotiation Journal* 4: 361–80.

Hornung, Rick. 1991. *One National Under the Sun: Inside the Mohawk Civil War.* Toronto: Stoddart.

Horowitz, Donald. 1985. *Ethnic Groups in Conflict.* Berkeley: University of California Press.

———. 1991. "Irredentas and Secessions: Adjacent Phenomena, Neglected Connections." In *Irredentism and International Politics,* edited by Naomi Chazan. Boulder: Lynne Rienner.

Houweling, Henk W., and Jan G. Siccama. 1985. "The Epidemiology of War, 1816–1980." *Journal of Conflict Resolution* 29:641–63.

Huertas, Thomas F. 1977. *Economic Growth and Economic Policy in a Multinational Setting: The Hapsburg Monarchy, 1841–1865.* New York: Arno.

Huntington, Samuel P. 1968. *Political Order in Changing Societies.* New Haven: Yale University Press.

———. 1991. *The Third Wave: Democratization in the Late Twentieth Century.* Norman: University of Oklahoma Press.

———. 1993. "The Clash of Civilizations?" *Foreign Affairs* 72, 3:22–49.

Huth, Paul, and Bruce Russett. 1993. "General Deterrence Between Enduring Rivals." *American Political Science Review* 87:61–73.

International Alert. 1993a. "Preventive Diplomacy: Recommendations of a Round Table on Preventive Diplomacy and the UN's Agenda for Peace." London, 28–30 January.

International Alert. 1993b. "Self Determination: Statement and Recommendations Arising from the Martin Ennals Memorial Symposium on Self-determination, Saskatoon Canada." London, 3–6 March.

Isaacs, Harold A. 1975. *Idols of the Tribe: Group Identity and Political Change.* New York: Harper and Row.

Jackson, Robert, H. 1990. *Quasi-States: Sovereignty, International Relations and the Third World.* Cambridge: Cambridge University Press.

Jackson, Robert, H., and Carl G. Rosberg. 1982. "Why Africa's Weak States Persist: The Empirical and the Juridical in Statehood." *World Politics* 35:1–24.

Jaimes, M. Annette, ed. 1992. *The State of Native America: Genocide, Colonization, and Resistance.* Boston: South End.

James, Alan. 1969. *The Politics of Peace-keeping.* London: Chatto and Windus.

———. 1996. "Peacekeeping and Ethnic Conflict: Theory and Evidence." In *The International Politics of Ethnic Conflict,* edited by David Carment and Patrick James.

James, Patrick. 1987. "Conflict and Cohesion." *Cooperation and Conflict* 22:21–33.

———. 1988. *Crisis and War.* Montreal and Kingston: McGill–Queen's University Press.

———. 1993. "Structural Realism as a Research Enterprise: Toward Elaborated Structural Realism." *International Political Science Review* 14:123–148.

James, Patrick, and John R. Oneal. 1991. "The Influence of Domestic and International Politics on the President's Use of Force." *Journal of Conflict Resolution* 35:307–32.

Jelavich, Barbara. 1983. *History of the Balkans.* Cambridge: Cambridge University Press.

Jenkins, David. 1980. "New Life in an Old Pact." *Far Eastern Economic Review,* 7–13 November, 26–28.

Jenkins, Craig J., and Augustine Kposowa. 1992. "The Political Origins of African Military Coups: Ethnic Competition and the Struggle over the Postcolonial State." *International Studies Quarterly* 36:271–92.

Jennings, Francis. 1993. *The Founders of America: How Indians Discovered the Land, Pioneered in It, and Created Great Classical Civilizations, How they Were Plunged into a Dark Age by Invasion and Conquest, and How They are Reviving.* New York: Norton.

Jervis, Robert 1976. *Perception and Misperception in International Politics.* Princeton: Princeton University Press.

———. 1978. "Cooperation Under the Security Dilemma." *World Politics* 30:167–214.

Job, Brian L. 1992. "The Insecurity Dilemma: National, Regime, and State Securities in the Third World." In *The Insecurity Dilemma: National Security of Third World States,* edited by Brian L. Job. Boulder: Lynne Rienner.

Kane, Joe. 1993. "With Spears from All Sides." *New Yorker* 27:54–79.

Kane-Berman, John. 1990. *South Africa's Silent Revolution.* Johannesburg: South/African Institute of Race Relations.

Kasfir, Nelson. 1979. "Explaining Ethnic Political Participation." *World Politics* 31:365–88.

Kaufman, Stuart. 1996. "Preventing Ethnic Violence: Conditions for the Success of Peacekeeping." In *The International Politics of Ethnic Conflict,* edited by David Carment and Patrick James.

Kaufman, Stuart. 1994–95. "The Irresistible Force and the Imperceptible Object: The Yugoslav Breakup and Western Policy." *Security Studies* 4 (winter): 281–329.

Kaye, G. D., D. A. Grant, and E. J. Emond. 1985. *Major Armed Conflict: A Compendium of Interstate and Intrastate Conflict, 1720 to 1985.* Ottawa: Department of National Defense.

Kelly, Philip L. 1986. "Escalation of Regional Conflict: Testing the Shatterbelt Concept." *Political Geography Quarterly* 5:161–80.

Kennan, George F. 1979. *The Decline of Bismarck's European Order: Franco-Russian Relations, 1875–1890.* Princeton: Princeton University Press.

Kennedy, Charles H., and David J. Louscher. 1991. "Civil-Military Interaction: Data in Search of a Theory." *Journal of Asian and African Studies* 26:1–10.

Keohane, Robert O., ed. 1986a. *Neorealism and Its Critics.* New York: Columbia University Press.

———. 1986b. "Realism, Neorealism and the Study of World Politics." In *Neorealism And Its Critics,* edited by Robert O. Keohane. New York: Columbia University Press.

———. 1986c. "Reciprocity in International Relations." *International Organization* 40:1–27.

Keohane, Robert O., and Joseph S. Nye. 1989. *Power and Interdependence.* 2d ed. Boston: Scott, Foresman.

Keyes, Charles, ed. 1981. *Ethnic Change.* Seattle: University of Washington Press.

Kinder, Hermann, and Werner Hilgemann. 1978. *The Anchor Atlas of World History.* Vol. 2: *From the French Revolution to the American Bicentennial.* Trans. Ernest A. Menze. New York: Doubleday Anchor.

King, Gary. 1986. "How Not to Lie with Statistics: Avoiding Common Mistakes in Empirical Political Science." *American Journal of Political Science* 30:666–87.

———. 1989a. *Unifying Political Methodology.* New York: Cambridge University Press.

———. 1989b. "Event-Count Models for International Relations: Generalizations and

Applications." *International Studies Quarterly* 33:123–48.

Kirby, Andrew M., and Michael D. Ward. 1987. "The Spatial Analysis of Peace and War." *Comparative Political Studies* 20:293–313.

Kissinger, Henry A. 1974. *American Foreign Policy.* Expanded ed. New York: Norton.

Klingman, David. 1980. "Temporal and Spatial Diffusion in the Comparative Analysis of Social Change." *American Political Science Review* 74:123–37.

Knight, David B. 1982. "Identity and Territory: Geographical Perspectives on Nationalism and Regionalism." *Annals of the Association of American Geographers* 72:514–31.

Kodikara, Shelton, U. 1985. *The Separatist Eelam Movement in Sri Lanka: An Overview.* Colombo: University of Colombo Press.

———. 1987. "International Dimensions of Ethnic Conflict in Sri Lanka: Involvement of India and Non-state Actors." *Bulletin of Peace Proposals* 18:637–48.

Kolsto, Pal. 1993. "The New Russian Diaspora: Minority Protection in the Soviet Successor States." *Journal of Peace Research* 30:197–217.

Krasner, Stephen D. 1981. "Transforming International Regimes: What the Third World Wants and Why." *International Studies Quarterly* 25:119–48.

———. 1985. *Structural Conflict: The Third World Against Global Liberalism.* Berkeley: University of California Press.

Kriesberg, Louis. 1982. *Social Conflicts.* Rev. ed. Englewood Cliffs, N.J.: Prentice-Hall.

———. 1989. "Transforming Conflicts in the Middle East and Central Europe." In *Intractable Conflicts and Their Resolution,* edited by Louis Kriesberg, Terrell A. Northrup, and Stuart J. Thorson. Syracuse, N.Y.: Syracuse University Press.

———. 1992. *International Conflict Resolution.* New Haven: Yale University Press.

Krueger, Chris. 1986. "Re-education and Relocation in Guatemala." *Cultural Survival Quarterly* 10:43–44.

Kuzmanic, Toni, and Arno Truger, eds. 1992. *Yugoslavia War.* Ljubljana/Schlaining: Austrian Study Centre for Peace and Conflict Resolution; Schlaining Peace Institute, Ljubljana.

Laitin, David. 1991. "The Four Nationality Games and Soviet Politics." *Journal of Soviet Nationalities* 2:1–37.

Lake, David A. 1992. "Powerful Pacifists: Democratic States and War." *American Political Science Review* 86:24–37.

Laurance, Edward J. 1992. *The International Arms Trade.* New York: Lexington.

Lee, H. P. 1986. "Emergency Powers in Malaysia." In *The Constitution of Malaysia: Further Perspectives and Developments,* edited by F. A. Trindale and H. P. Lee. Petaling Jaya: Oxford University Press.

Lee, Shin-wha. 1993. *Minorities at Risk Phase I Dataset: Users' Manual.* College Park: Center for International Development and Conflict Management.

Leistikow, Gunnar. 1950. "Co-operation Between the Scandinavian Countries." In *Scandinavia—Between East and West,* edited by Henning Friis. Ithaca: Cornell University Press.

Levine, Robert A., and Donald T. Campbell. 1972. *Ethnocentrism: Theories of Conflict, Ethnic Attitudes and Group Behavior.* New Haven: Yale University Press.

Levy, Jack S. 1989. "The Diversionary Theory of War: A Critique." In *Handbook of War Studies,* edited by Manus I. Midlarsky. Boston: Unwin Hyman.

Lian, Bradley, and John R. Oneal. 1993. "Presidents, the Use of Military Force, and Public Opinion." *Journal of Conflict Resolution* 37:277–300.

Licklider, Roy, ed. 1993. *Stopping the Killing: How Civil Wars End.* New York: New York University Press.

Lijphart, Arend. 1979. "Consociation and Federation: Conceptual and Empirical Links." *Canadian Journal of Political Science* 22:499–522.

Lindgren, Raymond E. 1959. *Norway-Sweden: Union, Disunion, and Scandinavian Integration.* Princeton: Princeton University Press.

Lizot, Jacques. 1976. *The Yanomami in the Face of Ethnocide.* Copenhagen: International Workgroup of Indigenous Affairs, Document no. 22.

Luard, Evan, ed. 1972a. *The International Regulation of Civil Wars.* London: Thames and Hudson.

———. 1972b. "Conclusions." In *The International Regulation of Civil Wars,* edited by Evan Luard. London: Thames and Hudson.

Lustick, Ian. 1979. "Stability in Deeply Divided Societies: Consociationalism Versus Control." *World Politics* 31:352–74.

Lyon, Peter. 1976. "Separatism and Secession in the Malaysian Realm 1948–65." In *Collected Seminar Papers on the Politics of Separatism,* edited by W. H. Morris-Jones. Collected seminar paper no. 19. Institute of Commonwealth Studies, University of London.

Mandel, Robert. 1980. "Roots of the Modern Interstate Border Dispute." *Journal of Conflict Resolution* 24:427–54.

Mandela, Nelson. 1994. *Long Walk to Freedom.* Boston: Little, Brown.

Maoz, Zeev. 1989. "Joining the Club of Nations: Political Development and International Conflict, 1816–1976." *International Studies Quarterly* 33:199–231.

———. 1990a. *National Choices and International Processes.* New York: Cambridge University Press.

———. 1990b. *Paradoxes of War: On the Art of National Self-Entrapment.* Boston: Unwin Hyman.

———. 1993a. "Domestic Political Change and Strategic Response: The Impact of Domestic Conflict on State Behavior, 1816–1986." Paper presented at the Conference on the International Dimensions of Ethnic Conflict, Florida State University, Tallahassee, Florida, 18–19 December.

———. 1993b. "The Onset and Initiation of Militarized Interstate Disputes in the Modern Era." *International Interactions* 19:27–47.

———. 1995. *Domestic Sources of Global Change.* Ann Arbor: University of Michigan Press.

Maoz, Zeev, and Nasrin Abdolali. 1989. "Regime Types and International Conflict, 1816–1976." *Journal of Conflict Resolution* 33:3–35.

Maoz, Zeev, and Bruce Russett. 1991. "Alliances, Contiguity, Wealth, and Political Stability: Is the Lack of Conflict Between Democracies a Statistical Artifact?" *International Interactions* 17:245–67.

Maoz, Zeev, and Bruce Russett. 1993. "Normative and Structural Causes of Democratic Peace, 1946–1986." *American Political Science Review* 87:640–54.

Marshall, Monty G. 1992. "Soviet Nationalities Policy: An Account of the Triumph of Reason." Unpublished manuscript.

———. 1993a. "States at Risk: Ethnopolitical Conflict in the Multinational States of Eastern Europe." In *Minorities at Risk: A Global View of Ethnopolitical Conflicts,* edited by Ted Robert Gurr. Washington, D.C.: United States Institute of Peace.

———. 1993b. "Collective Violence and War: Reconceptualizing the Problem of Political Borders in Security Studies." Paper presented at the annual meeting of the International Studies Association-Midwest, East Lansing, Michigan, 29–30 October.

———. 1995. "The Global Insecurity System: Protracted Social Conflict, Diffusion of

Threat, and Limitations on Developmental Growth." Ph.D. diss., University of Iowa.

Mason, John W. 1985. *The Dissolution of the Austro-Hungarian Empire, 1867–1918.* London: Longman.

Mastanduno, Michael, David Lake, and John Ikenberry. 1989. "Toward a Realist Theory of State Action." *International Studies Quarterly* 33:457–74.

May, Arthur J. 1951. *The Hapsburg Monarchy 1967–1914.* Cambridge: Harvard University Press.

May, Ronald J. 1990. "Ethnic Separatism in Southeast Asia." *Pacific Viewpoint* 31:28–59.

Mayall, James. 1990. *Nationalism and International Society.* New York: Cambridge University Press.

McClintock, Catherine. 1992. "Communal Strife in Peru: A Case of Absence of Spillover into the International Arena." In *The Internationalization of Communal Strife,* edited by Manus I. Midlarsky. London: Routledge.

McGarry, John, and Brendan O'Leary, eds. 1993. *The Politics of Ethnic Conflict Regulation.* London: Routledge.

McGowan, William. 1992. *Only Man Is Vile: The Tragedy of Sri Lanka.* London: Farrar, Strauss and Giroux.

McGrew, Anthony G., and Paul G. Lewis. 1992. *Global Politics: Globalization and The Nation-State.* Cambridge: Polity Press.

McRoberts, Kenneth. 1988. *Quebec: Social Change and Political Crisis.* 3rd ed. Toronto: McClelland and Stewart.

Meadwell, Hudson. 1989. "Cultural and Instrumental Approaches to Ethnic Nationalism." *Ethnic and Racial Studies* 12:309–28.

———. 1991. "A Rational Choice Approach to Political Regionalism." *Comparative Politics* 23:401–23.

———. 1992. "Transitions to Independence and Ethnic Nationalist Mobilization." Eighth International Conference of Europeanists, Chicago.

Means, Gordon P. 1970. *Malaysian Politics.* London: University of London Press.

Mearsheimer, John. 1990. "Back to the Future: Instability in Europe after the Cold War." *International Security* 15:5–56.

Miall, Hugh. 1992. *The Peacemakers: Peaceful Settlement of Disputes since 1945.* London: St. Martin's.

Micelmann, Hans, J., and Panyotis Soldatos, eds. 1990. *Federalism and International Relations: The Role of Subnational Units.* Oxford: Clarendon Press.

Midlarsky, Manus I. 1988a. *The Onset of War.* Boston: Unwin Hyman.

———. 1988b. "Rulers and the Ruled: Patterned Inequality and the Onset of Mass Political Violence." *American Political Science Review* 82:491–509.

——— 1989a. *Handbook of War Studies.* Boston: Unwin Hyman.

———. 1989b. "Hierarchical Equilibria and the Long-Run Instability of Multipolar Systems." In *Handbook of War Studies,* edited by Manus I. Midlarsky. Ann Arbor: University of Michigan Press.

———. 1992a. "Communal Strife and the Origins of World War I." In *The Internationalization of Communal Strife,* edited by Manus I. Midlarsky. London: Routledge.

Midlarsky, Manus I., ed. 1992b. *The Internationalization of Communal Strife.* London: Routledge.

Modelski, George. 1964. "International Settlement of Internal War." In *International Aspects of Civil Strife,* edited by James Rosenau. Princeton: Princeton University Press.

Moore, Will H., and David R. Davis. 1994. "Does Ethnicity Matter? Ethnic Alliances and International Interactions." Paper presented at the conference, International Spread and Management of Ethnic Conflict, La Jolla, Calif.

Morgan, T. Clifton. 1993. "Democracy and War: Reflections on the Literature." *International Interactions* 18:197–203.

Morgan, T. Clifton, and Sally H. Campbell. 1991. "Domestic Structure, Decisional Constraints, and War." *Journal of Conflict Resolution* 35:187–211.

Morgenthau, Hans, J. 1957. "The Paradoxes of Nationalism." *Yale Review* 46:481–91.

———. 1977. *Politics Among Nations.* 5th rev. ed. New York: Knopf.

Morrow, James D. 1991. "Electoral and Congressional Incentives and Arms Control." *Journal of Conflict Resolution* 35:245–65.

Most, Benjamin A., and Harvey Starr. 1980. "Diffusion, Reinforcement, Geopolitics, and the Spread of War." *American Political Science Review* 74:932–46.

———. 1989. *Inquiry, Logic and International Politics.* Columbia: University of South Carolina Press.

———. 1990. "Theoretical and Logical Issues in the Study of International Diffusion." *Journal of Theoretical Politics* 2:391–412.

Most, Benjamin A., Harvey Starr, and Randolph M. Siverson. 1989. "The Logic and Study of the Diffusion of International Conflict." In *Handbook of War Studies,* edited by Manus I. Midlarsky. Boston: Allen and Unwin.

Moynihan, Daniel P. 1993. *Pandemonium: Ethnicity in International Politics.* London: Oxford University Press.

Muller, Edward N., and Erich Weede. 1990. "Cross-National Variation in Political Violence: A Rational Action Approach." *Journal of Conflict Resolution* 34:624–65.

Nafziger, E. Wayne, and William L. Richter. 1976. "Biafra and Bangladesh: The Political Economy of Secessionist Conflict." *Journal of Peace Research* 13:91–109.

Nagel, Joanne. 1980. "The Conditions of Ethnic Separatism: The Kurds in Turkey, Iran and Iraq." *Ethnicity* 7:279–97.

Nagel, Joanne, and Brad Whorton. 1992. "Ethnic Conflict and the World System: International Competition in Iraq (1961–1991) and Angola (1974–1991)." *Journal of Political and Military Sociology* 20:1–35.

Nahaylo, Bohdan, and Victor Swoboda. 1990. *Soviet Disunion: A History of the Nationalities Problem in the USSR.* London: Hamish Hamilton.

Neilsson, Gunnar P. 1985. "States and Nation Groups: A Global Taxonomy." In *New Nationalisms of the Developed West,* edited by Edward A. Tiryakian and Ronald Rogowski. Boston: Allen and Unwin.

Neilsson, Gunnar, P., and Ralph Jones. 1988. "From Ethnic Categories to Nation: Patterns of Political Modernization." Paper presented at the annual meeting of the International Studies Association.

Neuberger, Benjamin. 1986. *National Self-Determination.* Boulder, Colo.: Lynne Reinner.

———. 1990. "Nationalisms Compared: ANC, IRA, and PLO." In *The Elusive Search for Peace: South Africa, Israel and Northern Ireland,* edited by Hermann Giliome and Jannie Gagiano. Cape Town: Oxford University Press.

The New York Times.

Nietschmann, Bernard. 1987. "Militarization and Indigenous Peoples: The Third World War." *Cultural Survival Quarterly* 11:1–16.

Nomikos, Eugenia V., and Robert C. North. 1976. *International Crisis: The Outbreak of World War I.* Montreal: McGill–Queen's University Press.

Nordlinger, Eric. 1972. *Conflict Regulation in Deeply Divided Societies.* Cambridge: Cambridge University Press.

Nye, Joseph S. 1971. *Peace in Parts: Integration and Conflict in Regional Organization.* Boston: Little, Brown.

Nye, Joseph S., and Robert O. Keohane. 1973. "Transnational Relations and World Politics: An Introduction." In *Transnational Relations and World Politics,* edited by Keohane and Nye. Cambridge: Harvard University Press.

Olzak, Susan, and Joanne Nagel, eds. 1986. *Competitive Ethnic Relations.* Orlando: Academic Press.

Ongkili, James P. 1985. *Nation-Building in Malaysia 1946–1974.* Singapore: Oxford University Press.

Oren, Ido. 1990. "The War Proneness of Alliances." *Journal of Conflict Resolution* 34:208–33.

Osgood, Charles E. 1962. *An Alternative to War or Surrender.* Urbana: University of Illinois Press.

Ostrom, Charles W., and Brian Job. 1986. "The President and the Political Use of Force." *American Political Science Review* 80:541–66.

Owen, David. 1996. *Balkan Odyssey.* New York: Harcourt Brace.

Paige, Jeffery M. 1975. *Agrarian Revolution: Social Movements and Export Agriculture in the Underdeveloped World.* New York: Free Press.

Pang, Eng Fong, and Linda Lim. 1982. "Foreign Labour and Economic Development in Singapore." *International Migration Review* 16:548–76.

Parsons, Talcott. 1951. *The Social System.* New York: Free Press.

Paul, John P. 1982. "The Greek Lobby and American Foreign Policy: A Transnational Perspective." In *Ethnic Identities in a Transnational World,* edited by John F. Stack Jr. Westport, Conn.: Greenwood.

Paul, T. V. 1992. "Influence through Arms Transfers: Lessons from the US-Pakistani Relationship." *Asian Survey* 32:1078–92.

Peretz, Don. 1990. *Intifada.* Boulder, Colo.: Westview.

Posen, Barry. 1993. "The Security Dilemma and Ethnic Conflict." *Survival* 35:27–47.

Premdas, Ralph R. 1991. "The Internationalization of Ethnic Conflict: Some Theoretical Explorations." In *Internationalization of Ethnic Conflict,* edited by K. M. de Silva and Ronald J. May. London: Pinter.

Premdas, Ralph, S. W. R. de A. Samarasinghe, and Alan B. Anderson, eds. 1990. *Secessionist Movements in Comparative Perspective.* London: Pinter.

Przeworski, Adam, and Henry Teune. 1970. *The Logic of Comparative Social Inquiry.* Malabar, Fla.: Robert E. Kreiger.

Putnam, Robert. D. 1988. "Diplomacy and Domestic Politics: The Logic of Two-Level Games." *International Organization* 42:426–60.

Ramet, Sabrina. 1992a. *Nationalism and Federalism in Yugoslavia, 1962–1991.* 2d ed. Bloomington: Indiana University Press.

———. 1992b. "War in the Balkans." *Foreign Affairs* 72:79–98.

Rapoport, Anatol. 1960. *Fights, Games, and Debates.* Ann Arbor: University of Michigan Press.

Rasler, Karen. 1992. "International Influence on the Origins and Outcomes of Internal War: A Comparative Analysis of the 1958 and 1975–6 Lebanese Civil Wars." In *The Internationalization of Communal Strife,* edited by Manus I. Midlarsky. London: Routledge.

Rawls, John. 1971. *A Theory of Justice.* Cambridge: Harvard University Press.

Ray, James Lee. 1993. "War Between Democracies: Rare or Nonexistent?" *International Interactions* 18:251–76.

Reardon, Betty. 1993. *Women and War*. London: Zed.

Richardson, Lewis F. 1960. *Statistics of Deadly Quarrels*. Pittsburgh: Boxwood.

Riker, William. 1986. *The Art of Political Manipulation*. New Haven: Yale University Press.

———. 1990. "Political Science and Rational Choice." In *Perspectives on Positive Political Theory*, edited by James Alt and Kenneth Shepsle. New York: Cambridge University Press.

Roeder, P. G. 1990. "Soviet Federalism and Ethnic Mobilization." *World Politics* 43:196–232.

Rosenau, James, ed. 1964. *International Aspects of Civil Strife*. Princeton: Princeton University Press.

———. 1990. *Turbulence in World Politics: A Theory of Change and Continuity*. Princeton: Princeton University Press.

Rosh, Robert. 1987. "Ethnic Cleavages as a Component of Global Military Expenditures." *Journal of Peace Research* 24:21–30.

———. 1988. "Third World Militarization: Security Webs and the States They Ensnare." *Journal of Conflict Resolution* 2:671–98.

Ross, Marc Howard, and Elizabeth Homer. 1976. "Galton's Problem in Cross-National Research." *World Politics* 29:1–28.

Rothchild, Donald, and Naomi Chazan, eds. 1988. *The Precarious Balance: State and Society in Africa*. Boulder, Colo.: Westview.

Rothman, Jay. 1992. *From Confrontation to Cooperation: Resolving Ethnic and Regional Conflict*. Newbury Park, Calif.: Sage.

Rothschild, Joseph. 1981. *Ethnopolitics: A Conceptual Approach*. New York: Columbia University Press.

Royce, Anya. 1982. *Ethnic Identity: Strategies of Diversity*. Bloomington: Indiana University Press.

Rubenstein, Richard. 1983. *The Age of Triage*. Boston: Beacon.

Rudolph, Joseph, and Robert Thompson. 1985. "Ethnoterritorial Movements and the Policy Process: Accommodating Nationalist Demands in the Developed World." *Comparative Politics* 17:291–311.

Ruggie, John Gerald. 1986. "Continuity and Transformation in World Polity: Toward A Neorealist Synthesis." In *Neorealism and Its Critics,* edited by Robert O. Keohane. New York: Columbia University Press.

Rummel, Rudolph. 1966. "Dimensions of Conflict Behavior Within Nations, 1945–59." *Journal of Conflict Resolution* 10:65–73.

Rupesinghe, Kumar. 1987. "Theories of Conflict Resolution and Their Application to Protracted Ethnic Conflict." *Bulletin of Peace Proposals* 18:623–36.

———. 1990. "The Disappearing Boundaries Between Internal and External Conflicts." *Peace and Security* 5:18–30.

Russett, Bruce. 1967. *International Regions and the International System*. Chicago: Rand McNally.

———. 1990. *Controlling the Sword: The Democratic Governance of National Security*. Cambridge: Harvard University Press.

———. 1993. *Grasping the Democractic Peace*. Princeton: Princeton University Press.

Russett, Bruce, and Thomas W. Graham. 1989. "Public Opinion and National Security Policy: Relationships and Impacts." In *Handbook of War Studies,* edited by Manus I. Midlarsky. Boston: Unwin Hyman.

Ryan, Stephen. 1988. "Explaining Ethnic Conflict: The Neglected International Dimension." *Review of International Studies* 14:161–77.

————. 1990a. *Ethnic Conflict and International Relations.* Brookfield, Vt.: Gower.

————. 1990b. "Ethnic Conflict and the United Nations." *Ethnic and Racial Studies* 13:25–49.

Said, Abdul, and Luiz R. Simmons, eds. 1976. *Ethnicity in an International Context: The Politics of Disassociation.* New Brunswick, N.J.: Transaction.

Sanders, William T., and Barbara J. Price. 1968. *Mesoamerica: The Evolution of a Civilization.* New York: Random House.

Schechterman, Bernard, and Martin Slann, eds. 1993. *The Ethnic Dimension in International Relations.* London: Praeger.

Schechtman, Joseph B. 1963. *The Refugee in the World: Displacement and Integration.* New York: A.S. Barnes; London: Thomas Yoseloff.

Schevill, Ferdinand. 1933. *History of the Balkan Peninsula from the Earliest Times to the Present Day.* Rev. ed. New York: Harcourt, Brace.

Schlesinger, Arthur M., Jr. 1991. *The Disuniting of America.* New York: Norton.

Schroeder, Gertrude E. 1992. "On the Economic Viability of New Nation-States." *Journal of International Affairs* 45:549–74.

Shaw, Stanford J., and Ezel Kural Shaw. 1977. *History of the Ottoman Empire and Modern Turkey.* Vol. 2: *Reform, Revolution, and Republic: The Rise of Modern Turkey, 1808–1975.* Cambridge: Cambridge University Press.

Sheffer, G., ed. 1986. *Modern Diasporas in International Relations.* Kent: Croom-Helm.

Shibutani, Tamotsu, and Kian M. Kwan. 1965. *Ethnic Stratification: A Comparative Approach.* New York: Macmillan.

Shiels, Frederick L., ed. 1984a. *Ethnic Separatism and World Politics.* Lanham: University Press of America.

————. 1984b. "Conclusion." In *Ethnic Separatism and World Politics,* edited by Frederick Shiels. Lanham: University Press of America.

Shih, Cheng-Feng. 1991. "A Multivariate Model of Ethnic Diversity and Violent Political Behavior." Ph.D. diss., Ohio State University.

Shoemaker, D. J., and S. J. Williams. 1987. "The Subculture of Violence and Ethnicity." *Journal of Criminal Justice* 15:461–72.

Simard, Pierre. 1991. "Compétition électoral et partage des pouvoirs dans un Etat fédéral." *Canadian Public Policy* 15:409–16.

Simmel, Georg. 1956. *Conflict and the Web of Group Affiliations.* Trans. Kurt H. Wolff and Reinhard Bendix. New York: Free Press.

Simon, Herbert, A. 1985. "Human Nature in Politics: The Dialogue of Psychology with Political Science." *American Political Science Review* 29:293–304.

Singer, J. David. 1990. "Reconstructing the Correlates of War Data Set on Material Capabilities of States, 1816–1985." In *Measuring the Correlates of War,* edited by J. David Singer and Paul F. Diehl. Ann Arbor: University of Michigan Press.

Singer, J. David, and Melvin Small. 1993. "The Correlates of War Project: International and Civil War Data, 1816–1992." Electronic Data File: January 1993.

SIPRI (Stockholm International Peace Research Institute). 1991. *World Armaments and Disarmament: SIPRI Yearbook.* Oxford University Press.

Sivard, Ruth Leger. 1991. *World Military and Social Expenditures 1991.* 14th ed. Washington, D.C.: World Priorities.

Siverson, Randolph M., and Harvey Starr. 1990. "Opportunity, Willingness, and the Diffusion of War." *American Political Science Review* 84:47–67.

————. 1991. *The Diffusion of War: A Study of Opportunity and Willingness.* Ann Arbor: University of Michigan Press.

Slater, Robert. 1993. "Conflict and Change in the International System." In *Global Transformations and the Third World,* edited by Robert Slater, B. Schutz, and S. Dorr. Boulder: Lynne Rienner.

Small, Melvin, and J. David Singer. 1982. *Resort to Arms: International and Civil Wars, 1816–1980.* Beverly Hills: Sage.

Smith, Anthony D. 1971. *Theories of Nationalism.* New York: Harper and Row.

———. 1980. "Nationalism and Classical Social Theory." *British Journal of Sociology* 24:18–31.

———. 1981. *The Ethnic Revival in the Modern World.* London: Cambridge University Press.

———. 1986a. "Conflict and Collective Identity: Class, Ethnic and Nation." In *International Conflict Resolution,* edited by Edward Azar and John Burton. Boulder: Lynne Rienner.

———. 1986b. *The Ethnic Origins of Nations.* Oxford: Blackwell.

———. 1990. "The Supersession of Nationalism." *International Journal of Comparative Sociology* 31:1–31.

———. 1991. *National Identity.* Reno: University of Nevada Press.

———. 1993a. "A Europe of Nations—or the Nation of Europe?" *Journal of Peace Research* 30:129–35.

———. 1993b. "The Ethnic Sources of Nationalism." *Survival* 35:48–64.

Snyder, Jack. 1993. "Nationalism and the Crisis of the Post-Soviet State." *Survival* 35:5–26.

Snyder, Louis L. 1982. *Global Mini-Nationalisms: Autonomy or Independence.* Westport, Conn.: Greenwood.

Spiro, Herbert J. 1968. "The Federation of Rhodesia and Nyasaland." In *Why Federations Fail,* edited by Thomas M. Franck. New York: New York University Press.

Sprout, Harold, and Margaret Sprout. 1965. *The Ecological Perspective on Human Affairs.* Princeton: Princeton University Press.

Stack, John F., Jr. 1979. *International Conflict in an American City: Boston's Irish, Italians, and Jews, 1935–1944.* Westport, Conn.: Greenwood.

———. 1981. *Ethnic Identities in a Transnational World.* Westport, Conn.: Greenwood.

———. 1986. *The Primordial Challenge: Ethnicity in the Modern World.* Westport, Conn.: Greenwood.

Starr, Harvey. 1990. "Modelling the Internal-External Linkage: Rethinking the Relationship Between Revolution, War and Change." Paper presented at the annual meeting of the American Political Science Association.

Stavenhagen, Rodolfo. 1987. "Ethnocide or Ethnodevelopment: The New Challenge." *Development: Seeds of Change* 1:74–78.

———. 1990. *The Ethnic Question: Conflicts, Development and Human Rights.* Tokyo: United Nations University Press.

———. 1991. "Ethnic Conflicts and Their Impact on International Society." *International Social Science Journal* 43:117–31.

Stedman, Stephen John. 1992. *Peacemaking in Civil War: International Mediation in Zimbabwe 1974–1980.* Boulder: Lynne Rienner.

Stern, Steve J. 1982. *Peru's Indian Peoples and the Challenge of Spanish Conquest.* Madison: University of Wisconsin Press.

Stohl, Michael. 1980. "The Nexus of Civil and International Conflict." In *Handbook of Political Conflict,* edited by Ted Robert Gurr. New York: Free Press.

Suhrke, Astri, and Lela Garner Noble, eds. 1977a. *Ethnic Conflict and International Relations.* New York: Praeger.

―――. 1977b. Introduction to *Ethnic Conflict and International Relations*, edited by Astri Suhkre and Lela Garner Noble. New York: Praeger.

―――. 1977c. "Spread or Containment: The Ethnic Factor." In *Ethnic Conflict and International Relations*, edited by Astri Suhkre and Lela Garner Noble. New York: Praeger.

Suzuki, David, and Peter Knudtson. 1992. *Wisdom of the Elders: Honoring Sacred Native Visions of Nature*. New York: Bantham.

Sylvester, Christine. 1994. *Feminist Theory and International Relations in the Postmodern Era*. Cambridge: Cambridge University Press.

Tanter, Raymond. 1966. "Dimensions of Conflict Behavior Within and Between Nations, 1958–1960." *Journal of Conflict Resolution* 10:41–64.

Tapie, Victor L. 1971. *The Rise and Fall of the Hapsburg Monarchy*. New York: Praeger.

Targ, Harry. 1976. "Global Dominance and Dependence, Post-Industrialism, and International Relations Theory, A Review." *International Studies Quarterly* 20:461–80.

Taylor, A. J. P. 1971. *The Struggle for Mastery in Europe, 1848–1918*. Oxford: Oxford University Press.

Taylor, Charles L., and David A. Jodice. 1983. *World Handbook of Political and Social Indicators*. Vol. 1. 3d ed. New Haven: Yale University Press.

Taylor, Charles L., and Michael C. Hudson. 1972. *World Handbook of Political and Social Indicators*. 2d ed. New Haven: Yale University Press.

Terrel, Lawrence. 1971. "Societal Stress, Political Instability and Levels of Military Effort." *Journal of Conflict Resolution* 15:329–46.

Thompson, David. 1966. *Europe since Napoleon*. 2d ed. New York: Knopf.

Thompson, John Eric Sidney. 1954. *The Rise and Fall of Maya Civilization*. Norman: University of Oklahoma Press.

Thompson, Richard H. 1989. *Theories of Ethnicity: A Critical Appraisal*. Westport, Conn.: Greenwood Press.

Thornton, Russell. 1987. *Native American Holocaust and Survival*. Norman: University of Oklahoma Press.

Tickner, J. Ann. 1992. *Gender in International Relations: Feminist Perspectives on Achieving Global Security*. New York: Columbia University Press.

Tihany, Leslie C. 1969. "The Austro-Hungarian Compromise, 1867–1918: A Half Century of Diagnosis; Fifty Years of Post-Mortem." *Central European History* 2:114–38.

Tillema, Herbert. 1989. "Foreign Overt Military Intervention in the Nuclear Age." *Journal of Peace Research* 26:179–93.

―――. 1991. *International Armed Conflict since 1945: A Bibliographic Handbook of Wars and Military Interventions*. Boulder: Westview.

Time Magazine, various issues.

Tiryakian, Edward A., and Ronald Rogowski, eds. 1985. *New Nationalisms of the Developed West*. Boston: Allen and Unwin.

Touval, Saadia, and I. William Zartman. 1989. "Mediation in International Conflicts." In *Mediation Research*, edited by K. Kressel and D. G. Pruitt. San Francisco: Jossey-Bass.

Tsebelis, George. 1990. *Nested Games: Rational Choice in Comparative Politics*. Berkeley and Los Angeles: University of California Press.

United Nations University. 1987. *Report on Ethnicity and Development*. Tokyo: United Nations University.

U.N. Document E/CN.4/GR.1987/7/Add. 12, 30 September 1987.

Van den Berghe, Pierre. 1987. *The Ethnic Phenomenon*. New York: Praeger.

―――. 1990. *State Violence and Ethnicity*. Niwot: University Press of Colorado.

Van der Merwe, Hendrik W. 1989. *Pursuing Justice and Peace in South Africa.* London: Routledge.

Vasquez, John A. 1992. "Factors Related to the Contagion and Diffusion of International Violence." In *The Internationalization of Communal Strife,* edited by Manus I. Midlarsky. London: Routledge.

———. 1993. *The War Puzzle.* Cambridge: Cambridge University Press.

Väyrynen, Raimo. 1984. "Regional Conflict Formations: An Intractable Problem for International Relations." *Journal of Peace Research* 21:337–58.

———. 1991. *New Directions in Conflict Theory: Conflict Resolution and Conflict Transformation.* Newbury Park, Calif.: Sage.

Vreeland, Nena et al. 1970. *Area Handbook for Malaysia.* Washington: American University Foreign Area Studies.

Wallace, Michael D. 1979. "Arms Races and Escalation: Some New Evidence." *Journal of Conflict Resolution* 23:3–16.

———. 1982. "Armaments and Escalation: Two Competing Hypotheses." *International Studies Quarterly* 26:37–56.

Waller, David V. 1992. "Ethnic Mobilization and Geopolitics in the Soviet Union: Towards a Theoretical Understanding." *Journal of Political and Military Sociology* 28:37–62.

Wallerstein, Immanuel M. 1974. *The Modern World System.* New York: Academic Press.

Walt, Steven. 1988. *The Origins of Alliance.* Ithaca: Cornell University Press.

———. 1992. "Revolutions and War." *World Politics* 44:321–28.

Waltz, Kenneth N. 1979. *Theory of International Politics.* New York: McGraw-Hill.

———. 1986. "Reflections on *Theory of International Politics:* Response to My Critics." In *Neorealism and Its Critics,* edited by Robert O. Keohane. New York: Columbia University Press.

Warren, Mark. 1992. "Democratic Theory and Self-Transformation." *American Political Science Review* 86:8–23.

The Washington Post, various issues.

Waters, Frank. 1963. *Book of the Hopi.* New York: Viking.

Watts, R. L. 1966. *New Federations: Experiments in the Commonwealth.* Oxford: Clarendon.

———. 1971. "The Survival or Disintegration of Federations." In *One Country or Two?* edited by R. M. Burns. Montreal: McGill–Queen's University Press.

Weatherford, J. McIver. 1988. *Indian Givers: How the Indians of the Americas Transformed the World.* New York: Crown.

———. 1991. *Native Roots: How the Indians Enriched America.* New York: Crown.

Wehr, Paul, and John Paul Lederach. 1991. "Mediating Conflict in Central America." *Journal of Peace Research* 28:85–98.

Weiner, Myron. 1971. "The Macedonian Syndrome: An Historical Model of International Relations and Political Development." *World Politics* 4:665–83.

———. 1987. "Political Change: Asia, Africa and the Middle East." In *Understanding Political Development,* edited by Myron Weiner and Samuel Huntington. Boston: Little, Brown.

———. 1992. "Peoples and States in a New Ethnic Order?" *Third World Quarterly* 13:317–33.

Wellhofer, E. Spencer. 1989. "The Comparative Method and the Study of Development, Diffusion, and Social Change." *Comparative Political Studies* 22:315–42.

Welsh, David. 1993. "Domestic Politics and Ethnic Conflict." *Survival* 35:63–80.

Wendt, Franz. 1981. *Cooperation in the Nordic Countries: Achievements and Obstacles*. Stockholm: Almqvist and Wiksell.

Werther, Gunther. 1992. *Self-Determination in Western Democracies: Aboriginal Politics in a Comparative Perspective*. Westport, Conn.: Greenwood.

Wiberg, Hakan. 1991. "States and Nations as Challenges to Peace Research." *Journal of Peace Research* 28:337–43.

Wilkenfeld, Jonathan, ed. 1973. *Conflict Behavior and Linkage Politics*. New York: David McKay.

Wilkenfeld, Jonathan, Michael Brecher et al. 1988. *Crises in the Twentieth Century: Handbook of Foreign Policy Crises*. New York: Pergamon.

Williams, Robert A. 1990. *The American Indian in Western Legal Thought*. New York: Oxford University Press.

Wilmer, Franke. 1993. *The Indigenous Voice in World Politics: Since Time Immemorial*. Newbury Park, Calif.: Sage.

Winant, Howard, 1994. *Racial Conditions*. Minneapolis: University of Minnesota Press.

Wittman, Donald. 1991. "Nations and States: Mergers and Acquisitions; Dissolution and Divorce." *American Economic Review* 31:126–29.

Wood, John. 1981. "Secession: A Comparative Analytical Perspective." *Canadian Journal of Political Science* 14:107–34.

World Almanac and Book of Facts. 1990. New York: World Almanac.

Young, Crawford. 1976. *The Politics of Cultural Pluralism*. Madison: University of Wisconsin Press.

———. 1982. "The Temple of Ethnicity." *World Politics* 35:652–70.

———. 1993. "The Dialectics of Cultural Pluralism: Concept and Reality." In *The Rising Tide of Cultural Pluralism: The Nation-State at Bay*, edited by Crawford Young. Madison: University of Wisconsin Press.

———. 1994a. "The Political Economy of Secession: The Case of Quebec." *Constitutional Political Economy* 5:221–45.

———. 1994b. *The Breakup of Czechoslovakia*. Kingston: Institute of Intergovernmental Relations, Queen's University.

Zamir, Meir. 1990. *The Formation of Modern Lebanon*. Ithaca, N.Y.: Cornell University Press.

Zartman, I. William. 1992. "Internationalization of Communal Strife: Temptations and Opportunities of Triangulation." In *The Internationalization of Communal Strife*, edited by Manus I. Midlarsky. London: Routledge.

Zimmermann, Ekkart. 1983. *Political Violence, Crises, and Revolutions: Theories and Research*. Boston: G. K. Hall; Cambridge: Schenkman.

Zinnes, Dina A. 1980. "Three Puzzles in Search of a Researcher." *International Studies Quarterly* 24:315–42.

CONTRIBUTORS

Gerald Alfred is an assistant professor of political science and director of the Center for Native Education at Concordia University. His publications include "Heeding the Voices of Our Ancestors" (1995).

Michael Brecher is Angus Professor of Political Science at McGill University. His publications include *Crises in World Politics* (1993) and *Crisis, Conflict and Instability* (1989).

David Carment is an assistant professor at the Norman Paterson School of International Affairs, Carleton University. His publications include articles in the *Journal of Peace Research* and *Third World Quarterly*.

David R. Davis is an assistant professor of political science at Emory University. His publications include articles in *Comparative Political Studies* and *American Political Science Review*.

Keith Jaggers is a doctoral candidate in political science at the University of Colorado. His publications include articles in *Comparative Political Studies* and *Journal of Developing Studies*.

Patrick James is professor and chair of political science at Iowa State University. His publications include *Crisis and War* (1988) and (co-edited with William James Booth and Hudson Meadwell) *Politics and Rationality* (1993).

Louis Kriesberg is professor of sociology and Maxwell Professor of Social Conflict Studies at Syracuse University. He is the author of *International Conflict Resolution* (1992).

Monty G. Marshall is an assistant professor of government and international affairs at the University of South Florida. His publications include "States at Risk: Ethnopolitics in the Multinational States of Eastern Europe" in *Minorities at Risk*, edited by Ted Robert Gurr (1993).

Zeev Maoz is professor of political science and director of the Jaffee Center at Tel Aviv University. His publications include *Paradoxes of War* (1990) and *National Choices and International Processes* (1990).

Manus I. Midlarsky is Moses and Annuta Back Professor of International Peace and Conflict Resolution at Rutgers University. His publications include *The Onset of War* (1988) and *The Internationalization of Communal Strife* (1992).

Will H. Moore is an assistant professor of political science at the University of California, Riverside. His publications include articles in *Studies in International Comparative Development* and *Western Political Quarterly*.

John F. Stack Jr. is professor of political science and acting director of the Institute for Public Policy and Citizenship Studies at Florida International University. His publications include *Ethnic Identities in a Transnational World* (1981) and *Primodial Challenge: Ethnicity in the Modern World* (1986).

Jonathan Wilkenfeld is professor and chair of government and politics at the University of Maryland, College Park. His publications include articles in the *Journal of Conflict Resolution* and (co-authored with Michael Brecher) *Crisis, Conflict, and Instability* (1989).

Franke Wilmer is an associate professor of political science at Montana State University. Her publications include *The Indigenous Voice in World Politics: Since Time Immemorial* (1993) and an article in *Political Science and Politics*.

Robert A. Young is professor of political science at the University of Western Ontario. His publications include articles in *Canadian Public Policy* and *Canadian Journal of Political Science*.

INDEX

Abdolali, Nasrin, 145
Activism, of indigenous peoples, 38–41, 42
Affinities, transnational ethnic, 9, 214, 224, 229–30, 263; and ethnic composition of states, 222–25; influence on domestic policies, 197, 199–200; and intervention in conflicts, 211–12, 257; pressure on multiethnic states from, 198, 209; and religion, 78
Africa: analysis of ethnic conflicts in, 176–93; colonial federations in, 51, 53, 59; lack of intervention in ethnic conflicts within, 196–97, 208; South Africa as example of escalation prevention, 247–48
African National Congress (ANC), 247–48, 269*n1*
Albania, in Balkan Wars, 68–69
Alger, Chadwick, 21
Alliance memories, 77; and etiology of systemic wars, 70, 72–73
Alliances, 39–40, 70, 136, 154; instability from, 71–74; as response to security dilemmas, 123–25, 134–45; in systemic wars, 76–79
Americas: analysis of ethnic conflicts in, 176–93; native sovereignty in, 26–27. *See also* Canada; U.S.
Anarchy, 7–8, 198
ANC (African National Congress), 247–48, 269*n1*
Anderson, Charles W., 225
Anglophilia, U.S., 20

Annexations: in irredentist cases, 210; resistance to, 72–73
Arab-Israeli wars, limitations on destruction in, 79
Arendt, Hannah, 83, 89, 91
Army, of former Yugoslavia, 75–77
Ascription, 13; in definition of ethnicity, 2, 82, 238
Asia, ethnic conflicts in, 176–93
Assimilation: coercive, 31–32; in cultural diffusion models, 43; culture of, 14; and ethnicity, 16–17, 20; justification for, 34–35; *vs.* shared identity, 242
Australia, state relations with indigenous peoples in, 36
Austria-Hungary, 69; and Bulgaria, 65–66; changes in balance of power of, 71–74; secession of Hungary from, 47–48, 50–60
Authoritarianism: ethnic conflicts repressed by, 164, 252. *See also* Regimes
Authority patterns, 150–51, 154
Autocracies: behavior to other countries, 127–47. *See also* Regimes
Axelrod, Robert, 128–29
Azar, Edward, 169

Balance of power, 18–19, 77; instability from changes in, 71–75
Balkanization, fear of, 196–97
Balkan Wars: effects of, 71–74; origins of, 66–68
Battenberg (Bulgarian king), 65–66

295

Bell, Daniel, 15–16, 21
Bismarck, Prince: attempts to balance power, 71–73; negotiating end to Russo-Turkish War, 61, 65
Bosnia-Herzegovina. See Yugoslavia, former
Boundaries, 84; cooperation in maintenance of, 196–97
Brain drains, as effect of insecurity, 111–12
Brecher, Michael, 117
Bremer, Stuart, 130
Britain, and breakup of colonial federations, 51, 55
Bueno de Mesquita, Bruce, 126
Bulgaria, 65, 68–69
Bureaucracies, and appeal of ethnic historicism, 21
Buzan, Barry, 118

Canada: as example of escalation prevention, 246–47; multiculturalism in, 31–32
Capital flight, as effect of insecurity, 111–12
Capitalism: and modernization, 28; vs. ethnicity, 14
Carment, David B., 27–28, 166–67, 175
Christians: in Balkan Wars, 68–69; in Bosnia-Herzegovina, 63–64
Class: importance in world systems theory, 196; vs. ethnicity, 17, 80
Cleavages, ethnic, 9; and ethnic composition of states, 220, 222–24; and involvement in protracted conflict, 229–31
Coercion. See Violence
Cohesion, internal: due to external threat, 84–85, 107; in secession process, 53, 60
Cold war, 114, 245; and ethnic conflict management, 256, 266n1
Cold war nationalism, and irrelevance of ethnicity, 20
Collins, John N., 208
Colonialism, British, breakup of federations from, 46, 49, 51, 55, 59
Colonization, activism against, 38–41
Communal conflicts: preventing and resolving, 232–51. See also Ethnic conflicts

Communal groups, 87, 238, 265n3; politicized, 152–53; relations among, 234–41. See also Ethnic groups
Communal violence: vs. systemic wars, 62. See also Ethnic conflicts
Confidence-building agreements (CBMs), 243–45
Conflict and Peace Databank, 156–57
Conflict behaviors, 98, 123; of different types of regimes, 125–47. See also State behavior
Conflict levels, determinants of, 134–43, 153–63, 155
Conflict management, 9–10, 114, 201, 239–46, 259–62; examples of, 246–50
Congress of Berlin, and Russo-Turkish War, 61, 65–66
Connor, Walker, 15, 17, 23–24
Conquest, law of, and subjection of indigenous peoples, 34–35
Consciousness raising, through activism, 40–41
Constitutions, in secessions, 56–58
Contiguity, importance of, 119–21, 130–31, 156–61
Cooperation, 127, 248; attempts to foster, 263; determinants of, 126, 156–63, 196–97, 227; and nonviolent options, 233–34, 237
Correlates of War (COW) data bases, 90, 100
Couldter, Robert T., 27
Courts, levels of sovereignty in, 42
COW (Correlates of War) data bases, 90, 100
Cox, Robert, 22
Crises, ethnic dimension in, 8, 166; analysis of, 174–90
Crisis management, 225–31; in ethnic crises, 170–71, 180–81
Crisis modes, of group political behavior, 6
Croats, 72; in modern Bosnia-Herzegovina situation, 74–80
Cultural diffusion models, assimilation in, 43
Cultural evolutionary process, Europe's set as model, 33

Culture, 13; European *vs.* indigenous, 26–44; importance of, 24–25; of violence, 84–85, 92, 114–15, 258

Davis, David R., 154
Deer, Kevin, 30
Defense issues: of Dual Alliance, 72–73; in secession agreements, 55–56
Delegitimation, in ethnic conflicts, 198
Deloria, Vine, Jr., 37–38
Democracies, 202; behavior of, 126–47, 258; conflict *vs.* cooperation in, 157–63; effects of systemic insecurity on, 107–13. *See also* Regimes
Democratization, effects of, 7; on other states, 126, 130–31, 144–45; on quantity of conflict, 132–34
Development, and indigenous peoples, 38–42
Diffusion, of violence and insecurity, 85–97, 195
Diffusion processes, 267*n*6
Discrimination, 32, 152; in communal relations, 234–37; levels of, 155, 157–63; and mobilization of ethnic groups, 223–24
Diversionary theory, of systemic insecurity, 84, 107–11
Domestic politics, 20, 123, 258; effects of, 195–96, 263; influence on ethnic conflicts, 116–47; influence on foreign policy, 127, 197–99, 204–11. *See also* Stability/instability
Dreikaiserbund (Russia, Germany, and Austria-Hungary), 65–66, 72
Dual Alliance (Germany and Austria-Hungary), 72–73

Eckstein, Harry, 108
Economic issues, 34, 75; and secession, 49, 55–56, 59–60. *See also* Resource inequalities; Resources
Elections, and institutional constraint, 202
Elites, 111–12, 231, 256–57; institutional constraint on, 202–12, 218–22, 226–31; motivations of, 199–201; national, 19–20, 51; use of ethnicity by, 88, 224–25, 259
Emerson, Rupert, 14–15

Enduring rivalries. *See* Protracted conflict
Environment, and indigenous peoples, 38–40, 44
Ethnic cleansing, in Yugoslavia, 76, 80
Ethnic cleavages, 198, 212–14
Ethnic conflicts, 2–3, 201–02, 207; causes of, 1, 116, 255–58, 262–63; effects of, 62, 258; explanation of increase in, 86, 164–65, 198–99; and interstate conflicts, 149–50, 155, 165–93, 195–99, 254; limitations on, 266*n*1, 267*n*3; locations of, 176–81; nature of, 23–24, 88–89; nonviolent options in, 233–34; prevention of, 195, 232–51; resolution of, 232–51, 259–62. *See also* Ethnic crises
Ethnic consciousness, 223–24
Ethnic crises, onset of, 169–70, 172, 177–78, 181; outcomes of, 172–74, 188–90, 244–46, 250
Ethnic diversity, within a state, 221–22, 226–29
Ethnic fragmentation argument on societal breakdown, 104–06
Ethnic groups, 33–34, 213; communal groups, 87, 152–53, 238, 265*n*3; in composition of states, 220–22; effects on transnational relations, 21–22, 154, 200–01; features of, 2, 221; and international conflict, 152–63, 200
Ethnic historicism, 21
Ethnicity, 23–24, 31–32, 62, 82; as attribute, 151, 156; as authority pattern, 150–51; connotations of, 11–12, 86; definitions of, 82–83, 87–88, 255; effects on international crisis, 168–74; importance of, 3, 12–15, 21–25; problems of, 83–115; *vs.* state, 253–54
Ethnic nationalism, 24
Ethnic pluralism, states accommodating, 43–44
Europe: culture of, *vs.* indigenous cultures, 26–44; ethnic conflicts in, 176–93, 268*n*8
Exclusivity, of ethnic groups, 2
Expulsions/removals, 236–37

Federations, secession from, 46–60
Ferguson, Yale, 150–51
Foreign policy, 18–20, 48, 267n5; affective motivation in, 153–55, 160–61, 199–201; crises due to irredenta or secession in, 213–18; effects of domestic politics on, 116–17, 201–12; effects of neighboring countries on, 122–31, 158–60; elites' convergence with masses on, 199–200, 231; influence on domestic policies, 198–99; strains of security dilemma on, 94–96; systemic perspectives on, 121–22
France, 79; Russian alliance with, 66–67, 72
Franz Joseph, in Hungary's secession from Austria, 55, 58

Gastil, Raymond, 223–25
Geertz, Clifford, 16–17
Germany, 79; changes in balance of power of, 71–73; and Yugoslavia, 61, 76
Gerson, Louis, 20
Glazer, Nathan, 17
Global culture, 23
Global interdependence, 21–22
Global organizations, intervention by, 171–72, 185–89; effectiveness of, 250, 254
Global reach, 119–20
Governments: accommodating ethnic pluralism, 43–44; strengthening for secession, 52–53, 57–58; systemic insecurity and rigidity of, 107–13. *See also* Regimes; States
Graduated reciprocation in tension reduction (GRIT) strategy, 245
Graham, Thomas W., 85
Great powers. *See* Major powers
Greece, in Balkan Wars, 69
Greenfield, Liah, 15
Grievances: level of, 157–63; ways to address, 239–41. *See also* Discrimination
GRIT (Graduated reciprocation in tension reduction) strategy, 245
Gurr, Ted Robert, 145, 152, 154, 200; on culture of violence, 85, 90; on foreign policy, 165, 267n5

Heraclides, Alexis, 200
Heterogeneity, extent of, 2
Hill, Ken, 223
Homer, Elizabeth, 267n6
Horowitz, Donald, 11–12, 196
Human rights: of indigenous peoples, 31–32, 41. *See also* Discrimination
Hungary, secession from Austria, 47–48, 50–60
Huntington, Samuel, 13, 24–25, 99

ICB (International Crisis Behavior) Project, 166–67, 175–90, 212–13
Identity, 150–51, 211–12, 265n1; communal, 232–33, 238; creating more shared, 241–42, 248–49; ethnic, 31–32, 255, 260; and ethnicity, 3–4, 17; ethnocultural, 33; group, 15, 83, 88; national, 15, 260
Ideologies, limitations on conflict over, 123–24
Immigrants, and U.S. Anglophilia, 20
Indigenous peoples, 27, 265n1; culture of, 4, 26–44, 35–38
Inequalities: as source of tension and conflicts, 241–42. *See also* Resource inequalities
Inhibited state theory, 196, 205–08
Instability. *See* Stability/instability
Institutionalization: of ideas, 123–24; of social structures, 266n1
Institutions, political, 9, 230, 258; constraints on elites by, 201–12, 218–22, 226–31; lack of neutrality in, 43–44
Integration: economic, 247–48; social, 236–37, 245
Intensity, of conflicts, 17, 77, 210
Interdependence, of communal groups, 234–37, 247
International Crisis Behavior (ICB) Project, 166–67, 175–90, 212–13
International environment, 117–18. *See also* Politically relevant international environment (PRIE)
International recognition: of Croatia, 76, 78; role in secession process, 55–56
International regions, and regional subsystems, 118

International relations: and causes of ethnic conflicts, 116; effects of ethnic conflict on, 7–8, 165–93; and state-centered paradigm, 21–24
International relations theory, 150–51, 195, 253–54; criticisms of, 84, 87
Interstate conflicts: ethnic, 166–67, 199–212; internationalization of communal violence, 61–63, 74–80; irredenta or secession as, 200, 213–18; relation to ethnic conflicts, 116–17, 123, 152–63, 165–93, 195–99
Interventions, external, 145–46, 237, 263; by African states, 196–97, 208; by global organizations, 185–89; by major powers, 171–72, 182–85, 254; to prevent escalation, 243, 248–50; reasons for, 122–23, 155, 162–63, 165, 190–91, 210
Irredenta, 121–22, 166–67, 194–231, 200, 210; analysis of, 213–18, 225
Isaacs, Harold, 16
Italy, in Balkan Wars, 68

Jackson, Robert, 196
Jelavich, Barbara, 64
Jureidini, Paul, 169

Kanesatake Mohawks, activism of, 39
Kasfir, Nelso, 2
Keohane, Robert, 13, 21
Keyes, Charles, 17
Klingman, David, 267n6
Krasner, Stephen, 41

Lalman, David, 126
Land, 31–32; contested, 67–69, 77; of indigenous peoples, 30, 37– 40; ownership of, 63–64
Language, importance in ethnic identity, 62
Leadership: substitutable, 91–92. See also Elites
League of Nations, effectiveness of, 185–86
Lee Kuan Yew, 49–51, 54
Liberalism, and ethnicity, 13–14, 20, 24
Lindgren, Raymond, 59

Litigation, in activism of indigenous peoples, 39
Luard, Evan, 150

Macedonia, and Balkan Wars, 67–68
Major powers, 71, 98, 171–72, 266n1; intervention by, 79, 182–85, 254; reach of, 119, 130–31
Malaysia, Singapore's secession from, 48–60
Mandela, Nelson, 248, 269n1
Mansbach, Richard, 150–51
Maoz, Zeev, 126–27, 130, 145–46
Marshall, Monty G., 90, 154
Marxism, and ethnicity, 23
Matthews, 110–11
McLaurin, Ronald, 169
Mediation, 165, 171–72, 191, 243–44
Memories, of past grievances, 74–75, 77, 242–43, 249
Metapower activism, 41
Middle East, diffusion of violence in, 94–96, 98–113
Migrations: forced, 236–37; and security dilemmas, 111–13
Military capabilities: effects of increasing, 127, 143; effects on alliances, 143–44; increases as response to security dilemmas, 123–24, 134–45; of protracted conflict region, 100–07
Military-security crises, 167
Minorities, 2, 8, 56–57, 239, 256; instability among, 84, 107–13. See also Ethnic groups
Minorities at Risk project, 152, 156–57, 225; use of data from, 110, 161–62, 212
Minor powers, 71, 266n1
Mistrust, as effect of ethnicity, 169
Mobilization: of ethnic groups, 200–01, 223, 255–58; of minority groups, 155, 157–63; political, 152
Mobilization wars, 79–80, 266n2
Modernization, 23–24, 28–29, 99; and indigenous peoples, 4, 31, 36
Modernizing elites, vs. indigenous peoples, 27, 30
Moore, Will H., 154
Most, Benjamin A., 90–91

Multiculturalism, in Canada, 31–32
Multiethnic states, 43–44, 197, 198, 237, 260
Multipolarity, 76, 256; in systemic wars, 69–70, 78
Muslims: and Balkan Wars, 67–69; in Bosnia-Herzegovina, 63–64, 74–80

National elites. *See* Elites
National identity, 15, 239
Nationalism, and ethnicity, 14, 19
Nationality, *vs.* ethnicity, 87
National perspectives, on global change, 125–31
National political culture: *vs.* indigenous peoples, 27. *See also* States
Nation building, 12–15, 266*n4;* process of, 33–34, 257–60
Nation-states, 24, 33–34, 265*n3*
Natural world, relations to, 35–38
Negotiations: over values, 260; to prevent escalation, 243–48; in secession process, 51–55
Neilsson, Gunnar, 225
Neoliberalism, and vulnerable states, 196–97
Neorealism, 22–23, 124–25, 196
Noble, Lela Garner, 150, 154, 155, 195
Norway, secession from Sweden, 48, 50–60
Nye, Joseph S., 21

OAU (Organization of African Unity), 197
Organization of African Unity (OAU), 197
Osgood, Charles, 245
Ottoman Empire, 64–65, 67–68

Pan-Arabism, as cross-national idea, 123–24
Patton, Charles, 30
PCRs (Protracted conflict regions), 268*n8;* diffusion of insecurity in, 93–98; Middle East as, 98–113
Plenary power, over indigenous peoples, 28–29, 35
Polarity: in ethnic crises, 175–93. *See also* Multipolarity
Political ethnicity, *vs.* ethnicity, 82, 87–88

Politically relevant international environment (PRIE), 119–27
Political participation, 2
Political parties: and constraint on elites, 205–06, 219; countrywide *vs.* ethnic, 249
Political transition, management of, 230
Politicized communal groups, 152–53
Politics, 14; allocation of values and resources in, 3–4, 27–28; of secession process, 45–60; world, 14, 18, 266*n1.* *See also* Domestic politics
Polities. *See* Regimes
Posen, Barry, 122–23
Power, *vs.* violence, 83
Preventive peacekeeping, 195, 232–51
Primordial ethnicity, 15–18, 80; in international relations theory, 253; *vs.* communal identity, 232–33. *See also* Ethnicity
PRIE (Politically relevant international environment), 119–27
Prisoner's Dilemma game, 128–29
Protest activism, of indigenous peoples, 40
Protracted conflict regions (PCRs), 268*n8;* diffusion of insecurity in, 93–98; Middle East as, 98–113
Protracted conflicts, 92–93, 177–78, 210–12, 245, 260; in ethnic crisis definition, 168–74
Public/private spheres, spread of violence and insecurity from, 84, 97, 110–11

Race, 43, 49, 238
Ransom, Jim, 37
Rapaport, Anatole, 127
Rationality: of ethnic identification, 257; of state behavior, 198–99
Realist theory, 7–8, 196, 198–99; and ethnicity, 12–13, 18–24; international relations in, 84, 124–25, 208; state-centeredness of, 150–51, 253
Reciprocity, and cooperation, 196–97, 243, 245
Reframing of conflicts, to prevent escalation, 243–44
Refugees, 111–13, 241, 268*n10*